MODERNITY AND TERRORISM

Studies in Critical Social Sciences Book Series

Haymarket Books is proud to be working with Brill Academic Publishers (www.brill.nl) to republish the *Studies in Critical Social Sciences* book series in paperback editions. This peer-reviewed book series offers insights into our current reality by exploring the content and consequences of power relationships under capitalism, and by considering the spaces of opposition and resistance to these changes that have been defining our new age. Our full catalog of *SCSS* volumes can be viewed at www.haymarketbooks.org/category/scss-series.

MODERNITY AND TERRORISM

From Anti-Modernity to Modern Global Terror

MILAN ZAFIROVSKI
DANIEL G. RODEHEAVER

Haymarket Books
Chicago, IL

First published in 2013 by Brill Academic Publishers, The Netherlands.
© 2013 Koninklijke Brill NV, Leiden, The Netherlands

Published in paperback in 2014 by
Haymarket Books
P.O. Box 180165
Chicago, IL 60618
773-583-7884
www.haymarketbooks.org

ISBN: 978-1-60846-381-7

Trade distribution:
In the U.S. through Consortium Book Sales, www.cbsd.com
In the UK, Turnaround Publisher Services, www.turnaround-psl.com
In all other countries by Publishers Group Worldwide, www.pgw.com

Cover design by Ragina Johnson.

This book was published with the generous support of Lannan Foundation
and the Wallace Action Fund.

Printed in Canada by union labor.

10 9 8 7 6 5 4 3 2 1

Library of Congress Cataloging-in-Publication Data is available.

MIX
Paper from
responsible sources
FSC® C103567

Dedicated to the past and present victims of counter-state and especially state terrorism

CONTENTS

INTRODUCTION

This is bound to be a fairly controversial work in at least four respects, not by intent but because of the nature, operation, and factors of the problem under examination, modern terrorism. First, the book will likely be seen as controversial in virtue of defining and considering terrorism in more comprehensive terms than usually. It defines and considers terrorism in terms of violent repression and physical coercion with certain specified attributes, and not only sheer violence or use of force as in most of the previous literature. This redefinition has the virtue or promise of being comprehensive enough to incorporate virtually all agents and actions of terrorism, as well as its functional equivalents, including inter-state wars of aggression prohibited by international rules, Draconian punishments for sins-as-crimes by certain, particularly Islamic and Puritan-rooted, governments, hate crimes, and genocidal acts by individuals, groups, and states, etc. Consequently, no relevant type and instance of modern terrorism is left out of consideration. Alternatively, the redefinition is also sufficiently specific and precise to exclude those social agents and actions that are not terrorist in the strict sense. This holds true despite the tendency of certain states and societies to brand these agents and actions as terrorist, for example, non-violent moral sins and peaceful oppositional political activities often defined and punished as anti-government "terror" or "crimes" by contemporary moralistic and repressive, especially Islamic and Puritan-based theocratic, governments.

Second, the book is likely to be controversial in respect of considering both counter-state and state terrorism in contrast to the prevalent emphasis on the first type in the previous literature. By giving due consideration and doing justice to state terrorism, the book attempts to correct the prior imbalance in the literature between, by and large, de-centering on the latter and centering on counter-state terrorism. Moreover, this is a relatively original, novel, and rare sociological work in that it centers equally and often more on state terrorism such as systematic government coercion and violent repression, including executions and other Draconian punishments of sins-crimes within society and aggressive wars against other societies, than on counter-state terrorism like anti-government violence. This is done on the grounds that state terrorism thus understood is as sociologically and historically relevant as, or even more so than, counter-state terrorism. Such relevance is in terms of magnitude of terrorism, for example, numbers of people killed, abused, and tortured for their moral sins and political dissent cum "crimes" by governments compared with non-governmental forces. It is also in terms of scope and intensity of terrorism, as witnessed in fascist and neo-fascist official and other totalitarian terrorism, as well as its persistence, as demonstrated by strikingly persistent theocratic or religiously grounded, especially Islamic and Puritan-grounded theocratic, "holy" terror, oppression, revolutions, and wars.

Alternatively, this book goes beyond just ritually condemning, though reaffirming the lethal, destructive gravity, of counter-state terrorism in the service of a government strategy and practice of counter-terrorism and consequently adopting a criminal justice or police perspective on counter-state terrorism (detecting, monitoring, apprehending, punishing terrorists, etc.) as too a limited stance for sociological and generally scientific purposes. Notably, it goes beyond paying only lip service to state terrorism as supposedly irrelevant compared to its counter-state form and even, as virtually all states claim about their actions, non-existent or irrelevant. This is an approach prevalent in the sociological and related literature and especially political discourse since at least September 11, 2001, yet hardly justified given the historical and continuing presence, salience, intensity, and expansion of governments as agents of terror.

Especially the book reconsiders and emphasizes state terrorism, because those very governments that are most vociferous and sanctimonious in condemning and countering "terror" tend to perpetrate multiple and serial acts of such terror. They do so through systematic government coercion and violent repression, including executions, long imprisonment, and other Draconian punishments, often of innocent persons, for sins-cum-crimes and aggressive inter-state wars, as witnessed in Islamic and Puritan-founded theocratic states, during the "war on terror" and before (the Cold War, WW II, interwar times, etc.). By focusing on state terrorism equally as, or even more than, on counter-state terrorism the book transcends such governmental biased definitions and conceptions of "terror." They follow the pattern of branding attacks on them as "terror", yet their tyranny or violent repression, including executions and mass imprisonment of innocent or sinful persons, and wars against other states, is extoled and believed, as in Nazism, Islamic countries, and America during neo-conservatism, at least its regions under revived Puritan-rooted fundamentalism, as "law and order" and "rule of law". Instead, the book sociologically reveals the proverbial tyrannical emperor as without democratic and with terror "cloths".

Third, the book will probably generate controversy, if not more, in respect of assuming, identifying, and anticipating the major and over-arching determinant and predictor of modern terrorism. The crucial factor and predictor of most modern terrorism is assumed, identified, and designated as anti-modernity. Anti-modernity consists in the adverse reaction to liberal Western modernity, i.e., antagonism to modern liberalism in the sense and form of liberal ideology, democracy, civil society, and culture. This is likely to be greatly controversial, disputed, or rejected, especially in contemporary America. In America, liberal modernity or modern liberalism has become since the 1980s through 2010s virtually condemned, defamed, and stigmatized by anti-liberalism such as neo-conservatism as "un-American" ("liberal" as the pejorative "L word"). And it is despite or perhaps because of liberalism's historical projection, creation, and sociological consolidation of the "new nation" as the "land of freedom" with "liberty and justice for all" from Jefferson and other Enlightenment-inspired liberal founders to the New Deal, the political democratization and cultural liberalization of the 1960s, and beyond.

Conversely, anti-liberalism has been defined and glorified as "all-American" as the "apple pie" involving an anti-liberal ideology, politics, society, and culture in the form of reactionary and repressive, notably theocratic, religious-political conservatism perpetually resurrected from "death". Conservative anti-liberalism therefore reproduces and celebrates triumphant "American exceptionalism" in relation to the "old" liberal Europe condemned and despised, and yet feared to change America–just as Islamic theocracies–beyond recognition through Western liberalism and modernism generally. In doing so, however, conservative anti-liberalism's outcome is seemingly "shocking" but ultimately almost predictable with proxy mathematical precision or high statistical probability—Islamic-like "American exceptionalism" or deviation from modern liberal Western civilization. For American conservatism and Islamic theocracies represent, each with national "pride and joy", the most intense, persistent, and radical forces of anti-liberalism and anti-modernism in recent times and thus the major, extreme forms of "exceptionalism" or deviation from Western liberalism as their shared main enemy. In sum, the authors expect denial and perhaps more among anti-modern and anti-liberal conservative forces and governments, especially in America and Islamic countries, in arguing, demonstrating, and predicting that anti-modernity, notably anti-liberalism in the specific sense and face of religious-political conservatism, is the prime societal source, explanation, and predictor of most (though not all) modern terrorism at the time of writing these lines.

Fourth, the present work will be likely controversial in respect of casting doubt on the ideas and practices of pacifying the main agents of modern counter-state terrorism, namely religious extremists like Islamic, "Christian", typically Protestant or evangelical, and other fundamentalists, by meeting their seemingly harmless and sensible demands for the "greater role of religion" in politics and society. The book contends and predicts that the pacification of social extremism, notably religious fundamentalism, never has worked, does not, and likely will not work during the *long durée* of centuries and even shorter periods (Kondratieff waves of 50–60 years and less). This was witnessed in a historical sequence of, for instance, pacifying tyrannical Calvinist Puritanism in England, totalitarian Nazism and other fascism in Europe, despotic fundamentalist Islam in Islamic and other countries, and theocratic primitive evangelicalism in American history and society. Extremism, notably theocratic fundamentalism and sectarianism, like fascism, can be "pacified" and made "happy" only at the price of instituting "holy" state terror and tyranny by extreme fundamentalist and sectarian forces once seizing power or critical influence through government systematic coercion and violent repression, including executions and mass imprisonment of "enemies" (the "ungodly" and "sinful") and aggressive wars against "evil" societies. Short of this "point of no return" to liberty and choice, democracy and inclusion, and human welfare, dignity and life, extreme religious, like fascist, forces will never be pacified, "satisfied", or "happy" with concessions to their demands for the "greater public role" of religion in modern society.

Hence, this work considers and envisions such seemingly "spiritual" demands for "faith-based" society as ultimately imposing or generating anti-democratic values, institutions, and practices denying and destroying democracy, liberty, and life. These negations and destructions are predictably in the guise of, as in Islamic countries and America, a "holy" war on liberalism and modernism as anti-Islamic and anti-American, and in the form of systematic government coercion and violent repression and to that extent state terror as defined in this book. In cost-benefit terms, the costs of meeting "greater public role of religion" demands consist in ultimately relapsing into religiously sanctified, "godly" state terror through theocratic coercion and violent repression in the manner of what Weber calls the "unexampled tyranny of Puritanism" in England and early America, and Islamic anachronistic despotism after the image of Taliban rule, as well as Nazi totalitarian terror. In turn, the "benefits", if any, involve ending counter-state terrorism by these forces once seizing political power either through violence or election, "bullet or ballot". Yet, the book suggests and predicts that the cost may well be greater than the benefit in this respect, given that state terror, especially its religious or theocratic form, has historically been, is presently, and likely will be in the foreseeable future more total, severe, and enduring than counter-state terrorism. This holds true in virtue of 'holy" theocratic and other tyrannical governments murdering, severely punishing, torturing, and coercing and repressing generally more individuals and groups, as well as attacking and destroying more societies and cultures, than do non-governmental forces. To that extent, the benefit does not seem worth the cost from the perspective of modern democracy, liberty, human well-being and ultimately life. For state terror is the magnified and expanded system of violent repression, severe coercion, war, destruction, torture, and death perpetrated by government in relation to counter-state terrorism committed by anti-governmental forces.

The point is that while counter-state terrorism by anti-government, especially religious, forces is a serious and growing danger for modern democratic societies, state terror in the form of government systematic coercion and violent repression never has been and likely will be underestimated with impunity. This specifically includes widespread executions and mass imprisonment of sinners-criminals and even innocent people within society and global aggressive wars against other societies. The latter was witnessed, for example, in Puritan "holy terror" once tyrannical sectarian Puritanism capturing political power in England and early America, Nazi and other fascist terrorist regimes seizing the state in inter-war Europe, Islamic fundamentalists ruling Iran and other Muslim countries, including extreme Taliban rule even by Islamic theocratic standards, and the evangelical capture or dominance of Southern politics and society (the "Bible Belt") and seemingly or conceivably all America. In light of the above, the authors write this book keeping in mind the victims of both counter-state and especially state terrorism. For example, these victims include thousands killed in the 1995 Oklahoma and 1996 Atlanta Olympic bombings, on September 11, 2001 and other anti-government violence. They also involve millions of others executed, often innocent and/or sinful, imprisoned, and tortured by, for instance, Puritan theocrats at Salem and New England, Nazi and other fascist totalitarians, Iranian, Taliban, and other fundamentalist Islamic states, as well as by the evangelical, religiously open or covert "original sin" grounded and sanctified death penalty and penal system in America, especially the Southern and other "Bible Belt".

The book is organized as follows. The first chapter reconsiders and redefines the concept of contemporary terrorism. It first registers the difficulty and complexity in defining terrorism and presents its various official and scholarly definitions. Then it proposes redefining modern terrorism by certain attributes, notably in terms of illegitimate, indiscriminate, methodical, and strategic physical coercion, and violent repression in general, and violence or force, war, and destruction in particular. The second chapter deals with the classification of modern terrorism. In particular, it elaborates on the prevalent typology into state and counter-state terrorisms, with an emphasis on the various forms of state terror, in conjunction with other types. The third chapter explores the social causes of modern terrorism. It outlines a sociological conception of terrorism revolving around the concepts modernity, anti-modernity, and pre-modernity. Specifically, it identifies anti-modernity as the primary and overarching cause, explanation, and predictor of most contemporary terrorism. In this context it identifies certain, four dimensions of anti-modernity as the particular explanatory and predictive mutually related and reinforcing factors of contemporary terrorism, first, anti-liberalism and anti-democracy, second, anti-secularism, third, anti-rationalism, and fourth, anti-globalism, anti-cosmopolitanism, and anti-universalism.

The fourth chapter analyzes the first specific dimension of anti-modernity, namely anti-liberalism and anti-democracy through the antagonism to liberal-democratic modernity, as the effective or potential cause and explanation of modern terrorism. Specifically, it rediscovers conservative anti-liberalism as the crucial determinant and predictor of modern terrorism, with special emphasis on fascism and religious fundamentalism as such particular factors. In this context, it reveals that the opposition to liberal democracy, in particular to political pluralism and culture diversity, operates as the potent factor and predictor of contemporary terrorism. The fifth chapter focuses on the second dimension of anti-modernity, such as anti-secularism expressed in the antagonism toward secular modernity, as the actual or likely cause and predictor of contemporary terrorism. In particular, it posits and identifies theocratic revolt as the special source and path of terrorism and theological orthodoxy as its sacred ground and justification. At this juncture, the relations between world religions and terrorism are reconsidered.

The sixth chapter centers on the third dimension of anti-modernity, anti-rationalism in the form of antagonism toward rationalistic modernity, as the real or probable cause and rationale of modern terrorism. In particular, it detects and investigates religious and related irrationalism as causing and justifying modern terrorism, including superstition and fanaticism in religion as well as the anti-Enlightenment as such causes and justifications. The chapter also identifies and examines the reasons why religious anti-rationalism generates and operates as terrorism, i.e., factors of "holy" terror and warfare. The seventh chapter investigates the fourth dimension of anti-modernity, anti-globalism, anti-cosmopolitanism, and anti-universalism involving antagonism toward global, cosmopolitan and universalistic modernity, as the effective or prospective cause and explanation of modern terrorism. In particular, this includes investigating the antagonism to globalization, notably global liberalization and democratization, secularization, rationalization, and modernization, as the actual or potential source and predictor of terrorism. In this connection, modern terrorism is analyzed, explained, and predicted within the framework of what is termed global-cosmopolitan liberal-democratic society and its enemies. Alternatively, the chapter analyzes whether and how social closure tends to generate and rationalize terrorism, particularly emphasizing aggressive nationalism or nativism as a strong cause and rationalization of terrorist agents and actions against "foreign" enemies and influences within society and across societies, including militarism and imperialism. The eighth chapter provides conclusions as well as tentative predictions and expectations concerning the "fatal attraction" between anti-modernity, especially anti-liberalism in the most intense, pernicious, and persistent form of religious-political conservatism, and modern terrorism.

CHAPTER ONE

THE CONCEPT OF MODERN TERRORISM

Defining Modern Terrorism

Defining and consequently identifying, explaining, and predicting modern terrorism is an increasingly salient sociological and political problem, as is the solution or response to it. This especially holds in light of the resurgence of terrorist agents, actions, and outcomes among contemporary societies during recent times. The sociological and related literature provides a variety of definitions of terrorism, just as do governments and other political organizations. Analysts register a "multitude of definitions" of terrorism (Lutz and Lutz 2004), such as "more than 100 diplomatic or scholarly definitions" (Krueger and Maleckova 2003), for example "109 different definitions" (Smelser and Mitchell 2002; Smelser 2007) in the social science literature, as well as among governments. They also suggest that defining terrorism is "difficult" (Krueger and Maleckova 2003), as is that of its equivalents or analogues (Blattman and Miguel 2010), when performed both by scholars and governments. Arguably, this applies even more to conceptualizing, explaining, and predicting this growingly manifest and salient phenomenon in contemporary societies, as indicated by the observed "dearth of explicitly sociological" analyses, conceptions, and explanations of terrorism (Turk 2004).

Terrorism is one of the most difficult categories of sociology and other social sciences to precisely define, just as to conceptualize, explain, and predict, in the sense of yielding a commonly accepted, non-controversial definition, as well as conception, explanation, and prediction, of the terrorist phenomenon. This is primarily because contemporary terrorism and its agents almost invariably are attributed a negative societal, notably political, connotation and interpretation or manipulation, thus ideological, partisan, and even emotional overtones and controversies. Terrorism and terrorists are thus virtually universally subject to the social definition or construction of negative meaning[1] in contemporary societies and by

---

[1] According to Turk (2004:271), terrorism "is a social construction [i.e.] not a given in the real world but is instead an interpretation of events and their presumed causes." In his

modern governments (Turk 2004), including those social groups and states committing, advocating, and supporting terrorist activities, as well as "cultures of violence" and "cosmic war" (Juergensmeyer 2003). Such social construction seems equivalent or analogous to the socially constructed universal negativity of concepts like "crime" and "criminals" whose special, grave cases "terrorism" and "terrorists" are usually considered, and to some extent aggressive inter-state war sometimes regarded as a particular form or proxy of terrorism. In short, in contemporary society terrorism has commonly been attached a "connotation of evil, indiscriminate violence, or brutality" (Lutz and Lutz 2004).

Yet, as is often said, what is/are for some scientific observers and especially governments "terrorism" and "terrorists" or "murderers", however defined, is/are "liberation" and "freedom fighters"[2] (Juergensmeyer 2003; Smelser and Mitchell 2002), "heroes", or visionary "revolutionaries" for others. This indicates a sort of social and political dualism and relativism in defining terrorism and terrorists[3] (Townshend 2002). Such dualism is a variation on the theme and experience that what is, as Simmel puts it, a great, loved ruler for one group and society is a tyrant for another, as well as what are domestic and war crimes and criminals for some are heroic acts and heroes for others, and generally the same thing may be experienced figuratively as a cure *and* a poison by different individuals, social groups, and societies or cultures. Defining terrorism and related societal phenomena paradigmatically epitomizes societal relativism or pluralism in the form of multiple social definitions and constructions of the same situation and reality by various groups, governments, and societies or cultures. A religious-theological variation or proxy of this sociological relativism is found in Protestantism. What is, in Weber's words, an understanding and benevolent "Father in Heaven" from the New Testament in original pre-Protestant Christianity becomes in Calvinism and its

---

view, the construction and selective application of definitions of terrorism are embedded in the dynamics of political conflicts, where ideological warfare to cast the enemy as an evildoer is a dimension of the struggle to win support for one's own cause (Turk 2004:273).

[2] Juergensmeyer (2003:9) observes that "a violent act is "terrorism" technically only in the eyes of the courts, more publicly in the eyes of the media, and ultimately only in the eyes of the beholder. 'One person's terrorist is another person's freedom-fighter'. The designation of terrorism is a subjective judgment about the legitimacy of certain violent acts as much as it is a descriptive statement." Similarly, Smelser and Mitchell (2002:16) note that "what is "terrorism" to some may be called "freedom fighting" by others."

[3] Townshend (2002:4) suggests that this social-political relativism, expressed in the "one person's terrorist is another's freedom fighter" dualism "is central to the impossibility of finding an uncontentious definition of terrorism".

sectarian descendant Puritanism an "absolutely transcendental God" after the image of a "hard king", "pitiless" (Harrold 1936) and "arbitrary" or "Oriental despot" (also, Artz 1998) like Islamic sultans, though, on a lighter note, not a "sultan of swing" given the Puritan hostility to and prohibition of dancing and non-religious music. This probably prompted even arch-Puritan Milton to say "though I may be sent to Hell for it, such a [Calvinist] God will never command my respect".

For instance, what the US and other Western governments consider to be Islamic terrorism and terrorists, as exemplified by the September 11, 2001 and other attacks in America, Europe, Russia, and elsewhere, is "liberation" and "freedom fighters" or "heroes" and "martyrs" for many Muslim groups, states, and countries (Glaeser 2004; Smelser and Martin 2002). In another instance, the Soviet Union denounced the Taliban *mujahideen* in Afghanistan and Chechnya as "terrorists" and the like. Yet, the US and other Western governments, alongside Islamic groups and states, extolled and supported, including funded and armed, these Muslim militants as "freedom fighters" waging a "holy" war, vicariously on behalf of America and the West and effectively for the Muslim world, against an "ungodly" (Townshend 2002) government as an anathema for both the "godly" American government (Bell 2002; Munch 2001) and theocentric Islamic states (Wall 1998). To take another example, the US government or the scientific literature regards the 1995 Oklahoma City and 1996 Olympics bombers (McVeigh et al.) and their organizations and activities, including the bombing of abortion facilities and the killing of physicians, as "terrorists" and "terrorism". Yet, these violent groups are defended and glorified by their supporters and sympathizers within revived evangelicalism, neo-fascism, and neo-conservatism overall. The latter thus praise them as "freedom fighters" and "all-American heroes" and "patriots" fighting a "cosmic war" for "liberty", "life", "nation", "honor", and "God", or "crusade for Christ" against a liberal-secular "big" and "ungodly" American government[4] and "liberals" as quintessential, according to Reaganism and all neo-conservatism, "un-American" enemies (Juergensmeyer 2003; Turk 2004) inspired by and evoking the ghost of McCarthyism as conservative

---

[4] Juergensmeyer (2003:32) remarks that *The Turner Diaries,* the book directly inspiring McVeigh's 1995 Oklahoma City bombing and various other terrorist agents and acts in America, "describes an apocalyptic battle between freedom fighters and a dictatorial American government. Such [bombings] were necessary because of the mindset of dictatorial secularism that had been imposed on American society as the result of an elaborate conspiracy orchestrated by liberals [etc.] hell-bent on depriving Christian society of its freedom and its spiritual moorings."

extremism (Bourdieu and Haacke 1995; Plotke 2002; Rydgren 2007a; Smelser and Martin 2002).

Furthermore, what is terrorism or terrorists, like criminals or murderers, can become "liberation" and "freedom fighters", "heroes", and "martyrs", just as conversely, for the same defining subjects, such as governments and domestic and international organizations over time. To exemplify this scenario, US officials such as secretary of state, etc. initially characterized the Kosovo Liberation Army, an Albanian Islamic group seeking to secede by a campaign of "terrorist tactics" (Lutz and Lutz 2004) from Yugoslavia during 1990s, as an "ethnic terrorist army" placed on the government International Terrorist List. Yet, they subsequently supported and incited this "terrorist army" militarily and financially as a "liberation" organization and its members as "freedom fighters" to the point of the US government and NATO forming an alliance with the latter by attacking this country virtually on behalf of these Muslim terrorists miraculously turned into "heroes", "allies", and "good guys" (Bauman 2001; Giddens 2000). Also, in an ensuing episode anticipated by the "liberation" of Kosovo in 1999, in 2001 NATO secretary general described as "murderers and criminals" the members of a branch of the Kosovo Liberation Army operating in Macedonia and seeking to secede or attain other political goals also by "terrorist" activities[5] (Lutz and Lutz 2004). Yet again, such "murderers" were later miraculously transformed into "freedom fighters" and consequently incited and supported in various ways, including funded and militarily helped, though less openly and massively, by the US government and private organizations associated with the military, UK and German governments, and NATO overall.[6]

In a reverse scenario, what are initially "liberation" and "freedom fighters", "heroes", and "good guys" can become "terrorism" and "terrorists" for the same governments and domestic and international organizations. The most salient and dramatic example is the case of the Taliban *mujahideen* and other Islamic volunteers (e.g., Osama bin Laden's organization) in Afghanistan during the Soviet occupation. As admitted and widely known, these Islamic groups were initially funded, armed, and politically

---

[5] Lutz and Lutz (2004:247) comment that "Macedonia has offered new programs and greater opportunities for its Albanian minority. The Albanian dissidents in Macedonia concluded that more was won by a few months of violence in Kosovo than in a decade of peaceful politics, thus leading them to adopt the same tactics in Macedonia."

[6] For example, like in Kosovo and Bosnia before, NATO forces literally saved these Islamic "holy warriors" cum "allies" or "friends" when surrounded by the Macedonian military in June of 2001.

supported by the US and other Western governments as "freedom fighters" against an "ungodly" government in Afghanistan. Yet later on these
very "freedom fighters" became "terrorists" and "evil enemies" of America
and the West to the effect of necessitating and implicating the entire
NATO in a protracted (more than 10-year, by the time of writing these
lines) Vietnam-style war against these former "freedom lovers", "good
guys", and "allies"[7] (Townshend 2002). Incidentally, these Islamic "holy
warriors", including elements of Al-Qaeda, as subsequently revealed by
the US government itself, also volunteered in the former Yugoslavia–first
Bosnia, then Kosovo, and also Macedonia–by joining their "Muslim brothers", notably the Bosnian Islamic and Kosovo "Liberation" armies in, as
they construed their activity, the "jihad" against "infidels" in the midst of
Europe. In passing, US government officials have routinely dismissed the
observation about domestic and foreign Islamic groups in Yugoslavia
fighting a sort of "jihad" on the "rational" grounds to justify their military,
financial, and political support of and alliance with these "freedom fighters", including NATO's massive, relentless, and indiscriminate bombing of
a sovereign country virtually on their behalf, thus acting as the "air force"
of the "ethnic terrorist [Kosovo Liberation] army" (Bauman 2001). Yet,
September 11, 2001 and some committed, uncovered, or averted terrorist
actions on the American soil and beyond by these very "good guys",
Muslims originating from Bosnia, Kosovo,[8] and Macedonia,[9] probably

---

[7] Townshend (2002:109) comments that "ironically, these hundreds of [Islamic] volunteers who had gone to Afghanistan to fight with the Taliban *mujahideen* against the Marxist
government were the fighters who were funded by their greatest enemies, the USA."

[8] Media reported that in March 2011 "two U.S. airmen were killed and two others
were wounded at Frankfurt airport when a man opened fire on them at close range with a
handgun, the first such attack on American forces in Germany in a quarter century.
The alleged assailant, identified as a 21-year-old Kosovo man, was taken immediately into
custody and was being questioned by authorities. Family members in Kosovo described
the suspect as a devout Muslim." Moreover, during the attack the attacker reportedly
exclaimed the typical battle cry (*Allah Akbar*) of Islamic terrorists." By contrast to such
growing instances of Albanian and other Muslims from the former Yugoslavia committing
and plotting terrorism against its strongest and most loyal "ally" and "friend", the US
government in their past and continuing "jihad" against Orthodox Christians, as well as
other Western "allies" and "friends" like the German and UK governments, there has never
been reported that any Serbs or non-Muslims have perpetrated or planned such actions
despite NATO's US-led act of inter-state terrorism by illegally attacking and indiscrimi-
nately destroying the country on behalf the Albanian-Islamic "terrorist army".

[9] In the fall of 2010 media reported the following: "An online music video praising
Osama bin Laden has driven home a troubling new reality: A radical brand of Islam
embraced by al-Qaeda and the Taliban is gaining a foothold in the Balkans. 'Oh Osama,
annihilate the American army'. 'Oh Osama, raise the Muslims' honor,' a group of
Macedonian men sing in Albanian, in video posted on YouTube last year and picked up by

should have opened the US government's "eyes" closed for long in the face
of such activities (Lutz and Lutz 2004) by its Islamic "allies" and "good
guys" in the Balkans, and given it a "second thought" on the matter.

Such are apparently what Merton (1968) would call the "perversities" of
defining and describing "terrorism" and "terrorists" by different social
groups and in diverse societal settings, including governments and societies, and by the same group and setting such as government and society,
over time, expressing sociological and political relativism or dualism in
this respect. Such "perversities" or complexities make a commonly agreed
definition of terrorism by social science and especially by government
exceedingly difficult. At least, this difficulty in providing a consensual,
"uncontentious" (Townshend 2002) definition of terrorism arises with
respect to certain individuals, groups, governments, and societies, in particular those characterized by cultural-political conservatism such as
revived religious fundamentalism as observed especially in the Islamic
world and America during recent times. This is so because their activities
are defined as "terrorism" and their members as "terrorists" by scientific
observers and most governments, and yet as "liberation" and "freedom
fighters", "patriots", "heroes", "martyrs", "saints", or "holier than thou" persons by these agents and their allies or supporters. The latter pattern is
especially shown by Islamic fundamentalists and Protestant evangelicals
such as "Christian" terrorist militias and related "Christian Right" movements (the "Tea Party", etc.) in America (Blee and Creasap 2010; Hedges
2006; Hout and Fischer 2002; Juergensmeyer 2003; Owens, Robinson, and

---

Macedonian media this August. 'In September 2001 you conquered a power. We all pray for
you.'" Furthermore, reportedly "experts are now seeing an increasing radicalization in
pockets of the country's Islamic community, particularly after armed groups from the ethnic Albanian minority, which forms a quarter of the population of 2.1 million, fought a
brief war against Macedonian government forces in 2001. It's a trend seen across the
Balkans and has raised concerns that the region, which includes new European Union
member Bulgaria, could become a breeding ground for terrorists with easy access to
Western Europe. Many fear that radicalized European Muslims with EU passports could
slip across borders and blend into society." For example, in 2009 "three ethnic Albanian
brothers originally from Macedonia were implicated—along with a Jordanian, a Turk and
a Kosovo Albanian living in the U.S.—in an alleged plot to attack the U.S. Army's Fort Dix
military base in New Jersey." In another example, in Serbia during 2009, 12 radical Muslims
"were sentenced to up to 13 years in prison for planning terrorist attacks, including on the
U.S. Embassy in Belgrade. The presence of radical Muslims in Sandzak, the poorest region
of Serbia, is linked to the advent of mujahedeen foreign fighters who joined Bosnian
Muslims in their battle against the Serbs in Bosnia's 1992–95 independence war". This gives
a sense of perversity or irony, because the US government was the main ally or supporter
of these Muslim groups in their "holy" wars in Bosnia, Kosovo, and in part Macedonia
against Christian "infidels", with the US military and NATO overall effectively becoming
the air force of Islamic "freedom fighters" by bombing Yugoslavia on their behalf.

Smith-Lovin 2010; Turk 2004), neo-fascist, right-wing groups in Europe (Rydgren 2007a), including reemerging neo-Nazis in Germany itself (Koopmans and Olzak 2004), and the like.

In addition, given the universally negative connotation of this concept in contemporary societies, virtually no modern individual, social group, state, and society or culture would define, or agree to defining, their actions as "terrorism" but it is always others, usually opposing or differing from them, that provide such definitions and descriptions[10] (Townshend 2002). These definitions are typically non-complimentary or "stigmatizing", thus making "terrorism" a concept amenable to political and other social contestation or manipulation, and having "rhetorical power but limited scientific precision"[11] (Smelser and Mitchell 2002). Hence, in contemporary societies one of the most effective ways to politically eliminate or ideologically discredit certain individuals, social groups, governments, and even entire societies or cultures seems to be characterizing them as "terrorist", just as generally "criminal" or "deviant". On this account, such a characterization has been become a sort of political alchemy in the sense of effective stigmatization to the point of demonization used by virtually all relevant agents, in particular conflicting collectivities like different religious denominations, sects, parties, etc., as well as governments and societies. Simply, "terrorism" or crime always represents the "evil" and different Other (Habermas, Cronin and De Greiff 1998), "people not like us", and never "us" or "people like us", expressions especially used by US religious/evangelical groups to differentiate and demonize outsiders from insiders (Lichterman 2008; also, Davis and Robinson 2009; Lindsay 2008).

The preceding makes terrorism a sociologically relative and highly emotionally charged concept that is difficult to define, at least officially by government, in a manner to produce a conceptually non-contentious and politically non-exploitable definition. As a result, no consensus reportedly exists in defining terrorism in the scientific literature and especially governments and society, as indicated by the observation that presently there is "no internationally accepted definition"[12] (Houen 2002). This holds

---

[10] In the view of Townshend (2002:3), "terrorist" is a description that has almost never been voluntarily adopted by any individual or group. It is applied to them by others, first and foremost by the governments of the states they attack."

[11] Smelser and Mitchell (2002:14) comment that the "term "terrorism" is a stigmatizing concept; as a result, definers, labelers, and the labeled are eager selectively to exclude themselves and their own actions under the term and, correspondingly, to include others and their actions under it; the result is that "terrorism" is a politically contested concept."

[12] Houen (2002:20–1) suggests that the "first recorded usage of "terrorism" is Burke's association of it with the "regime of terror" after the French Revolution, thus originally

even for the aftermath of September 11, 2001 as the critical point with respect to global counter-state terrorism followed by various transnational and domestic terrorist acts or plans mostly by Islamic fundamentalists in a "jihad" against "infidels" (Feldstein 2008), as well as by US Puritan-inspired evangelicals (Blee and Creasap 2010; Hedges 2006; Owens[13] et al. 2010; Turk 2004) also in a "crusade" on the "ungodly" both within America and the world. In the latter, such instances are anti-abortion evangelical groups and/or anti-government "Christian" militias and the ultra-conservative "Tea Party" movement following the 2008 Presidential election, involving killings of abortion personnel, the terrorist attack on the IRS office in Texas, "Tea Party" warriors attacking and threatening to kill "big government" officials, etc.

Official Definitions of Terrorism

Instead of an "internationally accepted definition" what exists in contemporary societies presently is a number of particular official definitions of terrorism by national governments, including the US government (i.e., various branches within it). Thus, the US federal statutes define an "act of terrorism" as "any activity that involves criminal violence that "appears to be intended (i) to intimidate or coerce a civilian population; (ii) to influence the policy of a government by intimidation or coercion; or (iii) to affect the conduct of a government by assassination or kidnapping" (Heymann 1999). In turn, according to the FBI definition, terrorism is "the unlawful use of force or violence against persons or property to intimidate or coerce a government, the civilian population, or any segment thereof, in furtherance of political or social goals" (Smith 1994). Also, the Department of State defines terrorism as "premeditated, politically motivated violence perpetrated against noncombatant targets by subnational groups

---

denoting a "repressive regime", with modern terrorism beginning in the mid 19th century with "the subversive militant tactics of the Russian Nihilists and Irish Fenians, developments in explosives and the advent of a mass media". Also, Townshend (2002:22–3) registers that terrorism "as a distinctive political concept got its name (and unattractive reputation) from the actions of the holders of state power, perhaps the first modern regime–the French Convention", and Lutz and Lutz (2004:195) remark that the "term terror was born during the Reign of Terror" in the wake of the French) Revolution. In turn, according to Heymann (1999:2–3; also, Angel 1994:), "although the word "terrorism" dates only from the time of the French Revolution, the acts it embraces go back to biblical times."

[13] Owens et al. (2010:492) register US "sectarian evangelical Protestants whose efforts animated the first wave of a Christian Right movement."

or clandestine agents, usually intended to influence an audience" (Krueger and Maleckova 2003). Most other Western governments reportedly have similar official definitions of terrorism (Krueger and Maleckova 2003; Smelser and Mitchell 2002).

The inherent and seemingly non-resolvable problem with government official definitions is "who, how, when, and why" in positions of governance or political power defines a certain social activity and individual/collective agent as "terrorism" and "terrorist", but not other activities and agents. Insofar as this is an intrinsic and irremediable problem of government and other politically or ideologically and religiously based definitions of terrorism and related actions and agents ("crime", "criminals", "deviance", "deviants"), most of them are "untrustworthy"[14] (Heymann 1999) for sociological and other scientific purposes. In short, these definitions are made in the view and function of attaining not scientific purposes but certain political or ideological and religious goals, thus being "self-serving" (Lutz and Lutz 2004). They are politically or ideologically and often religiously motivated definitions, thus biased in the sense of defining and recognizing terrorism incorrectly or dubiously, namely various terrorist or non-terrorist agents, actions, organizations, and societies[15] (Townshend 2002). Specifically, for political, ideological, and religious motives, governments and other political organizations either define non-terrorist agents, actions, organizations, and societies as "terrorist", or fail to do with respect of those that commit, advocate, incite, or support terrorism instead defined and rewarded as "freedom fighters" and "allies", or reclassified, especially "home boys", as just "ordinary criminals" vs. "evil" foreigners, including immigrants (Collins 2010; Turk 2004).

The tendency is exemplified by the definition of and hence the "war" against terrorism by the US and other Western, not to mention Islamic, governments. For instance, the US neo-conservative "godly" government, including self-described evangelical Presidents a la Reagan and his ideological epigones, have attempted, and neo-conservatism overall still does, to redefine non-violent agents and acts like drug trade and traders–and in

---

[14] Heymann (1999:17) comments that even Western democratic governments may look "weak or untrustworthy in a shared battle against particular forms of political violence, or—in the case of the U.S. sale of missiles to Iran—hypocritical".

[15] According to Townshend (2002:3–4), the problem with state definitions of terrorism is they "simply assume that the use of violence by "subnational groups" is automatically illegal. The very first revolutionary terrorists in the modern sense believed themselves justified in opposing with violence a repressive regime in which no freedom of political expression or organization was permitted (Tsarist Russia)."

extension the use and users of drugs–as genuine or proxy "terrorism" and "terrorists" by interlinking the military "war on terror" with the Puritan-style temperance "war on drugs" and other moral sins and vices (Bell 2002; Cooney and Burt 2008; Hill 2002; King 2008; Wagner 1997). Yet, US authorities reportedly tend to define only a "few" terrorist actions by "home-grown militants", including anti-abortion and anti-government extremists, as terrorism and their perpetrators as terrorists, instead "typically" neglecting or minimizing their "political significance" and depicting them as "apolitical criminal acts" committed by "deranged" individuals, outlaws or gangsters, or "imported" agitators[16] (Turk 2004; also, Collins 2010). An identical pattern is observed with respect to the US conservative government defining of terrorism associated with non-American agents and settings[17] (Turk 2004). This is the pattern of defining state "terrorism", as exemplified by branding "unfriendly" governments in Cuba, Nicaragua, Venezuela, and other South/Central American countries as "terrorist", and Iraq's alleged "terrorist" role in September 11, 2001, as well as counter-state "terrorism", for example, a label attached to progressive-democratic movements in opposition to military and other dictatorships in Latin and Central America (Chile, Argentine, Salvador, etc.) during the 1970s–80s and elsewhere.

The opposite pattern is also observed in a kind of omission by failing to define or describe effective state and counter-state terrorism as such. The first is epitomized in refusing or avoiding to characterize as state terror "friendly" military juntas and other dictatorships installed or incited and

---

[16] Turk (2004:272) notices that "the US has a long history of violence associated with political, labor, racial, religious, and other social and cultural conflicts. Assassinations, bombings, massacres, and other secretive deadly attacks have caused many thousands of casualties. Yet, few incidents have been defined as terrorism or the perpetrators as terrorists. Instead, authorities have typically ignored or downplayed the political significance of such violence, opting to portray and treat the violence as apolitical criminal acts by deranged or evil individuals, outlaws or gangsters, or "imported" agitators. In official public usage, terrorism is far more likely to refer to incidents associated with agents and supporters of presumably foreign-based terrorist organizations [al Qaeda] than with the violence of home-grown militants, for example, the American Coalition for Life Activists, "one of whose founders, Hill, was executed in Florida in 2003 for murder, not terrorism."

[17] Turk (2004:272) comments that governments, in particular the US government, "generally succeed in labeling their more threatening (violent) opponents as terrorists, whereas attempts by opponents to label officially sanctioned violence as "state terrorism" have little chance of success unless supported by powerful third parties (e.g., the UN). (In) the cold war, the concept of "state-sponsored terrorism" was given full credence. Bulgaria, East Germany, Libya, North Korea, and Syria were named as Soviet-controlled sponsors of anti-American terrorism (yet) adequate evidence was never presented to support the listing of these nations as sponsors, much less under Soviet direction."

supported by the US conservative government (the military, CIA, ambassadors, etc.). The paradigmatic instance of this pattern was observed during Pinochet's neo-fascist military dictatorship in Chile violently overthrowing a democratically elected ("socialist") government, thus committing counter-state terrorism, with the evidenced crucial US incitement and support (especially CIA) and subsequently perpetrating egregious and documented acts of state terror, including mass murders of dissenters. Yet, this paradigmatic instance of state terror was never characterized by the American administration as such in a "meeting of allies" (Heymann 1999).

Additional instances include similar, as a rule, conservative far-right, dictatorships as axiomatic systems of state terror, yet political or ideological or "allies", especially during the Cold War, of the US conservative government and consequently never called by their true terrorist "name". These include other military juntas in South and Central America during the 1970s–80s and various dictatorial states beyond. Also, as noted, the US government extended the pattern of not calling by its name either counter-state or state terror perpetrated by its "allies" to Islamic extremists and "holy" warriors supported, incited, and glorified as "freedom fighters" in various settings and times, from Afghanistan in the 1980s to Yugoslavia (Bosnia, Kosovo, Macedonia) during the 1990s and Russia until recently, and other parts of the world. For instance, recall the US and in part other Western governments defined the Taliban *mujahideen* initially as "freedom fighters" or "allies", yet eventually as "terrorists" and "enemies", and also Albanian and allied Muslim volunteer groups (including Al-Qaeda) in Yugoslavia (Kosovo, Bosnia, etc.) in a reverse order.

In particular, the US and other Western governments have often defined and recognized state, just as counter-state, terrorism in a dubious manner. This involves not defining as "terrorism" such terrorist acts as "secret state violence" against their own citizens (Heymann 1999) by governments as "allies" or "friends", as well as by "friendly" terrorist subversive movements against "unfriendly" states, especially during the Cold War and later, under the guise of protecting "American interests and values"[18] (Stiglitz 2002).

---

[18] For instance, Stiglitz (2002:487) registers that the US government in the 1990s "opposed the OECD initiative to combat money laundering through greater transparency of offshore banking centers—these institutions served particular political and economic interests—until it became clear that terrorists might be using them to help finance their operations. At that point, the balance of American interests changed, and the Treasury changed its position. Political processes inevitably entail asymmetries of information: our political leaders are supposed to know more about threats to defense (etc.) than ordinary citizens." In turn, Davis (2005:148) observes that the "Pentagon briefly (and surreally)

As noted, cases of state terrorism perpetrated by American and Western "allies" or "friends" abound and would require a separate chapter or even book to describe them. For instance, in addition to neo-fascist brutal military dictatorships installed or supported by the US conservative government in Chile and other Latin and Central American countries during the 1970–80s, they involve other violently oppressive regimes elsewhere in the world such as Africa and Asia, including Indonesia in its massive and brutal purges, similarly established and sustained.

Recent instances are the repressive and nationalistic states resulting from the collapse of Yugoslavia during the 1990s. An example involves the state-sponsored campaign of mass murder and expulsion of non-Croats and non-Catholics in a newly independent Croatia (Lutz and Lutz 2004), practices especially supported and incited by Germany's conservative government as its main past and present ally (Alesina and 2004), after the model or image of the "Ustasa [Nazi] terror" against the same groups during WW II (Rydgren 2007b), as well as endorsed or "understood" by the US administration. Identical practices of mass murder and expulsion have targeted "infidels" in Muslim-dominated Kosovo (and in part Bosnia) after its "liberation" by NATO forces and its independence, first recognized by its chief "allies" and "friends" like US, German, and Islamic governments. Apparently, "secret state violence against its own citizens" is hardly ever considered government-committed terrorism in "meetings of allies" (Heymann 1999), in this case the US and Western governments with their European and non-Western "friends", from Indonesia and Chile to independent Croatia, Bosnia, and Kosovo; and many more countries can also be mentioned during the Cold War and later on.

In criminal-justice terms, the US and other Western governments explicitly or implicitly define and hence punish terrorism and terrorists as a special case or analogue of crime[19] and criminals (Heymann 1999;

---

contemplated creating an online "market for terror" in which traders could speculate on various classes of tragedy, the better to gather information about possible attacks. (The presumption was that traders had incentives to invest in gathering relevant information and that price changes would reflect the appearance of new data relevant to possible attacks. Critics pointed out that the market created a potential investment opportunity for terrorists to cash in on future attacks)." Also, Roth (2007:41–3) remarks that "in July 2003 a proposed U.S. government-funded "prediction market" for terrorism related events was scrapped (as) "trade in death." There was also some concern that terrorists themselves shouldn't be encouraged to play such markets. The proposed prediction market for terrorist events met with vigorous denunciation, but general prediction markets have thrived, including some that include bets on various aspects of current events."

[19] For instance, Moore et al. (2009:6) include terrorism, alongside, in "rare serious crimes."

Moore, Clayton, and Anderson 2009). Alternatively, the US government, notably the neo-conservative administration since September 11, 2001, has attempted to redefine and thus punish as "terrorism" and "terrorists" both certain violent and non-violent forms of crime and criminals. These include not only murders and violent attacks, but non-violent drug trade/ traders and even use and users, alongside illegal immigration and immigrants (Collins 2010; Shamir 2005), a classification driven by typical conservative xenophobia or American-style jingoism as "a series of xenophobic lies about the essential depravity of foreigners contrasted with the natural goodness of one's own countrymen"[20] (Dugger 1998), and some foreign journalists.[21]

Specifically, the US neo-conservative government has aimed, and neo-conservatism overall still does, at interlinking the Puritan-style "war on drugs" and other culture, moralistic wars on sins with, as an integral part of, the "war on terror", making drug-war and other culture-wars "crimes and criminals" (Reuter 2005), like illegal non-violent immigration and immigrants (Collins 2010), a form of "terrorism" and "terrorists". Yet, from the prism of modern liberal-secular democracy—and *not* theocracy and fascism–drug-war and related sinful "crimes" and "criminals", including drug traders and users not using violence, are non-violent, effectively moral sins and sinners. They are in that sense, following human rights organizations' terminology, innocent prisoners of ethical and implicitly political conscience, thus the victims ("collateral damage") of the US neo-conservative religiously driven, especially in the "Bible Belt", "political economy" of mass imprisonment as well as executions (Sutton 2004; also,

---

[20] Dugger (1998) adds that "these stereotypes are easily and continually debunked, but they easily and continually reemerge in new forms. For example, international terrorist conspirators recently replaced international communist conspirators, but xenophobia has continued to benefit the powers that be." Also, Shamir (2005:202) registers the emergent "new conceptual link, associating poverty with the threat of terrorism (as) in the "War against Terror". Yet, even without the mediation of poverty, the link between immigration and terrorism increasingly shapes public consciousness and public policy. At the height of the Cold War the legal category of "alien" in the U.S. Immigration and Nationality Act of 1952 had assumed a new meaning. Whereas prior immigration policies focused on setting numerical and ethnic-based limits on immigration, newly conceived concerns translated into a focus on the ideological profile of new entrants (assuming) an ideological association", i.e., the threat of incoming subversives. For instance, in a "conceptual fusion between immigration and terrorism, the U.S. Department of Justice also announced that undocumented immigrants could be detained indefinitely, without bond, if the government provided evidence that their release might threaten national security" (Shamir 2005:207).

[21] For example, a hyper-conservative Senator branded in 2010 the founder of a website (WikiLeaks) "a high-tech terrorist."

Becky and Western 2004; Cooney and Burt 2008; Jacobs, Carmichael, and Kent 2005; Wakefield and Uggen 2010).

To that extent, the US neo-conservative government's neo-Puritan and Islamic-style expanded definition of "terrorism" and "terrorists" to include certain non-violent sinful acts and agents–plus, as in ultra-conservative Southern and other states, illegal immigrants–is arbitrary and extremely broad. It is thus potentially amenable, and has often actually been applied, to penal abuse by including in the category "terrorism" and thus punishing and otherwise mistreating like imprisoning and torturing those individuals and groups that objectively and reasonably do not belong to "terrorists" (Smelser and Mitchell 2002).

The US "godly" government attempted redefinition of "terrorism" to include non-violent sins like drug use and trade would have an aggregate perverse outcome of infinite escalation through long-standing conservative-authoritarian slogans of "law and order" (Dahrendorf 1979), including neo-fascism in Europe (Rydgren 2007a) and neo-conservatism, in particular, religious fundamentalism, in America (Bailey and Snedker 2011; Baumer, Messner, and Rosenfeld 2003; Danigelis, Hardy, and Cutler 2007; Jacobs and Carmichael 2005; Jacobs and Tope 2007; Owens et al. 2010; Sutton 2004). Simply, the redefinition would treat and punish virtually all Americans as proxy "terrorists", except for Puritan-like evangelical self-proclaimed saints-guardians and would-be total masters of America (Davis and Robinson; Hedges 2006; Lindsey 2008). It would so long as most Americans, however "godly" and "patriotic"–the first typically determining the second– are "no angels" (Block and Sommers 1995) or moral saints, but various sorts of sinners ("all too human").

According to the Puritan-rooted and Islamic equation of non-violent sins and pleasures with crimes as Pareto registers for Puritanism, they are actual or potential criminals, notably "terrorists". Hence, these are to be punished because of the "rule of law" and "no one is above the law", except for evangelical saints-rulers, with "Draconian severity" (Patell 2001) by the neo-conservative penal and death penalty system as a "unique anomaly" (Pager 2003) among modern Western and other civilized societies, and only rivaled by its Islamic versions (Jacobs et al. 2005; Jacobs et al. 2007). As a secondary theological note, that most Americans as humans are no saints is implied in the Bible by its forgiveness for moral sins ("who has not sinned"), and yet invoked, notably the dogma of "original sin", as the "sacred" ground and justification of the neo-conservative redefinitions and sanctions of sinners as criminals, including "terrorists", notably of the death penalty and mass long imprisonment as overly harsh punishments

(King 2008), in America, especially the "Bible Belt" (Texas, etc.). More importantly, sociologically this is also indicated by the common observation and public admission that most Americans, including Presidents and Congressmen, have used illicit drugs (marihuana and others) and committed other sins like excessive alcohol use and sexual offenses (adultery, prostitution, etc.).

According to the neo-conservative attempted linkage of the "war on drugs" and other culture wars with the "war on terror", thus the equation of non-violent drug and similar moral offenders with terrorists, those dozens of millions of Americans, including Presidents and Congressmen, having used illicit drugs would be classified and severely punished as "terrorists" and their sins as "terrorism". Notably, they would be so sanctioned if only government authorities like prosecutors cum persecutors made a "real effort" (Friedman 1997) after the perennial model of Puritanism and its moralistic reproduction and suppression of "witches" (Kaufman 2008; Munch 2001) or the reign of "holy" terror and theocratic coercion in old and New England (Merril 1945; Rossel 1970; Walzer 1963; Zaret 1989). At the minimum, this applies to those almost two third or majority of nearly 2.4 million of US, including Federal, prisoners (Becky and Western 2004), imprisoned for non-violent drug and other sinful offenses sometimes for life due to "three strike laws" and generally political-religious factors (Cooney and Burt 2008; King 2008; Sutton 2004; Wakefield and Uggen 2010). They would be treated and punished, as have been in a way since September 11, 2001, as "terrorists" following neo-conservatism's "new" definition of terrorism to include such and related sins.

In historical terms, however, this is *not* a new definition, but rooted in Puritanism's prototypical equation of sexual and all other sins and pleasures and sinners, including adultery, "fornication", and blasphemy and their subjects, with crime and criminals and thus by implication terrorism and terrorists. Recall New England's Puritan theocracy punished adultery, like blasphemy and sorcery, with execution, which even sympathetic Tocqueville deplores by identifying the "sectarian spirit" and "religious passions" as the driving force of "punishment by death" that, as he puts it, "has never been more used" in the Western world than by American Puritanism as the "most totalitarian" (Stivers 1994) subtype of Europe-born Calvinism. In retrospect of almost two centuries, this is a prophetic or predictive observation. The death penalty, just as life or excessively long imprisonment for moral sins, "is never more used" or advocated in today's Western society than by revived American evangelicalism and neo-conservatism overall (Cunningham and Phillips 2007; Jacobs and Carmichael 2005; Jacobs et al 2005; Jacobs et al. 2007; King 2008; Sutton 2004). The latter stands in and perpetuates the theocratic and "holy" terror tradition of Puritanism (Dunn and Woodard 1996; Munch 2001) and strives to recreate "Christian America" (Juergensmeyer 2003; Smith 2000), notably ruling the South *cum* the "Bible Belt" (Mencken 1982) as the perennial and proud world "leader" (Texas) in executions and mass imprisonment for sins-crimes, alongside Islamic theocracies and China and North Korea.

The above, especially the scenario of infinite escalation, however seemingly fantastic and Orwellian, inevitably opens the following dilemma. One wonders "who" in America are to be protected from "terrorism", domestic or international, *if* most Americans have "sinned" by being past or present *non*-violent drug, alcohol, and sexual sinners, thus belong to "terrorists" according to the neo-conservative Puritan-type definition linking the "war on terror" with the "war on drugs" and other temperance wars against "sin and vice". The answer is virtually no one among "regular Americans" or "little guys" remains to be protected from "terrorism" if they are moral sinners, thus actual or potential criminals and conceivably "terrorists". The exceptions are self-proclaimed, but actually sinful and hypocritical Puritan-style conservative saints claiming, as did early Puritans, to be God's anti-vice agents (Zaret 1989) or "fallen angels", rulers, and guardians, including "born again" evangelical Presidents, Congressmen and governors, or power-hungry and seeking evangelicals (Blee and Creasap 2010; Davis and Robinson 2009; Hedges 2006; Lindsey 2008; Owens et al. 2010), "reborn" from the past "fall" in sin and vice like drug and alcohol use.

A disclaimer is that even the US moralistic and "godly" conservative government did *not* openly equate non-violent moral sins, pleasures, and sinners with terrorism and terrorists. Instead, in the admittedly venerable Puritan-conservative tradition (Dunn and Woodard 1996) of "vigorous hypocrisy" (Gould 1996), it did and neo-conservatism does so covertly by interlinking the "war on terror" with the "war on drugs" and other moralistic wars against sins and vices (Cooney and Burt 2008), specifically by reclassifying and punishing drug traders and in part users as genuine or proxy terrorists, just as illegal immigrants, since September 11, 2001.

Furthermore, skeptics suggest that, just as its war on drugs and other repressive temperance wars within society, American neo-conservatism's "war on terror" is problematic on its own right (Pillar[22] 2001), especially on the account of its suppression of civil and other liberties[23] (Heymann 2003; Townshend 2002). In this view, the "war against terrorism", as conducted by the neo-conservative government (until 2009 and perhaps resuming from 2013), poses a threat to democracy and civil liberties (Vasi and Strang 2009), just as does the war on drugs and other culture wars, and represents a syndrome of imperialism and militarism (Abbott 2005, Acemoglu and Yared 2010; Steinmetz 2005), jingoism and xenophobia (Dugger 1998) yielding and rationalizing anti-immigrant ideas and policies (Collins 2010; Shamir 2005). To that extent, the neo-conservative military "war on terror", just as the repressive Puritan and Islamic style "war on drugs", may, if not has already, become part of the problem rather than the solution, analogous to Mannheim's (1936) surgeon whose "operation was a splendid success [but] the patient died", thus a sort of, to cite Keynes (1972), "remedy that cures the disease [of terrorism] by killing the patient [of liberal-secular democracy and civil liberties]".

Notably, the above Puritan-based governmental definition strikingly violates or perverts what is the consensual, non-contentious condition of terrorism in virtually all previous and subsequent governmental and scientific definitions considered below. This is that the use of violence (Sorrel 1919) or physical force (Goode 1972) is the fundamental condition and thus the defining attribute of terrorism, and conversely, non-violent

---

[22] Pillar (2001:4) comments that "dead, or potentially dead, Americans are obviously the most important aspect of the problem for American policymakers but not the only aspect. Such a narrow perspective overlooks other costs of terrorism (particularly when non-American victims are involved) and other effects of measures taken to counter it." Pillar (2001:5) infers that "if counterterrorism is conceived as a war, it is a small step to conclude that in this war there is no substitute for victory and thus no room for compromise".

[23] Heymann (2003:16) remarks that "its political posture was always aggressive, for the administration trusted that the American people would not demand greater deference to (civil liberties). War on terrorism is the wrong theme. Reliance on the military is the wrong set of priority activities. Continued domestic support will depend upon confidence that the administration is not proposing, as ""temporary" losses of democratic liberties, changes that could last for generations." Heymann (2003:18, 160) envisions that "if these were to be the practices of decades of a war on terrorism, the country's democracy would change fundamentally (e.g.) a strategy of preventing, after the fact, the operation of the separation of powers (denying the need for legislative oversight and the right of judicial review)." Also, Townshend (2002:35) registers the concern that the "biggest damage resulting from the counterterrorist reaction had been to the long-cherished American legal defences of individual freedom. Though nobody would dare to suggest publicly that such damage was greater than the mass killing in the Twin Towers, it may have a more pernicious long-term effect on the quality of our life."

acts and agents are as a rule, other things being equal, non-terrorist; otherwise, heresy, blasphemy, dissent, and Orwellian "thought crimes" would be defined and punished as "terrorist" or "criminal", just as Puritanism did and US Puritan-inspired evangelicals overtly or covertly advocate. On this basis, drug-war, sexual, and other culture-wars crimes and criminals or rather moral sins and sinners, if non-violent, however morally repugnant or "disgusting", do not belong to the terrorist category. This holds true unless one, as US "born again" evangelicals and other neo-conservatives do, redefines and thus punishes every offense and offend-ers, including heresy, dissent, and dissenters, if not "thought crimes", against the religious and moral purity of their moralistic-theocratic and militarist vision of America as "terrorism". The second scenario would thus usher in an Orwellian totalitarian world or rather revert to Puri-tanism's theocratic "paradise lost" retrieved by evangelicalism in the shape of "Christian America" (Blee and Creasap 2010; Davis and Robinson 2009; Hedges 2006; Lindsey 2008; Owens et al. 2010; Smith 2000), at least the Southern and other evangelical "Bible Belt" (Bailey and Snedker 2011; Bauman 1997; Messner, Baller, and Zevenbergen 2005) resurrecting New England's Puritan "Biblical Commonwealth", a paradigmatic case of Weber's "unexampled tyranny of Puritanism", from the "golden past".

Yet, among contemporary Western and even non-Western states, excluding most Muslim countries, the equation of moral sins and thus underlying sensual pleasures with crimes and in extension terrorism is a sort of another religious conservative-based Islamic-style "American exceptionalism" (Inglehart 2004). Thus, many Americans cynically des-cribe this conservative American-only, within the modern West, equation of pleasures with crimes saying that "if it feels good, the government prohibits and punishes it", from alcohol Prohibition to the war on drugs, perpetuating the Puritan fear and punishment of sensual pleasure or enjoyment (Scitovsky 1972), of course of non-Puritans given the legendary moral hypocrisy of Puritans. Pareto long ago identifies the motivation of such Puritan and related prohibition/punishment of pleasures for others in observing that it "springs from that envy which unknowingly and unintentionally the non-enjoyer resents in the enjoyer, or the eunuch in the virile man [sic]."

The above then yields the "only in America" under conservatism Orwellian or paradoxical outcome of "less [real] crime, more punishment" (Cooney and Burt 2008). Virtually none of Western and related demo-cratic states defines non-violent crimes and criminals such as drug trade and use, traders and users, and similar offenses as genuine or proxy "terrorism" but rather as moral sin and sinners or addicts needing appropriate non- or mildly punitive treatments typifying an enlightened and humane penal system (Reuter 2005; Rutherford 1994). Instead, they invariably define the category of "terrorism" by violence or use of force, thus as a particular kind of violent crime and criminals. Conversely, only the US Puritan-rooted neo-conservative (Federal) government, at least until its likely transient replacement in 2008, alongside the "Bible Belt", and Islamic theocracies like Iran, Saudi Arabia, and Taliban regions redefine and include into "terrorism" and crimes overall such non-violent moral sins and vices involving sensual pleasures and sinners, including drug, sexual, and similar offenses without violence.

If the US and other governments' efforts to define "terrorism" like crimes such as murder, robbery, rape, etc. have been "less than successful"[24] (Heymann 1999) than conventional definitions of these offenses, this holds true even more of the alternative approach of defining and punishing non-violent moral sins involving sensual pleasures and sinners, equated with "crime" and "criminals" Puritan-Islamic style, as "terrorist" and "terrorists". This is indicated or predicted by the fact that, except for US evangelical-conservative and Islamic fundamentalist governments or non-governmental groups, no contemporary Western and non-Western democratic government does so, instead following the basic condition and sanctioning of terrorism solely on grounds of violence, not moral non-violent sins, or Orwellian "though crimes", dissent, and blasphemy.

In sum, governmental, official definitions of terrorism tend to be, first, too narrow by excluding and thus exonerating certain "friendly" terrorist acts and agents by allies, as the US government traditional definition of international terrorism during the Cold War and later (in Latin America, Yugoslavia, etc.). Second, conversely they tend to be exceedingly broad by potentially including and punishing virtually any, including non-violent, offenses and offenders, as in the neo-conservative attempted linkage of the war on drugs and the war on terror after September 11, 2001. Also, governmental definitions "naturally" tend to focus and overemphasize anti-government or counter-state terrorisms and terrorists, while neglecting or downplaying their alternative forms, viz., nation-states as actual or potential "perpetrators of terrorism" (Krueger and Maleckova 2003)

---

[24] Heymann (1999:7–8) adds that "terrorist acts are both crimes and forms of warfare (but) as a crime, terrorism is different (i.e.) planned to force changes in government actions, people, structure, or even ideology as a means to whatever ends the perpetrators are seeking with whatever motivations drive them towards those ends."

through government violent repression or severe coercion in society and inter-societal war and destruction (Houen 2002; Townshend 2002).

Scholarly Definitions of Terrorism

In light of the above, sociological and other scientific or scholarly definitions of terrorism should and usually do avoid the above problems and shortcomings of its official definition by political bodies like governments. First, they should be neither too narrow nor too broad[25] (Smelser and Mitchell 2002). They should include appropriate types and agents of violence characterized with certain attributes specified below, as the consensual condition and defining trait of terrorism, and exclude others (Lutz and Lutz 2004), for instance, non-violent moral sinners, plus political dissenters, that especially Islamic and Puritan-rooted governments tend to falsely define and severely punish as "terrorists" or "criminals". Second, these definitions should also consider types and agents of terrorism other than their anti-government or counter-state forms central in governmental definitions, namely government or state as an effective and potential agent of terrorist practices and outcomes[26] (Krueger and Maleckova 2003).

A group of sociological theories define terrorism as control strategy and tactic, i.e., as calculated action. Thus, terrorism is defined in terms of attempted control, namely as "illegal" or "threatened" violence targeting "human or nonhuman objects" whereby terrorists aim to become from objects to "agents of social control" (Gibbs 1989). Arguably, the reason why terrorism is "illegal" is due to its undermining state control and seeking to spread "fear" among certain populations, and thus controlling their behavior by "deterrent vicarious social control"[27] (Gibbs 1989).

---

[25] Smelser and Mitchell (2002:14–5) propose that defining terrorism "too broadly will dilute and waste resources that could be put to more efficient preventive and defensive use. A too broad definition may catch in its net persons not at all engaged in undesirable activity and may violate their constitutional rights or international conventions. Defining terrorism too narrowly means that people will not be protected from unanticipated kinds of attacks.

[26] Krueger and Maleckova (2003:120) remark that "definitions used by scholars tend to place more emphasis on the intention of terrorists to cause fear and terror among a target audience rather than the harm caused to the immediate victims (and) also, often include nation-states as potential perpetrators of terrorism.

[27] Gibbs (1989:332) adds that the choice is of "control" rather than "social control" because the latter is only a subclass of "control over human behavior". In turn, "deterrent vicarious social control" is defined by that the "first party punishes or rewards the third party, presuming that this will influence second party's behavior" (Gibbs 1989:335).

For instance, some sociologists identify lynching and related forms of vigilantism in the US South as a "distinctive form of "terroristic social control" "in that "by creating a "climate of terror", the specter of lynching served as a "powerful tool of intimidation" against certain social groups (Messner et al. 2005; also, Bailey and Snedker 2011; Jacobs et al. 2005; King 2008).

In another sociological definition, terrorism "in its purest form" is defined as "self-help by organized civilians" by covertly inflicting "mass violence on other civilians" (Black 2004). Thus defined, terrorism has what is called "its social geometry—its multidimensional location and direction in social space", in which new technologies by making physical and social distance "increasingly irrelevant" cause terrorist violence to proliferate, and yet by reducing the "social universe" they also plant the "seeds of terrorism's destruction"[28] (Black 2004). For instance, such technologies include the new "communications and transport systems" accelerating the "pace of globalization", yet being "also at the disposal of terrorists" and other criminal groups, international (Fischer 2003; also, Ceobanu and Escandell 2010) as well as domestic, as exemplified by the September 11 terrorist attacks[29] and the 1995 Oklahoma City bombing, respectively. In a similar definition, the concept of terrorism signifies strategies recurring "across a wide variety of actors and political situations" rather than "causally coherent and distinct social phenomena" (Tilly 2004). For instance, some analysts suggest that for most contemporary, especially religious, terrorists, their acts of violence such bombings are "well calculated, with carefully chosen targets and identifiable issues" furnishing "the rationale for each attack", as exemplified by an "antigovernment, antilaw enforcement creed for the Oklahoma City bombers" and "alleged U.S. oppression of Muslims in the Middle East for the World Trade Center group" (Pillar 2001). Arguably, what defines terrorism is the "pursuit of political goals" by means of the "systematic use of terror alone" as a "free-standing, sufficient, and decisive political strategy", thus being defined by an "absolute, independent terror strategy" rather than terrorist actions *per se* (Townshend 2002). In particular, counter-state terror or anti-government violence is often viewed as a "product of [social] movement strategy" (Walder 2009).

---

[28] Black (2004:14) predicts that "because social distance historically corresponded to physical distance, terrorism lack(s) the physical geometry necessary for its occurrence: physical closeness to civilians socially distant enough to attract terrorism".
[29] Fischer (2003:4) says that "the events of 11 September 2001 could not have taken place before the current global era."

According to a related definition, terrorism is "almost always" the strategy or tactic of "powerless or purposely disempowered" subjects (Heymann 2003). Reportedly, for more than a century, namely since the late 19th century, terrorists resorted to assassinations, hostage-taking, hijacking of planes, and "conventional bombs"[30] (Heymann 2003). In this view, still "many[31] acts of political violence" are not tactical or calculated but "relatively uncalculated" instead representing a "desperate effort" for being "seen and heard" by forcing a "handful of people or their concerns" onto the national and international stage, with many terrorists either being "simply mistaken about their prospects" or "so angry" resulting in indifference, as shown by the Oklahoma City bomber McVeigh (Heymann 1999). In a similar account, terrorism is typified by the tendency to acting "straight off the chart of "common sense", namely "not only unjustifiable, but atrocious, mad, or "mindless", even though it sometimes appears "rational" (Townshend 2002). Also, terror and intimidation are implicitly defined as "tactics" that are used for the goal of "political control through exclusion" on ethnic and/or religious grounds, as observed in the Balkans since the 1990s, particularly by the Muslim "Albanians in Kosovo" (Giddens 2000) against non-Albanian and non-Muslim minorities (Lutz and Lutz 2004) following the 1999 war and the secession ("liberation") and eventual independence of the province from the former federal state.

Another group of sociological and related theories define terrorism as the act of collective indiscriminate violence and destruction. In such definitions, terrorism is characterized with "indiscriminate terror" (Coleman 1990) through a "method of random violence" (Townshend 2002), including "deadly indiscriminate assaults on random members of politically salient groups" (Kestnbaum 2009). In particular, terrorism is defined by "public acts of destruction" which are perpetrated "without a clear military objective" and causing a "widespread sense of fear" (Juergensmeyer 2003). According to another definition, terrorism as a form of "unilateral collective violence", including or alongside lynching, rioting, and vigilantism (Roche 2001). In this view, terrorism is primarily collective and sometimes individual violence, including serial killings and

---

[30] Heymann (2003:22) cites the following cases of terrorism: "(a) attention-getting but purposely limited violence by a small group; (b) a continuing campaign of such violence (France 1985–95); (c) the spectacular attempts to kill many Americans (Lebanon, Oklahoma City etc.); (d) the danger of terrorists' use of weapons of mass destruction."

[31] Heymann (1999:9) suggests that "the burning of African-American churches in the [US] South in 1996 fall[s]" in terrorism.

assassinations, some rioting, lynching, attacks between street gangs, and vigilantism (Roche 2004). For instance, terrorism involves violent "forms of vigilantism" (Heymann 1999) and so-called vigilante terror does not necessarily possess "any developed ideological basis"[32] (Townshend 2002). In addition, some analysts regard hate crimes as cases of terrorism (Heymann 1999; King, Messner, and Baller 2009), or at least its "close cousin[s]" (Krueger and Maleckova 2003) invariably expressing moral-religious, ethnic-racial, national, ideological, political, and other bigotry (King 2008). In this view, as an archetypical case of hate crimes, lynching in the post-bellum US South differed from other homicides in virtue of its initial aim or ultimate outcome was inciting "terror" and conveying a "message beyond the immediate victims" (King et al. 2009). Generally, terrorism is defined by the "deliberate" targeting and attacking of "more or less randomly selected victims" in expectation that their deaths or injuries will undermine "the opponent's will" for action in political or military conflict (Turk 2004). In sum, according to these definitions terrorism is typified by "indiscriminate violence" in virtue of usually targeting and attacking "innocent civilians" and causing "indiscriminate casualties among them" to the effect that these are "terrorized" (Lutz and Lutz 2004).

   Still another group of sociological theories defines terrorism in relation to, typically distinction from, war and crime. First, some theories distinguish between war and terrorism. In such a conception, the "core of nearly all definitions" of terrorism, namely the "use of violence for political ends", is "too similar" to the definition of war although the two phenomena are seen as "intimately related" (Townshend 2002; also, Blattman and Miguel 2010). This view suggests that war is "ultimately coercive", and terrorism "impressive", the first being "physical", and the second "mental" (Townshend 2002). An alternative definition proposes that the "essence" of terrorism" represents moreover the "negation of combat" and involves the "process of terror" as the mechanism thereby violent acts produce "political effects" (Townshend 2002). It infers that its "essence" consists in the "use of violence" as a rule by armed agents against unarmed ones, involving certain stages or objectives such as getting "attention" through "shock, horror, fear, or revulsion", sending the "message" ("what do terrorists want?"), "fight or flight?, and lastly the societal response" (Townshend 2002; also, Spilerman and Stecklov 2009).

---

[32] Townshend (2002:50) cites the "Loyalist terror campaign in N. Ireland".

Another definition proposes that, while being less distinguishable from "guerrilla warfare" than from "conventional military operations", terrorism is "distinctive" in virtue of targeting and attacking "civilians" (Turk 2004). Also, a sociological analysis distinguish terrorism from crime in that criminal activities and criminals seeking "financial gain", as through kidnappings and extortions, do not represent terrorist acts and agents although "extremely frightening" for their victims, while criminal organizations (the Mafia, etc.) and their actions are in "only indirect relationships to motives of financial gain" (Lutz and Lutz 2004). Yet another analysis suggests that terrorism is different from ordinary crime because of, by using the "standard of collective liability for perceived violations of normative expectations", its targeting and attacking an entire population, thus being the "most extreme" form of destructive violence (Turk 2004).

In a sociological summary, according to "a simple and straightforward definition" terrorism comprises agents and acts aiming to generate and spread "terror" (Smelser and Mitchell 2002). Reportedly, the "recurring definitional characteristics" of terrorism are the following: first, the "illegal use or threatened use of force or violence"; second, a tendency for coercing governments and societies through generating and spreading "fear in their populations"; third, a typical set of "ideological and political motives and justifications"; and fourth, "extra-societal" elements, either "outside" society for domestic terrorism or "foreign" for its international variant (Smelser and Mitchell 2002; Smelser 2007). According to another summary, terrorism is characterized with (a) "political aims and motives", (b) actual or threatened "violence", an intent for generating "fear in a target audience beyond the immediate victims", (d) violence through an "identifiable organization", (e) violence implicating "non-state actors as either the perpetrator, the victim of the violence, or both" and (f) such violent actions strive for political power (Lutz and Lutz 2004). In this view, all these elements form the necessary condition for a certain action and agent to be considered "terrorist", while being "interrelated" and implicitly mutually reinforcing (Lutz and Lutz 2004).

Redefining Terrorism

The following is a step toward tentative redefinition of the concept of modern terrorism for the purpose of the present work. At this juncture, modern terrorism is distinguished from, though considered in a certain basic historical continuity or affinity with, ancient or pre-modern "terrorism"[33] (Lutz and Lutz 2004, Rapoport 2003; Townshend 2002). Modern terrorism is defined as the complex of actions of violent repression and physical coercion in general, and sheer violence or force, destruction, and war in particular, that are, first, illegitimate and illegal or unlawful, second, undifferentiated or indiscriminate, third, systematic or continuing, and, fourth, strategic or tactical. These acts are committed, advocated, incited, or supported by individuals and especially collective agents, with the second involving social groups or organizations, states or governments, and entire societies or "cultures of violence" (Juergensmeyer 2003).

First, terrorism involves institutionally illegitimate, more precisely illegal or unlawful (Smelser and Mitchell 2002; Smelser 2007; Smith 1994) individual and especially collective (Abbink et al. 2010; Friedland 2002; Juergensmeyer 2003) agents and acts of violent repression and physical coercion (Townshend 2002) as a "distinctly antiliberal mechanism" (Dobbin, Simmons, and Garrett 2007), particularly violence or force, destruction, and war. These agents and acts operate as terrorist in virtue of deliberately transgressing or disregarding and suspending definite rules of "social games" (Dahrendorf 1979). These rules include intra-societal legal systems such as constitutions and their specification in various laws. They also involve inter-societal, global conventions and norms such as those of the UN concerning civil liberties and human rights, war and peace, including the Geneva Convention on prisoners—openly and unapologetically violated by the US neo-conservative government in its "war on terror" and "evil", just as by its Islamic fundamentalist enemies Al Qaeda and the Taliban–the prohibition of wars of aggression, and the like (Giddens 2000; Habermas 2001; Smelser and Mitchell 2002). In sum, the core element defining terrorism and terrorists is the use or threat of violence and destruction, including war, and in extension violent repression and severe coercion as the means of attaining certain political and other ends[34] (Cragin and Chalk 2003; Lutz and Lutz 2004; Morrill, Zald, and Rao 2003), yet which is considered normatively illegitimate or unlawful action

---

[33] Townshend (2002:100) distinguishes pre-modern and modern terrorism. Also, Lutz and Lutz (2004:4–19) remark that terrorism is "quite ancient. Some of the most notable examples go back centuries or even a millennium or more [i.e.] its long history as a political tool by various groups", including "political violence or terrorism in the Middle Ages in Europe". They cite the following "waves of violence" since the 19th century: the anarchist during the 1880s; the anti-colonial since the 1920s; the new left of the late 1960s; and the religious wave since 1979 (Lutz and Lutz 2004:19).

[34] In the view of Cragin and Chalk (2003:1), terrorism is the "deliberate creation and exploitation of fear through violence or the threat of violence in the pursuit of political

according to applicable rules and institutions within society and across societies.

Second, terrorism involves undifferentiated or indiscriminate (Coleman 1990; Kestnbaum 2009; Smith 1994), random (Townshend 2002), widespread (Juergensmeyer 2003), or unilateral (Roche 2001) actions of violence, destruction, and war in particular, and violent repression and physical coercion in general. Such acts and their agents operate as terrorist in virtue of targeting, attacking, and conceivably destroying virtually all social resources and human subjects. The latter include military-civilian, economic-noneconomic, active-passive, insiders-outsiders, adults-children, males-females, native-transnational, leaders-masses, guilty-innocent, etc., located in a given societal space such as institution, city, region, or country, and historical conjuncture like culture, civil, and global wars, economic and political crises, etc. For instance, U.S. conservative, right-wing terrorists typically resort to "indiscriminate violence", as witnessed in the 1995 Oklahoma City (Blee and Creasap 2010) and 1996 Atlanta Olympic bombings and the 2010 Texas attack on IRS, as the effective means of fulfilling their "political or social dreams"[35] (Smith 1994). These are condensed in the old Puritan master-dream of reconstructing America as evangelical, sectarian theocracy (Davis and Robinson 2009; Hedges 2006; Hout and Fischer 2002; Owens et al. 2010; Phillips 2006) *cum* the "godly community" (German 1995), "Christian society" strictly governed by primordial Biblical law (Juergensmeyer 2003; also, Lindsey 2008; Smith 2000).

Third, terrorism involves systematic or methodical, organizational, and constant or recurrent agents and acts of physical coercion and violent repression, particularly violence, destruction, and war (Bauman 1997; Lutz and Lutz 2004; Townshend 2002). These agents and acts operate as terrorist in virtue of devising and using certain systems or methods (Turk 2004) and forms of non-state, state, and transnational organization

---

change." Similarly, according to Morrill, Zald, and Rao (2003:402–6), terrorism is "covert (political) conflict or violent covert collective action". Also, Lutz and Lutz (2004:10) propose that terrorism involves "violence or the threat of violence. For (political) violence to qualify as terrorism, it must also affect a target audience beyond the immediate victims and influence such audiences as part of the attempt to gain the political objectives of the organization."

[35] Smith (1994:45) quotes KKK leader Robert Miles who stated, concerning the idea of a thirty-gallon barrel of cyanide being placed in the Washington water system, that "the ones who would be killed would not really matter. It would be a good cleansing", and comments that such statements reflect a "move toward more indiscriminate violence by right-wing terrorists" in America.

(Smelser and Mitchell 2002). In consequence, they tend to be continuous, persistent, or recurrent, and to that extent "chronic" (Spilerman and Stecklov 2009), thus involving a degree of tenacity, repetition, and so predictability (Adorno 2001; Arendt 1951; Bahr 2002; Lutz and Lutz 2004). They are such within certain social settings or power constellations such as the opposition to modern democracy and society, or as the instrument of dictatorship and theocracy, and historical conjuncture like economic and political crises, culture, civil and global wars, etc. No doubt, some terrorist agents and acts can be non-systematic, non-organizational or individual, and non-continuing or transient, as in the case of conservative "lone wolf terrorists" (Lutz and Lutz 2004) in America,, such as the 2010 plane attack reminiscent of September 11, 2001 by an unaffiliated person on the IRS office in Texas, and their Islamic variants. Still, these "lone wolves" and their terrorist actions are relatively insignificant compared to their collective and organized form, because, as observed for America and Islamic societies or groups, contemporary terrorism has been "seldom a lone act"[36] (Juergensmeyer 2003; also, Abbink et al. 2010; Friedland 2002; Smelser and Mitchell 2002; Smelser 2007).

Fourth, terrorism involves strategic (Black 2004; Gibbs 1989; Tilly 2004) and/or tactical (Giddens 2000) and to that extent Machiavellian (Mannheim 1936) agents and acts of violent repression and physical coercion, violence, destruction, and war particularly, as "part of a political strategy" (Heymann 2003). They operate as terrorist in virtue of actors acting strategically a la Machiavelli in that their actions are designed (Friedland 2001; Mises 1950; Smelser and Mitchell 2002), projected or planned and public (Juergensmeyer 2003), or deliberate (Turk 2004) as the efficient instrument of attaining predefined political, military, economic, religious, and cultural goals or "dreams". Therefore, this strategic/tactical tendency renders terrorism an "instrumental process" (Townshend

---

[36] Juergensmeyer (2003:11) observes, for example, "when Hill stepped from a sidewalk in Pensacola, and shot Dr. Britton and his security escort as they prepared to enter their clinic, he was cheered by a certain circle of militant Christian anti-abortion activists around the country. It takes a community of support (plus) a large organizational network for an act of terrorism to succeed. Because of the moral, ideological, and organizational support necessary for such acts, most of them come as collective decisions. Even those acts that appear to be solo ventures conducted by rogue activists often have networks of support and ideologies of validation behind them. Behind convicted bomber McVeigh (etc.) was a subculture of militant Christian groups that extends throughout the US". In short, there were many, if not most, "Christians in America who supported abortion clinic bombings and militia actions such as the bombing of the Oklahoma City federal building" (Juergensmeyer (2003:13).

2002). At this juncture, in terrorism the ends or dreams really justify the means or techniques used for their fulfillment, defining–as Pareto and Merton in his analysis of the "American dream" as the "sacrosanct" end consecrating "any means whatsoever"–suggest, Machiavellianism as what Mannheim (1936) calls the amoral "cold-blooded" exercise of the "technique of domination" (Bowles and Gintis 2000).

As observed, these ends of terrorism can be divided into two broad classes. The first class comprises realizing and reproducing such a classic and perennial Machiavellian desideratum as dominant permanent power, as well as superior wealth and social status, simply privilege (Jacobs et al. 2005), for its agents, advocates, and supporters (Black 2004; Gibbs 1989; Tilly 2004). The second consists of inducing, spreading, and maintaining mass fear or intimidation, despair, anger mostly about the perceived government's incapacity and/or corruption, anxiety, and widespread panic—i.e., simply, terror–among other, targeted groups. These conditions and collective emotions of terror are designed to occur and remain both within society (Collins 2004; Heymann 2003; Krueger and Maleckova 2003; Lutz and Lutz 2004; Messner et al. 2005), provoking certain societal responses (Spilerman and Stecklov 2009), and across societies, as via global terrorist actions in the way of Islamic fundamentalists (Feldstein 2008) and "preemptive" illegal imperial wars on the "evil" world (the Iraq Second War, etc.) after the model of the US neo-conservative government (Abbott 2005; Steinmetz 2005; Turk 2004). For instance, conservative forces in the US, especially the South and vigilante groups, use and advocate the death penalty as the strategy and means of preserving their "privileges with selective terror" (Jacobs et al. 2005) against non-privileged groups, notably strategically using the "spectacle of executions" in order to "terrorize" the poor and powerless "underclass" (Bauman 1997).

In sum, terrorism represents a complex of individual and especially collective agents and acts of violent repression and severe coercion and, in particular sheer violence, destruction, and war that, as a rule with secondary exceptions, entails four interconnected and mutually reinforcing properties (Table 1.1). Namely, these properties are, first, unlawful acts by the "rules of the social game", second, indiscriminate in their targets and attacks, third, systematic or persistent in their operation, and, fourth, tactical in their design. Hence, terrorism is defined, detected, and predicted by the presence of violent, warlike, destructive, and generally coercive and repressive-coercive agents and actions having these four defining properties (minimally, most of them). Alternatively, terrorism is not present if such agents and actions of violent repression and severe coercion, in particular sheer violence, destruction, and war, lack these four properties (or most of them). Hence, the definition considers and incorporates only specific types of violence, destruction, and war, in general violent repression and physical coercion—i.e., illegitimate, indiscriminate, systematic, and strategic—while not considering and excluding others, as the suggested prerequisite for its analytical usefulness[37] (Lutz and Lutz 2004).

The present definition of terrorism both builds on and is distinct relative to more than a hundred definitions in the literature (Krueger and Maleckova 2003; Smelser and Mitchell 2002; Smelser 2007). Its particular and secondary distinctiveness consists in incorporating, war, including both civil or intra-societal and military or inter-societal wars, if sharing the above four attributes of terrorism, thus warriors ("war lords"), into terrorist actions and agents. This is in contrast to most of the current literature (Blattman and Miguel[38] 2010; Townshend 2002; Turk 2004), with exceptions concerning religious "holy" cosmic wars within society and against other societies as the observed form or sacred framework, ground,

Table 1.1. Defining elements of modern terrorism.

I Illegitimate or unlawful physical coercion and violent repression, in particular sheer violence/force, destruction, and war

II Indiscriminate physical coercion and violent repression, in particular sheer violence/force, destruction, and war

III Systematic physical coercion and violent repression, in particular sheer violence/force, destruction, and war

IV Strategic-tactical physical coercion and violent repression, in particular sheer violence/force, destruction, and war

---

[37] Lutz and Lutz (2004:9) suggest that in order to be "useful", the "multitude of definitions" of terrorism "need to exclude as well as include different kinds of violence."

[38] Blattman and Miguel (2010) distinguish civil war from terrorism and "related forms of violence", including interstate war, coups, communal violence, political repression, and crime. They object that the "distinction" between civil wars and terrorism, as well as "other forms of political instability has largely been assumed rather than demonstrated" (Blattman and Miguel 2010:6). Blattman and Miguel (2010: 35–6) conclude that "theoretical progress in this area accelerated some years ago, and we now have a host of theories of rebel and terrorist organization."

and rationale of contemporary fundamentalist Islamic, Christian, and other religious terrorism (Hedges 2006; Juergensmeyer 2003).

At this juncture, in Clausewitz's terms, as a form of terrorism war within society and against other societies can be redefined as the "continuation" of domestic politics and foreign policy, respectively, by "other [violent] means". First, these means are unlawful according to constitutions, as in violent religious-culture "holy" wars American-style violating the Constitution, notably the Jeffersonian liberal-secular prohibition against the "government promotion of religion", or per international rules such as the UN prohibition of wars of aggression, including the Geneva Convention for the humane treatment of prisoners as an anathema for US neo-conservative warriors. Thus, according to the UN rules prohibiting wars of aggression, most postwar wars launched by the US conservative and Western governments have been effectively unlawful and consequently, if the definition of terrorism by unlawful violence is consistently applied (Smelser and Mitchell 2002), acts of inter-state terror. This is epitomized by the Vietnam War, the 1999 NATO bombardment of Yugoslavia, the 2003 invasion of Iraq, and other smaller or "forgotten" neo-conservative wars (Grenada, Panama, etc.), with the exceptions of the Korea War and the 1991 Iraq War in virtue of their UN authorization and thus being legitimate by the global rules of war and peace.

Second, Clausewitz's "other means" are indiscriminate through the use of weapons of mass destruction on virtually all societal targets, as witnessed in NATO's 1999 illegitimate (Bauman 2001; Giddens 2000) attack on Yugoslavia, not to mention the Vietnam War, targeting and seeking to destroy or "neutralize" its entire "capabilities", both its military and civilian infrastructure, including national television and Danube bridges causing the long-term contamination of the river and the environment. (For instance, to add insult to injury during its unlawful and indiscriminate bombardment of Yugoslavia in the Spring of 1999, on Orthodox Christian Easter the US military/NATO "adorned" their missiles with the cynical message "Happy Easter!", a kind of cynicism that their Islamic allies, including parts of Al Qaeda, in Kosovo likely shared and rejoiced.)

Third, these "other means" are systematic and permanent or constant, indefinitely continuous. This is exemplified by Islamic jihad as the never-ending struggle against "infidels" in society and across societies (Juergensmeyer 2003; Turner 2002) and its Christian or rather Protestant equivalent in the form of the US evangelical "Crusade for Christ" in the generic sense of a perpetual "holy" warfare against the "ungodly" in

America and beyond. This permanence is also implicit in the Orwellian permanent "war on terror" and "evil" cum peace, in the sense of, as US neo-conservative self-declared evangelical Presidents and other officials stated, continuing and not ending in "our lifetime", thus a proxy new crusade, as they also depicted it, yet mutating in inter-state terror in its own right so long as it assumes the form of unlawful aggressive wars.

Fourth, the means in Clausewitz's sense are strategic or tactical and in that sense Machiavellian. Admittedly, this is epitomized by the strategy of pursuing and perpetuating US and Western global military, political, economic, and cultural hegemony (Smelser and Mitchell 2002), as experienced by most non-Western countries. Alternatively, certain, collective elements of terrorism can be defined and conceptualized in terms of war or warfare[39] (Heymann 1999; Kestnbaum 2009) broadly understood and thus mass destruction and self-destruction[40] (Mises 1950).

Generally, the above definition is distinct compared to the present literatures by virtue of defining terrorism by a definite type of violent repression (Besley and Persson 2009), including Draconian punishment like the death penalty (Jacobs et al. 2005), and physical severe coercion (Heymann 1999) or compulsion, direct and indirect[41] (Townshend 2002), and not only by sheer violence or force, destruction, and war as their special cases. However, it does not define all violent repression and physical coercion by individuals, groups, states, and societies as terrorism but only their illegitimate, indiscriminate, systematic, and strategic Machiavellian type, as well as such types of sheer violence, destruction, and war. In particular, government repression operates as a type of terrorism or locates itself on what some analysts call a "political terror scale"

---

[39] According to Heymann (1999:7) terrorist action are also "forms of warfare". In this view, "as a form of combat, (terrorism) falls into the category of violent ways of pursuing political ends (which) includes war between states, civil war, guerrilla warfare, and coup d'état. It differs (in that) it is carried out during peacetime in secret, without occupying or claiming to occupy any significant territory, and without organizing large groups to defy government authority openly" (Heymann 1999:8).

[40] Mises (1950) states that "violent action and terrorism of every kind are not economic means. They are destructive means, designed to interrupt the movement of economic life. They are weapons of war which must inevitably lead to the destruction of society". Yet, like his colleague Hayek, Mises reveals his "libertarian" anti-labor bias in that he includes labor collective actions like strikes into terrorist acts (sic) and thus implicitly criminalizes them, which makes his "libertarianism" the atavistic ("stone-age") and self-contradicting doctrine of unlimited liberty for capital and repression of labor, Anarchy for plutocracy, Leviathan for workers.

[41] Townshend (2002:100) suggests that the "conception of indirect coercion is indeed vital to any view of terrorism as a rationally comprehensible instrumental process; but religious violence lacks this special dimension."

(Besley and Persson 2009). It does through illegitimate, violent, and systematic repression and coercion committing "civil and political rights violations" (Besley and Persson 2009; Vasi and Strang 2009), including executions and political murders of "enemies", dissenters, sinners-as-criminals, and "infidels", their long mass imprisonment[42] (Becky and Western 2004; Sutton 2004; Wakefield and Uggen 2010), and generally the aggregate counter-utopian Orwellian or Puritan-Islamic empirical outcome of "less [actual] crime, more punishment (Cooney and Burt 2008). In this respect, political or state terror involves any institutional as well as extra-institutional coercive and repressive activities violating civil and political liberties and rights, executing and imprisoning innocent, dissenting, and sinful, but not truly criminal, persons, and generally perverting legal justice by linking "less [actual] crime" with "more punishment."

Notably, this definition is different from–i.e., more specific than–the frequent and perhaps prevalent sociological definitions of terrorism in terms of strategic control (Black 2004; Gibbs 1989; Tilly 2004). The latter is, as understood in these definitions, a more general category logically and empirically incorporating violent repression and physical coercion or direct compulsion, yet not limited to the latter, as shown by non-coercive, voluntary control through the internalization of religious and other cultural values, as Durkheim and Parsons emphasize, and also Weber suggests by his ideal type of "value-rational" action induced by "ultimate values".

First, the present definition differs in the sense in which violent repression and physical coercion or direct compulsion on one hand and social control on the other differ as the particular and the general, respectively. Namely, they differ in the sense of violent repression and physical coercion or direct compulsion being special cases of or attempts at control that is actually or potentially repressive and non-repressive, coercive and non-coercive, compulsive and non-compulsive.

Second, violent repression, including Draconian punishment, and physical coercion or direct compulsion, like sheer violence, operate as the mechanism, instrument, and "process" of terrorism, as demonstrated by systematic and widespread executions and imprisonment, especially of political dissenters and moral sinners cum criminals, in repressive states

---

[42] Besley and Persson (2009:294) measure government repression by a "political terror scale ranked from 1 to 5" such as that a cutoff of 3 and above is used to classify a country as "repression". Substantively, they suggest that "this implies that civil and political rights violations such as execution, imprisonment and political murders/brutality are widespread" (Besley and Persson 2009:294).

(Besley and Persson 2009), particularly Islamic and Puritan-rooted evangelical governments like Iran, Saudi Arabia, Taliban-ruled regions, Texas
and the "Bible Belt" overall. Notably, this includes the use of the death
penalty as the ultimate means of "selective terror" (Jacobs et al. 2005),
especially used to "terrorize" the poor and powerless underclass (Bauman
1997) through reproducing a sense of "terror" among them (Smelser and
Mitchell 2002), by the US federal government and most states, plus
anti-government vigilante groups by lynching and other violence, as well
as their using life imprisonment based on Draconian "three strikes" laws
for non-violent moral sins-crimes for the same aim.

In this dynamic sense, government and related political coercion and
violent repression represent the "process of terror", which especially
applies to executions and mass incarceration, notably of innocent
persons or non-violent drug, sexual, and other moral sinners in America
under revived evangelicalism and Islamic theocracies. Through this
process, coercive-repressive, largely religiously motivated and sanctified,
actions and agents such as Islamic and evangelical governments (aim to)
produce strong and enduring political and social effects (Townshend
2002). These notably include the effect of "terror" or "ambient fear"
(Bauman 2001) within society and beyond, for instance, "shock and awe"
not only, as via wars of aggression, "evil" societies but the US "sinful" population, including labor and "un-American" minorities and immigrants,
subjected to the ever-increasing threat and practice of repression and
coercion, including execution and mass long imprisonment (Becky and
Western 2004; Jacobs et al. 2007; Sutton 2004; Uggen and Manza 2002;
Wakefield and Uggen 2010), under neo-conservatism (Pryor 2002).

By contrast, with a few exceptions[43] most sociological definitions
defining terrorism in terms of control consider the latter to be its
ultimate end or aggregate outcome, thus being teleological that is in itself
problematic. A compromise solution is proposing that terrorism proceeds
or operates through illegitimate, indiscriminate, systematic, and strategic
Machiavellian violent repression and/or physical coercion, in particular
sheer violence, destruction, and war in order to attain and consolidate
social or oppositional control (Gibbs 1989), including mass intimidation
or fear, public anger and despair, and widespread panic—simply to induce

---

[43] For instance, Messner et al. (2005:636) characterize lynching as a "distinctive form of
"terroristic social control," while adding that "by creating a "climate of terror", the specter
of lynching served as a "powerful tool of intimidation"" . Yet, this implies that coercion via
lynching and other vigilante violence is the mechanism or process, and control in the form
of intimidation, the outcome or end of this form of terrorism.

the feeling of "terror" (Smelser and Mitchell 2002)–among targeted populations. However, it is this type of violent repression or physical coercion, in particular violence and war as the means or process, and not control in itself as the end or outcome, including fear, despair, anger, and panic or insecurity, that primarily defines terrorism and related actions.

In sum, violent repression and physical coercion with these four characteristics, specifically violence, destruction, and war within society and against other societies, are the invariant hallmark of terrorism, and control its variable desideratum, a teleological state that may or may not be attained. To that extent, this renders the sociological definition of terrorism by systematic violent repression and physical coercion[44] with the above properties more adequate than by control, although the latter concept is closely related to the former as the end to the means, respectively.

---

[44] Houen (2002:9) considers the treatment of terrorism in the aesthetic literature and suggests that its "focus on the fictional and the figurative obscures the physical effects of terrorist violence." In his view, "so much terrorism has been about contesting history. [In] McVeigh's bombing (the) date of the attack was carefully chosen as a response to the disaster in Waco, Texas (April) in which US Federal forces attacked the camp of a separatist, religious group (so) protesting against the Federal government's perceived interference in the local affairs of the nation's states (and) inspired by right-wing conspiracy theory (i.e.) the idea that the US Federal government is operated by a host of secret organizations masquerading as the "New World Order"—of which the UN is the public face—was common currency. Such paranoia also literally involved fiction in the form of novels", the most notorious and influential being the Turner Diaries (Houen (2002:13). Houen (2002:14) infers that "such terrorism is not just a rupture in history, but [also] of history, in which the anachronistic and the utopian are made inexplicably incarnate". In turn, Houen (2002:20, 236) comments that "literary and critical theorists contend (moving) from modernity to postmodernity, capitalism to "late-capitalism", structuralism to poststructuralism (with the contrasting) ways that modernism and postmodernism (examine) terrorism", although so-called the new "postmodern terror" "does not necessarily amount to a disappearance of state politics" contra Baudrillard and other post-modernists.

CHAPTER TWO

CLASSIFICATION OF MODERN TERRORISM

Typologies of Modern Terrorism

Certain overlapping sociological typologies of terrorism follow from the preceding definition and consideration. One typology encompasses individual, group, state, and societal terrorisms in which individuals as such ("lone wolves"), social groups or organizations, states or governments, and entire societies or cultures operate as agents of terrorist activity, incitement, advocacy, and support, respectively (Juergensmeyer 2003). This typology can be restated, as usual in the literature, as a dichotomy involving individual and collective terrorism, with the second, as the more relevant type (Abbink et al. 2010; Friedland 2002; Juergensmeyer 2003), subdivided into group-organizational, governmental-state, and societal terrorist agents and activities. Another typology comprises state or governmental, official or institutionalized terrorism (Baudrillard 1994; Einolf 2007; Habermas 2001; Lutz and Lutz 2004; Piven and Cloward 1977; Piven 2008; Torpey 1998; Townshend 2002) on one hand, and counter-state or oppositional, rebellious (Blee and Creasap 2010; Collins 2010; Gibbs 1989; Juergensmeyer 2003; Roche 2004; Smelser and Mitchell 2002; Smith 1994; Turk 2004) terrorism on the other. Each type contains its subtypes or functional equivalents. A complete classification and plausible conception of terrorism includes both counter-state and state terrorisms, although in the current scientific literature, just as the official definitions, an asymmetrical emphasis is put on the first type[1] (Gibbs 1989; Lutz and Lutz 2004; Townshend 2002).

---

[1] Gibbs (1989:330) recommends that it is "desirable to limit the definition of terrorism to non-state terrorism and to seek a different definition of state terrorism", adding that not all violence "by state agents is terrorism." (Juergensmeyer 2003:5) comments that ""terrorism" has more frequently been associated with violence committed by disenfranchised groups desperately attempting to gain a shred of power or influence", as does Townshend (2002:53) commenting that terrorism "is most commonly conceived [as] a strategy of assault on the state". Moreover, Lutz and Lutz (2004:12) state that terrorism involves "situations in which either the perpetrators of the political violence, the victims, or both are not states or governments. Actions between states, including war, (are) not included. [Yet] if both state and non-state actions are defined as terrorism, equality is established between dissident groups and governments. Limiting a definition of terrorism to exclude

This chapter and book overall aims to redress this imbalance in favor of counter-state terrorism by giving equal and even greater consideration to state, including inter-state, terrorism. The asymmetry is hardly justified given that state terrorism by means of government severe coercion and brutal repression, including executions, torture, and imprisonment, has been equally manifest and salient historically and presently (Arendt 1951; Bahr 2002; Besley and Persson 2009; Cooney 1997; Cooney and Burt 2008; Harris, Evans, and Beckett 2011; Jacobs et al. 2005; Lutz and Lutz 2004; Phillips and Cooney 2005) as, and even more so than, its counter-state variant. This salience has often reached the point of states or governments reportedly being the "most prolific users of terroristic violence" surpassing the "puny efforts of rebels" and thus a more destructive or threatening force to "liberal norms and public confidence"[2] in democratic societies (Townshend 2002). In this sense, the "most successful" and notably "most deadly" type of terrorism is that committed by states, namely the "direct state use of terrorism" (Lutz and Lutz 2004).

The latter is exemplified by Nazism in interwar Germany and Stalinism in the Soviet Union (Lutz and Lutz 2004). It is also epitomized by Islamic theocracies in Iran and Taliban-ruled regions. Another epitome is, alongside McCarthyism (Smelser and Mitchell 2002) as its source or precursor (Plotke 2002), repressive neo-conservatism with its design of "American theocracy" (Phillips 2006) or "Christian fascism" (Hedges 2006) via mass long incarceration and executions, often of innocent and typically of sinful and thus within the context of liberal democracy, non-criminal persons. As noted, neo-conservatism therefore generates and reproduces the perverse "only in conservative America" theocratic, Puritan and Islamic-style outcome of "less crime, more [Draconian] punishment" (Cooney and Burt 2008; also, Harris, Evans, and Beckett 2011). These and related practices form elements on a "political terror scale" (Besley and

---

actions between states, however, does not excuse or ignore the violence that states undertake." For instance, they remark that "terrorist attacks by the groups being victimized by [Nazism] would hardly have deserved any negative evaluations" (Lutz and Lutz 2004:9).

[2] According to Townshend (2002:23), "governments have been on any quantitative measure the most prolific users of terroristic violence. Yet there is no hint of this in the dominant official discourse, whether of national or international law (as) terrorism is used by extremists-rebels against the established order–the state (the hypocrisy or double standards)." In his view, "state terror has dwarfed the puny efforts of rebels in the 20th century. State terror may not fit the common model of clandestine terrorism, but (has) played a bigger role in undermining liberal norms and public confidence" Townshend (2002:45). Townshend (2002:52) infers that state terror shows "the tension between "terror" as a semi-random by-product of massive repressive violence, and terrorism as a deliberately focused product of demonstrative violence".

Persson 2009). In particular, this holds for the death penalty as "selective terror" (Jacobs et al. 2005) reportedly used to "terrorize" (Bauman 1997) especially lower classes or powerless groups and generally to repress the population (Pryor 2002) in America. Notably, the latter includes the "Bible Belt" (Texas, etc.) as the Western and even global "leader", along with Islamic theocracies, in executions, often of innocent persons as axiomatic state terror, just as the "undisputed world champion" in imprisonment for sins-as-crimes (ahead of China).

Regionally, the "Bible Belt" (notably, Texas) remains or appears to outsiders as the American and generally Western leader in religiously driven and sanctified genuine or proxy state terror, including the death penalty and other Draconian punishment like long mass imprisonment. The latter is applied not only to moral sinners like non-violent drug/sexual offenders, etc. in the Puritan and Islamic manner. It is also often to innocent people, as repeatedly proven by DNA evidence yet usually "too little and too late" for such persons, on overtly or covertly "godly" fundamentalist grounds a la "original sin" and the like. At this juncture, the term "Western" is a misnomer, however. For such "faith-based" Draconian punitive practices typifying state terror in the "Bible Belt" are unknown in and thus outside of the setting and thinking of modern Western civilization, simply deeply non-Western and uncivilized, and instead found only in the non-Western, especially Islamic, world.

For instance, only Islamic theocracies like Iran, Saudi Arabia, Sudan, and Taliban-ruled regions are serious challengers to the "Bible Belt" (Texas) long-standing proud world leadership in executions and long imprisonment, often of innocent or sinful persons—which is equivalent from the prism of modern liberal democracy that does not criminalize moral sins–and to that extent state terror openly or secretively driven and rationalized by religious fundamentalism cum evangelicalism or Biblicism. On this account, the "Bible Belt" and "Christian America" overall appears to outsiders and even many Americans as a sort of "Christian Taliban" (Mansbach 2006) in the midst and consequently outside of modern Western civilization. No doubt, this is a description that Southern and other US evangelical culture and "holy" warriors declaratively repudiate, while reportedly or secretly admiring Islamic theocracies governed by religious Sharia law, just as they strive to make America ruled by "Christian law" (Juergensmeyer 2003) through their persistent attempt or dream of seizing federal and all government and make it conform with their theocratic beliefs (Lindsey 2008) via systematic coercion and violent repression (Hedges 2006) and in that sense state terror. At this juncture, they may appear as what some magazines (*the Economist*) call Southern "fried crazies", yet in doing so they reveal a sort of rational "method in the madness" (Smith 2000) of government severe coercion and violent repression, notably executions and mass imprisonment of sinners and/or innocent persons, thus of state terror in the "name and mind of God" (Juergensmeyer 2003).

Notably, through their monopoly and apparatus of force and coercion, including punishment, above all executions and mass imprisonment, often regardless of actual crime, as in America during neo-conservatism (Cooney and Burt 2008; Hill 2002; Wagner 1997), states can and usually are the most potent actual or potential agent of terror. Thus, in an unlawful manner–either by their own legal norms (constitutions, etc.) or international rules—they conceivably can and likely historically did kill, abuse, and torture more individuals or exterminate more groups, as well as, via wars of extermination, "enemy" governments and societies than counter-state agents and actions. This is especially exemplified by totalitarian or authoritarian fascist, communist, and conservative political systems (Cooney 1997) premised on ideological monism (Dahrendorf 1959) or religious and political absolutism (Cooney and Burt 2008; Habermas 2001). It is also manifested in formally democratic yet substantively theocentric (Wall 1998) "godly" societies like America during the societal resurgence, predominance, and prestige of religious-political conservatism such as what Weber calls "Protestant sectarianism" (also, Clemens 2006; Jenness 2006; Lipset 1996) or Puritan-rooted evangelicalism (Davis and Robinson 2009; Lindsey 2008; Munch 2001), as during most of American history. In the latter case, as in most others, the fact or possibility of a government killing more persons and exterminating more groups and societies than anti-government forces is due to a mutually related and reinforcing mixture of state and inter-state "holy" terror, i.e., official, institutionalized terrorism within society and against other societies.

Predictably, "holy" state terror and warfare involves what Comte calls government "violent repression". Alternatively, the latter is indicated by a "political terror scale" comprising executions, mass imprisonment, and related violations of human liberties and rights (Besley and Persson 2009) within society. Such violent repression, in particular Draconian punishment with death and mass long imprisonment, has been especially directed against organized and disorganized labor (Piven 2008; also, Hayagreeva, Yue, and Ingram 2011; Western and Rosenfeld 2011) and the low-class and powerless population as a whole in America (Bauman 2001; Pryor 2002). For instance, the above "political terror scale" comprises mass, life-long imprisonment for sinful moral offenses—ranging from repeated drug use and trade to illicit alcohol consumption, prostitution and pornography and various other non-violent sexual activities, etc. (Cooney and Burt 2008; Hill 2002; Wagner 1997)—and the persistent and pervasive use of the death penalty as "selective terror" (Jacobs et al. 2005).

Both types of punishment are applied on overt or covert moralistic and "godly," including covertly "original sin" grounds, and often inflicted on innocent persons for fabricated murders, rapes, and other serious crimes, as especially witnessed in the "Bible Belt", notably Texas, judging by after-the-fact, usually too late DNA evidence. As noted, this underlying, though hidden, religious "original sin" perpetuation and sanctification of mass incarceration and executions, often irrespective of actual crimes and even sins, (patho)logically results in "less crime, more punishment" as a seemingly Orwellian fantasy within Western modernity, yet too a real historically primitive and comparatively Puritan and Islamic-style outcome in America during revived evangelicalism and neo-conservatism in general. At this juncture, if there is such thing as institutional state terror within modern Western society, then it is "less crime, more punishment" by government at all levels observed during the rise and hegemony of neo-conservatism in America since the 1980s through the 2010s. And if such a phenomenon exists or germinates in America, it does primarily in the form of "less crime, more punishment" by states on mostly fundamentalist "original sin" grounds in the evangelical "protototalitarian" (Bauman 1997) Southern "Bible Belt" (Alabama, Georgia, Kentucky, Mississippi, Oklahoma, South Carolina, Tennessee, Texas, etc.).

Generally, the government, like non-governmental or vigilante, execution of innocent–and in extension, within modern liberal democracy, sinful but non-criminal—individual is an axiomatic form of state and any terror in all societies and times, alongside, for instance, its collective form genocide or war of extermination, including ethnic cleansing. Recall Tocqueville observes that punishment by death was "never" more frequently prescribed and used in recent Western history than by New England's Puritan theocracy which punished in this manner, driven by what he calls deplorable religious sectarian "passions", virtually all non-violent moral sins and religious offenses, from adultery (and "fornication"?) to witchcraft and blasphemy or dissent. At this juncture, if anything was "pure" in Calvinist Puritanism as the self-proclaimed "pure" and "only true" Christian church, yet strictly speaking a "pure sect" in Weber's sense (or "cult"), then it was the rigorous and consistent use of the death penalty for moral and religious sins, apart from what he and Hume before detect as "pure" and "vigorous" hypocrisy (Gould 1996). And this Puritan "purity" or "favorite pastime" of executions for virtually "everything sinful and ungodly under the sun", including punishment by death for sexual sins, superstitious and cruel witch-trials, the extermination of the "pagan" Native Americans, and the persecution of Quakers, Catholics, and other non-Puritans, has yielded an apparent over-determination by or path dependence in this respect on Puritanism (Munch 2001). Overall, the latter has become, in Tocqueville's view, the "destiny" of America in the sense of its main religious and cultural heritage (Clemens 2007; Hillmann 2008b; Inglehart and Baker 2000; Jenness 2005; Kaufman 2008; Lipset 1996; Munch 2001) or parentage (Dunn and Woodard 1996).

Comparatively, no contemporary state in the Western and entire world, excluding Islamic theocracies Iran, Saudi Arabia, Taliban-ruled regions, and dictatorships North Korea and China, applies punishment by death for sins-crimes equated (Cooney and Burt 2008; Friedman 1997; Wagner 1997) more frequently, sanctimoniously, and arbitrarily—as when executing innocent or sinful and powerless persons—than does the "godly" US government at national and state levels. This sheds the new light or rather, from the stance of human liberty, dignity, and life, darkness on the celebrated conservative "phenomenon of American exceptionalism" (Inglehart 2004) as a striking deviation (Inglehart and Baker 2000), primitive in historical respect after the image of the "Dark Middle Ages" and Islamic-like in comparative terms, from Western modernity. No wonder that the resurgence and dominance of religious fundamentalism cum evangelicalism and generally neo-conservatism (King 2008) has been diagnosed or predicted as historically the "New Dark Ages" (Bauman 2001; Berman 2000), or perhaps the "Dark Middle Ages" never ended in Puritan evangelical America (Gould 1996; Stivers 1994). Comparatively, it has designed and even reconstructed Islamic-like theocracy in the form of "Christian" fascism (Hedges 2006) or extremism (Blee and Creasap 2010; Hout and Fischer 2002; Owens et al. 2010) defined by "holy" terror and warfare in, as Pareto would expect, the "name of the Divine master" and "the mind of God" (Juergensmeyer 2003).

Predictably, in addition to the federal government when under conservative control, the punishment by death and otherwise in a Draconian manner for sins-as-crimes especially holds for the Puritan-rooted evangelical states of the "Bible Belt", epitomized by Texas as the leading death penalty and imprisoning machine in the Western and, excluding Islamic theocracies, entire world, seemingly with pride and joy perhaps according to "everything [except reason, liberty, and life] is big in Texas". These states are manifestly or implicitly induced and self-justified in such "selective terror", plus mass long imprisonment for moral sins like non-violent drug, alcohol, and sexual offenses, etc., by sectarian religious "passions", including openly or covertly "original sin", as was Puritanism's "Biblical Commonwealth" as the perennial model for the "Bible Belt" and "Christian [read evangelical] America". At this juncture, sociological analyses identify the US neo-conservative death penalty system, as established in the federal government and most states, notably the "Bible Belt", as functionally equivalent to those in Iran's Islamic theocracy and implicitly Taliban-held regions in terms of frequency of executions as well as religiously fundamentalist "original sin" and related bases and sanctifications[3] (Jacobs et al. 2005; King 2008), alongside North Korean and Chinese non-religious dictatorships.

In turn, inter-state "holy" terror is historically and paradigmatically manifested in the Puritan-initiated apparently genocidal war of extermination (Mann 2005) driven by the idea of "manifest destiny" against the Native Americans (Gould 1996; Munch 2001). This also applies to other offensive and imperial (Abbot 2005; Steinmetz 2005) wars. For example, such wars more or less are exemplified by, alongside the war of extermination or dispossession of the Native Americans, by the Mexican conquest and subjugation, the Spanish war, Puerto Rico's re-colonization, military interventions in South and Central America, Vietnam, Grenada, Panama, Yugoslavia, Iraq II, etc. As least since WW II no Western state has waged more, invariably offensive "preemptive" wars by attacking other sovereign states than the US government especially (though not only) under conservative control, which, alongside the emerging and ever-growing military-industrial complex, would probably turn the founders like Jefferson and Madison (and even Eisenhower) in their graves given their largely pacifist or non-militarist ideas. And all these wars have been primarily induced and justified by religiously based nationalism—i.e., God's assigned "manifest destiny" to rule and save the world joined and reinforced with national "superiority"–a la triumphant Americanism (Baudrillard 1999; Bell 2002; Friedland 2001) as the civil religion (Beck 2000; Lipset 1996) with its "American myth of origins" (Dessí 2008).

---

[3] Jacobs et al. (2005:672) find that in the US "religious views account for all death sentences" to the effect that "religious fundamentalism leads to increased death sentences". Also, King (2008, 1355) observes that "Christian fundamentalists" in the US "generally favor harsher criminal sanctions".

Generally, theocratic and other "truly repressive" states can and do reportedly murder and otherwise illegally punish and harm "more people, especially the innocent" than all counter-state terrorist agents and actions, including those that claim to fight "for freedom or democracy" (Lutz and Lutz 2004). This is because in contrast to the latter governments are capable and wiling to resort to "terror on a mass scale", thus contradicting the mostly government-reproduced myth that terrorism is an "exclusive" activity of "non-state actors" (Lutz and Lutz 2004). In this view, what makes government violent repression and physical coercion, notably executions and other Draconian sanctions like torture and long incarceration, genuine or proxy state terrorism is identifying, repressing, and eliminating a "target group" that extends beyond the "victims and a political objective" and encompasses the "general population" (Lutz and Lutz 2004). The pattern was exemplified by Nazism[4] (Gestapo, etc.) in interwar Germany and the US government's "dispossession" of American Indians (e.g., the Cherokee Nation in Georgia[5]), as well as inciting, encouraging, or supporting attacks by paramilitary, vigilante, and semi-official groups against such "enemies"[6] (Lutz and Lutz 2004). Virtually all "authoritarian governments" are observed to tend to create, control, and manipulate "subdued or terrorized populations" (Torpey 1998) such that public officials commit or incite "terrorist acts". They thus commit or encourage

---

[4] Lutz and Lutz (2004:189) observe that "Gestapo in Nazi Germany was a gray presence everywhere, ready to detect any trace of treason or anti-government activity. Governments [often acquiesce] in violent activities [targeting] certain groups in their societies because of their unpopularity with the general population." According to their account, in Germany after WW I "paramilitary groups often used force against the left while the government did little to stop the violence (and) before Hitler came to power, the police frequently did not interfere with attacks by the stormtroopers against leftist political activities. The courts were more likely to punish communists for violence that occurred than the Nazis" (Lutz and Lutz 2004:190).

[5] Lutz and Lutz (2004:197) cite "the gradual dispossession of members of the Cherokee Nation of their lands in Georgia as a consequence of the actions of the state government and the inaction of the national government in the first quarter of the (19th) century (provides) an example of government complicity in terrorizing a minority group that was unpopular with the majority". In their view, "while many groups of American Indians were forced off their lands in the history of the US, the case of the Cherokees involved a consistent and concerted effort by the Georgia government for more than 20 years to support violence by private groups in order to achieve its desired goals" (Lutz and Lutz (2004:199).

[6] Lutz and Lutz (2004:190) remark that "governments may participate in terrorism when they permit and even support paramilitary groups, vigilante organizations, and semi-official groups that use violence in efforts to support government policies", citing the SA and the Nazi party in Germany, as well as Indonesia, inferring that "when the state tolerates and even encourages such terrorism, it is an example of state terrorism."

"a sort of state terrorism" for the sake of subjugating and controlling the "populace" (Juergensmeyer 2003). They do so, although such "secret state violence against its own citizens" is hardly ever considered terror in "meetings of allies" (Heymann 1999), as those of the US government during the Cold War (e.g., Chile and other Latin American military dictatorships, Indonesia, etc.) and afterwards (Croatia and Kosovo in Yugoslavia, etc.).

In sum, undemocratic states tend to exert social control through the "spread of terror" and by punishment, including torture, imprisonment, and execution, of those individuals and groups, other government and societies, identified as "enemies of the state (Einolf 2007). In particular, the "terrorist violence of single-party dictatorships", such as theocratic-conservative, fascist, communist, and others, tend to eliminate or subvert "constitutional protections internally", just as war of aggression as a sort of inter-state terrorism does externally by violating international rules and convention such as the UN prohibition of such wars (Habermas 2001). For instance, sociological studies find that in America a kind of state "terror" (Piven 2008) has been exerted primarily by a conservative government in coalition with the capitalist class, thus reproducing a sort of capitalist dictatorship "made in the USA" as an oppressive anti-labor "free enterprise system" and so a perversion of a liberal, free-market economy (also, Pryor 2002; Schutz 2002). In this view, such an activity has been the "principle means of social control" targeting especially, though not solely, labor and its collective organizations (Piven and Cloward 1977; Piven 2008; also, Western and Rosenfeld 2011) within society and through "US [inter] state terrorism" (Clairmont 1993) against "evil" societies. Moreover, post-modern theorists extend such diagnoses to Western society contending that its people are "hostages to a system" depicted as "terroristic" as that of the non-Western world, including Eastern Europe's former communist systems, and that "an escalation in the psychological balance of terror" proceeds through "world capitalist oppression" and "moral predation" (Baudrillard 1994).

State and Counter-State Terrorism

Forms of State Terrorism

By assumption and in reality, state terrorism implicates states or governments and political institutions in general as the agents of terrorist advocacy, action, and incitement, permission or support (Cooney 1997; Cooney and Burt 2008; Einolf 2007; Lutz and Lutz 2004; Townshend 2002). Thus, a subtype or functional equivalent of state terrorism is theocracy. For the present aim, theocracy is defined as the theological design and institutional system of "holy" terror and warfare against "infidels" or the "ungodly" within society and other societies and of tyranny or despotism in general (Dombrowski 2001; Juergensmeyer 2003; Merrill 1945; Oberschall 2004; Walzer 1965; Zaret 1989; also, Cooney 1997, Cooney and Burt 2008). Reportedly, theocracy is connected with and established through members of "the dominant or majority religion" committing or advocating terrorism, i.e., violent repression and ultimately elimination of other religious and secular groups (Lutz and Lutz 2004), though theocratic, including Islamic and Christian evangelical, states are typified with "internal contradictions" (Oberschall 2004).

This "holy" state system of terror and tyranny spans, for example in the Christian world, from what Pareto calls the "Roman theocracy" through Calvin's theocratic government in 16th century Geneva (Gorski 1993; Mansbach 2006; Walzer 1965) to, in Weber's expression, the Puritan "theocracy of New England" (Munch 2001) cum the "Biblical Commonwealth" only to be "disestablished" during the 19th century after precisely two centuries of official establishment. It also encompasses, with prudent qualifications, the reportedly fundamentalist, backward, illiberal, and undemocratic Southern "Bible Belt" (Acemoglu and Robinson 2008; Amenta and Halfmann 2000; Bauman 1997; Cochran 2001; Gould 1996)– plus from totally Mormon-ruled Utah–as heir apparent of the Puritan "Biblical Commonwealth," and conceivably all evangelical America (Davis and Robinson 2009; Lindsey 2008; Owens et al. 2010; Smith 2000) as the last effective or prospective Christian-Protestant theocracy, alongside in part post-communist hyper-religious Catholic Poland. Beyond the Christian world, the system is paradigmatically epitomized by contemporary Islamic theocracies in Iran, Saudi Arabia, and Taliban-ruled regions, as the most severe and pervasive systems of "holy" state terror, warfare, and tyranny. For instance, some analysts (Phillips 2006) identify an effective or prospective "American Theocracy" and in that sense the societal system or theological design of "holy" state terror, warfare, and tyranny by means of systematic government violent repression and coercion, including religiously "original sin" motivated and sanctified mass long imprisonment and executions for sins-crimes and often of innocent persons, since the 1980s through the 2010s. Furthermore, others identify evangelical "American theocracy" premised on Calvinist-inspired Dominion theology of the "Kingdom of God on Earth" with "Christian fascism" (Hedges 2006) or extremism (Blee and Creasap 2010; Friedland 2002; Hout and Fischer 2002; Juergensmeyer 2003).

For example, an historical study finds that Puritanism's theocratic "Holy Commonwealth" in England during the 1640s–60s was designed and functioned as the systematic "Puritan terror", embodied by Cromwell as the self-proclaimed "Lord of the Domain" and 100-odd self-declared "divines" as described by Hume in his classical account, while Puritan congregations in England instituted a "kind of local terrorism" enforced by the "godly elders" just as its national form was by an "elite of saints" a la Baxter et al. (Walzer 1963). This yields the inference that Puritanism's historical achievement was not, contrary to what is assumed in historically Puritan societies like America and in part Great Britain, as well as by sociologists like Parsons (1967) with his "Puritan heritage" (Alexander 1983), freedom and democracy. It was rather "terror" in virtue of designing and creating a tyrannical "holy commonwealth" and forcing people to be "godly" and "pure" through "a nervous lust for systematic repression and control" attempted to "universalize" with an intensity and to an extent, after the Calvinist model or image of society as a total monastery and open prison, with "no parallel among statesman or traditional moralists" (Walzer 1963). In short, as a sociological analysis suggests, Puritanism's main creation was a primitive "coercive theocracy" as the system of "holy" repression or terror in its own right realizing the Puritan medieval-based ideal of "godly politics" rather than modern liberal democracy (Zaret 1989). Moreover, due to their "theocratic revolt against the increasing secularism of 17th century English politics", Puritans are considered "precursors of modern antisecular radicals" (Juergensmeyer 1994). These are specifically US Protestant evangelicals and Islamic fundamentalists as functionally equivalent extremists and terrorists driven by the idea of a "cosmic" war, i.e., crusade and jihad in the broadest meanings, against "infidel", "impure", "sinful", and "evil" forces, in political translation modern liberal-secular democracy and civil society (Juergensmeyer 2003).

In another more salient and enduring instance, like its short-lived variant in England and the longer one in Scotland, Weber's Puritan "theocracy of New England" (Munch 2001; also, Kaufman 2008) lasting exactly for two centuries from the 1630s-1810-30s was reportedly the "reign of terror" as well as "suspicion and martyrdom of innocent people", as exemplified in the "deplorable witchcraft delusion at Salem" (Merrill 1945). In short, the theocratic "Puritan Babel tower" in its "reign of terror" planted the "germs of its own destruction" (Merrill 1945), i.e., failure and formal "disestablishment" during the 1830s. Note that this Puritan theocracy was disestablished about half a century after the American Revolution, primarily due to the ungodly and "wicked" Jefferson and his constitutional prohibition of "government promotion of religion" and the "wall of eternal separation of church and state" (Baldwin 2006; Dayton 1999; German 1995; Gould 1996; Hillmann 2008b; Kloppenberg 1998).

A contemporary survival or revival and extension of New England's Puritan theocracy and thus by implication, if not openly, its "reign of terror" is the perennial theological design, even the partially instituted theocratic system of "Christian [evangelical] America" (Davis and Robinson 2009; Hedges 2006; Lindsey 2008; Smith 2000; Juergensmeyer 2003). Minimally, it is the one of the new South redesigned as and transformed into the fundamentalist "Bible Belt" (Bauman 1997; Boles 1999; Gould 1996) following the anti-liberal, anti-secular, and anti-rationalistic "Great Awakenings" during the 18th-19th centuries (Archer 2001; German 1995; Means 1966; Rossel 1970). As registered, Puritan-inspired "born again" American evangelicalism seeks and even, as in the Southern and other "Bible Belt", succeeds to realize the fundamentalist vision of a "Christian theocratic state" in America by merging church or religion (the preferred term) and state in a "new" society and beginning ruled and marked by "religious law" (Juergensmeyer 2003). To show that they practice what they preach, reportedly many US fundamentalists, such as "Christian Identity" groups implicated in the 1995 Oklahoma City and 1996 Atlanta anti-government bombings and other terrorist acts, especially anti-abortion attacks and murders, have made the "rational choice" (following the "rational choice model" of religion) to lead, like their Islamic equivalents, a "holy" life in "theocratic societies" such as "Christian" ("Freeman" and "Aryan Nations") compounds (Juergensmeyer 2003). In so doing, these "holy" warriors and their supporters like the conservative "moral majority" apparently strive to redesign and reconstruct America as a whole after their own image, plan, and lifestyle of theocracy as "Christian fascism" (Hedges 2006) or the political rule of the extreme "Christian Right" (Blee and Creasap 2010; Hout and Fischer 2020; Owens et al. 2010) as almost totally established and exerted in the Southern "Bible Belt" and similar regions (Utah, etc.).

Hence, revived evangelicalism in America overtly or covertly redesigns and reconstructs, after the venerable and enduring model of Puritanism (Dunn and Woodard 1996; Kaufman 2008; Munch 2001), a system of "holy" state—and when outside government counter-state–terror in America against the "ungodly" as supremely "un-American" (Edgell, Gerteis, and Hartmann 2006), as does Islamic fundamentalism against "infidels" within society and via militarist jihad across societies. Evangelicalism does so through the extensive and intense government use of force, physical coercion, and systematic violent repression. This include Draconian punishments like mass long imprisonment and executions for sins-crimes, often of innocent people rendered ritual human sacrifices to the Puritan-rooted neo-conservative "obsession with sin and vice" (Wagner 1997) and in extension "original sin", couched in "tough on crime" paranoid and irrational–or, as many Americans call them, "dumb"–laws and policies. Recall that almost two thirds or majority of nearly 2.4 million prisoners in America (Becky and Western 2004; Cooney and Burt 2008; Sutton 2004; Uggen and Manza 2002; Wakefield and Uggen 2010) at the time of writing these lines are imprisoned, often for life thanks to Draconian "three strike" laws in most US states, for non-violent moral sins and vices such as drug (mostly marihuana) use, possession, and trade, and sexual offenses without violence (prostitution, viewing the Internet and other pornography, consensual sex, in part adultery, etc.).

And this leaves a sour taste of déjà that only Puritanism and cognate hyper-moralistic and theocratic religions like Islam can leave and is reminiscent of an Orwellian world of perpetually recurring waves of tyrannical repression, destruction, death, and wars. For American sinners could and were punished, including being imprisoned potentially for life, for committing the sin of alcohol consumption during Prohibition as another Puritan-style precursor–alongside capital punishment for adultery and other sins in the Puritan "Bible Commonwealth," witch-trials at Salem, "Monkey trials", etc.–of the "war on drugs" and related admittedly "futile" culture, yet often violent or coercive, wars (Bell 2002; Hill 2002; King 2008).

And these wars continue to engulf the "new nation" by the early 21st century (Blee and Creasap 2010; Bell 2002; King 2008; Singh 2002), as they did Puritan-ruled New England in the 17th century and the "old" Europe around two centuries ago or so (Dombrowski 2001), as during and following the Enlightenment and the French Revolution counterattacked by the "mindless" eventually lost battle of "religious orthodoxy" (Habermas 2001). On the account of such Puritan-initiated and inspired never-ending culture wars to describe, as do US super-patriotic sociologists and economists, America as the "new exceptional nation" in an invidious distinction of superiority or triumph from the "old decadent" Europe is not only empirically ungrounded. It is also a sort of "cruel joke" for those millions of "proud to be Americans" punished, including imprisoned and executed, for violating the "new temperance" and paying a high price of liberty and life to the conservative "obsession with sin and vice" (Bell 2002; Cooney and Burt 2008; Wagner 1997) and in extension "original sin", a punitive treatment virtually unknown or, as with the punishment of drug use, "more humane" (Reuter 2005) in modern Western societies.

In this connection, these sinful Americans represent within the context of Western liberal democracy innocent prisoners of ethnical and in part political conscience. To that extent, they are victims of "holy" and moralistic state terror and warfare in the form of near-total and severe violent repression, coercion, and Draconian punishment sanctified on religious Biblical grounds, thus of what Hume classically identifies as Puritan-style "wretched fanaticism" and generally "madness with religious ecstasies" or religiously induced "insanity" (Pareto's word) and hysteria. Furthermore, many innocent persons, as increasingly but after-the-fact proven by DNA evidence, have been executed or are on death row and imprisoned for life or decades due to unproven and fabricated crimes like murders and especially, given the Puritan-rooted conservative perpetual morbid obsession with "Sex [plus Money and God]" (Friedland 2002), rapes and other sexual offenses.

On this account, those innocent and/or sinful Americans suffering from the conservative pathological obsession with sins and vices, ultimately "original sin", notably "Sex [and God]", are the ultimate victims and true living or rather dead and ruined proofs of Puritan-style and Islamic-like "holy" state terror and warfare driven and justified by religious fanaticism or fundamentalism-induced madness in the "Bible Belt" and beyond in evangelical ("red") regions. Simply, even if not executed, a sort of miracle if they are accused of capital offenses given the perverted presumed *guilty* presumption due to "original sin" and legal proceedings (especially against those accused of sexual offenses and hence presumed *non*-innocent) reminiscent of Puritan witch-trials, it is far from a "happy-ending". For their lives have been effectively destroyed or harmed and disrupted beyond recognition and repair (e.g., permanent mental damage, failure to form or loss of family, etc.) by long imprisonment with its Puritan-style severer punishment like slave-style hard long labor often of several decades.

They are, in the US military's infamous terminology, the "collateral damage" of a Draconian and consequently unjust, unbalanced, and arbitrary death penalty system that is religiously sanctified, especially in the "Bible Belt," notably, Texas as the state "leader" in executions and incarceration, by Biblical law a la "eye for eye", the dogma of "original sin", and the like, just as are Islamic penal systems by Koran Sharia law. In this connection, recall sociologists observe that both the US government, notably Southern ultra-conservative states, and anti-government violent vigilante groups a la Ku Klux Klan (Cunningham and Phillips 2007; Lutz and Lutz 2004) though lynching, use or support the death penalty as a kind of "selective terror" against certain groups (Jacobs et al. 2005; also,

Cunningham and Phillips 2007; Jacobs et al. 2007). Notably, these "godly" powers and groups are observed using the "spectacle of executions" as the weapon to "terrorize" low and powerless classes into submission, resignation, indignity, and slave-like existence (Bauman 1997).

For example, some magazines (*The Economist*) regularly describes conservatives, including "born again" religious fundamentalists, in the South as "Southern-fried crazies" embodying the US "crazy right". Yet, as the interwar experience with the madness of Nazism and fascism overall showed, "crazy" Southern and US fundamentalism and conservatism overall can never be underestimated with impunity, as observed since the 1980s and before, from the 1920s "Monkey Trials" against science and KKK through McCarthyism to Reaganism and to the 1994 "Conservative Revolution" and the "Tea-Party" ultra-conservative extremist reaction and seeming triumph of the 2010s. After all, its parent and model Calvinist Puritanism initially proved that one could underestimate its "wretched fanaticism" detected by Hume only at one's own peril, as witnessed at Salem and in its New (and old) England theocracy overall.

In sum, the historical experience shows and predicts that various forms of religious-political conservatism could and can be underestimated only at society's peril, specifically counter-state and ultimately state terror, no matter how mad or crazy they appear. Cases in point comprise Puritanism in early England and New England, Nazism and other fascism in interwar and postwar Europe, revived Puritan-inspired evangelicalism and neo-conservatism in contemporary and historical America, and Islamic fundamentalism in Muslim countries and beyond. No wonder that these four varieties of conservatism have been the main historical and present forces and sources of terrorism, as elaborated and demonstrated in the rest of the book.

In retrospect, during the early 20 century Pareto presciently predicts this practice of institutional moralistic coercion and violent repression and to that extent institutionalized "political terror" (Besley and Persson 2009) in America under religious or conservative control. He does by diagnosing a century ago that the US conservative government has an undemocratic and illiberal–in virtue of its adverse effects on democracy and liberty–tendency for and systematic practice of enforcing, as a rule, Puritan-based "morality by law", as a sort of "favorite pastime" of its officials. In his observation, the US moralistic and "godly" government consequently tends to commit "gross abuses" of power or acting as "malignant power" in contrast to other governments in Western societies without such moralist and religious "restrictions" on individual moral liberty and privacy which Puritanism has reportedly never respected (Walzer 1963) and apparently, via Puritan-rooted evangelicalism with its assault on private liberties and choices, hardly ever will. Generally, Pareto predicts that the more government interferes with private morality and life, the more it will commit "abuses" of political power and thus eliminate or pervert democracy and freedom overall. His US contemporary, Mencken (1982) similarly observes and predicts that the "worst" government is the moralistic one, as epitomized by the Puritan and generally evangelical, sectarian type of governance in the US, notably the "Bible Belt" ruled by Baptist and Methodist repressive fundamentalism ("barbarism") for long, as since the Great Awakenings.

Pareto's and Mencken's observations have proven prophetic with respect to the US typically Puritan-type or moralistic "godly" government as well as fascist states, including the Nazi state, and Islamic governments. All these political systems share religiously grounded moralistic interference with and intrusion in private life and the consequent destruction or perversion of democratic politics and free civil society. Apparently, some things never change, or the "more things change, the more they stay the same" since Pareto-Mencken's diagnosis, in the US "faith-based" moralistic federal government, especially "Bible Belt" states (from South Carolina, Alabama and Tennessee to Texas and Oklahoma). Such a political system is driven by Puritan-inspired or Islamic-style fanatical obsession with and warfare against sins and vices recriminalized (Cooney and Burt 2008; Friedman 1997; Hill 2002) like alcohol and drug use as if these were—and remade by the government-media puritanical propaganda apparatus daily–the gravest and most pressing (alongside of course the sexual lives of others) problems of the "land of freedom." These sins and vices are consequently harshly punished as true crimes, thus sinners as real criminals, through the coercive and even often lethal imposition of "morality by law". To that extent, the moralistic government and "godly" states in the "Bible Belt" and beyond tend to commit genuine or proxy state terror. This holds true so long as systematic coercion and violent repression, notably unjust Draconian punishment like the death penalty and mass long a la 99 or more year imprisonment for sins-as-crimes and of innocent persons, as observed in America under theocratic evangelicalism and Islamic theocracies (Jacobs et al. 2005), belong to the "scale of political terror" (Besley and Persson 2009) and totalitarianism overall. Of course, the latter is a totalistic terrorist political system in its own right.

Another subtype or functional equivalent of state terrorism is fascism as essentially conservative-based "right totalitarianism" (Dahrendorf 1979;

Giddens 1979; also, Blee and Creasap 2010; Einolf 2007; Mannheim 1936; Rydgren 2007a). Thus, Mannheim (1936) implies this by observing first-hand during the late 1920s and early 1930s that, from a sociological viewpoint, fascism, notably Nazism, was the ideology and movement of terrorist, subversive or "putschist" (also, Lutz and Lutz 2004), and extremely conservative (Lipset 1955; Moore 1993) groups seizing political power through the Machiavellian manipulation or exploitation of the "crises of modern society" and by attracting the "explosive irrational elements in the modern mind". Fascism basically remains a type of terrorism through neo-fascism, including neo-Nazism, in contemporary Europe in the shape of or within extreme new conservative, radical-right movements (Rydgren 2007a).

In America, neo-fascism also tends to arise and operate within the "extended family" of neo-conservatism (Blee and Creasap 2010), notably merging or allying with revived religious fundamentalism, with outcome being or likely to be what analysts call "Christian fascism" (Hedges 2006) or "Christian Right" political dominance (Hout and Fischer 2002; Owens et al. 2010). This indicates that, like early fascism a la KKK et al. (Cunningham and Phillips 2007), neo-fascism in American tends to mostly assume the "godly" and so "all-American" form of "Christian" terrorist militias and allied or similar groups (the "Tea Party" movement, radio-television neo-fascist, right-wing hosts, etc.) exemplified by McVeigh et al. (Blee and Creasap 2010; Juergensmeyer 2003; Turk 2004). Moreover, the myth and subsequent reality of the "Fascist and Nazi seizures of power" by counter-state terrorism or using the procedures of democracy—for example, free elections by Nazism in Germany–in order to destroy it in interwar Europe was "probably the most potent fantasy" and the realization of state and all terrorism in the "modern age" (Townshend 2002).

And this fascist seizure essentially continues to exert fascination on and inspire counter-state terrorism by neo-fascism, in particular neo-Nazism, in Europe through extreme conservative, right-wing groups and America. In the latter it does so predictably via "Christian fascism" such as neo-Nazi "Christian" militia and related fundamentalist ultra-conservative movements a la "Christian Identity", "Christian warriors", "Tea Party", etc., also and perhaps more inspired by the Puritan "Bible Commonwealth" as "paradise lost", while admiring Islamic theocracies[7] (Juergensmeyer 2003). In essence, akin to Mannheim, Dahrendorf (1979)

---

[7] Juergensmeyer (2003:212) remarks that US fundamentalism regards the "Protestant governments of the early American colonies", namely Puritan New England, grounding

suggests that what calls the "anti-philosophy of fascism" was and, via neo-fascism, remains the design and ultimately practice of state terrorism in the form of totalitarian government coercion and violent repression, Draconian punishment, mass murder, and warfare once in power, just as of counter-state terrorism or anti-government violence when not in governance. And this is pattern and method that fascism/neo-fascism evidently shares with theocracy and religious, including Islamic and Protestant "Christian", fundamentalism.

As known, totalitarian fascism as a paradigmatic type and system of state terrorism incorporates, first and foremost, Nazism being the system of "Nazi terror" in Germany (Adorno 2001; Arendt 1951; Bahr 2002; Barnes 2000; Horkheimer and Adorno 1993; Lemert 1991; Rydgren 2007; Savelsberg and King 2005). As observed, in terms of state "terror and repressive measures", fascism, specifically Nazism, invariably moves and does "*beyond*" its proclamations and intentions such that fascist totalitarianism recognizes "no limits" and leaves no "breathing spell" in its "conquest with absolute domination, complete extermination of the chosen foe" (Adorno 2001; also, Horkheimer and Adorno 1993). In a similar observation, the nature of Nazi and other fascist totalitarianism is the "combination of its essence of terror and its principle of logicality", with "total terror" generating "total loneliness" and the latter enabling "total power"[8] (Arendt 1951). For instance, in this account, while "anti-utilitarian only by normal standards of utility maximization", Nazi concentration camps as the ultimate instruments of total state terror had, by Nazism's standards, their dual "usefulness" in, first, exterminating "objective enemies", and, second, producing the "model citizen" of fascist totalitarianism[9] (Bähr, 2002).

The preceding perhaps applies in some degree to the conservative or, as in the "Bible Belt" (particularly Texas), fundamentalist-based death penalty, prison, and generally penal system in America. It does on the account of the penal system using, like anti-government violent vigilante

---

their "constitutions in biblical law" as a model or precedent for a "new kind of Christian government", and "admires the attempts of Muslims in Iran, Sudan, and Afghanistan to create regimes grounded in Islamic law."

[8] Arendt (1951:34) adds that "in the background there lurked the terror of the Gestapo and the fear of the concentration camp for those that got out of line or who had been" against Nazism.

[9] Evoking Arendt, Bähr (2002:811) proposes that modern totalitarianism like Nazism is "a type of regime that, no longer satisfied with the limited aims of classical despotisms and dictatorships, demands continual mobilization of its subjects and never allows the society to settle down into a durable hierarchical order (and) predicated on an experience of mass superfluity".

groups, from KKK (Cunningham and Phillips 2007; Lutz and Lutz 2004) to recent anti-immigrant vigilantes, executions as the means of "selective terror" against "enemies" or "un-American" persons, not to mention non-Americans or foreigners (Mexicans and other in Texas, for example), notably to "terrorize" the low class (Bauman 1997), and the "ungodly" (Edgell et al. 2006). This holds true in virtue of the overall "Draconian severity" (Patell 2001) of the conservative religiously grounded, notably "Bible Belt", criminal justice, system, thus its exceptional attribute of a "unique anomaly" (Pager 2003) among contemporary Western and other societies, excluding Islamic theocracies and other dictatorships (North Korea, China, etc.). To avoid misunderstanding or worse, this does not posit an equation between Nazi and conservative/fundamentalist criminal justice "Bible Belt" systems, but an approximation in the sense of proxy comparability, similarity, or affinity between the two.

For instance, some observations (Bauman 2001; Bourdieu 1998; Miliband 1969; Wacquant 2002; Wagner 1997) imply that the US conservative penal system evinces the following dual tendency. First, it tends to construct the material capacities for Draconian punishment, including the death penalty and life-term or long mass imprisonment. Then, it aims to fully and "efficiently", in particular, profitably through "free" private enterprise in the prison system, utilize these capacities rather than leaving them "empty" and "idle" by inhabiting them with sinful and often legally innocent humans (e.g., drug, alcohol, sexual, and other non-violent offenders) usually "beyond capacity", as in Texas, California, and other states, a dual practice initiated or climaxed in the Nazi totalitarian regime as a paradigmatic system of state terror. Simply, this is the practice of building prisons (camps) first and then filling them with an interrupted stream of prisoners (inmates). The latter increasingly include innocent or–which is the same from the angle of modern liberal democracy–sinful persons imprisoned and executed or placed on death row, as revealed usually too late by DNA evidence in Texas and elsewhere. In the process, considerations of innocence and guilt have become increasingly irrelevant or perverted from "presumed innocent" into "presumed guilty"— sanctified by "original sin" presuming constant and perpetual human guilt–through neo-conservative "tough on crime" temperance wars a la the war on drugs.

These moralistic wars and their Draconian punishments are overtly or covertly motivated and sanctified by fanatical religious fundamentalism a la the Biblical "eye for eye", "original sin", etc. They thus follow New England's Puritan theocracy driven in its punishment by death for a myriad of moral-religious sins, including adultery, fornication, blasphemy, and sorcery, by what Hume and even sympathetic Tocqueville deplore as "wild" and "wretched" fanaticism and sectarian "passions" defying and destroying human reason and even common sense. And these religious forces still do defy, insult, and pervert reason and common sense as via puritanical evangelicalism (increasing the legal age limit for alcohol consumption from 18 to 21 years by Reaganism, etc.).

Hence, the outcome is a perverse form of crime or rather sin control, including "vice police", that reproduces rather than reduces sins and vices cum crimes[10] (Wagner 1997), thus reproducing mass and long imprisonment primarily for moral like non-violent drug offenses (Becky and Western 2004; Sutton 2004; Wakefield and Uggen 2010). This is a pattern shared by other forms of fascism in interwar Europe, as well as contemporary Islamic theocracies like Iran, Saudi Arabia, and Taliban-ruled regions. Generally, some analysts suggest such affinity or convergence between European fascist and US conservative penal systems observing that "never" in contemporary Western society, except for Nazi Germany and fascist Italy, have been more human and material resources employed in "police and other repressive duties" (Miliband 1969) than in America during conservatism and even more neo-conservatism. In such an account, this tendency has reached the no-return point of a true police or policing–and, as usually connected, warfare—state and thus maximal unlimited government for the "populace".

And such government is perversely joined with a "welfare state", so a small limited government for the privileged, thus those who objectively and even subjectively–as judging by some of its members' public statements–need not governmental financial assistance (Bourdieu 1998) like obsessive neo-conservative "tax cuts" revealing what prominent economists call "fiscal madness" (Stiglitz 2010). Especially, though not only, those of the US South and other "red" regions are genuine or proxy police as well as warfare, bellicose, and anti-welfare states. Predictably, this is exemplified by the deliberately exceptional–even within the neo-Puritan South and America as the last remaining Puritan society (Munch 2001)– and proud state of Texas in which two separate police forces wage a sort of moralistic war against the sin of alcohol consumption, not to mention

---

[10] Wagner (1997:175) asks "what if the [US] state builds more and more prisons and then (surprise!) begins to fill them up with more and more prisoners?" and infers that "crime control produce(s) crime rather than the opposite" by for example the Puritan-rooted "seek and ye shall find" practice.

illicit drugs and sexual sins, as violating its "true spirit of freedom" and subjected to legal restrictions (21-year limit, etc.) or outright prohibition ("dry" counties), like most of the "Bible Belt" (Merton 1968). Incidentally or rather not, Islamic theocracies like Iran, Saudi Arabia, and Taliban-ruled regions also use multiple police forces against alcohol use, almost invariably prohibited, and all kinds of, especially sexual, nonviolent sins and vices through "commissions for the prevention of vice and the promotion of virtue".

Them above thus confirms what sociologists identify as the affinity (Turner 2002) or commonality (Friedland 2002) between Puritan-inspired evangelicalism in America and fundamentalist Islam in terms of government moralistic coercion and violent repression, including Draconian punishments like executions and long imprisonment for sins-crimes, eventually eliminating individual and civil liberties, rights, and choices (Bauman 2001; Hedges 2006; Vasi and Strang 2009), and in that sense "holy" political terror (Besley and Persson 2009). In a way, Weber predicts such a commonality between contemporary Protestant and Islamic fundamentalism by identifying various affinities or similarities of Puritanism and Calvinism overall with Islam (including Calvin and Mohammad) in terms of "holy" violence and tyranny, namely the shared concept and practice of religious revolution and wars. In functionalist terms, Puritanism, like Calvinism as a whole, and Islam have historically been functional equivalents or substitutes in "holy" terror or war, and remain such through their respective revivals, Puritan-inspired revived US evangelicalism and contemporary Islamic fundamentalism in Iran, Taliban-regions, and elsewhere.

In turn, the police state is the subtype or mechanism of state terrorism through systematic government coercion and violent repression, including executions and long mass imprisonment, in its own right. The police state is paradigmatically epitomized in Nazism and all fascism, including neo-fascism, and other totalitarianism like Stalinism and other totalitarian communism. It is also witnessed in Puritanism and its long and even, via the "Bible Belt", "undying" or revived theocracy embodied by the strict "Puritan policeman" (Merril 1945) in America, as well as in Islamic theocracies. By analogy and in typical conjunction and mutual reinforcement with the police state, the warfare state is the mechanism or means of inter-state terrorism in the form of offensive wars against other states. This is also exemplified in Nazism, all fascism, and other totalitarianism, as well as American conservatism from Puritanism to neo-conservatism and neo-fascism, and in Islamic theocracies.

By contrast, the welfare state, especially its liberal type, as the antipode and antidote of the police-warfare states, is typically the opposite and antidote to state and inter-state terrorism, as witnessed from Scandinavian social democracies to the US New Deal. And it is because the liberal welfare state is democratic within society and reasonably pacifist or peaceful in relation to other societies alike and thus "small government" on both accounts, as paradigmatically epitomized by contemporary Scandinavian and other Western European welfare states. This is the typical non-violent pattern of the modern liberal-democratic welfare state despite US conservatives' deceptive allegations of "big government," "socialism", and "tyranny." These allegations aim and seemingly succeed to convince most Americans that figuratively "the sun revolves around the earth", as seen in the rise of the extremely conservative or neo-fascist and theocratic, thus potentially terrorist or violent "Tea Party" movement mostly due to such deceptions and defamations by neo-conservatives (right-wing media, present and former Congress members, etc.) as the foremost masters in this art of Machiavellianism.

That the modern welfare state is as a rule non-violent holds true both for its Western European comprehensive versions and its American minimal variant since the Great Depression and the New Deal through the Great Society and to the Great Recession, the anti-crisis economic stimulus, and the universal health care reform. And to reiterate, it does in virtue of the welfare state being typically both liberal-democratic and thus reasonably non-violent, non-coercive, and non-repressive or tolerant within society and pacifistic or non-warlike and non-militaristic toward other societies. This is paradigmatically epitomized by contemporary Scandinavian and other European social democracies, Canada, etc., though with a few past and transient exceptions like Bismarck's conservative-authoritarian anti-liberal welfare-warfare state in Germany (Feldstein 2005; Habermas 1989; Hicks, Misra, and Ng 1995; Mann 1993). Not surprisingly, liberal-democratic and pacifist welfare states like Scandinavian and cognate societies (Denmark, Finland, Sweden, Norway, Holland, Austria, Switzerland, Canada, Australia, New Zealand, etc.) are regularly observed as the "happiest nations" and the "best places to live" in the world.

Conversely, conservative-authoritarian police and warfare states, including Islamic and other theocracies and in part America under neo-conservatism are also unsurprisingly found to be among the least or less" happy" and the "worst" places to live. An almost identical pattern is also observed within America itself. Typically, liberal "blue" states are the "happiest" and "best places to live", just as richest in social capital or most trusting, and conservative, especially Southern "Bible Belt", "red" invariably vice-police states the least or less "happy" and "worst" in this sense, as well as poorest in this observed factor of happiness or in trust (Putnam 2000).

In turn, Nazism in Germany and then, via the Nazi *anschluss* (Barnett and Woywode 2004), Austria was not the only type of fascism and thus state terrorism, as the latter also encompassed other fascisms in interwar Europe such as Italy, Spain, Portugal, Central and Eastern Europe (Croatia, Hungary, Bulgaria, etc.). In Europe during WW II, for example, a relatively obscure case is what is called the "Ustasa [fascist] terror" by a Nazi-puppet government in "independent Croatia" against non-Croat (Serbian), non-Catholic (Orthodox Christian), and other minority or dissenting groups (Rydgren 2007b) to the point of genocide[11] (Lutz and Lutz 2004) whose barbarity or cruelty in some concentration camps reportedly disgusted even its Nazi masters. As a better known instance, in virtue of its "exaltation of violence, its ethos of war both external and internal, its remorseless attempt to project combat into all spheres of life" and hence destroying or undermining "stable" social rules and expectations interwar Italian Fascism functioned "as terrorist in effect if not in intent" (Townshend 2002). This holds true a fortiori of Nazism as the paradigmatic and even axiomatic, alongside Stalinism, as well as Islamic and Puritan or evangelical tyrannical theocracy, exemplar of state terrorism[12] (Townshend 2002). For instance, in interwar Germany and Italy, fascist systems and their typically conservative creators or allies (Blinkhorn 2003; Lutz and Lutz 2004) resorted to "torture and other terror techniques against political opponents, prisoners of war, populations of occupied territories, and members of outsider groups" (Einolf 2007). These practices are also characteristic for neo-fascist and neo-conservative groups and governments in contemporary societies, notably the US government under neo-conservatism in the "war on terror" (Einolf 2007; Vasi and Strang 2009; Turk 2004) and other "patriotic" wars against "evil" countries before.

Also, fascism as the exemplary type and system of state terrorism comprises to some extent its forms or substitutes and proxies in postwar

---

[11] Lutz and Lutz (2004:194) observes that "in 1941 Germany and its allies invaded Yugoslavia and quickly defeated the armed forces of the country [that] was dismembered with Hungary, Germany, Italy, and Bulgaria directly acquiring territory. A German puppet state of Croatia was set up under the Croatian fascist and nationalist Ustashe party. The government of Croatia under the leadership of Ante Pavelich practiced both genocide and ethnic cleansing [as] hundreds of thousands of Serbs were murdered."

[12] However, Townshend (2002:44) suggests that the "Nazi measures against the Jews" were not a case of terrorism (but rather genocide).

America, including McCarthyism as a fascist equivalent or proxy and its derivations or "ugly" legacies in American politics and society, particularly neo-conservatism and its own product or ally neo-fascism (Bourdieu and Haacke 1995; Lipset 1955; Plotke 2002; Rydgren 2007a; Smelser and Mitchell 2002; Vasi and Strang 2009). In general, admittedly proto-fascist or "extremist" political movements were manifested in "two disturbing episodes of stereotyping and group punishment" in the US during the 20th century (Smelser and Mitchell 2002). These were, first, the "red scare of the early 1920s" characterized with "government intimidation and actual raids" in the function or setting of a "great national fear of Bolshevism", second, as its sequel or reflex, "McCarthyism in the late 1940s and early 1950s" arising in the "context of a state of high national anxiety" over the acquisition of nuclear arms by the Soviet Union, etc. (Smelser and Mitchell 2002). Even though both movements were "limited in duration", their legacy was more enduring by leaving "ugly scars on the body politic" through "seriously" undermining the "civil liberties and livelihood of some citizens" (Smelser and Mitchell 2002), including imprisoning and prohibiting certain "un-American" persons and groups from public and even private employment through "government and private loyalty programs" (Vasi and Strang 2009). As an aggregate effect of McCarthyism and in extension its parent or "extended family" traditional conservatism, America during the 1950s was made no less than "proto-fascist" [sic!] in some descriptions (Putnam 2000).

Fascism thus understood also comprises postwar and contemporary neo-fascism, including neo-Nazism, defined as the new fascist type and system of state–and, when, outside government power or in opposition, counter-state–terrorism. Just as original fascism was the totalitarian and terrorist subtype and product or ally of traditional conservatism in interwar Europe as well as contemporaneous and postwar America exemplified by KKK, McCarthyism, etc., neo-fascism is invariably an extreme neo-conservative or radical-right (Rydgren 2007a) system of would-be totalitarianism and terrorism. And like its original form, neo-fascism spans from Europe such as neo-fascists in Italy and elsewhere and neo-Nazis in Germany, etc. through America (Blee and Creasap 2010) involving neo-Nazi fundamentalist "Christian" militias and allied extreme-right a la "Tea Party" and similar movements to other parts of the world such as South America under military dictatorships during the 1970–80s (Townshend 2002). For instance, in postwar Europe "neo-fascist terrorism" reportedly was "grimly in evidence" during and has been since the 1960s, as witnessed in Italy and other countries (Townshend 2002), thus resurrecting from the presumed death of fascism, notably Nazism "in the ruble and fire of Berlin and Dresden" (Manent 1998), following WW II (Giddens 2000). While this resurrection has been largely in a counter-state terrorist form directed against liberal-democratic and secular governments, neo-fascism's ultimate goal, like of fascism in interwar years, is a sort of slightly adapted state terrorism in the form of totalitarian violent repression and coercion through its capturing of power. For instance, this has happened in Italy via neo-conservative-neo-fascist coalitions, some German states, and briefly Holland and Switzerland via similar alliances of neo-conservatism and neo-fascism or extreme right groups in the 1990s–2010s.

In turn, in postwar America "neo-fascist terrorism" assumes the typical form of or is intertwined with "godly" and "born again" fundamentalist extremism and thus forming the composite of "Christian fascism" (Hedges 2006), exemplified by neo-Nazi "Christian" terrorist groups a la "Christian Identity" and "Dragons of God" with members like McVeigh et al. (Blee and Creasap 2010; Juergensmeyer 2003; Turk 2004). Historically, it was conceived during and in adverse reaction to the liberal-secular 1960s, appeared during the 1980s, culminated first in the 1995 Oklahoma City bombing by the members of these "godly" and anti-government groups, and seemingly ready to culminate or explode once more at the time of writing these lines. "Neo-fascist terrorism" has persisted and even, especially during and following the 2008 Presidential election, resurrected and escalated since the Oklahoma City bombing and related terrorist acts of the 1990s. This is indicated in the aftermath of 2008 by the frantic and unprecedented buying and stocking of arms by militia members and other "patriotic" persons. Notably, it is shown by the rise of the extreme and potentially violent anti-government "Tea Party" movement instigated and directed by neo-fascist or neo-conservative persons and organizations (including extremist radio-television media, Congress members, lobbying firms, "think-thanks", etc.) and attacking and threatening, including threats of killing, "big government" institutions and representatives especially prior to and after the anti-recession economic stimulus and health care reform.

Like its somewhat less "godly" variant in Europe, neo-fascism and its creator or ally revived religious and political neo-conservatism in America has resurrected fascism or its "godly" equivalent Puritanism and conservatism in general from its presumed death (Dunn and Woodard 1996). Also, like in Europe, while such resurrection has initially been and continues to be mostly in the shape of counter-state terrorism against "big government" while not being in power, as shown by anti-government neo-Nazi "Christian" militias and the anti-welfare state "Tea Party", the design or dream of neo-fascism or revived fundamentalism seems to be manifest and salient, or the worst kept secret. This is full-blown "holy" state terror and Puritan-style tyranny institutionalized as "Christian fascism" called "Christian America" and operating in the form of total violent repression and coercion, culture and military "cosmic" war a la "Crusade for Christ" against domestic and foreign "enemies". The latter include not only, as axiomatically, unbelievers and agnostics as foremost "un-American" persons (Edgell et al. 2006). They also comprise non-evangelical Christians, including to some extent Catholics and in part moderate mainline Protestants (Lutherans, Anglicans, etc.) redefined by "born again" evangelicals, notably, Southern Baptists and related funda-mentalist sects and cults, as "anti-Christian" deserving complete extermi-nation through such a crusade or at least exclusion from society (Edgell et al. 2006) as the "best" outcome they can expect and obtain.

Predictably, like the "reign of terror" operating as the mechanism of New England's Puritan theocracy, such "holy" violence or "cosmic" war within society and against other societies is conducted as the only or most effective instrument of reconstructing "American theocracy" (Hedges 2006; Phillips 2006) via "Christian Right" total rule (Owens et al. 2010) cum "Christian America" (Blee and Creasap 2010; Juergensmeyer 2003; Smith 2000). It is the means and path of finding "paradise lost", namely the "disestablishment" of Puritanism and its "Biblical Commonwealth" due to "ungodly" forces such as Jeffersonian liberalism and secularism (Archer 2001; Gould 1996; Kloppenberg 1998). And such a theocratic design has been in part so far implemented in the "Bible Belt" through what is described as "Christian fascism" (Hedges 2006; also, Friedland 2002; Juergensmeyer 2003). In particular, this involves what analysts call Puritan-rooted "friendly [moral] fascism" (Bonefeld 2002; Gross 1981) in the sense of moralistic violent repression and coercion, notably execu-tions and other Draconian punishments for sins-crimes and in extension or by implication "original sin", often of innocent persons sanctified by the latter dogma of immutable eternal human guilt or "lost innocence". These practices thus reenact or evoke Weber-Ross' identified tyranny of Puritanism enforced by the police state as the agent of official terror or the terrorist government in its own right, notably the explicit vice (Wagner 1997) and implicit "religious police" (Infantino 2003).

In another instance, in Latin America neo-fascism as a type of state and counter-state terrorism was paradigmatically exemplified by Chile under

Pinochet's neo-fascist and terrorist military dictatorship[13] (Heymann 2003; Tilman 2001; Townshend 2002), just as by a similar fascist regime in Argentina[14] (Lutz and Lutz 2004). Chile's military junta was, as well-known by now, installed and maintained with the crucial military, financial, and political support of the US conservative government (CIA, etc.) as well as the Chicago economic school ("boys") of dictatorial anti-labor cum "libertarian" capitalism. Evidently, neo-fascism thus understood in Latin America was distinct from that in postwar Europe and America in more fully succeeding to establish and longer maintain itself in power, at least during the 1960s-80s, and thus to achieve the typical fascist as well as religious-fundamentalist ideal and trajectory. The latter is moving from initially counter-state to ultimately state terrorism, as exemplified by Nazism in interwar Germany, Islamic fundamentalism in Iran and Taliban-ruled regions, and in part Protestant evangelicalism in the "Bible Belt" and its disdained functional equivalents like Mormon-ruled Utah. Yet, like that in Europe and America, state terrorism in Latin America was conceived during, anticipated by, and effectively continued initial counter-state terrorism—as manifested in anti-government attacks or threats by various subversive military or paramilitary, mostly conservative, right-wing groups—by means of capturing, controlling, and using government power against "enemies." At this juncture, state terrorism with reference to both South America and Europe and America can be redefined a la Clausewitz as the "continuation" of the politics of anti-government violence or counter-state terrorism by "other means", official governmental power like the police state exerting violent repression and coercion within society and the military waging aggressive wars against other societies.

Included in the totalitarian subtype of state terrorism is communism (Moore 1993; also, Juergensmeyer 2003), more precisely Russian Stalinism,

---

[13] Townshend (2002:46) observes that the "military regimes in Chile (and other South American countries) taking the socialist threat as justification, unleashed full-blown systems of terror [in which] whole armies and police forces seem to have participated enthusiastically, [involving]) not just killing, but a perhaps more sinister and subversive structure of arbitrary imprisonment, torture, and "disappearance". Though these [were] "systems" of terror, they were not comprehensible as such—rather the apparently uncontrolled action of variegated and overlapping security forces created a nightmarish situation [as] Kafkaesque". Also, Heymann (2003:159) remarks that "Chile's Pinochet or his generals (were) violators of international humanitarian law."

[14] Townshend (2002:47–8) registers that "total terrorism" in Argentina included "death squads" "formed to bolster the state's repressive efforts" and its "institutionalization of torture." Also, Lutz and Lutz (2004:190) note that "one of the most deadly forms of state assisted terrorism" involves death squads, as in Argentina and other South American countries.

Chinese Maoism, and their variants in other countries (Romania, Cambodia, etc.), as the radical or left-wing form of totalitarianism or authoritarianism (Cooney 1997; Habermas 2001; Wrong 1979). An exemplar is the "Stalinist reign of terror" (Straughn 2005) in the Soviet Union and its ramifications or proxies in other countries like Eastern Europe, except for Yugoslavia abandoning Stalinism during the late 1940s (Schutz 2001) and in part "liberalized" Hungary and Poland since the early 1980s, and Asia (China, Cambodia, etc.). For all intents and purposes, communism, in particular Stalinism, can be considered and pronounced virtually *caput mortuum* (clinically dead) now, and so can its brand of state and other terrorism (Lutz and Lutz 2004). This is in stark contrast to fascism, religious fundamentalism, and generally conservatism still looking "well and alive" and even perpetually resurrected from death (Dunn and Woodard 1996). Thus, it is revived through neo-fascism in Europe (Rydgren 2007), including neo-Nazism in Germany, and via neo-conservatism and fundamentalist revivals in America (Blee and Creasap 2010) such as the neo-conservative revolt against the liberalization of the 1960s and the evangelical or neo-fascist revival since the 1980s, including the 2008 Elections and ensuing reforms, respectively.

At least, communism in Eastern Europe and even the Soviet Union realized after less than half a century and seven decades respectively that the system "does not work" and has lost social legitimacy, and thus it is the time to "go" more or less peacefully and dignified (Habermas 2001; Schelling 2006) saying basically "sorry, I will not do it again"; and yet conservatism, including religious fundamentalism and fascism, virtually never did, does, and likely will do so. For example, even after five centuries religious conservatism in America from Puritanism to revived evangelicalism has not yet reached and likely never will reach the functionally equivalent realization that theocracy as the system of "holy" terror and tyranny, like communism, does not work or, as Pareto predicts referring to theocratic aristocracy, does not last, and thus it is the time to admit the systemic failure and "leave" peacefully and with dignity (and not being what Americans call a "bad loser").

Instead, with what Hume prophetically diagnoses as Puritan "unreasonable obstinacy" and generally Weber's registered Calvinist "iron consistency", US conservatism persists in resurrecting from the dead past or reconstructing the "Biblical Commonwealth" cum the "Kingdom of God on Earth" and so "paradise lost and found", as shown by the "eternal" theocratic design and established system of the Southern "Bible Garden" and "Christian America" up to the 21st century, just as does

Islamic fundamentalism in its perennial blueprint and regime of an "Islamic state". To that extent, Puritan-rooted evangelicalism, like Islamic fundamentalism and fascism, and conservatism as a whole in America reportedly has been, continues and will likely continue to be a more enduring, actually perpetual, systematic, sanctimonious, and unapologetic force and source of terror, tyranny, warfare, destruction, and death in the long run of centuries than any non-religious ideology and political system, including short-lived and self-euthanized European communism (Juergensmeyer 2003). Simply, US evangelicalism, like Islamic fundamentalism and fascism, and conservatism overall virtually never did, does, and will likely say "sorry, I will not do it again", from the witch-trials at Salem through "Monkey Trials" to executions of innocent people in the "Bible Belt". Instead, it persists with what Hume prophetically diagnosed as Puritan "wretched fanaticism" and consequently "demonic energy" (Tawney 1962) in perpetrating counter-state and especially state terror and thus "evil as distorted good" and in establishing an eternal, millennial "Kingdom of God." This is a crucial difference that is usually overlooked or downplayed in the sociological and related literature as well as official politics and political discourse. US evangelicalism and generally conservatism, alongside Islamic fundamentalism and fascism, is the purported "holy" eternal or persistent, virtually never-ending, and rigid design, system, or source of terror vs. communism and other non-religious ideologies and systems as the comparatively transient and changeable.

In a way, communism was reportedly perhaps an instance of the proverbial "road to hell" being "paved with good intentions" like "social justice" and the like, unlike fascism, religious fundamentalism, and conservatism overall generating the same outcome but with an evidently "bad intent" through "cosmic" war, holy terror and tyranny, and destruction[15] (Juergensmeyer 2003). Conservatism's overt intent or design and ultimate outcome has invariably been and remains via neo-conservatism, notably neo-fascism and revived evangelicalism, making life for most humans, as Tawney (1962) observes for theocratic Puritanism, "hell in this world." It makes and reproduces such "living hell" as the overt or covert punishment for human "original sin" and to be compensated, as for "born again" US

---

[15] Juergensmeyer (2003:217) observes that "in the more humane versions of Marxist conflict theory, persons can be separated from their class roles: capitalists, for instance, can be reeducated [etc.]. Religious concepts of cosmic war, however, are ultimately beyond historical control, even though they are identified with this-worldly struggles. A satanic enemy cannot be transformed; it can only be destroyed."

evangelicals, with "heaven" in the beyond (Lemert 1999; Wuthnow 1998) as what Simmel calls a "compensatory substitute" and Mises would call ersatz-bogus replacement or safety valve.

In fact, Calvinism, including Puritanism, stipulates and enforces a sort of double "hell" both in this life and the world beyond. In the latter it does through Calvin's predestination doctrine that the vast majority of humans are predestined into "everlasting death", thus denied access to heaven reserved only to a few as what Weber calls the "aristocracy of salvation". In this life it does by the argument, apparently derived from and justified by the dogma of predestination, that, as Winthrop proclaimed, most people are preordained to be in a "mean condition" and "subjection" to their Divinely ordained aristocratic or oligarchic rulers like himself. On the account of this dual "hell" for most people, Calvinism, Puritanism in particular, reverses or deviates from original Christianity. For the latter allows access to "eternal life" in heaven to everyone such that the "house of God" is open to all (Lucas 2000), thus universal salvation through the church, subject to certain conditions like "good" intentions and works, "words and deeds", as the ultimate compensation for the temporal suffering of the masses in society at the hand of the elite or "hell in this world". This simply implies that the "last in this world will be the first in the world beyond," though this expression is also used for social conditions through the "second coming" of Christ or Messiah as the "savior" of the suffering masses. No wonder that Calvinism, including Puritanism, due to Calvin's doctrine of predestination with its, in Weber's words, "extreme inhumanity" and "particularism of grace", and the consequent exclusionary and violent practices of "holy" terror and tyranny a la Winthrop and Cromwell, has often been experienced or perceived as anti- or non-Christian, as implied in Franklin's rejection of his inherited Calvinist theology as "inimical to morality" (Byrne 1997) and by implication to Christianity and its "scale of moral values" (Tawney 1963).

While "good intentions" do not justify "bad" social outcomes such as state terror in communism and any ideology and social system (Friedman 1982), recall that original pre-Protestant Christianity was and Catholicism remains what Weber calls a "religion of intentions" and "good works" as the composite condition for humans attaining universal salvation through the church as an "hierocratic organization". As noted, original Christian salvation universalism on the condition of "good" intensions and deeds was reversed by Calvinism, including Puritanism, characterized by, in Weber's view, the anti-universalism or "particularism of grace" monopolized by the self-proclaimed "aristocracy of salvation" or "heavenly" oligarchy (Zaret 1989) in accordance with the dogma of pre-destination to heaven and "everlasting death" regardless of human merits (also, Friedman 2011). "Good" intentions and works formed the defining attribute of original Christianity to be perverted cum "reformed" by Protestantism, notably Calvinism and its Anglo-Saxon sectarian product Puritanism, vehemently rejecting such intentional and actual "goods" through its theological predestination dogma's "extreme inhumanity" and, sanctified by it, equally inhumane theocratic practices of "holy" terror and war in Calvinist-Puritan theocracies throughout Europe, Great Britain, and America.

Needless to say, "good intentions" generate both social "goods" and "bads" (Friedman 1982), as in original Christianity itself, including Catholicism, as Pareto suggests by observing the development of the "religion of Christ" from one seemingly "especially made for the poor and humble" to the "Roman theocracy". Yet "bad intentions" almost never do anything but "living hell" in the form of "holy" terror and tyranny, war, suffering, destruction, and death, as in Puritanism and Calvinism generally due to the anti-universalistic aristocratic or oligarchic and inhu-mane dogma of predestination (Divine "election" and "damnation"), Puritan-rooted revived evangelicalism, fundamentalist Islam, and Nazism and all fascism.

Generally, "modern totalitarian dictatorships", fascist, communist, theocratic and others, reportedly rely or entail the prospect of an "almost total reliance on terror as a basis of rule", though such social systems are "transitory in the long run" (Wrong 1979). However, this transiency evi-dently has applied more to European fascism and especially communism than to theocracy. At least, this is witnessed by the persistence of Islamic theocracies in Iran, Saudi Arabia, Taliban-ruled regions, etc. in third-world countries. It is also observed in the Western world, alongside the Vatican church-state, by the Divine theological design" or "eternal dream" of "American theocracy" (Friedland 2002; Hedges 2006; Owens et al. 2010; Phillips 2006), though never so called but couched and sugar-coated as "Christian America" or a "Bible Garden", spanning from Puritanism to revived evangelicalism. For example, Nazism or Hitlerism and Stalinism are usually classified as totalitarian and "terrorist regimes" (Townshend 2002). Yet they proved more transitory or less resilient and successful in long terms than Islamic, Christian-Protestant, and other theocracies, either institutionalized in Iran, Saudi Arabia, Taliban regions, etc., or "divinely" designed and to be reestablished in the "Bible Belt", as "holy" systems of terror and tyranny. Overall, totalitarianism is observed to rely on the "use of secret police and terror" as its "necessary" instrument and feature, and also authoritarian governments resort to "repressive measures" of control over their populations and "extraordinary mechanisms" of suppressing "dissidents and other opponents" (Lutz and Lutz 2004).

Still another compounded subtype of state terrorism is what can be described as theocratic or religiously grounded fascism and Nazism or fascist-Nazi theocracy involving a mix of theocracies and fascisms. Such were interwar Italian, Spanish, and other Vatican-supported fascisms, and their contemporary variations or proxies in these societies, especially in Italy during the new conservative governance through the 2010s, and also in post-communist Poland, including partly "godly" Nazism and neo-Nazism in Germany and elsewhere. Theocratic or religiously-supported fascism is also exemplified in institutionalized neo-fascism in Catholic South America. Predictably, this includes Chile's, Argentina's, and other South American fascist-military murderous dictatorships regularly supported and often installed by the U.S. conservative government thanks to their pro-capitalist and anti-communist core (Heymann 2003, Townshend 2002; Tilman 2001) extolled by Hayek et al. and imported by the "Chicago Boys" of hardline anti-liberal, falsely "libertarian" laissez-faire pro-capital, anti-labor economics.

As indicated, a consequent subtype and/or instrument of state terrorism is the theocratic Islamic, "Bible-Belt", fascist, communist, and other totalitarian police or policing states (Bourdieu 1998; Cable, Shriver, and Mix 2008; Wacquant 2002). The latter include the "intelligence state" as reportedly recreated in America by neo-conservatism during the "war on terror" and "evil" (Heymann 2003) and embodied in the "homeland security" department organized and operating, aside from anachronistic stringent anti-labor rules, after the image of Leviathan and evoking "eerie images of police states" (Cable et al. 2008; also, Vasi and Strang 2009). Historically and presently, the police state is a common element shared by all repressive social systems, including theocracies or "holy" tyrannies, fascism, communism, and other modern totalitarianism or authoritarianism, as well as paleo-conservatism in Europe and America (McCarthyism), and European, British, and especially "American neo-conservatism, particularly resurgent fundamentalism and neo-fascism.

At this juncture, the police state can be redefined as the legal-penal or criminal-justice—cynics may say truly criminal, including murderous–institutional mechanism and instrument of state terrorism through violent repression and coercion inherent and common to such social systems, thus a terrorist type of government. This in particular applies to what can be described as the vice-police state that is axiomatically intrinsic, in various forms or proxies, to theocracies as invariably moralistic "godly" tyrannies as well as mostly moralizing fascism, including Nazism, and puritanical yet "ungodly" communism (Wallerstein and Zukin 1989), especially its Soviet and Chinese versions, and also invariably moralistic neo-conservatism, especially religious fundamentalism and neo-fascism, notably its American versions. Recall a paradigmatic exemplar among Western societies is what is described as the "Puritan policeman" (Merril 1945) in early New England on the ground of Puritanism declaring itself and acting as "God's [anti] vice regent" (Zaret 1989), as the prototype and model or precursor of the contemporary true or proxy vice-police state in America, especially the "Bible Belt" and similar theocratic and ultra-conservative "red" regions (Utah, etc.). This even more holds true of the Islamic peculiar version of a police state, as represented by the "commissions for the prevention of vice and the promotion of virtue" in Iran, Saudi Arabia, Taliban-ruled regions, etc., among non-Western countries, although such commissions or multiple police forces fighting sins and vices and in extension punishing "original sin" are also found in the "Bible Belt" like Texas with its special separate anti-alcohol police force as if regular police were not sufficiently "big" and effective.

Hence, repressive undemocratic social systems, notably theocracy, fascism, communism, and (neo) conservatism, especially fundamentalism, are designs and regimes of state terrorism or terrorist types of political system in virtue of functioning, in criminal-justice or penal terms, as police states. In particular, they and especially Islamic and Puritan theocracy, fascism, Soviet-Chinese communism, and American neo-conservatism, including notably revived religious fundamentalism and neo-fascism, are such because of their functioning, once seizing political power, as vice-police states, based on or mixed with some version or proxy of "religious police", in criminal-justice terms. For instance, Nazism was an axiomatic system of state terrorism due to the fact that Nazi Germany's legal-penal system was the police state or "terroristic police force" (Arendt 1951; Bahr 2002), in particular the vice police state in virtue of its moralistic attack on "corrupt" persons, lifestyles, and art (Bourdieu and Haacke 1995), though less so than Italian and other Catholic fascism's states in interwar Europe as well as the US conservative "born again" evangelical version in the "Bible Belt" and beyond. Also, observers imply that the policing state, almost invariably in a vice-police moralistic and "godly" form, in America arises and functions as a form and means of state terror (Bourdieu 1998; Wacquant 2002) or "terrorist government"

(Townshend 2002), including the "intelligence state" and a "state of per-petual war" both posing the grave "danger to democracy"[16] (Heymann 2003; also, Cable et al. 2008; Habermas et al. 1998; Turner 2002; Vasi and Strang 2009).

A next subtype or functional equivalent of state terrorism represents the interlinked and mutually reinforcing complex of imperialism and militarism (Acemoglu and Yared 2010; Steinmetz 2005), typically founded on and driven and rationalized by aggressive nationalism (Brubaker 2009), religious (Friedland 2001) and/or secular (Calhoun 1993). Speci-fically, the "twin brothers" of imperialism and militarism–and by implica-tion aggressive nationalism as their prime mover–represent inter-state terrorism by assumption directed against other societies. Moreover, when joined with and grounded in totalitarianism or authoritarianism like fascism or theocracy as analogously intra-state terrorism, they are also eventually directed against their own society, as in the case of military dictatorship in Nazism as well as the bellicose military-industrial complex in American conservatism, especially during McCarthyism, the Cold War, and the "war on terror". Within the complex of imperialism and militarism as well as aggressive nationalism, a paradigmatic instance of inter-state terrorism is what Spencer denotes and somewhat over-optimistically predicts to disappear as offensive war, and international rules such as UN conventions prohibit as wars of aggression (Clairmont 1993; Habermas 2001; Juergensmeyer 2003; Schelling 2006; Turk 2004).

As noted, offensive war is a subtype of inter-state terrorism because or so long as it is what Clausewitz would call the "continuation" of bellicose or nationalistic foreign policy and imperialistic politics by "other", terror-istic means. These means are unlawful as per the UN prohibition of wars of aggression. They are also indiscriminate or involve, as US neo-conservatives love to say, overwhelming force like attacking and killing civilian populations, as in WW II (Houen 2002; Lutz and Lutz[17] 2004) and before, in the aggressive wars against Vietnam[18] (Juergensmeyer 2003),

---

[16] Heymann (2003:166) predicts that "creating either a state of perpetual war or an "intelligence state" (in the USA) will not greatly reduce the danger from (counter-state) terrorism, although it will gravely increase the danger to democracy."

[17] Lutz and Lutz (2004:12) suggest that "the bombings of Rotterdam and London by the Germans and the bombings of Hamburg, Tokyo, and Hiroshima by the Allies during WW II were all designed to create terror as well."

[18] Juergensmeyer (2003:5) remarks that the US "has rightfully been accused of terrorism in the atrocities committed during the Vietnam War, and there is some basis for considering the nuclear bombings of Hiroshima and Nagasaki as terrorist acts, and (Houen 2002:2) also registers "the nuclear mushroom-clouds of Hiroshima and Nagasaki."

Yugoslavia, and Iraq II (Turk[19] 2004; Vasi and Strang 2009). And they tend to be systematic or near-permanent such as the Cold War and the "war on terror", and strategic or Machiavellian, for example, for the sake of assuring and sustaining global military and other dominance (Smelser and Mitchell 2002) by the US conservative government and its "allies". According to this, but not necessarily other, definition, offensive "preemptive" wars, as especially conducted by the US (and UK) conservative government in recent times and before at least since the Vietnam War as well as before (the Mexican wars of aggression, etc.), objectively present or qualify as cases of inter-state terrorism. This also applies to the aggressive wars launched by Nazism and other fascism, as well as by Islamic expansionism, exemplified by the Ottoman Empire (Kuran 2004) and its perceived genocide (still a highly emotional issue for the Turkish government) of Armenian Christians, and by other Muslim expansionist states or groups, past and present, driven by the jihad as the total "holy" war against "infidels" within both society and across societies (Christian, Hindu, pagan, liberals, secularists, and even some "not true" Muslims, etc.).

In general, especially what Kant and Simmel call the war of extermination represents a paradigmatic or ultimate subtype of state terrorism, including intra- and inter-state terrorism, depending on whether the entity to be exterminated is within society and in other societies, or in an alternate and intermediate position (e.g., Native Americans). For such a type of war is unconstrained by any legal-moral rules and historical conventions concerning the use of force and the mutual treatment of combatants. This pattern typifies religious and conceivably all-out nuclear wars[20] (Habermas 2001) that are openly or secretly planed or envisioned by US arch- and neo-conservatives (Schelling 2006), especially by "born again" evangelicals as the most bellicose, militarist, and nationalist (Blee and Creasap 2010; Friedland 2002; Turner 2002), including jingoistic or xenophobic (Dugger 1998), "godly" group, driven by the "sadistic intolerance to cultural [and any] otherness" (Bauman 2001) in contemporary America. It is epitomized by Islamic jihads as intra- and inter-societal

---

[19] Turk (2004:281) registers the US "military action against a sovereign government" like Iraq during the 2000s, thus implication an act of inter-state terrorism in virtue of violating national sovereignty and thus the UN prohibition of wars of aggression, as would conceivably be an equivalent action by (a coalition of) other nations against the "sovereign American government", but apparently US militarist neo-conservatives with their Orwellian "double thinking" consider only the second scenario terrorist.

[20] Habermas (2001:47) registers in general "the time-honored pattern of deflecting internal conflicts with military adventures abroad", in particular the "mad calculations of a balance of terror" (MAD) during the Cold War.

"holy" wars or struggles (Juergensmeyer 2003; Mansbach 2006; Turner 2002) against "infidels" to be exterminated or subjugated and converted. It is also in Christian, especially Puritan evangelical, crusades in the same sense of "cosmic wars" within society, including partly violent culture wars, and across societies such as the "war on terror" and the "axis of evil" described by an Evangelical President as a "crusade".

Another epitome involves the aggressive wars by Nazism and other fascism. For instance, Pareto observes that German nationalistic religious conservatism "preaches militarism, war and extermination against the enemies of Germany and also against those who, though not her enemies, refuse to be her slaves". His observation is prophetic for WW I and WW II initiated by traditional conservatives in Germany (and Austria) and the "new conservatism" cum Nazism (Blinkhorn 2003; Lutz and Lutz 2004) sharing pan-German nationalism, racism, militarism, and aggressive war.

In his own terms, a common attribute of all wars of extermination, be they Islamic, evangelical, Nazi-fascist, and others, is that the exterminating and in that sense the genocide of the "ungodly" or "enemy" is a sort of Pareto-optimum, the "best option" or the "final solution". In turn, anything short of genocide, including enslavement, subjection, or conversion represents only the "second best" or temporary expedience and tactical compromise if the first cannot be attained. Hence, if any type of war meets the four defining conditions of terrorism, then this applies to wars of extermination, especially their religious "cosmic" forms (Juergensmeyer 2003) like Islamic jihads and evangelical "Christian" crusades as understood. These religious wars inherently aim at (Angel 1994) or eventually commit genocide of "infidels" such as Armenian or other Christians and "pagans" like Native Americans by Islamic and Puritan "holy" warriors, as "enemies of God", thus according to what Weber calls, referring to Calvinism as the "church militant," the Divine Will and consequently exterminating or killing, as Pareto sarcastically puts it, for the "divine master". Moreover, if any form of "terror [is] in the mind of God" (Juergensmeyer 2003) supposedly "revealed" to "godly" self-designated agents and warriors like Islamic "warriors" and US evangelical cum Christian "soldiers", it is the "holy" war of extermination of the "ungodly" a la jihad and crusade, respectively.

A related subtype or instrument and facet of state, including both intra- and inter-state, terrorism is government torture (Einolf 2007; Heymann 2003) and other physical and mental abuse of both citizens through the system of government theocratic tyranny or fascist violent repression and coercion within society and especially non-citizens or foreigners during offensive wars against other societies. Thus, all theo-cratic and fascist and generally conservative systems tend to invariably commit extensively and intensely both forms of torture and thus state terror, sometimes reaching the point of sadism in torturing the "ungodly" or "enemies", as especially witnessed in Calvinism, notably Puritanism, and Nazism (Adorno 2001; Fromm 1941; McLaughlin 1996). For instance, Pareto observes that such Puritans as Scottish Presbyterians "experience great delight in tormenting themselves and others" and a "kind of insanity", exhibiting a sort of composite sadism-masochism or the "sado-masochistic personality" attributed to Calvinism and contemporary fas-cism as their shared attribute (Adorno 2001; Fromm 1941; McLaughlin 1996). Predictably, sadistic torture and related abuses especially typify Nazism and all fascism before and during WW II, American conservatism from Puritanism to McCarthyism and to neo-conservatism, in particular revived fundamentalism and neo-fascism, in its various crusade-like wars within society and against other societies, including the Cold War and "war on terror"[21] (Einolf 2007), as well as fundamentalist Islam via its jihads and its equivalents domestically and globally.

Finally, and perhaps most controversially the death penalty in the form of executions or killings of individuals as well as groups and, via wars of aggression, societies can be considered and reclassified as a subtype of state terror, including both intra- and inter-state terrorism, depending on whether those executed are natives or foreigners. Thus, some analysts incorporate executions and even imprisonment into state terrorism or a "political terror scale" indicating government repression (Besley and Persson 2009). The treatment of executions, as well as mass long impris-onment, as a kind or instance of state terrorism is not implausible espe-cially so long as the ultimate punishment is advocated, incited, applied, and supported as a kind of "selective terror" (Jacobs et al. 2005) in a cruel, degrading and inhumane manner against innocent or sinful—i.e., non-criminal within modern liberal democracy–and powerless persons and

---

[21] Einolf (2007:105–7) observes that "today, torture is rarely practiced by liberal democracies against their own citizens, but occasionally practiced by (them) against suspected terrorists and prisoners of war. When (democratic states) engage in torture, it is primarily against noncitizens and under conditions of extreme threat, such as in response to terrorist attacks". For instance, he registers that the "US and Great Britain have used torture against Iraqis and other prisoners in the global war on terror" (Einolf 2007:113). Einolf (2007:116) concludes that a reason "why 20th-century conflicts have caused an increase in the use of torture is that torture has been used as a way of inflicting terror and imposing control upon the civilian populations of occupied territories" as done by Nazi Germany.

groups (Bauman 1997; Matsueda et al.[22] 2006), and in violation or disregard of applicable norms like national constitutions and international rules, for example, UN conventions on human rights and civil liberties (Cole 2005). Reportedly, in the US, especially during neo-conservatism with its resurrected religious fundamentalism, since the 1980s "powerful", almost exclusively conservative fundamentalist, groups apply and support the death penalty for the sake of protecting their "privileges with selective terror" (Jacobs et al. 2005) against sinners-criminals, not only murderers but potentially non-violent drug-traders, as stipulated by the Federal government, and some sexual offenders, as in Texas and other parts the "Bible Belt". In general, as noted, neo-conservative forces reportedly use the "spectacle of executions" as the strategic means to "terrorize" low and powerless classes, notably the growing underclass (Bauman 1997).

In regional terms, U.S. states applying the "death sentence most often" also had the "highest lynching rates" (Jacobs et al. 2005) in the past, predictably virtually all of them being hyper-conservative, including evangelical, and located in the South. The latter notably includes Texas as the perennial leader accounting for about half of all executions in America and thus the entire Western world, perhaps in accordance with, as Texans love to say, everything, including the death penalty and mass long imprisonment inflicted often on innocent and regularly on sinful and powerless, persons, is "big in Texas". Hence, Southern ultra-conservative states exhibit a sort of path dependence or remarkable continuity and trajectory from counter-state vigilante terrorism to state "holy" terror through executions and other Draconian punishments such as mass long or life imprisonment for sins-crimes and in perverse extension "original sin" by criminalizing (by "dumb laws") and harshly punishing non-violent immoral acts like drug and sexual offenses involving no violence, etc. As indicated, executions and imprisonment as neo-conservative "tough on crime" preferred practices ("favorite pastimes") are elements of a "scale of political terror" especially if they are applied, as in the "Bible Belt", on overt or covert religious Biblical "original sin" and thus arbitrary grounds enacting or approaching theocracy as the system of "holy" terror, warfare, and tyranny. Also, these practices are such if punishing not only guilty criminals-sinners but often innocent persons, as proved by DNA evidence in

---

[22] In general, Matsueda et al. (2006:118) find that "policies of getting tough on crime always resonate well in the U.S. political arena [yet are] based more on ideology than empirical research on punitive practices", as exemplified by California's "Three Strikes laws." They conclude that "increasingly harsh punitive crime policies [persist] in the US in the face of this growing body of research" (Matsueda et al. 2006:118).

Texas, notably the "cowboy" Dallas county as the US and so the Western leader of executing or keeping on death row and long imprisoning individuals with eventually proven but immaterial "too late" legal, yet not religious "original sin", innocence, and other parts of the "Bible Belt" and beyond.

The above trajectory of terrorism holds true in the sense of "selective terror" through the death penalty as well as long imprisonment used in the service of attaining and preserving the power and privileges of neo-conservatives. They particularly include "reborn" power (and in that sense almost literally blood) thirsty evangelicals especially for control of the federal government with neutral despised bureaucracy identified as the main obstacle to their "sacred" theocratic ambitions (Davis and Robinson 2009; Hedges 2006; Lindsey 2008; Owens et al. 2010), whose dominance is already almost total in the "Bible Belt" and other "red" regions. Perhaps, such ultimate or severe punishment is also used in the function of "feeling good" about their "godliness" and Puritan-style "purity" in punishment by death and other Draconian sanctions, but, as Weber would put it with respect to evangelical "emotionalism", "only a neurologist or perhaps rather Freudian psychoanalyst or psychiatrist could tell" given what Hume identifies as religious "fanaticism" and in that sense a type of hysteria. As known, religiously driven, notably evangelical, and other conservative hysterias have been endemic in American history. Recall that they span from Puritan witch-trials and other hysterical acts through the hysterical or irrational Great Awakenings to the "red scare" and the Cold War hysteria to the neo-conservative anti-liberal, anti-government, specifically, anti-welfare state—yet never anti-police or anti-warfare state–and anti-immigration hysteria, since Reaganism through the "Tea Party".

Most minimally, the above path holds to the extent that the death penalty is applied to innocent individuals or groups, as witnessed both in vigilante violence past and present and in executions by government, notably Southern states like Texas and others. For if any act of government is truly state terror, it is its killing of innocent humans through ritual executions on sacred, including covertly or subconsciously "original sin", and any grounds, which is evidently a long-standing tradition in America, particularly in Puritan New England and the "Bible Belt".

The pattern thus starts with Puritanism as the point of origin and its massive use of punishment with death against a myriad of sins cum crimes like adultery, fornication, blasphemy, sorcery, etc. to the point, if Tocqueville is right, "never" being used more before and after, except for

Nazism and Islamic theocracies, against the "ungodly", "impure" and "witches", not to mention the genuine or proxy genocide of the Native Americans (Campbell 2009; Gould 1996; Mann 2005; Munch 2001). The pattern continues or climaxes in the neo-conservative, including, as in the "Bible Belt" (Texas, etc.), fundamentalist, death penalty and prison system as the destination point of the Puritan origin. At this juncture, the Puritan lethal penal code of "holy terror" is the extant overt or covert historical and religious basis and justification or precedent of the neo-conservative criminal justice system also using, like anti-government conservative vigilante groups, the death penalty as "selective terror", given that American conservatism continues with pride and joy to "stand" in the tradition (Dunn and Woodard 1996) of theocratic, intolerant, violent, and Draconian Puritanism and its "reign of terror" (Merril 1945; also, Kaufman 2008; Munch 2001). Recall that Puritanism in virtue of its initial "theocratic revolt" against secularism in 17th century England and, to add, in 18th century Jeffersonian America represented the prototype or precursors of contemporary terrorists or anti-secular violent radicals within Protestant evangelicalism and Islamic fundamentalism, thus both counter- and state terrorism on such religious grounds (Juergensmeyer 1994).

At this juncture, the extreme or most comprehensive subtype of both intra- and inter-state terrorism is probably genocide. The latter can be described as the "ultimate stage of terrorist regimes"[23] (Townshend 2002; also, Lutz and Lutz[24] 2004) and a sort of mass or collective death penalty, indiscriminate execution or destruction of certain groups and societies through the war of extermination within a society and/or against other nations. In this respect, genocide is the prime goal or ultimate outcome of the war of extermination, and conversely, the second being the effective means or path of attaining the first. Hence, if any type of death penalty broadly understood qualifies as a subtype of terrorism, it is at

---

[23] Townshend (2002:44) says that "the deadly pinnacle of genocide, the special crime of the 20th century, [is] the ultimate stage of terrorist regimes. Mass murder is unquestionably a terrifying phenomenon; but there are problems in classifying genocide–as distinct from mass murder–as a terrorist act. Its very modernity points to its logic, which is ethnic rather than ideological", as exemplified by the "Turkish roundup of Armenians during the WW I."

[24] However, Lutz and Lutz (2004:193) suggest that the "actual efforts at extermination do not constitute examples of government terrorism. The intent of the Ottoman Turks and the German Nazis [etc.] was not to influence a target audience but to commit mass murder. Since the elimination of a group is not the goal, neither government-sponsored nor government-supported terrorism qualify as genocide. Ethnic cleansing is an example of such government terrorism to achieve political objectives."

least genocide as collective indiscriminate execution religiously or ethnically grounded and justified. This is analogous to widespread governmental executions and long imprisonment of innocent, sinful, so objectively non-criminal, and powerless individuals as partly witnessed and recently documented by DNA evidence in the U.S. neo-conservative criminal justice system, especially its fundamentalist variant in the "Bible Belt" (Alabama, Georgia, Mississippi, South Carolina, Tennessee, Texas, etc.).

Instances of Counter-State Terrorism

In contrast and often opposition to state terrorism, counter-state terrorism consists in individual and collective public acts of violence or force, destruction (Juergensmeyer 2003; Roche 2001), war, and physical coercion directed against government agents and agencies. However, reportedly the "historic record" of counter-state terrorism is observed to be "generally" its defeat by the "immensely more powerful repressive forces of dictatorial states" (Heymann 2003), thus by implication by state terrorism, and its rare victory over the latter.

Counter-state terrorism operates either directly by attacking and destroying government and other political, as well as economic and cultural, facilities and institutions or indirectly through targeting and killing or wounding civilian populations (Smelser and Mitchell 2002; Turk 2004). Counter-state terrorism is hence manifested in various past and contemporary attacks on, killing, and destructions of government representatives, resources, and institutions, as well as civilian populations, in Europe, America, and other societies. For example, in interwar Europe counter-state terrorism was exemplified in a wide range of anti-government attacks and conspiracies, such as Nazi-fascist violent putsches (Lutz and Lutz 2004; Mannheim 1986) and similar subversive anti-state violence and destruction in Germany, Italy, Spain, and other European countries (Portugal, most of central and eastern Europe) eventually succumbing to the "totalitarian temptation" (Cohen 2003) of fascism. While European fascism, notably Nazism, and its system of state terror (to be) established through victorious counter-state terrorism, was disposed of "in the fire and rubble of Berlin and Dresden" (Manent 1998) and discredited, alongside its parent conservatism, in postwar times (Giddens 2000), neo-fascism and the conservative extreme right overall (Rydgren 2007a) continues to adopt or admire the "good old" fascist methods of counter-state terror or anti-government and other violence in contemporary Europe, including neo-Nazism in Germany, though so far with less success than during interwar years.

Also, during recent times, especially since the 1990s through the 2010s, counter-state terrorism in America has assumed the form of attacks on or treats to federal "big government". For instance, such a pattern of anti-government neo-conservative rhetoric and extremist violence (Blee and Creasap 2010) climaxed in the 1995 Oklahoma City bombing in apparent response to the 1992 Elections resulting in a "big" government (President, Congress) and to its actions (the 1993 Waco episode, etc.), just as did international, specifically Islamic, terrorism in the September 11 2001 attacks. And this pattern threatens to climax again or resume on an ever-large scale with the rise of "Tea Party" and related neo-fascist or fundamentalist, ultra-conservative movements adopting and even intensifying the familiar anti-government rhetoric and attacks or threats in vehement reaction to the 2008 Elections yielding yet another "big government". This thus gives a sense of déjà vu in that the history of counter-state terrorism may repeat itself in America during recent times. At this juncture, "big" undemocratic government has become the "all-American" neo-conservative, including neo-fascist and fundamentalist, label demonizing what is actually a minimal "liberal" welfare state condemned in favor of the conservative composite police-warfare state, especially in the "Bible Belt" like Texas, as "small" government according to neo-conservatism's inverted logic and in, perhaps via its successful indoctrination of, most Americans' minds.

Such are what Merton (1968) would call the "perversities of social logic", in this case the prevalent neo-conservative collective definitions of the situation involving liberal-welfare vs. conservative police-warfare states, perpetuating the "reign of error" (and ultimately terror). This involves an inverted logic or perverse outcome, because virtually everywhere in the Western world and beyond, except for America during neo-conservatism, modern welfare and generally liberal states are experienced or regarded as "small", democratic governments, as epitomized by Scandinavian and similar West European social democracies as the commonly agreed paradigmatic exemplars of democracy and liberty. Conversely they are nowhere defined or viewed as "big", undemocratic governments, while police-warfare states are universally socially constructed as the latter, with the exception of, according to the neo-conservative definition, US police-warfare state. Yet, these neo-conservative perversions of logic and social reality would likely delight or at least not surprise the old US conservative Emerson admitting long ago that conservatism has a sort of built-in tendency for "seeming and trickery" as the only available or efficient means to attain and maintain power and privilege, because of its always having the "worst of arguments". He thus admits or implies that since argumentation does not typically function for US conservatives, primarily because their lack or disdain arguments of science and education, they tend to use "true lies" as well as violence against the welfare state and liberal democracy cum "big" government and the like.

Instances of counter-state terrorism also involve serial killings, assassinations, and vigilantism (Blattman and Miguel 2010; Roche 2004; Smith 1994; Townshend 2002) such as lynching (Bailey and Snedker 2011; King 2008; Messner et al. 2005) and related violence in historical and in part contemporary America, especially, but not only, the post-bellum South (Jacobs et al. 2005). They also include "hate crimes" seen as the instance or at least "close cousin" of terrorism in general (Krueger and Maleckova 2003). It is a sort of individual, micro variation and perhaps the initial stage or anticipation and thus predictor of genocide as a kind of "hate crime" on a collective, macroscopic scale. Both acts are invariably driven and justified by various bigotries, especially ethnic-religious bigotry, as observed for political conservatism and Protestant "Christian" fundamentalism in America (King 2008).

As noted, genocide is typically attained or conducted through the war of extermination against "evil", "infidel", or "inferior" groups and societies such as "heathen" and "impure" Native Americans by New England's Puritan theocracy. Also, hate crimes are committed as acts within the process of or during culture and other intra-societal wars, as especially intense and persistent in America under conservatism since Puritanism through neo-conservatism, against equivalently defined, "ungodly" or "un-American" persons and activities. Thus, the war of extermination represents the means of attaining the "higher" end of genocide as "macro-hate crime" within state terrorism. Analogously, culture and related wars provide the instrument or rationale for hate crimes as, say, "micro-genocides" in the sense of personal destructions, vigilante violence, and other forms of counter-state terrorism. Hate crimes against the "ungodly" are especially, but not only, witnessed in America and supported or sanctified by religious conservatism, most manifestly and saliently in the Southern "Bible Belt" (Bailey and Snedker 2011; Jacobs et al. 2005; Messner et al. 2005) in the past and present.

Other Types of Terrorism

Still another typology incorporates conservative, counter-revolutionary, or reactionary and radical, revolutionary or "progressive", also described, not always accurately or scientifically, as, respectively, right-wing and left-wing (Habermas 1989; Lutz and Lutz 2004; Townshend 2002), terrorism in contemporary societies, including America[25] (Borgeson and Valeri 2009; Smith 1994), each further subdivided. In turn, conservative and radical terrorisms each can be of state and counter-state variety, involving government and non-government terrorist agents and activities.

Thus, subtypes or instances of the first type include feudal master-servant[26] (Steinberg 2003), theocratic or religiously based and justified, and fascist (Smith 1994), including Nazi as well as neo-fascist and neo-Nazi terrorisms. The latter are committed and advocated by "law-and-order" conservative or right[27] (Heymann 1999) forces in Europe as well as, through their "godly" fundamentalist versions a la the "Christian Identity Movement" (Smith 1994), in America. Notably, in America since the 1980s reportedly right-wing, invariably conservative or fundamentalist, terrorism has "far" surpassed in size as well as intensity and persistence its left-wing or radical variant (Smith 1994; also, Borgeson and Valeri 2009; Juergensmeyer 2003; Lutz and Lutz 2004; Townshend 2002). Generally, in a historically classification, conservative, right-wing counter-state terrorism is represented by the Nazi party's putschist "storm-troopers" in Weimar Germany before Nazism's seizure of power, "neo-fascist groups" in Italy and other European countries provoking government authoritarian reaction in postwar times. It is also manifested in the "US militias and patriot groups" culminating in the "bombing of the federal office building in Oklahoma City and the "neo-Nazis" in Germany and elsewhere in Europe, as well as America, especially growing since the 1990s and targeting and attacking immigrants or foreigners[28] (Lutz and Lutz 2004).

---

[25] Smith (1994:2) observes that "terrorists in America come from many philosophical, ideological, and religious backgrounds. They are neo-Nazis, Marxist revolutionaries, Puerto Rican nationalists, and anti-Castro Cubans. Yet [they] share an important commonality [i.e.,] willing to use indiscriminate violence to further their political or social dreams." Also, Heymann (1999:3) remarks that "political violence (is not) new to the US. We have lost four presidents and two senators to assassination [plus] groups such as the Ku Klux Klan dedicated for decades to terrorizing an important segment of our population."

[26] Steinberg (2003:458) finds that in the UK "the law still operated *in terrorem* [i.e.,] as a substantial threat used by employers for labor discipline. Free labor, in fact, did not come into being until the Workmen's and Employers Act of 1875."

[27] Heymann (1999:10–1) notices that "for terrorists of the law-and-order Right, acts of random violence, disguised as acts perpetrated by insurgent radicals, can be "addressed" to the attention of security forces in the hope of provoking a coup and a military takeover (as in Italy in the 1970s)".

[28] Lutz and Lutz (2004:166) add that "right-wing neo-Nazi violence has increase[d] since the 1990s (and) against migrants and anyone or anything that is considered foreign.

Such variations of the non-conservative type are bourgeois or "liberal", including Jacobin (Delanty 2000; Michels 1968; Mises 1957), and communist or Marxist terrorism (Juergensmeyer 2003; Lutz and Lutz 2004). For instance, Michels (1968) uses the expression the "confused years of the Terror [by] Robespierre" and Mises (1957), seemingly, like Hayek and other "libertarian" economists, following Burke as the anti-revolutionary role model, the "reign of terror" following, as Tocqueville also observed and in part lamented, the liberal-egalitarian or bourgeois, anti-feudal, and anti-monarchic French Revolution (Acemoglu et al. 2011; Moore 1993; also, Lutz and Lutz 2004). Generally, the French Revolution's aftermath and ramifications were "the specter of social disorder, terror, and revolutionary change" resulting in a liberal-democratic or bourgeois and egalitarian republic (Acemoglu et al. 2011), temporarily replaced by the "conservative and counter-revolutionary decades of the Restoration" of the *ancien regime* or the monarchy (Delanty 2000).

However, terrorism in liberalism, including liberal democracy, dismissed and attacked by conservative anti-liberals a la Burke and Maistre as "utopia", is an aberration or exception[29] (Habermas 1989) and defensive action "in response to the threat" (Acemoglu et al. 2011), internal and external, to the new democratic political system, as during the Jacobin "reign of terror" (Townshend 2002). Thus, this comprised the hostility and threats of Austrian, Prussian, and British monarchies and aristocracies to destroy and their military attack on the revolutionary regime" in France[30] (Acemoglu et al. 2011). If anything, this suggests that such a "defensive war" of the new liberal-democratic political system against these external as well as domestic enemies was by definition a legitimate defense for the sake of survival rather than "state terror" in the strict sense as Burke et al. accused. Instead, the offensive wars or invasions by these European monarchies, including Burke's Great Britain, against the French

---

Groups linked with neo-Nazi or other racist organizations have appeared in most European countries". In general, "right-wing groups have resorted to violence in the US and Europe" (Lutz and Lutz 2004:244).

[29] According to Habermas (1989:69), a "critique of utopia that has issued dire warnings against Jacobinism has been wrong in denouncing the supposedly unavoidable marriage of [liberal] utopia and terror."

[30] Acemoglu et al. 2011, 3289) add that the "first war between revolutionary France and the major European powers—the so-called War of the First Coalition—did not break out until 1792. Contrary to almost everyone's expectations, the armies of the new Republic were victorious in an initially defensive war. France's borders were thus expanded with an eye towards creating an effective buffer between the new Republic and the hostile monarchies of Prussia and Austria".

liberal-democratic and egalitarian Republic appeared objectively as acts of inter-state terror, according to the present definition of terrorism.

This is in stark contrast to anti-liberalism, notably conservatism, including fundamentalism and fascism, in which terrorism is a rule, pattern, constant, and offensive action. For instance, the Jacobin "reign of terror" admittedly took place because the French Republic established in the aftermath of the Revolution, specifically the "deposition and execution of King Louis XVI in autumn 1792", was gravely threatened from and occasionally attacked by "foreign invasion and internal rebellion"[31] (Townshend 2002; also, Acemoglu et al. 2011). In addition, the Jacobin-like "reign of terror" is not exceptional but to some extent typical of virtually all liberal-democratic and other revolutions (Moore 1993) or post-revolutionary constellations facing counter-revolutionary rebellion or adverse reaction by the old order. This includes the American Revolution with its various proxy state terror measures, viz., "Sedition laws", etc. (Hull 1999; Lipset 1996; Vasi and Strang 2009), as well as during social crisis and war, such as the US in WW I and II times. Admittedly, according to its liberal-bourgeois agents, the French Revolution was "under threat" and attack during the early 1790s, namely threatened and counter-attacked by "both external and internal enemies", making revolutionary violence "natural" for the sake of resisting "oppression" and preserving "liberty against tyranny", an indicative instance being the "counter-revolutionary rebellion at Lyon" (Townshend 2002). In a similar account, during the "Reign of Terror" the revolutionary government was in a way forced to seek and eliminate its various enemies "before" their succeeding to overthrow of the new liberal-democratic and egalitarian state[32] (Lutz and Lutz 2004) and restore the *ancien* despotic feudal regime and aristocracy (Acemoglu et al. 2011; Markoff 1997). It is for the latter that Maistre, Burke, in part Tocqueville, and other arch-conservatives did shed a river of tears (Parsons 1967;

---

[31] Townshend (2002:36–7) adds that "in July the National Assembly had declared *la patrie en danger* (the fatherland in danger), and in August 1793 it decreed a *levée en masse*, mobilizing the whole French nation to defend the country Finally, in October, it declared terror 'the order of the day', to preserve the revolution against its enemies, kings and aristocrats. The Committees of Public Safety and General Security, even more than the Convention from which they sprang, represented the progressive avant-garde of the French Revolution. They pioneered representative democracy and equality before the law. The Reign of Terror was informed by the Enlightenment assumption that the social order can be changed by human agency."

[32] Lutz and Lutz (2004:196) add that "over 90 percent of the executions ordered by courts between the spring of 1792 and summer of 1794 were directed against individuals accused of conspiring with enemies of the revolutionary state."

Schmidt 1996) and their conservative and neo-conservative followers a la Hayek et al. seemingly still do.

In general, the "prime exponents" of state terrorism "from above" reportedly have been and remain either conservative, including reactionary or counter-revolutionary, "overtly repressive autocracies and despotisms" or "radical revolutionary regimes" (e.g., the Bolsheviks, Stalinists, Maoists) as a rule, and secondarily and as an exception their liberal antipodes (Townshend 2002). Thus, only "in times of crisis" did and do liberal-democratic constitutional states, including the US government during non-conservatism, reportedly undertake "ferocious repressive action" to preserve their constitutions and liberties[33] (Townshend 2002). Moreover, in this account certain acts of what is initially characterized as liberal and radical terrorism may be "good" or "justified" in historical perspective such as the assassination of tyrants (tyrannicide) and by implication the overthrow of tyrannical or repressive regimes by force such as through revolutions (Townshend 2002). By implication, such an outcome is epitomized by the French and American Revolution. Recall that both revolutionaries were explicitly or implicitly defined as proxy "terrorists" or "criminals" by the ruling powers. Admittedly, this is because such liberal and in part radical agents, notably revolutionaries exemplified by those of the French and American (Lutz and Lutz 2004) Revolution and their Enlightenment precursors a la Voltaire and Jefferson genuinely did and do believe in and create a "free and nonviolent society"[34] (Townshend 2002) as well as promote the pursuit of happiness or joy in life (Phelps 2007). In stark contrast and opposition, conservative "terrorists of the right" (Townshend 2002) seek to establish or maintain an opposite type of society, and violent religious ascetics, notably those in Islamic

---

[33] Townshend (2002:38) comments that the US federal government reportedly at least tolerated, and the Southern states during the Jim Crow era actively supported or colluded with, the "persistent, systematic terrorization" by the Ku Klux Klan of definite racial-ethnic minorities (Blacks, Catholics, immigrants) in the post-bellum South.

[34] Specifically, Townshend (2002:20) states that "good terrorists are those whose actions are justified by the oppressiveness of the system they oppose [as] unlike terrorists of the right, they genuinely believed in a free and nonviolent society." In his view, the specific and "perfect deed of the good terrorist is assassination. Classical tyrannicide was valorized because it could remove the oppressor with the minimum force" (Townshend 2002:21). Generally, Townshend (2002:53–4) suggests that "the criteria for revolutionary change – social transformation, or at least major social and economic change–are generally fulfilled only (in) existing nation-states" and that radical terrorism "with this aim emerged as a consistent and coherent strategy in the late 19th century." However, he thinks that "Western revolutionary terrorist groups have relied on pure terrorism mainly as a result of political weakness or marginality. When detached from the wider revolutionary movement terrorism is self-defeating" (Townshend 2002:73).

fundamentalism and in Puritanism and its heir evangelicalism, advocate and enforce suffering and even literal sacrifice of humans for higher Divine and related, national causes.

During recent times, as since the 1980s through the 2010s, conservative, right-wing counter-revolutionary, including religious, as well as nationalistic (Brubaker 2009; Townshend 2002), terrorism has been prevalent and overwhelming, particularly in America (Blee and Creasap 2010; Friedland 2002; Juergensmeyer 2003; Lutz and Lutz 2004; Smith 1994; Turk 2004), plus Islamic countries (Feldstein 2008; Pillar 2001; Smelser and Mitchell 2002), and Eastern and Western Europe. Reportedly, in contemporary America conservative, usually religiously grounded "terroristic violence" committed by persons and organizations "on the right" has continuously and even dramatically increased by comparison with its radical version, just as historically being more numerous and intense such that "even at the height of violence from the left" US fundamentalist-racist groups committed "more terrorist activities", though the first attracted "more" attention by the media (Lutz and Lutz 2004) and the "godly" government. This has been a general pattern observed in Western and other societies, especially since the late 1980s, alternatively, the sustained decline of radical, left wing and secular, and the explosive growth of conservative, right-wing or neo-fascist terrorist agents and actions[35] (Lutz and Lutz 2004), notably those religiously motivated and rationalized, as in America and by Islamic groups.

In another classification intimated above, terrorism can be classified into religious or pseudo-religious and non-religious or secular terrorism. The first type is premised on and driven and sanctified by certain religious, typically fundamentalist, concept of what Weber calls, as a shared trait of Islam and Calvinism, including Puritanism, "religious revolution" or "holy" cosmic war between "good" and "evil" forces of the world. Invariably, agents and acts of terrorism ("we") claim to supposedly represent "good" and "God" and so a "higher law", and the second "evil," "enemies of God", "infidels" or "unbelievers", and outsiders ("they") or Satan (Blee and Creasap 2010; Juergensmeyer 2003; Lutz and Lutz 2004). As implied, religious, like conservative, terrorism has been more manifest, salient, and intense than its secular and radical variant in recent times. This is especially witnessed in America, not to mention Islamic groups

---

[35] Lutz and Lutz (2004:148) register that "after the demise of communist states in Europe terrorism from the left declined, and the initiative in the use of terror and violence passed to groups on the extreme right."

and theocracies committing counter-state and state terrorisms, as paradigmatically exemplified by the Taliban and Al-Qaeda when both in opposition and power, respectively[36] (Juergensmeyer 2003; Pillar 2001). In turn, both religious or pseudo-religious and non-religious terrorisms can be counter-state and state alike, although the typical pattern is that the first mostly tends to intermingle or intersect with conservative, and the second with radical, terrorism.

Included into still another classification of specifically counter-state terrorism are domestic or national and international or global terrorisms (Abadie 2006; Beck 2000; Béland 2005; Bergesen and Lizardo 2004; Blattman and Miguel 2010; Cetina and Bruegger 2002; Feldstein 2008; Giddens 2000; Lutz and Lutz 2004; Phillips and Cooney 2005; Scott 2004; Shamir 2005; Smelser and Mitchell 2002; Shamir 2005; Tilly 2004; Turk 2004). While both domestic and international or global terrorism (Lutz and Lutz 2004) are self-explanatory in geographical or territorial terms, the second type seems more complex and thus less easy to define, even if paradigmatically exemplified and culminating during recent times in Islamic fundamentalists" September 11, 2001 terrorist acts in America.

Still, international terrorism is usually defined as involving terrorist agents and acts supported or incited by external forces such as "outside governments, drugs, illegal trade in arms, or plunder" (Giddens 2000; also, Kestnbaum[37] 2009; Lutz and Lutz 2004) and in turn attacking or targeting "citizens or property of more than one country" (Abadie 2006) through "covert mass violence by organized civilians against other civilians"[38]

---

[36] Juergensmeyer (2003:5) note that "some [terrorist] groups have been inspired by purely secular causes [i.e.] motivated by leftist ideologies". However, he suggests that "although left-wing movements subscribe to what seem(s) a similar idea—the concept of class conflict—ordinarily this contest is thought to take place only on a social plane and within the temporal limitations of history. In fact, in the more humane versions of Marxist conflict theory, persons can be separated from their class roles: [e.g.,] capitalists can be reeducated" as in China during Mao's cultural revolution (Juergensmeyer (2003:217). Moreover, Pillar (2001:217) observes that as left-wing terrorism "is eradicated altogether [e.g., the Red Army Faction]—a different and perhaps even more threatening problem emerges" such as Al-Qaeda, epitomizing Islamic and other religious terrorist agents. Specifically, the "frequency of international terrorist (actions) was cut in half from its level during the mid-1980s to the rate that existed for most of the 1990s" (Pillar 2001:2).

[37] Kestnbaum (2002:244) proposes that "terroristic forms of violence may be further bolstered by religious or other ideological justifications for militant opposition against broadly defined enemies, and may spill over into—or be organized primarily as—terror undertaken in foreign lands."

[38] For Phillips and Cooney (2005:352), terrorism is one of "forms of international violence [i.e.,] covert mass violence by organized civilians against other civilians. Terrorism

(Phillips and Cooney 2005). For example, the role of such transnational forces in terrorism was reportedly witnessed in the Balkans during the 1990s-2000s and exemplified by the "Albanians in Kosovo" receiving various, including financial and even military, forms of support and/or information from their kin in Western Europe like Switzerland (Giddens 2000) and perhaps governments in some European countries such as Germany during the neo-conservative government. Such and other terrorist groups (Bauman 2001), or alternatively "freedom-fighters", causing, as in Bosnia, Kosovo, and Macedonia, and waging these new wars in the form of nation-state conflicts was and is "political control through exclusion", relying on "intimidation and terror" as their strategies or tactics (Giddens 2000). Another example of supporting and even sponsoring by outside governments or countries of "terrorist groups" reportedly includes the US government, namely the Reagan neo-conservative administration, "support for the Contras in Nicaragua" and thus their "terrorist actions" (Lutz and Lutz 2004).

Furthermore, governments or countries can not only support, sponsor or incite transnational terrorism, as did the US government by supporting and inciting Islamic Albanian and in part Bosnian terrorists cum "freedom fighters" in the former Yugoslavia, as well as such groups in Latin America and elsewhere. They can also directly commit terrorist actions either through their representatives and agencies in a clandestine way or overtly via offensive wars against "enemies", or both. These two scenarios were exemplified by Nazism and other interwar fascism. They were also manifested in the communist Soviet Union and the conservative US government during the Cold War (Lutz and Lutz[39] 2004), as well as the neo-conservative administration in the "war on terror" and the "axis of evil", for example, the continuing support for proxy terrorist or anti-government groups in Latin America like Cuba and Venezuela and offensive "preemptive" wars against "axis of evil" (Vasi and Strang 2009) enemies a la Iraq.

---

grows out of strong partisanship (without a steady supply of supporters, it will simply wither away). Hence, close and distant ties are likely to be essential for its understanding."

[39] Lutz and Lutz (2004:46) remarks that "some [global] violent activity is carried out by state agencies. During the Cold War the CIA and KGB were quite active in violent activities. Sometimes, the actions involved agents of allied states." In addition, in their view, "a foreign government [can] effectively [control] political groups that [are] willing to undertake violent activities even when the groups had a base in their local societies. [E.g.] the [Nazi] Parties in Austria and Czechoslovakia were reflections of right-wing discontent within the Austrian and Czech governments. They respond[ed] to directives from the Nazi Party in Germany and after 1933 the German government (Lutz and Lutz 2004:47).

Historically, instances and "acts of violence by transnational terrorism (Beck 2000) during postwar times are classified as some "phases of colonial struggles, hostage-taking, hijacking, assassination, explosive bombing, and suicidal vehicle and airplane bombing"[40] (Smelser and Mitchell 2002). In this view, what often characterizes contemporary international terrorism is the property of statelessness and lack of territorial boundedness, instead mostly operating through "territorially fluid" and "relatively unreachable" (by political or diplomatic channels) social networks[41] (Smelser and Mitchell 2002) that act as "globally operating terrorist organizations" (Cetina and Bruegger 2002). At this juncture, global terrorism arises as a "newly articulated form of organized trans-national violence" (Shamir 2005; Tilly 2004), especially in the "semiperipheral zones of the world-system" during the process of rapid globalization involving the decline of the "dominant state"[42] (Bergesen and Lizardo 2004), with such processes reportedly affecting, specifically permitting and expanding, "every form of organizing (including) terrorist cells" (Scott 2004).

Transnational terrorism is increasingly seen as a "global threat" in virtue of undermining or casting doubt on nation-states' "ability" of protecting their citizens (Béland 2005) and even institutions or values such as democracy and civil liberties vs. national security in America and to a lesser extent other Western societies. Predictably, this in particular applies to Islamic-based "global terrorism" exploding during the 1990s–2010s through its "attacks in Europe, in North America, and in Asia" (Feldstein 2008), as well as to its "Christian" and other religiously driven and sanctified variants in these societies, especially in the US (Juergensmeyer 2003). Still, reportedly most agents and acts of contemporary terrorism are domestic or national rather than global or international[43] (Abadie 2006;

---

[40] Smelser and Mitchell (2002:11–2) state that "the evolution of terrorism from WW II—through the phases of colonial struggles, hostage-taking, hijacking, assassination, explosive bombing, and suicidal vehicle and airplane bombing—shows a certain mercilessness in the perpetration of violence: any target, at any time, in any place, and by any means."

[41] Smelser and Mitchell (2002:35) add that the "preferred organizational form for terrorism is organizational networks or networks of network-based organizations." In their view, "because much of the glue of terrorist organizations is commitment to an extreme ideology in a group with extreme solidarity, this generates a special range of issues of maintaining internal control (and) One additional vulnerability, characteristic of all ideologically extreme and rigid organizations, is the constant danger of schismatic ideological tendencies from within" (Smelser and Mitchell 2002:36–7).

[42] According to Bergesen and Lizardo (2004), "waves of terrorism appear in semiperipheral zones of the world-system during pulsations of globalization when the dominant state is in decline."

[43] However, in Abadie's view (2006:50), global or international terrorism as defined represents only a small fraction of terrorist activity. For example, for the year 2003

Lutz and Lutz 2004). For instance, the 1995 Oklahoma City bombing by "all-American" anti-government and "godly" terrorists resulted in killing "more people" than did "all the recorded international incidents that year" (Lutz and Lutz 2004). In turn, as implied, domestic and international terrorism each can be religious and non-religious, as well as conservative and radical terrorism.

Alternatively, a classification of specifically state terror incorporates intra- and inter-state, i.e., within and across society, terrorisms. As implied, subtypes and instances of within-society terrorism, namely what Comte calls in reference to Puritanism "violent repression", are theocracy as "holy terror" and tyranny, then fascism, communism, and other totalitarianism, as well as government executions in violations of applicable domestic and international rules. Forms and cases of inter-state or across-society terror are, alongside torture and abuse of foreign persons and groups, militarism, imperialism, wars of aggression, and the consequent conquest and violent occupation (Bauman 2001; Clairmont 1993; Giddens 2000; Habermas 2001; Turk 2004). In particular, offensive "preemptive" wars against other societies represent instances or proxies of inter-state terror in that via total war the "boundless violence" of governments destroys or subverts the "barriers of international law", for instance the UN prohibition of military aggressions (Habermas 2001).

As noted, a recent instance or proxy of wars of aggression as acts of inter-state terrorism is NATO's, according to international rules, illegitimate as well as indiscriminate, unprovoked, and undeclared attack on Yugoslavia effectively in, to add insult to injury, the service of a religious-ethnic (Islamic-Albanian) "terrorist army". The second element made this attack terrorist in a double way, namely not only a war of aggression against a sovereign country as inter-state terrorism in its own right, but allying with and on behalf of certain terrorist agents, couched in the rhetoric of "human rights", "liberation", and the like, within the attacked nation, probably an unprecedented event in postwar times. Simply, if admittedly the "intervention in Kosovo" was "not" explicitly legitimized by

---

(were reported) 1,536 events of domestic terrorism, but only 240 events of international terrorism." Similarly, Lutz and Lutz (2004:19) register that "by far the majority of terrorist acts that do occur are domestic ones (and) only a small portion of all terrorist attacks can be classified as international." In turn, Turk (2004:277) comments that "most of what is known about terrorist organizations is now outdated. Even distinctions such as "international" and "domestic" terrorism are decreasingly meaningful because technological advances (electronic communications, transportation networks) and corporate globalization facilitate more complex and flexible ways to organize terrorist activities, frequently involving cooperation among various "international" and "domestic" parties."

the UN (Giddens 2000) and thus unlawful in international terms (Smelser and Mitchell 2002), a "charge of aggression" and thus inter-state terrorism is logically, though not politically as unrealistic, suggested "against NATO forces"[44] (Bauman 2001). In particular, this attack qualified as an act of inter-state terrorism by attacking and destroying not only military targets and personnel but also the civilian infrastructure, and in the process killing civilians as merely "collateral damage" such as "lines of communications", including the bridges on and contaminating the Danube river and "economic facilities in Serbia proper"[45] (Lutz and Lutz 2004), and not just in Kosovo as the nominal and militarily, according to time-honored war conventions, sole legitimate site of combat and bombardment.

Another recent instance or proxy of offensive wars as acts of inter-state terrorism is the US/UK joint invasion of Iraq (Turk 2004) increasingly recognized as a "mistake" but evidently "too late" given the numbers of people killed, including US soldiers and especially Iraqis civilians, tortured, and the scope of "high-tech" destruction ("destroy to rebuild"). Its costs also include the exorbitant economic cost (4 trillion dollars in some estimates), incidentally, converting the budget surplus of the previous "liberal" administration into a huge deficit, which neo-conservatives, including the "Tea Party" and related movements, dramatize only after the "small" neo-conservative government that had performed this reverse budget alchemy was replaced by another "big" liberal government in 2009. This war qualifies as such an act of inter-state terror in virtue of being illegitimate and unprovoked war by international rules such as the UN prohibition of aggressions,[46] for which the Yugoslavia case served as a precedent (as the President and other officials and the British prime minister insisted). Yet, such and any international rules are irrelevant for

---

[44] Bauman (2001:208–9) also approvingly cites the view that the International Tribunal for Yugoslavia which "designated [a former Yugoslav President] a war criminal loses its credibility if, following the same criteria, it refrains from the inculpation of Clinton and Blair [etc.] and all those who violated simultaneously all forms of decency and the laws of war".

[45] Lutz and Lutz (2004:105) remarks that "Yugoslavia was subjected to an aerial bombing campaign launched by the US and other Western countries. The attacks targeted (not only) military units (but), lines of communications, and economic facilities in Serbia proper", thus implicitly characterizing it as terrorist.

[46] Turk (2004:281) comments that "the decision to launch an essentially unilateral invasion of Iraq was a huge departure from generally and increasingly accepted [outside the US] international norms for reviewing interstate grievances and providing for a collective (Security Council) decision authorizing military action against a sovereign government." Turk (2004:282) adds that "as the world's superpower, the US has weighed and accepted the political costs of ignoring the UN".

US bellicose, nationalistic neo-conservatives, including religious fundamentalists (Blee and Creasap 2010; Friedland 2002) and neo-fascists.

For instance, like virtually all US and UK newspapers and TV media,
with rare notable exceptions such as BBC, a British dogmatic laissez-faire
economically conservative though socially mostly liberal magazine initially supported the US/UK invasion and occupation of Iraq, just as NATO's
attack on Yugoslavia, by adopting the government rationale, only to
subsequently admit that this war was a "mistake". So do in one way or
another most of these outlets, excepting a hardline conservative business
journal which despite its pretended "libertarian" seriousness cannot be
taken seriously or can be taken seriously only, apparently living up its title,
as the brazen apologetic of capitalist plutocratic-oligarchic dictatorship
(Wall Street), as well as evangelical theocracy "made in the USA", not to
mention a television channel described by most Americans as a naked
partisan perversion or "joke" of journalism. In so doing they follow conservatism's old pattern of never repenting or apologizing for even most egregious acts, set, for instance, by warlike and violent yet self-righteous
Puritanism for Anglo-American settings.

Such admissions unwittingly imply that the Iraq war was a genuine or
proxy instance of inter-state terror—if it was a "mistake", then it was an
illegitimate and unjustified and to that extent terrorist act by one state or
a "coalition of the willing" states against another. However, such admission almost never rise the issue of individual or collective responsibility,
for one wonder if the war was a mistake, then someone or some must have
been responsible and thus sanctioned for making it because of its grave
human, social, ands material consequences, which make the term "mistake" an under-statement or misnomer. Apparently, demanding and
reaching individual responsibility is obstructed by enduring nationalism
domestically–the likelihood that US Congress and even the UK Parliament
will punish the former President and Prime Minister as "home boys" and
even "heroes" for the Iraq "mistake" is exactly zero. It is also unrealistic
globally, as the probability of UN or its World Court sentencing them as
war criminals like others from the former Yugoslavia, Africa, etc. is near
zero. A fortiori, the collective responsibility, for example, of the US
Congress and the UK Parliament for authorizing with near "bipartisan"
consensus (exceeding two-thirds majorities) such a "mistake" has never
been and will be seriously demanded or achieved, because of the mix of
such nationalistic and global factors, thus destined to remain "collective
irresponsibility". Hence, by failing or refusing to demand and enact such
individual and collective responsibility, those hundreds of thousands and

perhaps millions killed, tortured, or incapacitated by the Iraq invasion will remain merely a sort of "collateral damage", i.e., dead or living proofs, of this "mistake" perpetrated by these leaders or governments and solemnly authorized and even, as with Congress, incited or encouraged by their "honorable" legislatures.

In general, this reveals a certain asymmetry in this respect. While most agents of counter-state terrorism are eventually punished in one way or another (killed, apprehended, suicidal acts, etc.), this is not necessary the case with those of state and inter-state terror. And the stronger the state, the less likely those terrorist actors or supporters of wars of aggression to be sanctioned as war criminals, as seen in the US/UK invasion of Iraq and NATO's illegal bombing of Yugoslavia, and conversely, as witnessed in the UN Court proceedings against perpetrators of war crimes in weaker states such as Yugoslavia, some African countries, etc. Apparently, military might still counts as right when it comes to committing or supporting inter-state terror through unlawful wars of aggression by the "great powers" today, just as before (Vietnam, Grenada, Panama wars of aggression, etc.).

Furthermore, aggressive inter-state wars are genuine or proxy inter-state terrorism in eventually being nihilistic or self-destructive; recall destruction is a defining and integral element of terrorist agents and actions. They are through the possibly ultimate use of nuclear and related weapons of mass destruction, as especially envisaged and threatened by US bellicose conservatives, particularly religious fundamentalists, in and outside government, including "evangelical" Presidents, Congress, etc. (Schelling 2006). Ultimately, these wars are likely to result in a truly MAD outcome in global societal terms (mutually assured destruction) for both the victim and the aggressor[47] (Habermas 2001). (Table 2.1 summarizes the preceding typologies of contemporary terrorism.)

---

[47] Habermas (2001:47) comments that "the mad calculations of a balance of terror–MAD was the self-ironic abbreviation for mutually assured destruction–did prevent the outbreak of a war with two super-powers gone wild. The Cold War [was] a high-risk process of the self-domestication of nuclear alliances. This is also an apt description for the peaceful implosion of a global empire, whose leadership recognized the inefficiency of a supposedly superior mode of production, and admitted defeat in the economic race rather than following the time-honored pattern of deflecting internal conflicts with military adventures abroad", the latter apparently referring to the former Soviet Union before and during its disintegration."

Table 2.1. Typology of Modern Terrorism.

I Individual and collective terrorisms
   Individual terrorism–Terrorist persons ("lone wolves")
Group terrorism–Terrorist groups and organizations
State terrorism–Terrorist states or governments
Societal terrorism–terrorist societies or cultures
II State and counter-state terrorisms
State, governmental, official, institutionalized terrorism
      Theocracy–"holy" terror
Fascism–right totalitarianism
    Nazism, neo-fascism and neo-Nazism
    McCarthyism
   Communism—left totalitarianism
    Stalinism, Maoism, etc.
Theocratic, conservative-fascist, communist police states
Mix of theocracy and fascism–Theocratic fascism/Nazism and
   neo-fascism/neo-Nazism
Imperialism and militarism–inter-state terrorism
  wars of aggression
  government torture of foreign (and domestic) enemies
Death penalty–executions of innocent persons and for moral sins as not
   crimes in liberal democracy
Genocide via war of extermination and ethnic cleansing
Counter-state or oppositional, rebellious terrorism
  Anti-government attacks and subversions
Assassinations and putsches
Vigilante violence
  Lynching and hate crimes
III Conservative and radical (right-wing and left-wing) terrorisms
Conservative, counter-revolutionary, reactionary terrorism
   Master-servant terrorism
   Theocratic-religious terrorism
Fascist-Nazi terrorism
Radical, revolutionary, "progressive" terrorism
   Bourgeois, "liberal" (Jacobin) terrorism
Communist-Marxist terrorism
IV Religious and non-religious terrorisms
Religious or pseudo-religious terrorism
   Islamic, Christian, Hindu terrorism, etc.

Table 2.1. (*Cont.*)

Non-religious, secular terrorism
V Domestic and global terrorisms
Domestic/national counter-state terrorism
International/global counter-state terrorism
VI Intra- and inter-state terrorisms
Intra-state, within-society state terrorism
Inter-state, across-society state terrorism

CHAPTER THREE

ANTI-MODERNITY AND MODERN TERRORISM

What Causes and Justifies Terrorism in Western and non-Western Societies?

An especially relevant sociological and political problem consists in the actual and potential causes and by implication societal solutions to modern terrorism. Simply, one wonders "why there is terrorism" (Jonsson et al. 2009) in contemporary society. This is the problem of explanatory factors of and perhaps implied remedies for terrorism and its high human and social costs[1] (Jackman 2002), including its undemocratic[2] (Gibbs 1989) and related political adverse[3] (Heymann 1999) or other effects (Blattman and Miguel 2010; Collins 2004) on society, notably civil and other liberties (Béland 2005; Cable et al. 2008; Smelser and Mitchell 2002; Vasi and Strang 2009).

The present chapter aims to specify the main social determinants and thus likely predictors and by implication "cures" of terrorism in contemporary Western and non-Western societies, especially though not only America and Islamic settings, respectively, in which terrorist agents and actions have proliferated and intensified to the no-return point of "holy" terror and wars and mass destruction (Juergensmeyer 2003) during recent times. Terrorism is a complex and perhaps historically "nearly universal" (Lutz and Lutz 2004), sociological phenomenon in virtue of having multiple societal causes (Smelser and Mitchell 2002; Smelser 2007; Turk 2004),

---

[1] Jackman (2002:396) points to "the terrible costs of terrorism and war with profound material, psychological, and social repercussions." Battaglini and Coate (2007:139) imply economic and political costs by observing that the "value of public goods" at a certain time is "stochastic" in virtue of reflecting "terrorist threats" as well as wars.

[2] According to Gibbs (1989:335), the outcome of terrorist "provocational" strategy can be an "authoritarian regime", in which, however, the "incidence of terrorism may decline because repressive measures become more effective."

[3] Heymann (1999:2) suggests that terrorism "can and does affect the policies of modern democratic states", especially if "operating in a country whose population is already severely divided into suspicious and hostile groups", as in Northern Ireland, India, and Spain. In this view, "when a government deems acceptance of the terrorist demands, even considering the effect of acquiescence on the frequency of future demands, as far less onerous than the ongoing campaign of terror" (Heymann 1999:12).

just as a multiplicity of far-reaching social repercussions[4] (Houen 2002). In this respect, terrorism's crucial determinants and predictors involve a variety of interconnected "sociological factors" (Heymann 1999). Before proceeding further, it is to be noted that the sociological and related literature assumes, observes, and predicts multiple social determinants of terrorism, just as its various social-political effects[5] (Smelser and Mitchell 2002).

One strand of the sociological and economic literature identifies and emphasizes economic conditions as effective or likely causes and predictors of terrorism, particularly in Islamic and other under-developed or "third-world countries. These economic conditions include poverty and related conditions such as extreme wealth-income disparities, and low education primarily among developing non-Western countries (Smelser and Mitchell 2002; Smelser 2007; yet see Krueger and Maleckova 2003; Turk 2004), and secondarily in some regions or strata within Western societies, especially America. Some analysts identify also cyclical economic crises as the factor of terrorism (Lutz and Lutz 2004), specifically recurring recessions typically originating in advanced capitalist economies, above all America during conservatism, and spreading beyond such as the "Great Recession" of the 2000s.

---

[4] Houen (2002:278) comments that analyzing terrorism's "impact in relation to a variety of cultural factors resist(s) solidifying it into a structure greater than it is. For whether it is West German terrorists linking their violence to Fascism, or Baudrillard rooting hostage-taking in global capitalism, the effect of such magnification is frequently to magnify the terrorism itself. One way to separate terror from its 'ism' is to try and map the multiplicity of factors involved in it."

[5] Smelser and Mitchell (2002:47) register several adverse political effects of terrorism. First, the "tension between the exigencies of national security and the preservation of civil liberties [is] real and perhaps inevitable in times of political crisis. This tension between vigilance and liberty is of special significance and is likely to be a running sore in the context of American democracy, because of the nation's commitment to civil liberties". The second effect involves "discrimination against and scapegoating of relevant minority groups in the domestic population, sometimes encouraged or even executed by the government", citing "the "negative actions taken against German Americans during WW I and Japanese Americans in WW II" (Smelser and Mitchell 2002:47). The third effect is the "confusion of political opposition with lack of patriotism" (Smelser and Mitchell 2002:47). Also, Béland (2005:25) observes that "the terrorist attacks of September 11, 2001, have increased the general concerns regarding the protective duties of the modern state as they exacerbate the tension between the respect of individual rights and the imperative of national security The 'war on terrorism' heightens the tensions between the imperative of national security and individual rights and freedoms (as) the current crusade against terrorism. The strengthening of national security is widely perceived as a threat to basic civil and constitutional rights of citizenship created during the long-term bargaining process between state officials and civil social movements."

As observed, the "Great Recession" was generated (Stiglitz 2010), just as the "Great Depression", by self-destructive (Pryor 2002; Schutz 2001; Trigilia 2002) American "unfettered capitalism" premised on "market fundamentalism" in its "cancer stage" (McMurtry 1999)–though New Deal-type of measures have temporarily "saved" it, just as during the 1930s–and diffused via global social contagion to contaminate and inflict both Western European welfare capitalisms and the under-developed world. A related identified or hypothesized variable in the literature pertains to developing countries' grievances against the perceived "injustice" such as "unfair" trading, lending, and investment practices, then resource "predation", labor "exploitation", and other "neo-colonial" or "neo-imperialist" practices like structural dependency, onerous policy conditions imposed on them by wealthy Western societies (Abadie 2006; Bergesen and Lizardo 2002) via West- and particularly America-controlled international financial and trade institutions, such as the IMF, the World Bank, and (in part) the WTO (Stiglitz 2002).

The current literature especially identifies or assumes the complex of expanding and accelerating economic, political, and cultural globalization (Ceobanu and Escandell 2010; Fischer 2005) as an actual or potential factor or rationale of terrorism. In such accounts, globalization generates violent or negative responses primarily among various strata in traditional non-Western countries, and additionally some conservative, nationalistic, and xenophobic regions or populations in advanced Western societies (Bendix 1984; Bergesen and Lizardo 2002; Cragin and Chalk 2003; Fischer 2003; Lutz and Lutz 2004; Turk 2004). The later comprise Europe, including neo-Nazis in Germany, etc., and America, especially the Southern and other "Bible Belt" pervaded by hyper-conservatism, aggressive religious nationalism, bellicosity, militarism, and paranoid xenophobia (Bauman 1997; Blee and Creasap 2010; Cochran 2001; Friedland 2002; Juergensmeyer 2003).

The sociological and related literature also observes and predicts a range of non-economic social, mostly interconnected and mutually reinforcing, explanatory variables of contemporary terrorism. One subgroups of these variables comprises religious causes and justifications of contemporary terrorism and cognate kinds of violence within a society and against other societies through "holy" wars, most notably committed by reinvented and reinvigorated religious fundamentalism, especially by Islamic fundamentalists and American evangelical groups like "Christian" militias (Angel 1994; Emerson and Hartman 2006; Feldstein 2008;

Friedland 2002; Juergensmeyer 2003; Lutz and Lutz 2004; Smelser and Mitchell 2002; Smith 1994; Townshend 2002; Turk 2004). Another subgroup of non-economic variables of terrorism incorporates ethnic and national (Juergensmeyer 2003; Lutz and Lutz 2004; Townshend 2002; Williams 1994; also, Tawney 1920), racial[6] (Bailey and Snedker 2011; Jacobs et al. 2005; Heymann 1999; Messner et al. 2005; King et al. 2009), and similar determinants or rationales of terrorist agents and actions in the Western world, including the Great Britain, Spain, France, the USA, etc., and the non-Western, spanning from the former Yugoslavia to the Soviet Union and its successor states and to India, etc. Still another, related subgroup of non-economic determinants and predictors of terrorism identified in the literature entails ideological and political variables, including clashes between ideologies and government severe and expanding oppression, especially theocratic or fascist tyranny, and alternatively, state collapse or breakdown, constitutional and parliamentary crises and instability (Jackman 2002; Lutz and Lutz 2004; Morrill, Zald, and Rao 2003; Oberschall 2004; Smith 1994; Turk 2004).

In addition, within the non-economic category the sociological, unlike economic and in part political-science, literature emphasizes and predicts general cultural conditions and settings of terrorism (Alexander 2004; Smelser and Mitchell 2002). These settings are terrorist or violent and warlike cultures, especially in Islamic countries under resurgent fundamentalist Islamism and America during "born again" Protestant evangelicalism, both pervaded by "cultures of violence", including "holy" cosmic war or revolution against "evil" forces within society and against other societies (Juergensmeyer 2003; Townshend 2002). Lastly, a subgroup of the non-economic variables of terrorism is identified in the form of socio-psychological determinants or motivations of terrorist agents and actions (Lutz and Lutz 2004; Olick 1999; Smelser and Mitchell 2002; Smelser 2007; Townshend 2002).

In sum, in the current sociological and related literature terrorism is explained as conditioned and anticipated by a "blend of historical, economic, political, cultural, motivational, and technological factors"[7]

---

6 Heymann (1999:18) remarks that "the only truly dangerous setting for resisting terrorism: a society already severely divided along racial, religious, or ethnic lines."

7 Smelser and Mitchell (2002:19–20) observe that "the historical, social, political, and cultural conditions that constitute a favorable soil in which terrorism can take root and grow, provide a continuously changing mix of support and discouragement for terrorism, and constitute one of the main audiences for terrorists" and distinguish these conditions from the "immediate motivational, ideological, group, and organizational determinants"

(Smelser and Mitchell 2002). However, the "search for a single or even a few causes" is regarded as misguided, and generally the cause-effect logic as inappropriate with respect to its "origins and contexts" because these include "remote background conditions", "facilitating circumstances" and "precipitating factors", just as "inhibitory factors" (Smelser and Mitchell 2002; also, Lutz and Lutz 2004, Smelser 2007). At this juncture, these "historical, social, political, and cultural conditions" representing a "favorable soil" of terrorism are distinguished from its "immediate motivational, ideological, group, and organizational determinants" (Smelser and Mitchell 2002; also, Lutz and Lutz 2004). In short, the "likelihood and strength" of terrorism are reportedly dependent on a complex of "sociological factors",[8] notably prior divisions and conflicts with society (Heymann 1999) and related "basic facts" of social existence, notably power asymmetries and their violent consequences[9] (Pillar 2001).

Nevertheless, the theory, as well as the empirical evidence, of the determinants and predictors of contemporary terrorism is comparatively undeveloped by being in an embryonic phase[10] (Krueger and Maleckova 2003), including its limited scope in relation to the multiplicity and complexity of terrorist types (Abadie 2006), despite recently reported "theoretical progress" (Blattman and Miguel 2010). Notably and perhaps surprisingly to sociologists, what is admittedly "rare" are distinctly sociological explanations of contemporary terrorist agents and actions[11]

---

of terrorism. They propose that "the explanations at each level are separate, though they overlap and articulate with one another as one regards the total picture" (Smelser and Mitchell 2002:20).

[8] Heymann (1999:7) proposes that "the likelihood and strength of (terrorism) depends upon sociological factors (i.e.) the danger to the society in which (it) takes place depends upon the divisions within it before (it) occurs".

[9] Pillar (2001:217) predicts that "the long history of terrorism is reason enough to expect that it will always be a (significant) problem. It is a product of such basic facts of human existence as the discontent that is sometimes strong enough to impel people toward violence, the asymmetries of the weak confronting the strong, and the vulnerability of almost every facet of civilization to physical harm at the hands of those who find a reason to inflict harm. If there is a "war" against terrorism, it is a war that cannot be won. Counterterrorism, even though it shares some attributes with warfare, is not accurately represented by the metaphor of a war." In short, "terrorism cannot be 'defeated'—only reduced, attenuated, and to some degree controlled" (Pillar 2001:218).

[10] Krueger and Maleckova (2003:120) comment that "evidence on the determinants of terrorism is just beginning to be assembled." In particular, (Abadie 2006:50) proposes that "the determinants of international terrorism, however, are not necessarily informative about (those) of domestic terrorism. Much of modern-day transnational terrorism seems to generate from grievances against rich countries."

[11] Turk (2004:282) registers "the "dearth of explicitly sociological studies of terrorism" and comments that "developing a sociological explanation of terrorism is a politically and

(Turk 2004), despite recent pertinent theoretical and empirical contributions to the emerging field of the sociology of terrorism (Black 2004; Gibbs 1989; Juergensmeyer 2003; Smelser and Mitchell 2002; Smelser 2007; Spilerman and Stecklov 2009).

A Sociological Framework for Analyzing Modern Terrorism

The present work's main purpose is to contribute toward building and establishing the sociology of terrorism in its theoretical, empirical, and, whenever scientifically feasible, applied dimensions, as the relatively new, emerging and legitimate sociological endeavor and field. The contribution is hence intended to be three-fold, of which the first two aspects are explicit and the third is mostly implicit or conditional on them. The first aspect is to contribute toward theorizing, explaining, and hence possibly predicting terrorism by providing a theoretical, explanatory, and predictive framework for a scientific sociological analysis of terrorist agents and actions in contemporary societies. The second aspect is to contribute toward (re)discovering or identifying and interlinking historical and current, and whenever realistic, predicting or anticipating, future agents, acts, instances, and types of terrorism in contemporary societies. The third aspect, largely implied and conditional on the first two, is to contribute toward finding sensible responses, solutions, or effective remedies to the commonly perceived societal and global problem of contemporary terrorism through applying the sociological theory and evidence of its causes to acting on this phenomenon and its multiple adverse societal effects, notably economic, human and social costs by appropriate institutional arrangements and policies.

In classical sociological terms, the first two objectives would contribute toward a better understanding–in the sense of Webber's *Verstehen*– knowledge or science and hence possibly prediction of terrorism, like any other social phenomenon. And the third would contribute to a more effective societal actions, notably institutions and policies, in acting on or responding to this persisting and even growing problem in contemporary societies evoking Comte's classical sociological and rationalistic credo "from science [knowledge], comes prediction, from prediction, comes action". In essence, building on and developing the present sociological

---

intellectually formidable task." In turn, Lutz and Lutz (2004:16) caution that terrorism "is such a complex phenomenon that no one theory can be sufficient as an explanation for all occurrences."

and related literature, this work constructs, substantiates, and applies a distinctly sociological framework for explaining, predicting, and conceivably solving or mitigating the problem of contemporary terrorism. It does so by assuming and documenting the major societal determinants and hence probable predictors of terrorism, and implicitly applying such assumptions and knowledge to helping address this growing societal and global problem.

The present sociological framework assumes, documents, and predicts that the crucial social determinant and predictor of contemporary terrorism is the profound antagonism and vehement revolt against the project and reality of modernity as a type of idea, society, and historical period superseding pre-modernity. In short, in this framework contemporary terrorism is mostly, though not always, caused, explained, and hence predicted by anti-modernity as the main and overarching explanatory factor. Anti- or counter-modernity is understood in the sense of initial adverse reaction and persistent opposition to modernity in favor of pre-modernity or what Weber and Mannheim call traditionalism seen as destroyed and discredited by modernism and to be restored through violent struggle and counter-revolution[12] (Townshend 2002), notably "cosmic" war a la evangelical crusade and Islamic jihad (Juergensmeyer 2003), against the latter.

Alternatively, the framework theoretically hypothesizes, historically and empirically identifies, and, whenever possible, predicts or envisions that anti-modernity, as the negative obverse of traditionalism, has been, is, and likely will continue to be the critical and overarching societal factor and rationale of terrorism in Western and non-Western societies, especially though not only America and Islamic settings, respectively. In a sense, it suggests that modernity represents a sort of major agent provocateur of modern terrorism as its unintended, notably perverse, outcome (Boudon 1982; Giddens 1984) or Merton's (1968) latent function

---

[12] Townshend (2002:12) suggests that "counter-revolutionary, right-wing or reactionary [vs. revolutionary] 'white terror' is often precipitated by revolutionary change or the threat of it, and is characteristically pro-state but if the state is seen as already under alien domination, such groups can be impelled to attack the state they claim to be defending". In his view, "the most spectacular and disturbing recent outbreak of this syndrome is the libertarian or white-supremacist 'militias' in the US, who hold that the Federal government and its agencies (the FBI) are under the control of a 'Zionist world government' (or indeed lizards) dedicated to the destruction of American liberty", as exemplified by McVeigh et al. (Townshend 2002:12–3). (Also, Townshend 2002:53) remarks that "in cases where ethnic identity rather than progressive ideology is the driving force, resistance movements can be remarkably conservative – if not indeed reactionary".

by unwittingly causing or provoking terrorist agents and activities against itself and its ideas, values, and institutions. Hence, modernity and modern terrorism relate according to what Parsons would call the sociological "law" of positive societal aggregate action and adverse collective and individual reaction (Parsons and Smelser 1956). The advent of modernity is an instance of such aggregate societal action initially within Western society and subsequently beyond. Modern terrorism is a special case of negative reaction, specifically a violent, destructive form of anti-modernity and by extension of pre-modernity or traditionalism turned, as Mannheim (1986) remarks, "self-reflective" in reacting to the modern societal condition, becoming "conservatism."

In this connection, contemporary, especially religiously conditioned and rationalized, terrorism emerges and acts as violent revolt against the alleged "discrediting" of traditional religious and other values by Western modernity (Juergensmeyer 2003). This is an allegation or perception especially shared by US and Islamic as well as virtually all forms of religious traditionalism and absolutism (Habermas 2001), notably fundamentalism, thus inducing and rationalizing their terrorist acts and "holy" wars or revolutions, such as new crusades and jihads in both military and general terms (Turner 2002). For instance, US "born again" evangelical groups claim that their "new religions" (sic!) have "ancient roots" and represent "revivals of the original forms of their traditions" or "defenders of ancient faiths"[13] after the model of "Church of Jesus Christ" in the generic sense

---

[13] Juergensmeyer (2003:223–4) adds that US as well as Islamic fundamentalists use the "language of traditional religion to build bulwarks around aspects of modernity that have threatened them. The need for ['hard' and 'ancient'] religion was a response to the soft treachery they observed in the new societies [i.e.,] the perceived failures of public institutions. The government—already delegitimized—is perceived to be in league with the forces of chaos and evil". In this account, the "result of this disaffection with the values of the modern West [is] a 'loss of faith' in the ideological form of that culture, secular nationalism [as] the principle that the nation is rooted in a secular compact rather than a religious or ethnic identity (as) an alien cultural construction [of] 'the project of modernity' [causing] religious alternatives to [modernity and] secular ideologies [to have] extraordinary appeal", as exemplified in Iran's "rejection of a modern Western political regime and the creation of a successful religious state" (Juergensmeyer 2003:226). Juergensmeyer (2003:227–8) comments that "yet what lies beyond modernity is not necessarily a new form of political order, religious or otherwise (but) cultural anarchism" as in the former Soviet Union, because the combination of violence and war with religion "in acts of religious terrorism [is] a potent assertion (indicating) "deprivatization" of religion. [Everywhere] attempts (are) made by defenders of religion to reclaim the center of public attention and authority, religious terrorism is often the violent face of these attempts. The postmodern religious rebels (are) neither anomalies nor anachronisms". For instance, "the Christian, Jewish, Muslim, Hindu, Sikh, and Buddhist cultures of violence"

of embarking on "Crusade for Christ" by fervent and suicidal "Christian soldiers", and a cacophony of other "Christian" churches and warriors, more precisely Protestant sects in Webber's sense and cults in America (Juergensmeyer 2003). Such a Protestant type of religious fundamentalism and sectarianism (King 2008) cum revived evangelicalism (Lindsey 2008) is reportedly opposed to Western modernity or disaffected with the "values of the modern West", including secular "big" government, effectively a minimal welfare state, demonized as belonging to the "forces of chaos and evil" (Juergensmeyer 2003). This also applies to other religiously and otherwise traditionalist groups in America (Houen 2002; Turk 2004) that stand in opposition "against modern society" (Lutz and Lutz 2004; Munch 2001) and induced and self-justified by anti- or counter-modernism into committing or inciting acts of violence, murder, mass destruction, and "cosmic" war, simply "holy" terror both when outside of and in government control.

Similarly, in Islamic and other traditional non-Western countries, the advent or potential of "competing religious forces, especially nonreligious secularism" and the spread of "ideas of freedom, rights, and democracy" from the West result in undermining "traditional and authoritarian political cal values and institutions" (Smelser and Mitchell 2002). It thus yields anti-modern antagonism among certain traditionalist or conservative groups, serving as the inducement and justification (Turk 2004) for their terrorist acts or plans seeking to reverse modernization and restore traditionalism through "holy" war a la jihad against "infidels" within society and across societies. Evidently, what is common to and even substantively unites (Davis and Robinson 2009; Friedland 2002; Hedges 2006; Juergensmeyer 2003; Turner 2002) these nominally "mortal enemies", American and Islamic fundamentalists and other religious conservatives is the shared opposition to modern secular-democratic government and generally to Western modernity as a "particular social order". This is a kind of antagonism that functions as a generating and rationalizing force of terrorism by providing the overarching source and rationale for terrorist agents and acts[14] (Blee and Creasap 2010; Turk 2004).

---

today "rely on [their] precedents and [theological] justifications for their own acts of religious violence" Juergensmeyer (2003:218).

[14] Turk (2004:278) infers that for Islamic and American fundamentalists "opposition to authority or a particular social order [modernity] is more likely to stem from a reasoned position than from pathology or deficient socialization. Reasoning in cosmological, religious terms is increasingly characteristic of the rationales by which terrorists justify their acts to themselves and others."

The shared elements of Islamic and American fundamentalists, as well as other religious traditionalists, thus their common driving forces or justifications of terrorism are reportedly at least two-fold. The first is Western modernity's perceived tendency to confine religion to the "private sectors of social life" and to separate sacred power from "formal roles in government, economics, and eventually education, medicine [etc.]", notably the legal separation of church and state (Emerson and Hartman 2006). The second is the presence of a "variety of religious and nonreligious ideologies", as predicted by secularization theory, as the cause of relativizing religion, an outcome "foreign" to and thus opposed by "most religions, especially those with a singular god" (Emerson and Hartman 2006) like Christianity (though, as Weber notes, not monotheistic in the strict sense) and Islam. Namely, what unites and drives into terrorism mutually hostile Islamic and Protestant "Christian" fundamentalists contesting for global religious and military dominance via what Weber calls "propaganda of faith" and "holy" wars is the shared perception that "sacred" tradition is violated. Hence, presumably the "godly" and "righteous", as US and Islamic fundamentalists both describe themselves, are prevented from reaching victory in their "holy" revolution and war a la crusade and jihad against "infidels" and "evil", as a sort of ultimate "injustice" to them, by the process of modernization, in particular liberalization and secularization.

In sum, anti-modernity is understood in the sense of a complex of initial adverse reaction and persistent opposition to and ultimate reversal of modernity and of restoration of pre-modernity as traditionalism. Thus understood, anti-modernity seems to be the overarching main content of religious fundamentalists' "beautiful minds" and the driving force and justification of their admittedly "mindless" acts and plans of terrorism, i.e., unlawful and indiscriminate violence, war, (self) destruction, physical coercion and violent repression in general. Such content would permit some understanding–Webber's *Verstehen*–or empathy for these terrorist groups and actions. Yet, it does not, as Weber admonishes, mean pardoning of or sympathy for them on these grounds, namely secular modernity's violation of "sacred" religious tradition or tearing of the traditional "sacred canopy" as the culprit and thus a sort of overt or covert justification for religiously based terrorism in its counter-state and state and interstate forms, especially by "our" native-grown and "holy" warriors[15] and

---

[15] Emerson and Hartman (2006:129) observe that in modernity "religion comes to be relegated to the private sectors of social life, divorced from formal roles in government,

"patriots" (Emerson and Hartman 2006; also, Eliasoph and Lichterman 2003; Lindsay 2008; Grim and Finke 2007; Smith 2000). Religious fundamentalists and other anti-modern conservatives are thereby somehow made to look not as atavistic or backward as usually seen, given the typical view of the "backwardness" of fundamentalism after the model or image of the Southern "Bible Belt" (Acemoglu and Robinson 2008; Amenta and Halffman 2000; Bauman 1997; Cochran 2001; Gould 1996; Hicks 2006) in urban-liberal, secular "blue" America and other Western societies, and even as "good-intentioned guys". This especially applies to "born again" US fundamentalists rechristened and supposedly reinvented as "evangelicals", including both grass-root members (Smith 2000) and leaders (Lindsey 2008), as presumably different, i.e., no or less violent, coercive, repressive, and theocratic, from their "Monkey Trial" fundamentalist ancestors (Boles 1999; Davis and Robinson[16] 2009; Evans and Evans 2008; Martin 2002).

In this connection, some sociologists (Emerson and Hartman 2006; Eliasoph and Lichterman 2003; Lindsay 2008; Grim and Finke 2007; Smith 2000) explicitly or implicitly question revived religious fundamentalism's imputed link with terrorism by asserting that not all or even most fundamentalists commit or support terrorist and related acts, which is probably correct. Yet, it is perhaps also correct to say not all fascists, including Nazis, especially rank-and-file members "just following orders" (including a Pope, etc.), as distinguished from their order-giving leaders, perpetrated counter-state or state terrorism, war crimes, and other violence in inter-war Europe. Second, it is equally correct to observe and predict, as stated in this work, that contemporary religious fundamentalists tend to commit or support terrorism, just as fascists and neo-fascists, more than do others, such as non-fundamentalists and seculars. In this sense, such an assertion and prediction only is sensible and relevant in sociological comparative-historical terms, while those stating that "not all" fundamentalists or fascists are terrorists (or murderers) are trivial and irrelevant. In purely methodological terms, the first is a substantive proposition and

---

economics, and eventually education, medicine [etc.]. [Also] exposing people to a variety of religious and nonreligious ideologies (secularization theory) relativizes religion, a concept foreign to most religions, especially those with a singular god. Modernization rips the sacred canopy."

[16] Davis and Robinson (2009:1305) observe that "Protestant fundamentalists in the United States did [themselves from society] for several decades following their defeat in the Scopes trial of 1925, or [became] "public" religious movements that work to remake or sacralize the public sphere."

prediction, or testable hypothesis, subject to confirmation or falsification, the second a truism not needed to confirm or falsify, thus methodologically redundant and unimportant.

Notably, US evangelicals reportedly seek to capture and retain by virtually any effective means political power at all levels, especially to seize and control the federal government, notably the Supreme Court. This is deemed the most effective instrument of realizing the theocratic design of "godly" society a la "Christian America" (Blee and Creasap 2010; Davis and Robinson 2009; Hedges 2006; Hicks 2006; Keister 2008; King 2008) and (re)establishing themselves as "preordained" rulers by "God's Plan", as portrayed in empathetic sociological accounts (Lindsey 2008). ("God's plan" is the expression used by an evangelical politician when asked about the reasons for being selected as the 2008 conservative vice-presidential candidate.)

The above also applies to Islamic fundamentalists as extreme religious conservatives among most Muslim countries and groups, including those in America as witnessed in and after September 11, 2001 (Collins[17] 2004). It does so long as these agents and their acts of terrorism or "holy" war are justifiable or pardonable as "martyrs" and "martyrdom" by their self-righteous anti-modernity (Oberschall 2004), typically anti-Western views, and rigid traditionalism based on Koran law, not just, as Weber would allow, to be "understood" via empathy, though not sympathy.

Following this rationale, also fascists and their terrorist actions and plans could be "justified" or "pardoned" on the ground of anti-modernity, namely reacting to, opposing, and reversing "corrupt" modernity and restoring the "glory" and "honor" of traditionalism. This epitomizes the pattern of anti-modernist reaction and traditionalist restoration in fascism and all conservatism, such as opposing the minimal welfare state as liberal "big" government and the "restoring honor" of the police-warfare and theocratic state by American neo-fascism, fundamentalism,

---

[17] Collins (2004) proposes, in apparent reference to the September 11 2001 terrorist attacks, that terrorism, like social conflict in general, "produces group solidarity in four phases:(1) an initial few days of shock and idiosyncratic individual reactions to attack; (2) one to two weeks of establishing standardized displays of solidarity symbols; (3) two to three months of high solidarity plateau; and (4) gradual decline toward normalcy in six to nine months. Conflicts arise over access to centers of ritual attention; clashes occur between pragmatists deritualizing security and security zealots attempting to keep up the level of emotional intensity. The solidarity plateau is also a hysteria zone; as a center of emotional attention, it attracts ancillary attacks unrelated to the original terrorists as well as alarms and hoaxes. In particular historical circumstances, it becomes a period of atrocities."

and neo-conservatism overall such as extremist "Tea-Party" and related movements. Fascism, including Nazism, has been and remains, via neo-fascism or the radical right (Blee and Creasap 2010; Rydgren 2007a), the most extreme form of anti-modernism (Habermas 2001), notably anti-liberalism (Dahrendrof 1979). Alternatively, fascism has been the new version of medievalist traditionalism, along and usually allied and eventually, as in contemporary America, merged, like political conservatism overall (King 2008), with religious fundamentalism (Friedland 2002; Hedges 2006), as embodied by "Christian" neo-Nazi militias and warriors.

In turn, both fascism and fundamentalism are the extremist and "godly" subtypes of the "extended family" of conservatism. Conservatism has always been and remains, with some embellishments or disguises (Bourdieu 1998), overarching anti-modernism and pre-modernism or traditionalism reinvented and become "self-reflective" in facing, aversely reacting to, and persistently opposing modernism, notably liberalism condemned initially as its "immediate antagonist" (Mannheim 1986) and subsequently as its perpetual "enemy". Consequently, modernism has been condemned by religious conservatism or orthodoxy declaring and waging a "holy" and "mindless" war against modernity, particularly the liberal Enlightenment (Habermas 2001), through the "papal struggles" against liberalism (Burns 1990) and their Protestant variants (Dombrowski 2000) such as Puritan fundamentalism or evangelicalism. In particular, in America Puritan-rooted evangelical Protestantism emerged and remains as a "reaction against the individualism of the Enlightenment" condemning and attacking the latter's modern principle of "individual judgment as the touchstone to truth" (Davis and Robinson 2009). Modernism, notably the Enlightenment, has also been denounced by fascism, notably Nazism, attacking and destroying anything "modern" and "liberal" (Blinkhorn 2003) and continues to be by neo-fascism, including neo-Nazism, in Europe and America alike (King et al. 2009; Rydgren 2007a).

In sum, most modern terrorism expresses and results from the revolt against modernity through anti-modern reaction and counter-revolution. It is a radical, violent expression and outcome of the opposition against modernism and alternatively of the attempted restoration of traditionalism, specifically medievalism, by anti-modernity such as conservatism, including fascism, neo-conservatism, revived religious fundamentalism, and neo-fascism. In this sense, as a form or part of total war and a type of rebellion, terrorism arises and functions as, in Clausewitz's terms, the ultimate "continuation" or escalation of the "politics" of anti-modernity and pre-modernity or traditionalism by "other means" such as illegitimate and indiscriminate violence, destruction, and violent repression and severe coercion overall. As such, most modern terrorism, especially during the 1990s–2010s, represents a sort of "normal pathology" (Gouldner 1970) or pathological normalcy, the integral radical element and predictable violent product of anti-modernity in the prime and most persistent and intense shape of conservatism as an ideology and societal system, including religious fundamentalism and political fascism.

Modernity, Anti-Modernity, and Pre-Modernity Revisited

For the purpose of the analysis of modern terrorism, the two key concepts and terms, modernity and anti-modernity, and therefore the associated secondary concept of "pre-modernity", are more fully and precisely specified as follows. By "modernity" is specifically understood liberal, democratic, secular, rationalistic, and cosmopolitan-global Western modernity or modernism in the sense of a social system and historical period. "Modernity" thus encompasses modern societies defined by liberalization, secularization, rationalization, and cosmopolitanism and globalization, as interlinked and mutually reinforcing processes and conditions, within the West and its extensions, such as the US, Canada, Australia, and New Zealand, and its emulators or imitators like Japan, etc. "Modernity" has developed since the late 18th century, namely the Enlightenment and its political sequel the French Revolution (Acemoglu et al. 2011; Dahrendorf 1979) and in part American Revolution in its Jeffersonian design or interpretation through the global trends toward economic, political, and cultural modernization during the early 21st century (Inglehart and Baker 2000; Inglehart and Norris 2004; Norris 2004; Munch 2001). At this juncture, as the intertwined and mutually reinforcing complex of liberalism, secularism, rationalism, and cosmopolitanism and globalism, modernity or modernism is usually considered the "child" and legacy of, first and foremost, the 18th century European Enlightenment (Barnes 2000; Davis and Robinson 2009; Delanty 2000; Habermas 2001; Mokyr 2009; Schmidt 1996).

By "anti-modernity" is specifically meant the initially medieval-rooted, including feudal-based, conservative antagonistic reaction to the point of violent revolt and counter-revolution against modernity in an attempt at restoration of pre-modernity. This conservative anti-modern antagonism assumes certain successive but interconnected and mutually reinforcing forms such as medievalist religiously orthodox, fascist, and neo-conservative, in particular revived fundamentalist and neo-fascist, adverse reactions to the advent and expansion of modernity. Hence, pre-modernity is understood in the sense of medievalism, including feudalism, and traditionalism in general subjected to the Schumpeterian process of "creative destruction" through revolutionary innovation by modernism, namely liberalism, secularism, rationalism, and cosmopolitanism and globalism, including capitalism defined in these terms (his preferred term is technological, market-economic, and organizational "invention"). The modernizing, notably liberalizing-democratizing, secularizing and rationalizing, process has been opposed and attempted to halt and reverse through the restoration of the "golden past" and "paradise lost", including the "honor", of pre-modernity, thus via reactionary counter-revolution (Bourdieu 1998), by anti-modernity, primarily conservatism, including medieval-based religious orthodoxy, fascism, and neo-conservatism, in particular revived fundamentalism, and neo-fascism. These particular forms of conservative anti-modernity arise and operate in a historical sequence and basic sociological continuity, convergence, and affinity.

A historical analogue or precedent is, in Pareto's account, that what Simmel and Parsons describe as the humanistic artistic Renaissance was "halted" by the Protestant Reformation, notably the Calvinist theocratic "disciplinary" Revolution (Gorski 2003; Hillmann 2008a; Loveman 2005; Walzer 1965). Thus it was reversed in those sections of Europe where the "Reformed Church" was victorious, such as initially and transiently France (the Huguenots' ruled parts), especially Switzerland (Geneva), Holland, Prussia (the royal court), and via Presbyterianism and Puritanism Scotland and England. In particular, as Weber suggests, this outcome occurred in Great Britain due to Puritan anti-artistic practices and influences. The result of these practices was what he describes as the striking suppression and retrogression of the arts (music, painting, etc.), as well as, in Mill's words, "amusements" (e.g., Shakespeare's theater, Sunday sports), and even, as Hume classically recounts, "science and learning" (also, Zaret 1989), through Puritan "holy terror" (Walzer 1963). And in a sense anti-humanistic, anti-artistic, and hyper-ascetic Puritanism as "American Calvinism" (German 1995; Hillmann 2008b; Munch 1981) effectively prevented the Renaissance from ever "coming to America" since the establishment of its New England theocracy during the early 17th century through the disestablishment in the 19th century, almost half a century after the American Revolution (Dayton 1999; Gould 1996) and beyond.

The legacy of what Weber calls the Puritan "antagonism" to art or "sensuous culture" continues to pervade contemporary America, including the government's depreciation and, among Western societies, unrivalled low spending on the arts (Throsby 1994) as involving forbidden pleasures (Scitovsky 1972) cum sins—and in extension "original sin"–and hence crimes, as Pareto registers for Puritanism. Such antagonism or depreciation causes, in Weber's words, the "adverse fate" of artistic culture in the "new nation", making it a sort of "cultural desert" (Baudrillard 1999), especially the "Bible Belt" as what Mencken (1982) calls anti-cultural "Sahara desert" ruled by evangelical primitivism in the form of what he calls Baptist-Methodist "barbarism [sic]".

Perhaps the above case is more than just an analogy or precedent. It is insofar as, first, the artistic and humanistic Renaissance heralded or anticipated modernity (Eisenstadt 1998; Habermas 2001), notably the rationalistic, liberal-secular Enlightenment. Second, contemporary religiously grounded anti-modernity mostly assumes the form of revived Protestant fundamentalism *cum* evangelicalism in America, alongside the Vatican Church, like Islamic fundamentalism in Muslim societies. To that extent, just as, if Pareto is correct, the Protestant Reformation, notably the Calvinist-Puritan Revolution, "halted" the Renaissance in Northern Europe and Great Britain, and prevented its artistic and humanistic ideas and legacies from ever fully spreading to the "new nation", American sectarian Protestantism and neo-conservatism overall aims and achieves an equivalent outcome. Namely, it seeks and reportedly (Inglehart 2004; Norris 2004; Ruiter and Tubergen 2009) succeeds to halt and even via recurring anti-modern evangelical revivals or neo-conservative counter-revolutions in the US—for example, those in 1980, 1994, 2000, 2010–reverse or subvert modernity.

Notably, this involves halting or reversing and subverting liberal-secular democracy and civil society as "un-American" by making liberalism the stigmatized "L-world" in politics and beyond (King 2008; Tiryakian 2000; Vasi and Strang[18] 2009), in America, particularly the South

---

[18] Vasi and Strang (2009:1716) report that "in the years since the 9/11 terrorist attacks, some 400 local governments passed "Bill of Rights" [BOR] resolutions in opposition to the USA PATRIOT Act." Moreover, they suggest that "this campaign [BOR] is the broadest grassroots effort to protect civil liberties in the history of the United States" (Vasi and Strang 2009:1718). Vasi and Strang (2009:1719–20) also register that the USA PATRIOT Act "passed the House on October 24, 2001, by a vote of 357 to 66 and passed the Senate the next day by a vote of 98 to 1" in a striking, but typical during US history, "bipartisan" attack on civil and political liberties and rights in America during objective or fabricated crises, essentially a permanent state of war and emergency (Habermas et al. 1998). In general, reportedly "this is a recurring issue in American history, as elsewhere. The term "civil liberties" was devised in response to the Espionage and Sedition Acts of 1918, which made it illegal to defame the government. At the height of the Cold War's Red Scare, Congress barred Communists from public employment and outlawed the Communist Party;

(e.g., Texas, etc.) where "liberal" has become almost equated to "criminal", "immoral", or "blasphemy", as was in Nazism and is in Islamic theocracies. (For instance, like others in the South, a "true" conservative Texas governor labeled with apparent pleasure and joy an electoral opponent from another political party as a "liberal" apparently expecting that this labeling will work in and by itself as a winning formula in Texan elections and politics overall, thus having no need of saying or doing much else. It seems as if simply just say liberal" and "no" to liberalism, "liberals need not apply" in politics and "you win" in the "Bible Belt" and other "red" US regions, as witnessed in the 2010 elections and before since hysterically anti-liberal triumphant Reaganism.)

This is indicated by the finding that for "born again" US Protestant fundamentalists *no* education and knowledge–let alone religious or home schooling widespread, especially in the "Bible Belt" on a scale unknown in modern Western societies–is "better" than its Enlightenment-rooted modern liberal-secular and rational form condemned as a grave threat to sacred and secular powers (Darnell and Sherkat 1996). (How *human* education and other action can be a grave threat to supra-human Divine authority, what Weber would call an "impossible contra-diction", only US evangelicals as well as Islamic fundamentalists holding the same view seem to know and fear.) Admittedly, US "conservative Protestants" tend to be more hostile or critical and skeptical toward science, including evolutionary biology, stem-cell research, and global warming theory, and in extension secular education and even technology and medicine than "other Americans" (Evans and Evans 2008) and a fortiori Westerners. In sum, conservative Protestantism, especially Calvinism and its Anglo-Saxon sectarian transplant Puritanism, has been and remains via revived Protestant fundamentalism in America an exemplary type of anti-Renaissance and counter-Enlightenment, and in that sense anti-modernity. Generally, religious, like political, conservatism, including Protestant, Catholic, and other Christian alike, reportedly reinvented and reinvigorated itself during the late 18th and early 19th centuries as the counter-Enlightenment (Nisbet 1966) and to that extent anti-modernity.

---

over 11,000 lost their jobs because of government and private loyalty programs. In the wake of al Qaeda's terrorist attack on September 11, 2001, efforts to secure the newly minted American homeland verged into the same territory [e.g.] rampant reports of abuse. The U.S. Department of Justice declared the Geneva Convention void with respect to "enemy combatants," hundreds of whom have been held incommunicado at Guantanamo Bay pending the successful resolution of the "war on terror" (Vasi and Strang 2009:1717).

At this juncture, modernity is what Schumpeter would extol and "libertarian" Hayek (1955) deplores as the creative "destroyer" of traditionalism as pre-modernity, notably medievalism's complex of feudalism, despotism, and theocracy as economic, political, and total societal systems. This is exemplified by the Enlightenment's "creative destruction", perhaps initiated or anticipated by the Renaissance as its precursor, of the Dark Middle Ages. Modernity is commonly considered the "child" or aggregate project and outcome of the Enlightenment (Berman 2000; Delanty 2000; Garrard 2003; Mokyr 2009; Phelps 2007; Smart 2000) and in extension of the Renaissance as the anticipation or precursor of the latter. Alternatively, anti-modernity in the form of conservatism arises, operates, and remains as the positive design and system of restoring and rehabilitating from "death" and discredit pre-modernity, traditionalism as the "golden past", notably medievalism and its economic feudalism, political despotism, and societal theocracy named *Civitas Dei* (godly society) a la *Christiana Respublica* (Black 1997; Gorski 1993) as "paradise lost" and in that sense of the Dark Middle Ages. Conservatism has historically been and essentially remains through neo-conservatism, including revived fundamentalism and neo-fascism, a paradigmatic exemplar of anti-modernity. In particular, it has been the counter-Enlightenment (Nisbet 1966) and thus axiomatic anti-liberalism (Mannheim 1986), despite some conservative "modernist" embellishments (Bourdieu 1998) and, as Michels (1968) observed and anticipated, democratic disguises and deceptions (Blee and Creasap 2010; King 2008; Rydgren 2007a).

In sum, "pre-modernity" is understood mostly as medieval traditionalism involving the "holy trinity" of the economic system of feudalism, the political system of despotism, and the total societal system of theocracy in the form or image of the Dark Middle Ages. "Modernity" means the four-fold complex of liberalism, secularism, rationalism, and globalism, universalism, and cosmopolitanism superseding through revolution, i.e., "creative destruction" of, medievalism and invented or projected by the Enlightenment. And "anti-modernity" signifies (primarily) conservatism, spanning from arch-conservatism, including medievalist religious orthodoxy, to fascism and to neo-conservatism, particularly revived fundamentalism and neo-fascism, striving to restore pre-modernism in the form of medievalism and to reverse modernism via counter-revolution and radical revolt overall (the above is summarized in Table 3.1).

In essence, within the present sociological framework "modernity" signifies modern liberalism as a project, social system, and historical

Table 3.1. Specification of pre-modernity, modernity and anti-modernity.

Pre-modernity

Medievalism—the Dark Middle Ages (the 4th-18th century AD, "Christian
   civilization")
   feudalism as an economic system
   despotism as a political structure
   theocracy as a total social system (*Civitas Dei*)
Pre-medieval traditionalism
   classical antiquity (Ancient Greece, Rome, etc.)
   other

Modernity

Liberal Western modernism (from the mid 18th century AD, the
   Enlightenment)
   liberalism–liberal democracy and society
   secularism–secular polity and society
   rationalism–rationalistic culture, including scientism
   globalism and cosmopolitanism–globalization and universalism

Anti-modernity

Anti-liberal conservatism (from the late 18th century AD)
   arch-conservatism in initial adverse reaction to modernity
      medievalist religious orthodoxy–the Vatican Church, orthodox
         Protestantism
   (Calvinism/Puritanism), etc.
   fascism
      Nazism in Germany
      McCarthyism and vigilantism (KKK, "red scare", etc.) in America
   neo-conservatism in America and Europe
      revived religious fundamentalism and theocracy in America
         (Protestant sectarianism and evangelicalism)
      neo-fascism (the radical right)
         neo-Nazism in Germany
   resurgent Islamic fundamentalism

conjuncture alike. Liberalism is understood by analogy to capitalism, as
incidentally its integral, economic element, with qualifications to include
liberal-democratic capitalist economies and exclude capitalist dictatorships like Chile (under Pinochet), Singapore, and other third-world

dictatorial economies, as well as America and Great Britain during repressive anti-labor neo-conservatism. In turn, "anti-modernity" means primarily contemporary conservatism also in the triple sense of an idea, social structure, and period analogously to medievalism as its historical source and persistent overt or covert ideal. Conservative anti-modernity specifically comprises, first, arch-conservatism, including medievalist religious orthodoxy, in adverse reaction to modernity, second, fascism as the extreme product or subtype of conservatism, and, third, neo-conservatism as its recent slightly modified revival, including revived fundamentalism and theocracy as an original and perennial design and reality, and neo-fascism as arising or operating in the neo-conservative "extended family". And conservative anti-modernity essentially strives to reverse modernity and restore "pre-modernity" in the form of medieval traditionalism comprising feudalism, despotism and theocracy.

Anti-Modernity and Modern Terrorism

At first glance, there is nothing new, original, and outrageous, let alone shocking, in the above dual definition of the primary concepts of "modernity" and "anti-modernity" in terms of respective liberal and conservative ingredients. This is how both concepts are typically defined or understood in the sociological and related literature. It is also how their adherents self-define and self-perceive themselves, i.e., liberals, classical and contemporary alike, and conservatives from arch-conservatives through fascists and neo-conservatives, including "reborn" religious fundamentalists or theocrats and neo-fascists. They simply do as the moderns and the anti-moderns or traditionalists respectively, with secondary variations and disguises, as in neo-conservatism. This applies even more to the definition of the secondary concept of pre-modernity in terms of traditionalism, especially medievalism incorporating medieval feudalism, despotism, and theocracy.

What is likely to be perceived as partly novel and original by liberals and moderns, or completely outrageous and "shocking" by conservatives, including "born again" religious fundamentalists, in America, Islamic countries, and beyond is something else. This is the uncovered and predicted linkage of conservative, including arch-conservative, fascist, and neo-conservative, in particular revived theocratic or fundamentalist and neo-fascist, anti-modernity with most, though not all, contemporary terrorism. The newness or "shock" is (re)discovering and predicting that anti-modernity in the primary form of conservatism has been, is, and likely will continue to be the main and overarching determinant, explanation, and predictor of terrorism in contemporary societies during the late 20th and early 21st century.

Recall that anti-modern conservatism involves an historical sequence and basic sociological continuity spanning from arch-conservatism, including medievalist religious orthodoxy, through interwar fascism like Nazism to neo-conservatism, notably revived theocratic fundamentalism and neo-fascism such as neo-Nazism. It is not the intention of this work to "shock" in this sense but, to use another adage, only to reveal, explain, and predict that the anti-modern *cum* primarily conservative, i.e., arch-conservative, fascist, neo-conservative or theocratic-fundamentalist, and neo-fascist, emperor "has no cloths." The latter expression is used with respect to conservative anti-modernity advocating, committing, and supporting terrorism as a sort of "sweet revenge" or the "last stand" of a *caput mortuum* ("presumed dead") world and time against liberal-democratic, secular, rationalistic, and global-cosmopolitan universalistic modernity. If this is construed as a shocking or "indecent proposal", it is only an unintended effect (latent function) of the main intended objective of this work. Recall this is identifying, documenting, and predicting the main sources and rationales of modern terrorism; and even here probably "one cannot please everyone", least of all probably anti-moderns like conservatives, fascists, theocrats, fundamentalists, etc.

In general, the present work intends only to restate, rediscover, and tentatively predict what has been widely assumed and even known or suspected not only by the agents and supporters of modernity (the moderns) but also, even when denying it, deeply in their "hearts" by those of anti-modernity, i.e., conservatives of all types and times such as arch-conservatives, fascists, and neo-conservatives, including reborn theocratic fundamentalists and neo-fascists. This is that anti-modern conservatism has been, is, and likely will be the prime source and mover of contemporary terrorism and even, especially in its ultimate form of theocracy or religious fundamentalism and fascism, constitutes and functions as terrorism in its own right. On this account, this study would hardly "shock" anyone, including most sensible conservatives, from arch- to neo-conservatives, including "reborn" theocratic fundamentalists and neo-fascists, in America, Islamic countries, and Europe but rather say what virtually "every schoolboy knows" (Bateson 1979). This is simply that the "emperor" of anti-modernity cum conservatism "has never had cloths" or qualms in respect of advocating, inciting, committing, and supporting terrorism as violent repression, ranging from medievalist arch-conservatism through fascism to neo-conservatism, the "new" theocracy and religious fundamentalism, and neo-fascism.

In sum, conservatism renders terrorism the effective ultimate means to suppress and reverse liberal modernity and restore pre-modern traditionalism. As noted, the latter especially involves medievalism, as the point of origin and perennial ideal of conservatism (Dunn and Woodard 1996; Mannheim 1986; Nisbet 1966) and neo-conservatism (Bourdieu 1998), including fascism and neo-fascism (Blinkhorn 2003; Rydgren 2007a) as the conservative final destination or ultimate outcome, as witnessed in interwar and postwar Europe and contemporary America. In sum, anti-modernity in the specific, primary form of conservatism, old and new, tends to exhibit "fatal attraction" with contemporary terrorism, including counter-state and state terror depending on the position of conservative forces within societal power constellations, viz., outside of or in government control.

Societal and Historical Conditions of Anti-Modernity and Terrorism

In particular, this study specifies, explores, and predicts under which societal conditions and/or historical conjunctures conservative anti-modernity as the systematic antagonism to liberal modernity especially generates and even becomes itself and operates as the design and system of terrorism in contemporary society. To wit and anticipate the argument and observations presented in the rest of the work, anti-modernity in the shape of conservatism generates and even itself develops in terrorism, in particular state or institutional terrorism, under four analytically independent but in reality interconnected and mutually reinforcing social conditions and historical conjunctures anticipated above.

The first of these social conditions and historical conjunctures involves the social system or design of medieval-like theocracy as invariably a conservative creation and "holy tyranny" in adverse reaction against and predating liberal-secular modernity. Theocracy naturally implicates religious conservatism or orthodoxy, notably fundamentalism, as its theological design, foundation, and sanctification a la "God's Kingdom on Earth" (Munch 2001) and the like to be (re)constructed and perpetuated by any means and at any cost. These means and costs include violence or brute force, wars, destruction and deaths, and severe coercion and systematic violent repression, thus eventually state and counter-state terrorism as the enactment and emanation of "holy" cosmic war or revolution[19] within society (Juergensmeyer 2003; Townshend 2002) and against "unholy" societies. Theocracy's ultimate means and cost is mass death or collective suicide and self-destruction for the "glory of God", a MAD (Habermas 2001) outcome analogous to and perhaps likely to be reached through nuclear "mutually assured destruction" reportedly envisioned or threatened by US religious-political conservatism from paleo- to neo-conservatives (Schelling 2006). As observed, theocracy is especially a shared ultimate end and vision of Islamic and American religious conservatism or fundamentalism (Oberschall 2004). This is exemplified by Iranian, Taliban, and other Muslim theocracies, and evangelical "American theocracy" (Phillips 2006; also, Davis and Robinson 2009; Hedges 2006; Owens et al. 2010) at least as a perpetual design or "eternal dream", minimally the Southern "Bible Belt" (plus Utah) as the nearly-established theocratic proto-totalitarian (Bauman 1997) or the most fundamentalist (Hicks 2006) and "theocentric" (Wall 1998) regional system within modern Western society.

The second social condition and historical conjuncture in which conservatism engenders or mutates into counter-state and state terrorism is fascism, including Nazism, as its extreme subtype, i.e., conservative, "right totalitarianism" (Dahrendorf 1979; Giddens 1979; Mannheim 1986; Rydgren 2007a). This was witnessed in interwar Europe, most dramatically Germany, and in part contemporaneous and postwar America, in the proxy form of McCarthyism (Bourdieu and Haacke 1995; Lipset 1955; Smelser and Mitchell 2002; Vasi and Strang 2009) and through violent vigilante "Christian" Southern and other groups a la the Ku Klux Klan (Bailey and Snedker 2011; Jacobs et al. 2005; Lutz and Lutz[20] 2004; Messner

---

[19] Townshend (2002:99) registers that the aim of contemporary terrorism is a "kind of cosmic revolution. While the exact processes of modern terrorism may often be obscure, their core principle is the modern assumption that society can be changed by human agency."

[20] Lutz and Lutz (2004:153) note that "terroristic violence in the US has increasingly been from groups on the right. Even at the height of violence from the left, racist groups were responsible for more terrorist activities [yet the first] received more media attention. [E.g.] the surviving elements of the KKK and the Aryan Nations, dissident groups [with] a religious orientation, tax resistors, those who fear a takeover of the US by traitors who favor one-world government, the militia movement and associated patriot groups." In particular, such groups "see the traditional values of the country being threatened by outsiders [while] committed to what they see as their Second Amendment rights to have weapons [believing] that [it] refers to individuals rather than the rights of states to run militias" (Lutz and Lutz 2004:153). Conversely, "even though the US was normally seen as the center of the system of global capitalism and was also held responsible for the Vietnam conflict, domestic violence from the left was relatively subdued in the late 1960s and 1970s" (Lutz and Lutz 2004:120).

et al. 2005) and their contemporary vestiges or revivals such as "Tea Party" and related extreme-right movements (Blee and Creasap 2010). A predictable variation on this social condition or historical conjuncture of conservatism is neo-fascism, including neo-Nazism, as analogously the extreme outcome and subtype or the standard ally of neo-conservatism, as shown in postwar Europe and America alike.

The third social condition and historical conjuncture in which conservatism generates or becomes terrorism in a way combines and replicates or evokes the first two. This is the merger or alliance of traditional theocracy and religions conservatism, notably fundamentalism, with fascism, including Nazism, as well as with neo-fascism and neo-Nazism. The merger between theocracy or religious orthodoxy and fascism was witnessed in Europe during interwar times and WW II, including Catholic-fascist countries like Italy, Spain, Portugal, Croatia, and others, as well as to some extent Nazi Germany. The merger or alliance between theocracy or religious conservatism and neo-fascism or neo-Nazism has also been observed in postwar Europe, including Spain and Portugal under fascist dictatorships, in part in Italy under allied neo-conservatism and neo-fascism (Berlusconi et al.'s coalitions), etc., as well as America especially since the 1980s through the 2010s.

In America, the merger is shown particularly in the "marriage" or "fatal attraction" and "flirt" between "born again" American religious fundamentalism with neo-fascism resulting in the composite of "Christian fascism" (Hedges 2006). The first seeks and even to some extent succeeds to reconstruct "Christian America" *cum* evangelical theocracy (Davis and Robinson 2009; Friedland 2002; Hedges 2006; Owens et al. 2010; Phillips 2006) a la the "Bible Belt" premised on the Calvinist vision of God's Dominion/Kingdom on Earth and modeled after or inspired by New England's Puritan "Biblical Commonwealth". The second is exemplified by neo-Nazi "Christian" terrorist militias and similar "godly" fascist movements (Blee and Creasap 2010; Juergensmeyer 2003; Turk 2004). Historically, these are traced to the Ku Klux Klan as a proto-fascist "godly" group yet resurging in the effectively or potentially violent "Tea Party" movement arising in hostile reaction to the 2008 Presidential and Congressional elections ("big government") and determined to "take America back" through not only institutional peaceful means like voting, as in part happened in 2010, but also, if these are ineffective, "holy" anti-government violence and thus counter-state terrorism, simply by "bullet" literally when "ballot" is not won. For instance, that the "Tea Party" movement really "means business", namely counter-state terrorism via violent attacks on "big" government, is indicated by the reported plan of one of its "Bible Belt" branches (Oklahoma) in natural alliance with conservative officials to "create a new volunteer militia to help defend against what they believe are improper federal infringements on state sovereignty" with its leader recruiting such "volunteers" by publicly exhorting people to "buy more guns, more bullets". Curiously, such "state-rights" statements replicate or evoke the virtually identical arguments by the Southern Confederate states against the federal government intervention during slavery and segregation, as if for "Bible Belt" conservatives the Civil War never ended, notably the military defeat of the "godly" South did not happen, and the Jim Crow system were not ever abolished and discredited.

In general, US "born again" religious fundamentalists or would-be-theocrats tend to merge or ally with and even seemingly act as "American fascists" (as described in Hedges 2006). And the merger or alliance of "godly" ultra-conservative "Tea Parties" with neo-Nazi militias today is just one recent instance of a long historical pattern of conservatism's "fatal attraction" with fascism and thus both counter-state and once in power state terrorism since postwar times (Adorno 2001) and especially the 1980s through the time of writing these lines.

The fourth generalized structural condition or historical conjuncture in which conservatism generates or becomes terrorism has been implied, the merger or coalition between social-political conservatism in general and fascism, including Nazism. This scenario was witnessed in interwar Europe, notably Italy and Germany, respectively (Blinkhorn 2003), as well as in part early postwar America during McCarthyism as the product or ally of American paleo-conservatism (Bourdieu and Haacke 1995; Lipset 1955; Smelser and Mitchell 2002). A variant of this condition is the merger or alliance between neo-conservatism and neo-fascism, including neo-Nazism, though the latter being of a type with relatively less pronounced theocratic ambitions or practices than that in the US, perhaps except for post-Communist Poland. This is observed in European societies like Germany and Austria through continuous open or covert neo-conservative and neo-Nazi coalitions or mutual sympathies, Italy by neo-conservative-neo-fascist regular joint governments, and others, such as even Holland and Switzerland for some time. It has also been found in Latin and Central American countries under military dictatorships, with Pinochet's Chile as the most notorious, but not isolated exemplar of such a mix resulting in murderous state, usually conservative terrorism (e.g., Argentina, Guatemala,[21] El Salvador, etc.).

In sum, in all or any one of these four sets of social structures and historical conjunctures conservative anti-modernity has generated in the past, generates in the present, and is likely to generate in the future counter-state and especially state terrorism as the ultimate, violent destructive weapon against liberal modernity in contemporary societies. Moreover, conservative anti-modernity tends toward evolving, as witnessed in theocracy and fascism as conservative creations, into a terrorist ideological (Lutz and Lutz 2004) or theological design and an institutional system in its own right. Alternatively, these four structural conditions and historical scenarios each cause and predict, with proxy mathematical precision, at least high statistical probability, that conservative anti-modernity will almost invariably itself become, as through religious fundamentalism or theocracy and fascism, the design and system of terrorism in its own right, or generate and perpetuate terrorist agents and actions in modern societies.

An opposite assumption is that if these four conditions or conjunctures are not met, then conservative anti-modernity will not generate or become the design and the system and process of terrorism. However, this assumption is not corroborated by historical and present experience, as argued and demonstrated throughout this work. Absent these four and related conditions, conservative–i.e., medievalist arch-conservative, fascist, and neo-conservative, notably theocratic or fundamentalist and neo-fascist–anti-modernity would voluntarily subject itself to a sort of Keynes' "euthanasia" proposed for absentee capitalist rentiers. It would thus end as "we know it", the foremost, though not the only, and implacable enemy and would-be destroyer of liberal-democratic, secular, rationalistic, and cosmopolitan-globalized, universalistic modernity. As US neo-conservatives, including "born again" fundamentalists, like to say, "failure" or "quit" in their perennial and even escalating and intensifying crusade-style culture and military wars, including terrorist violence (Juergensmeyer 2003; Turk 2004), against liberal-secular modernity

---

[21] For instance, the second author personally met, interviewed, and assisted some victims of state terror committed by Guatemala's conservative government since the middle 1950s through the late 1980s. Guatemala is the probably first or early postwar case of conservative state terror in South and Central America providing a template or precedent for such more notorious cases as terrorist states in Chile Argentina, El Salvador, etc. over the 1970s–80s.

(Munch 2001) is not in their dictionary or an option, but rather a kind of supreme expression of celebrated conservative-American "can-doism" in terms of violent repression, coercion, (self) destruction, and war. On this account, so long as conservative anti-modernity continues to be what was born and has always invariably been–the supreme and irreconcilable antagonistic force and vehement revolt against modernity–these four sets of structural conditions and historical constellations will likely persist or recur (summarized in Table 3.2). And in consequence terrorism will persist or recur as the ultimate, violent expression of this anti-modern antagonism of conservatism, including state and counter-terrorisms alike.

Dimensions of Anti-Modernity and Modern Terrorism

The preceding represents a relatively original, well-specified, and comprehensive sociological framework for theorizing, evidencing, predicting, and conceivably helping solve or mitigate the problem of contemporary

Table 3.2. Social Conditions and Historical Conjunctures of Conservative Anti-Modernity and (State) Terrorism.

I Theocracy—conservative "holy" tyranny
   old and "reborn" religious fundamentalism in world religions
      revived Islamic fundamentalism and "born again" Protestant
         evangelicalism
      Islamic Republic of Iran, Taliban-ruled regions, etc., "Christian
      America", the "Bible Belt"
II Fascism—conservative (right-wing) totalitarianism
Nazism, neo-fascism, and neo-Nazism
   Neo-fascism (the "far right"), including neo-Nazism, in contemporary
      Europe and America
III Merger/alliance of theocracy and religious fundamentalism with
      fascism
   merger of theocracy/religious fundamentalism and neo-fascism
"Christian fascism" in interwar Europe (Italy, Spain) and prewar and
   postwar America (KKK, Dominionism, etc.)
IV Merger/coalition between conservatism in general and fascism
   merger of neo-conservatism and neo-fascism
      neo-conservative/neo-fascist coalitions in Europe, "Christian"
         neo-Nazi militias in America

---

terrorism in relation to previous theory, research, predictions, and their applications in this respect in sociology and related disciplines. First, though often intimated or implicit in the sociological literature (Bendix 1984; Eisenstadt 1999; Friedland 2002; Habermas 2001; Juergensmeyer 2003; Smelser and Mitchell 2002; Smelser 2007; Turk 2004), the framework is in part original in virtue of rarely, if ever, being explicitly and systematically used and/or elaborated before in its current formulation.

Especially, what renders the framework partially novel and well-specified is the thesis of antagonism toward specifically *liberal Western modernity* as providing the overarching and primary social condition, thus explanation or prediction, of contemporary terrorism. This holds true insofar as modernity and hence the antagonism toward it can assume divergent and often contradictory forms, namely "multiple modernities" (Eisenstadt 2003; Jepperson 2002; Sachsenmaier and Eisenstadt 2002), including liberal and non-liberal, Western and non-Western, in particular "Enlightenment West" and "Enlightenment East" (Angel 1994), and consequently multiple anti-modern antagonisms. If the thesis of "multiple modernities" is considered valid, the present work specifically centers on their liberal and Western, and probably theoretically and historically prevalent, variant and the antagonism toward it, while abstracting from their non-liberal and non-Western alternatives and their respective antagonisms. And if the above thesis cannot be, as in part Weber and Parsons imply by their focus on its Western rationalistic form, deemed plausible, then the work simply adopts the prevalent conception or meaning of "modernity" as liberal modernity in the West.

Hence, it is not just antagonism to modernity (Bendix 1984; Smelser and Mitchell 2002) or modernism (Angel 1994; Juergensmeyer 2003) that is relevant for explaining and predicting terrorism, but to its specifically liberal Western as distinct from its alternative form, simply modern liberalism. Alternatively, it is not only antagonism to liberal democracy, including the secular state (Juergensmeyer 2003), that is so, but also to liberal-secular civil society and culture, including science, education, technology, medicine, etc., as also constituents or subsystems of liberal Western modernity as a "total social system" and historical time (Eisenstadt 1999; Habermas 2001).

Second, while well-specified, the framework is also relatively comprehensive in the sense of having a reasonable large scope of explanation, prediction, and application. It is so in virtue of encompassing or implicating most of the relevant explanatory social, including economic and non-economic, factors, as assumed or registered in the literature, of contemporary terrorism. As a consequent aspect of its comprehensive quality, the framework can potentially help explain and predict most, although not all, types of contemporary terrorism as classified before, for example, counter-state, state, and inter-state terrorisms. In doing so, it elaborates on, expands, and corrects the literature that features a primary emphasis on counter-state (Black 2004; Blattman and Miguel 2010; Blee and Creasap 2010; Gibbs 1989; Juergensmeyer 2003; Krueger and Maleckova 2003; Roche 2004; Smelser and Mitchell 2002; Smelser 2007; Smith 1994; Turk 2004) and international (Abadie 2006) terrorism, and a secondary interest in state and domestic alternatives (Bahr 2002; Einolf 2007; Torpey 1998). In turn, such comprehensiveness of the framework reflects the comprehensive or overarching character of the assumed prime mover and predictor of contemporary terrorism, the antagonistic reaction toward liberal Western modernity. For this is a kind of antagonism that is almost total in the sense of opposing virtually all relevant dimensions and outcomes of modernity and of being manifested in multiple, seemingly innumerable, forms, shades, and colors. Hence, this sociological framework aims to do justice to the comprehensive character and manifold facets of its primary explanatory variable, thus being empirically plausible or realistic, which then makes its comprehensiveness an analytical virtue, rather than a disadvantage, as one might be objected.

The present sociological framework posits that the antagonism to liberal Western modernity or simply anti-modernity, as the prime mover of contemporary terrorism, functions as such a factor in definite ways and paths that are typically observable and predictable in interconnection and mutual reinforcement. The first way and path is the antagonism to modern liberal democracy and society, i.e., the opposition against the process of liberalization and democratization. The second is the antagonism to modern secularized politics and culture, the opposition against the process of political and cultural secularization. The third is the antagonism to modern cultural, notably scientific, rationalism, the opposition against the process of societal rationalization. The fourth is the antagonism toward modern globalism and cosmopolitanism, thus universalism (and humanism), the opposition against the process of economic and non-economic globalization and cosmopolitan, universalistic society (and humanization). In short, anti-modernity operates as comprehensive and multifarious antagonism toward (a) liberal-democratic, (b) secular, (c) rationalistic, and (d) global-cosmopolitan, universalistic (and humanistic) Western modernity.

Hence, such four-fold antagonism to modernity generates four classes of interconnected and mutually reinforcing factors of contemporary terrorism, all of them expressing and operationalizing ("loading on") anti-modernity as the overarching, prime factor. The first class of anti-modernity factors of contemporary terrorism comprises the antagonism to liberal-democratic Western modernity through opposition against modern liberal democracy and society. The second class of these factors involves the antagonism to secular Western modernity through adverse reaction against modern secularized polity and society. The third class incorporates the antagonism to rationalistic Western modernity through adverse reaction against societal, particularly scientific, rationalism. The fourth class of anti-modernity factors of contemporary terrorism includes the antagonism to global-cosmopolitan, universalistic Western modernity through adverse reaction against modern globalism, including economic, political and cultural globalization, cosmopolitanism, and universalism. In short, these four anti-modernity variables are, first, anti-liberalism and anti-democracy, second, anti-secularism, third, anti-rationalism or irrationalism, and fourth, anti-globalism, anti-cosmopolitanism, and anti-universalism.

In aggregate, through these four interconnected and mutually reinforcing factors, anti-modernity operates as the encompassing and main source and rationale of contemporary terrorism in most of its types, including counter-state and state terrorisms. In turn, liberal modernity, including democracy, is a sort of agent provocateur of contemporary terrorism by virtue of provoking conservative, including fundamentalist and fascist, anti-modernity, and its theocracy and totalitarianism, and in consequence terrorist agents and actions in counter-state and state forms. Alternatively, terrorism is the "perverse" outcome (Boudon 1982; Giddens 1984) of liberal modernism through the latter's "provocation" of conservative anti-modernism. In Merton's terms, contemporary terrorism is, first and foremost, the manifest function, intended outcome of conservative anti-modernity, including theocratic fundamentalism and totalitarian fascism, and the latent function, the unintended, more precisely perverse, effect of liberal modernity.

In sum, the determinants and predictors of contemporary terrorism consist of four categories that operate in conjunction and mutual reinforcement and all express ("load on") the antagonism to liberal Western modernity, i.e., anti-modernity as the comprehensive and main determinant and predictor. They are, first, anti-liberal and anti-democratic factors in opposition to liberal-democratic modernity, second, the anti-secular opposing secular modernity, third the anti-secular in adverse reaction to secular modernity, and fourth the anti-global and anti-cosmopolitan antagonistic to global and cosmopolitan, universalistic modernity. Anti-modernity factors oppose and seek to eliminate or subvert, first, liberal democracy and society, second, secularized society and politics, third, scientific and other cultural rationalism or the process of societal rationalization, and fourth, globalism, cosmopolitanism, and universalism in the form of economic, political, and cultural globalization. These determinants are indicative and predictive of the specific social structures and historical conjunctures in which individuals, groups, states, and societies tend to advocate, commit, and support terrorism, thus of the societal sources of terrorist agents, actions, and outcomes.

In the present sociological framework, those economic and non-economic factors effectively or potentially conditioning terrorism that do not derive from or directly relate to anti-modernity are controlled for (control variables) by analogy to Weber's treatment of the non-Calvinist, non-religious conditions of modern capitalism in the *Protestant Ethic*. Instances of economic control variables are poverty (Abadie 2006; Smelser and Mitchell 2002) or affluence, under-development (Cragin and Chalk 2003) and social class (Smith 1994), including education[22] (Krueger and Maleckova 2003; Turk 2004), unemployment, inflation, and economic crises like depressions or recessions (Lutz and Lutz 2004). They also involve wealth and income inequalities especially in underdeveloped economies, including their resentment or grievances against advanced Western societies (Abadie 2006; Bendix 1984; Bergesen and Lizardo 2004; Krueger and Maleckova 2003; Kuran 2004; Turk 2004), and also among certain, mostly rural, uneducated, hyper-religious, or conservative segments in the latter, particularly America (Juergensmeyer 2003) and the South within it. Instances of non-economic control variables include government repression or lack of civic and political liberties (Abadie

---

[22] Krueger and Maleckova (2003:142) suggest that "on the demand side, terrorist organizations may prefer educated, committed individuals. [E.g.] religious schools, in Pakistan (are funded by wealthy industrialists and (they) deliberately educate students to become foot soldiers and elite operatives in extremist movements around the world. "Most madrasahs offer only religious instruction, ignoring math, science, and other secular subjects important for functioning in modern society". This holds true, with certain qualifications, of most US religious or fundamentalist private schools or home schooling opposing secular science and education (Darnell and Sherkat 1997).

2006; Krueger and Maleckova 2003), civil, culture, and foreign wars (Lutz and Lutz 2004), including the use or threat of using nuclear and other weapons of mass destruction[23] (Schelling 2006).

Other instances are modern political and social crises or instabilities and emergencies, mostly in developing countries and occasionally in developed societies, particularly America, as well as racial and ethnic or national, religious, and linguistic fragmentation and tensions, gender, age, geographic location, climate, etc. (Abadie 2006; Bergesen and Lizardo 2002; Blattman and Miguel 2010; Heymann 1999; Jackman 2002; Juergensmeyer 2003; Krueger and Maleckova 2003; Mannheim 1936; Morrill et al. 2003; Oberschall 2004; Turk 2004; Williams 1994). In the literature, except for the widely but not universally observed positive effects of young age (Turk 2004) and male gender (Juergensmeyer 2003) on counter-state religious and other terrorisms, the exact impact of most economic and non-economic control variables, in particular race, ethnicity, climate, and geographic location, is not well-established. Also, the impact of these factors is often observed to be non-significant or non-existent, ambiguous, and complex (curvilinear, etc.), as in case of most economic and political variables, including poverty, wealth inequality, education, unemployment, developing countries' grievances against Western economies, civil and other wars, government crises and repression, etc.

---

[23] Schelling (2006:936) admonishes that the "next possessors of nuclear weapons may be [also] possibly some terrorist bodies. There is no Soviet Union to deter [and] terrorists cannot be deterred anyway. The most effective use of the bomb, from a terrorist perspective, will be for influence. Possessing a workable nuclear weapon, if they can demonstrate possession [without detonating it] will give them something of the status of a nation. Threatening to use it against military targets, and keeping it intact if the threat is successful, may appeal to them more than expending it in a purely destructive act. Even terrorists may consider destroying large numbers of people less satisfying than keeping a major nation at bay."

Appendix 3.1. A Simple Model of Anti-Modernity and Modern Terror

The present sociological framework can formally be represented by a simplified model as follows:

$$\gamma = \alpha + \beta_1 X_1 + \beta_2 X_2 + \beta_3 X_3 + \beta_4 X_4 + \beta_5 X_5 + \epsilon,$$

where γ is a vector of likelihoods (log odds) of advocating, committing, and supporting terrorism, α_i a vector of regression constants, β_1 a vector of logistic regression coefficients (logits) for the category of anti-liberal and anti-democratic determinants, X_1 a matrix of anti-liberal and anti-democratic variables, β_2 a vector of logistic regression coefficients for the category of anti-secular determinants, X_2 a matrix of anti-secular determinants, β_3 a vector of logistic regression coefficients for the category of anti-rationalistic determinants, X_3 a matrix of anti-rationalistic determinants, β_4 a vector of logistic regression coefficients for the category of anti-global and anti-cosmopolitan determinants, X_4 a matrix of anti-global and anti-cosmopolitan determinants, β_5 a vector of logistic regression coefficients for economic and non-economic control variables, X_5 a matrix of control variables, and ϵ_i a vector of residuals indicated unexplained variation in γ (represented in Figure 3.1).

Table 3.1. Terrorism, explanatory variables, hypotheses, and hypothesized effects.

Explanatory variables	Hypotheses	Hypothesized effects	Dependent variable Contemporary terrorism
I. Anti-liberal and anti-democratic variables			
Opposition to liberal democracy	H1	→→ (+)	
Opposition to pluralism and diversity	H1A	→→ (+)	
Conservatism, fascism, anti-liberalism	H1B	→→ (+)	
Political absolutism and monism	H1C	→→ (+)	

(*Continued*)

Table 3.1. *(Cont.)*

Explanatory variables	Hypotheses	Hypothesized effects	Dependent variable Contemporary terrorism
II. Anti-secular variables			
Opposition to secular politics and society	H2	→→ (+)	
Opposition to Enlightenment values	H2A	→→ (+)	
Religious orthodoxy, dogmatism	H2B	→→ (+)	
Religious fundamentalism, literalism	H2C	→→ (+)	
Evangelicalism, strict Koran application	H2D	→→ (+)	
Theocracy, "godly politics"	H2E	→→ (+)	
III. Anti-rationalistic variables			
Opposition to modern rationalism	H3	→→ (+)	
Irrationalism in general	H3A	→→ (+)	
Pre-scientific irrationalism	H3B	→→ (+)	
Religious superstition and fanaticism	H3C	→→ (+)	
Beliefs in Satan	H3D	→→ (+)	
IV. Anti-global and anti-cosmopolitan variables			
Opposition to globalized-cosmopolitan society	H4	→→ (+)	
Exclusion, nationalism, ethnocentrism	H4A	→→ (+)	
Opposition to globalization	H4B	→→ (+)	
Opposition to global humanistic society	H4C	→→ (+)	
Control variables			
Poverty		→→ (?)	
Unemployment		→→ (?)	
Inflation		→→ (?)	

Table 3.1. (*Cont.*)

Explanatory variables	Hypotheses	Hypothesized effects	Dependent variable Contemporary terrorism
Lack of education		$\rightarrow\rightarrow$ (?)	
Wealth-income inequality		$\rightarrow\rightarrow$ (?)	
Grievances against wealthy economies		$\rightarrow\rightarrow$ (?)	
Civil and other wars, political crises		$\rightarrow\rightarrow$ (?)	
Government repression, lack of civil liberties		$\rightarrow\rightarrow$ (?)	
Race-ethnicity		$\rightarrow\rightarrow$ (?)	
Male gender		$\rightarrow\rightarrow$ (+?)	
Young age		$\rightarrow\rightarrow$ (+?)	
Geographic location		$\rightarrow\rightarrow$ (?)	
Climate		$\rightarrow\rightarrow$ (?)	

Note: $\rightarrow\rightarrow$ (+) positive effects, $\rightarrow\rightarrow$ (?) unknown, ambiguous, or complex effects, $\rightarrow\rightarrow$ (+?) seemingly, but not invariably, positive effects

Appendix 3.2. Defining Terrorism and Government

Critics and skeptics (Bauman 2001; Cable, Shriver, and Mix 2008; Clairmont 1993; Heymann 1999; Townshend 2002; Vasi and Strang 2009) suggest a kind of cynicism or irony in respect of conservatism and terrorism. In this view, it is cynical or ironic that the US conservative, to be distinguished from non-conservative, liberal (if ever), government to define and so stigmatize "enemy" governments and non-governmental groups and entire societies as "terrorist" so long as it itself commits or supports various forms or proxies of terrorism in America and the world. Following this critical line of reasoning, within American society such genuine or proxy actions of state "terror" involve systematic and intense conservative-government violent repression and physical coercion or direct compulsion as a general defining element of terrorism. These actions are epitomized or approximated by conservative-driven repressive moralistic, temperance wars, such as the "war on drugs" and Prohibition before. These wars result in mass life or long imprisonment for sins-crimes like sinful drug and sexual activities, reaching by the 2010s almost 2.4 million of prisoners of whom no less than almost two third or at least the vast majority are sinners-criminals such as non-violent drug users (Cooney and Burt 2008; Becky and Western 2004; Harris et al. 2011; Wakefield and Uggen 2010).

These and related non-violent offenders are effectively, in the language of international human rights organizations, innocent prisoners of ethical and implicitly political conscience, thus victims of state terror or the "political economy of imprisonment [and execution]" (Sutton 2004), sacrificed to higher, typically theocentric "godly" and moralistic Puritan-style causes. Specifically, these millions of "sinful" Americans are defined as victims from the stance of modern Western liberal-secular democracies superseding the primitive equation of moral sins and their sensual pleasures with crimes. Yet, this equivalence is instead evidently perpetuated in America under predominant religious-cultural conservatism such as Protestant sectarianism and evangelicalism (Clemens 2007; Davis and Robinson 2006; Jenness 2006; King 2008; Lipset 1996; Munch 2001; Owens et al. 2010), notably the theocratic "Bible Belt" (Texas,[24] etc.), just as in Islamic theocracies like Iran, Saudi Arabia, and Taliban-ruled regions.

---

[24] Also, as news media reported, one observer said with respect to the Texas persisting and pervasive gun culture that "anywhere in the civilized world you would be able to make

Cynically or ironically, non-violent drug offenders cum moral sinners appear as innocent prisoners of ethical conscience even according to the FBI conventional classification of crimes. This classification contains, as of yet, *no* special explicit category of drug use, possession, and related non-violent sinful offenses, thus implicitly admitting what is the rule in all modern Western and many other societies. This is simply that moral sins and vices and in extension sensual pleasures are *not* crimes, instead the first equated with the second and thus harshly punished only by US religious conservatives within Western society, alongside Islamic funda-mentalists in the Third World. Yet, US neo-conservatives (and media) make appear and most Americans believe as if vices drug and alcohol use and sexual sins adultery, prostitution, "fornication", pornography, etc. were precisely the most serious "crimes" in America, even more so than murders and other violent crimes, just as did their Puritan "parents" (adultery was punished by death by New England's Puritans) and do their Islamic theocratic "brothers in arms". Hence, in a cynical or ironic twist, following the very governmental crime classification in the US those two third of nearly 2.4 million of prisoners imprisoned for non-violent drug use and possession are truly innocent prisoners of ethical conscience in virtue of committing "crimes" that do *not* exist in the "books", i.e., moral sins and thus sensual pleasures, rather than, as portrayed by the federal government and most states, "criminals" or even, as are drug traders, "terrorists". And so long as mass long, notably arbitrary and unjust, impris-onment belongs, alongside executions, to the "scale of political terror", these millions of drug-war prisoners, not to mention those executed and imprisoned on fabricated evidence or unproven guilt for especially rapes and related sexual offenses, are the living proofs, or rather "dead men walking", of state terror at both federal and state levels, especially in the "Bible Belt" like Texas, couched in and rationalized as "tough on crime" neo-conservative laws and policies.

Notably, acts of true or proxy state terror are exemplified by govern-ment executions, as a paradigmatic act of state terror or official murder (Popper 1973), as well as mass long imprisonment, for example, up to 99 and even 100-plus years on the bizarre assumption that humans could live that long and so escape the full extent of "justice" by shorter sentences. Especially executions and incarceration represent terror acts when applied to innocent or sinful but not criminal persons and unproven

---

the argument that everybody should be able to be against illegal guns. But we're not in the civilized word. We're in Texas."

crimes, particularly fabricated rapes and similar sexual offenses often punished more severely than murders (e.g., "murders of passion" against adulterous wives) by the Puritan-rooted conservative government or "Bible Belt" states like Texas, as by Islamic theocracies Iran and Taliban regions. Thus, executing or imprisoning for life or long time innocent people is not an Orwellian fantasy but "all too real" governmental activity for the "glory of God", the "Crusade for Christ." This has been repeatedly proven by DNA evidence exonerating such persons—typically too late not only for those already executed but on death row and imprisoned because their lives have been likely ruined–especially in Texas (e.g., the Dallas county) as the "proud" perennial Western world "leader" in the death penalty as well as mass long imprisonment for sins-as-crimes.

(Now, as one might expect in a region pervaded by xenophobia as a sort of mild collective madness or anti-foreign sentiment, the application of the death penalty in Texas and the "Bible Belt" overall is permeated by xenophobic, just as low-class, bias against non-Americans and immigrants and in favor of native-born Americans. As an almost "iron" rule, if non-Americans or immigrants from Mexicans to Europeans commit, or even are just simply and often falsely accused of committing, murder of an American, they will be invariably sentenced to death and executed in Texas and the "Bible Belt" as whole. Conversely, if native-born Americans murder a non-American or immigrant, the death penalty is hardly ever used or demanded, as a rule, and only as an exception, in this proud American and Western leader in executions. Thus, typically state prosecutors do not demand or, if they do, juries do not recommend, and judges do not apply the death penalty for such cases in Texas[25] and the "Bible Belt" overall. This is sobering and frightening for non-Americans or immigrants in Texas and the rest of the "Bible Belt", because they literally risk their life, let alone liberty, by residing in and even visiting this region if they not only actually commit a crime but just being, not rarely falsely, accused of

---

[25] A recent instance is the reported savage killing of an Indian taxi driver by several Texans in the 2010s, yet the state prosecutor decided that the murder of a "foreigner" did not merit the death penalty; and this is not an isolated case or exception, but a rule, especially when the victims are Mexicans. Instead, a rare exception, a sort of miracle is that prosecutors in Texas and the "Bible Belt" overall demand and/or juries recommend and judges apply the death penalty when foreigners or immigrants are murdered by Texans and other Americans. Conversely, it is exceptional or miraculous that these agents of the penal system do not do so in the opposite scenario. In passing, this xenophobic perversion is mostly an overlooked or unexamined aspect of the death penalty system in Texas and the other South, and cannot be hidden, even if disguised or embellished, even by the purest Puritan-style conservative hypocrisy.

committing it, simply "in the wrong place at the wrong time". The "Bible Belt" criminal justice system makes for them legal "justice" not worth the paper on which it is written, actually criminal injustice as if their grave crime were not having been "born in the USA", in particular not "native Texan".)

Recall that both executions and long mass imprisonment, especially for unproven offenses and/or non-violent moral sins, belong to the "political terror scale" as the measure or dimension of government violent repression and physical coercion, just as does the perverse legal outcome of "less crime, more punishment" reportedly observed in America during neo-conservatism, including the evangelical South, during recent times.

Comparatively, such repressive practices, unknown or unparalleled among modern Western democracies, express and enact the conservative religiously sanctified wars on "crime". Crucially, these wars involve the "new temperance" war perpetuating the Puritan-rooted "obsession with sin and vice" (Wagner 1997; also, Bell 2002; Cooney and Burt 2008; Harris et al. 2011) redefined and punished as crimes, while committed (e.g., adultery, prostitution) with impunity by neo-Puritan "born again" evangelical "saints" in accordance with what Hume detects as and Weber calls the "pure hypocrisy" of Puritanism as self-proclaimed "God's vice regent" (Zaret 1989). The outcome of these temperance or culture wars is perverting presumed innocence into a presumption of guilt for sins-crimes such that humans are "presumed guilty"—overtly or covertly because of "original sin"–unless *they* prove otherwise rather than the government proving their guilt. This seems a legal-procedural perversion in a way predicting and rationalizing state and any type of terror and tyranny overall, including the "less crime, more punishment" perverse link defining Puritan and Islamic criminal justice systems as truly *criminal* ones and state terror, and prefiguring an Orwellian dystopia.

As noted, in effect, US religious warriors against sins-crimes allege or imply that the presumption of guilt is rooted and so people are "presumed guilty unless proven otherwise" due to "original sin" committed by first humans, yet for which by association all their descendants shall expiate and be punished or responsible by "judgment before an omnipotent God" (Dunn and Woodard 1996) and in consequence by Divine ordained rulers' "holy" terror or theocratic violent repression. Within predominant Puritan-inspired Protestant sectarianism (Lipset 1996), "omnipotent God" is what Weber calls–and even Puritan Milton deplores as not commanding his respect–the non-understanding, merciless, and despotic "God of Calvinism" (also, Artz 1998). In turn, Divine ordained rulers are Puritans and their evangelical heirs as self-proclaimed "God's [anti] vice regents" (Zaret 1989) establishing, practicing, and seemingly enjoying as the only or chief pleasure the reign of "holy" terror, as in England (Walzer 1963) and New England by means of the "Puritan policeman" (Merrill 1945) or the vice-police state pervasive in the "Bible Belt" (Texas, etc.) and beyond. In sum, US crusaders against sin-crime overtly or covertly and perhaps subconsciously use the dogma of "original sin" as the sacred ground for their perversion of the modern legal rule and procedure of presumed innocence into its opposite. In consequence, they exploit this dogma for their "holy state terror, including executions and mass long imprisonment of sinful (e.g., non-violent drug and sexual sinners) and innocent persons, as well as counter-state terrorism when not in political power, as in the wake of the 2008 elections and other times (the 1960s, 1993–4; etc.).

Thus, the open or covert ground and sanctification for this mutation of presumed innocence into its perverted form of "presumed guilty" in the US conservative penal system, especially in the "Bible Belt" (Texas, etc.), is the dogma of "original sin", at least its evangelical Puritan-rooted interpretation and rendition. For according to US evangelicalism, like Puritanism and Calvinism in general, notably Calvin himself, there is *no* such thing as human innocence or innocent humans, excluding evangelical saints-would-be-masters (Lindsay 2008), owing to "original sin". This religious dogma consequently, overtly or covertly, perverts presumed innocence as the basic legal-penal principle of modern democratic and civilized society into that of presumed guilt defining theocracy as well as fascism, notably Nazism, and other totalitarianism. Ultimately, though almost invisible, it is the evangelical Puritan-Calvinist redefinition or Machiavellian strategic manipulation of the dogma of "original sin" that makes the US neo-conservative, especially the "Bible Belt", criminal justice system a polar opposite of a just penal code, a proxy criminal-murderous and injustice system. This is a fact hidden from most Americans and even sociologists, a sort of "best kept secret" in America.

Yet, it is fully visible and prefigured in New England's long (and England's shorter) "unexampled tyranny of Puritanism", including its mass death punishment in, as Tocqueville quotes, the "name of God" and by implication because of Adam's "original sin," as Calvin postulates in his theology and implemented in his Geneva theocracy as the model for Calvinists of all times and places, including Winthrop et al. (Walzer 1965). For example, following Calvin an arch-Puritan solemnly declared centuries ago, that "thou art [you are] guilty of Adam's [original] sin [and] prone by nature to all evil in the world", hence to be punished "without mercy".

And this is what the Puritan-rooted conservative penal system essentially does in contemporary America, at least in the "Bible Belt" like Texas, etc. (also, Bluestein[26] 1977).

In an exemplary display of Puritanism's invariant rage and hatred for and severe punishment, including death, of humans as innately and utterly "depraved", this hard-core Calvinist and Puritan pioneer (William Perkins) raged against "original sin" apparently consumed with infinite hate and disgust for humans as Adam's innately sinful and depraved and thus criminal descendants to be tormented and ultimately disposed of as unworthy of life in the 'Kingdom of God." In his own words, "First, that thou art guilty of Adam's sin [sic]. Secondly, that thou art prone by nature to all evil in the world. Thirdly, that for these thou art subject to the wrath of God and to all the curses of his wrath" (also, McGiffert 1988), an indictment/imputation not surprising from an author of works like "Discourse of the Damned Art of Witchcraft" perpetuating and intensifying the medieval superstition in and persecution of "witches" seen in the "compact with Satan" (Teall 1962). Similarly, an American Puritan during the early 18th century proclaimed a la Calvin that "Man is guilty of Adam's Sin" and hence is "destitute of original Righteousness" such that his "whole Nature" and life being "corrupt" (Goodwin 1968). In consequence, humans are to be (mis)treated accordingly, i.e., invariably constrained, controlled, tormented, and punished, including imprisoned and executed–regardless of one's *own* actual sins-crimes by "imputing Adam's sin to his posterity" (Breitenbach 1984) in accordance with the dogma of "imputation" characteristic of hyper-moralistic Puritanism.

Reportedly, according to the Calvinist "doctrine of imputation" in early 18th century Puritan New England "the first actual Sin of Adam" is being imputed to all his "Posterity by ordinary Generation" independent from and antecedent to any "Regard to the Corruption of human Nature"

---

[26] Also, Bluestein (1977:205) comments that in Puritanism "human beings in their very nature are deemed bestial and subject to an overwhelming determinism according to the will (or whim) of an omnipotent God. The political implications are equally clear; if man is a beast then he ought to be in a cage, watched over by an armed keeper. That is to be expected (and even welcomed) [sic] by a race which reproduces in every generation and in every individual the sins of its parents-and not in simply symbolic terms, but quite literally." In turn, he remarks that (referring to Hawthorne's *The Scarlet Letter*) that "vicious punishment not only mirrors the depravity of the society itself but often results in the opposite of what it was intended to accomplish" (Bluestein 1977:213), which seemingly could apply to the death penalty in America, notably the "Bible Belt" like Alabama, Georgia, Mississippi, Oklahoma, Tennessee, Texas, etc., where virtually all US executions have been conducted during recent times.

(Goodwin 1968), thus regardless of humans' real-life sins-as-crimes. This therefore implies that the Puritan penal system, of which predictably the death penalty was, as Tocqueville remarks, the most salient and pervasive element, effectively operated on the basis of this theological doctrine and so on the presumption of *guilt* with utter disregard of actual sins-crimes. It therefore perverts the time-honored assumption or implication of presumed innocence–probably since the Roman Law– which confirms what Comte detects as the barbarian or primitive ("Biblical") uncivilized properties of Puritanism and Calvinism generally. Puritanism apparently continues to do so through the largely Puritan-rooted criminal justice, notably death penalty, system in America during revived evangelicalism and neo-conservatism overall, above all in the "Bible Belt" like Texas, where the Calvinist "doctrine of imputation" of Adam's "original sin" to humans here and now is seemingly still applied, even if covertly or unconsciously and hypocritically. This is at least indicated by the virtually unapologetic execution and especially imprisonment of innocent persons and/or sinners-as-criminals. And if such Puritan punitive practices, thus premised on and justified by the "Sin of Adam" imputed to posterity, in New England were characterized as the "reign of terror" (Merrill 1945), this holds, with slight modification, for their contemporary neo-conservative reenactments or proxies in evangelical America such as the "Bible Belt."

In retrospect, this "original sin", "no human innocence" evangelical basis and the consequently perverted legal principle of presumed *guilt* helps understand and explains, at least in part, why the imprisonment has exploded (Cooney and Burt 2008; Harris et al. 2011; Sutton 2004; Wakefield and Uggen 2010) and executions, including those of innocent and/or sinful persons, increased in America, notably the "Bible Belt", with the resurgence of evangelicalism and neo-conservatism overall during recent decades since Reaganism (Jacobs et al. 2007). In prospect, it helps to predict or anticipates the identical outcome in the future, i.e., more innocent, dissenting, or sinful yet not truly criminal Americans to be imprisoned and executed largely regardless of their actual guilt or sins, so long as evangelicalism and neo-conservatism generally continues to dominate the ideological and political landscape of America, at least the "Bible Belt" where it exerts near-total rule. Thus, the more of the same "no or less crime, more punishment" reverse link in the foreseeable future is almost certain so long as religious conservatism claims or implies la Calvin and Winthrop that no innocent humans exist, except for its saints, and that the principle of presumed innocence is a liberal, foreign European and so "un-American" lie and conspiracy.

Historically, evangelical "Christian" America, minimally the "Bible Belt", has been and will likely remain the expanded version of Calvin's Geneva theocracy premised on the dogma of "original sin" and so eternal human guilt and non-innocent humans, as well as its own extension and replica Puritan ruled New England's "Biblical Commonwealth" founded and ruled by his theocratic "child" Winthrop (Gould 1996; Kloppenberg 1998; Munch 2001). To that extent, penal justice in this setting has been and will probably remain what Weber calls an "impossible contradiction" and economists an "impossibility theorem", simply, as Americans would say in despair or doubt, a joke, and instead degenerates into the system of "holy" terror sanctified by humanity's "original sin". In effect, legal justice or the "rule of law", like government and society overall, in this setting becomes the servant of religion or theocracy a la "Biblical law", thus descending into the Dark Middle Ages, not being the worth the paper on which it is printed, just as does in Islamic states one of Sharia law reportedly emulated and even admired by US ever power-thirsty evangelicals (Juergensmeyer 2003).

If this "original sin" explanation and prediction of the unparalleled and persistent severity and inhumanity, within Western modernity, of the US conservative criminal justice system sounds exaggerated or worse, as conservatives would accuse, one should recall the millions of Americans imprisoned either formally innocent proved by DNA evidence or as non-violent and thus substantively non-guilty moral sinners (drug users, etc.), and especially those executed with subsequently, yet too late, proven innocence. And all these acts have been, continue, and likely will continue to be committed by evangelical saints-would-be-masters, at least in the "Bible Belt" like Texas, etc., with Puritan-style self-righteousness and non-repentance (e.g., archetypically revealed at Salem's witch-trials) and thus on the overt or covert assumption of presumed guilt and no human innocence due to humanity's supposed inherent sinfulness and depravity. To that extent, these are acts of "holy" state terror grounded and sanctified by the dogma of "original sin" in its evangelical construction or manipulation, for the essence of terror is imprisoning, executing, and otherwise torturing, tormenting, abusing, and punishing innocent persons in legal terms on whatever "sacred" religious or other ideological and "patriotic" grounds.

In regional terms, if the "original sin" theorem of the US neo-conservative penal system sounds dubious, then the "Bible Belt" (Texas, etc.) provides a partial "proof in the pudding" or at least "food for thought." It does by becoming or looking as a sort of forced overarching monastery after the model of Puritanism and Calvin's vision and even a massive open prison in which everyone can be imprisoned or executed largely regardless of legal innocence, but openly or covertly because of imputed human sinfulness and depravity, as of course "no one is above the [Biblical] law", minus its evangelical masters, just as none is above Sharia law in Islamic states, except for their fundamentalist rulers. Simply, if one does not know what the "original sin" foundation or mechanism of this legal system is, one knows it when one sees Mencken's "Bible Belt" ruled by what he calls evangelical Baptist-Methodist "barbarism". In passing, sociologists have registered the religious and related basis and rationale of the US neo-conservative criminal justice system (Cooney and Burt 2008; Jacobs et al. 2005; Jacobs et al. 2007; King 2008; King, Messner, and Baller 2009), especially in the "Bible Belt" (Bailey and Snedker 2011; Messner et al. 2005). Yet, virtually none has identified the evangelical version of the "original sin" dogma as such a factor, especially in the explosion of prisoners and the increase of executions, including of innocent or sinful persons, during the rise and political dominance of evangelicalism and generally neo-conservatism. While at first sight it seems perhaps dubious, if not worse, at least the "original sin" theorem of "tough on crime" US neo-conservatism, in particular revived evangelicalism, deserves more consideration by sociologists and other analysts than usually given or suspected.

Another consequent outcome is inflicting punishments with Draconian harshness, as effective acts of state terror, let alone injustice, in their own right in virtue of violating what Durkheim calls the fit or balance between crime and punishment as the definition of penal justice. This hence reveals the "less crime, more punishment" neo-conservative link in America as a process and system of institutional terrorism and/or of radical negation and perversion of this universal legal principle at least within Western modernity. In passing, Durkheim never did or would envision the "less crime, more punishment" reverse "fit" in civilized modern Western society[27] (also, Wakefield and Uggen 2010), but rather in

---

[27] Wakefield and Uggen (2010:392–3) observe that during neo-conservatism in America "rising punishment is thus a policy choice rather than a natural response to sustained increases in crime. Increases in the use of incarceration are "intensely political". The emergence of crime as a salient political tool [the politicization of crime] is strongly linked to changes in sentencing practices, most notably the greater enforcement and severity of American drug laws. In short, the process and outcome is "indiscriminate over-incarceration" (Wakefield and Uggen 2010:394) and in that sense institutional terrorism (recall a defining element of the latter is indiscriminate coercion, repression, or violence).

primitive societies dominated by religious absolutism and repression (Cooney and Burt 2008). And he was probably correct as this reversal historically hardly ever materialized, except in interwar Nazi Germany and other fascist countries, especially in West Europe during postwar times. This sheds another light or rather penal darkness of state terror and injustice on conservative reproduced and glorified "American exceptionalism" revealing it as an Islamic and pre-modern primitive deviation from modern Western legal-political systems in which "less crime" is simply linked with "less punishment".

Such an outcome is exemplified by Draconian "three strikes" laws punishing with life imprisonment repeated sins like drug possession and petty non-violent crimes and enforced in most US states, including supposedly "liberal" California (Akerlof 2002; Matsueda, Kreager, and Huizinga 2006). In passing, these offenses punished with life imprisonment often appear so trivial or minor (stealing pizzas, chocolates and vitamins from stores, "hot" checks, etc.) that most Westerners unaffected by the American conservative "tough on crime" hysteria likely remain in disbelief and doubt the sanity or rationality of "law and order" religious-political neo-conservatives perpetuating or evoking what Hume and Pareto describe as Puritan religious "madness" and moralistic "insanity". In the process, such comparatively exceptional government activities at local, state, and federal levels reportedly pervert the US criminal justice system with its striking primitive "Draconian severity" (Patell 2001) into a "unique anomaly" (Pager 2003) among modern Western societies. They do so through committing or approaching "holy" state terror in the form of religiously sanctified violent repression and severe coercion, including extremely harsh punishment such as executions and mass long imprisonment (Jacobs et al. 2007; King 2008) frequently of legally innocent and usually "sinful" and so substantively innocent persons (even for the Bible's "who has not sinned") within Western liberal-secular democracy.

For instance, even a pro-American magazine (the *Economist*) comments in an editorial entitled "Rough Justice In America Too Many Laws, Too Many Prisoners" (2010) that "never in the civilised world have so many been locked up for so little." As commented, "Justice is harsher in America than in any other rich country. Between 2.3m and 2.4m Americans are behind bars, roughly one in every 100 adults. As a proportion of its total population, America incarcerates five times more people than Britain, nine times more than Germany and 12 times more than Japan. Overcrowding is the norm. Federal prisons house 60% more inmates than they were designed for. State lock-ups are only slightly less stuffed."

For instance, the US prisoner rate is 748 prisoners per 100,000, the highest in the entire world (exceeding Russia's 600). In this view, specifically the US criminal justice system "has three big flaws": "First, it puts too many people away for too long. Second, it criminalises acts that need not be criminalised. Third, it is unpredictable. Many laws, especially federal ones, are so vaguely written that people cannot easily tell whether they have broken them". In particular, "the number of drug offenders in federal and state lock-ups has increased 13-fold since 1980". Furthermore "severe drug laws have unintended consequences. Less than half of American cancer patients receive adequate painkiller [as]. doctors are terrified of being accused of drug-trafficking if they over-prescribe. In 2004 William Hurwitz, a doctor specialising in the control of pain, was sentenced to 25 years in prison for prescribing pills that a few patients then resold on the black market." In general, "half the states have laws that lock up habitual offenders for life. In some states this applies only to violent criminals, but in others it applies even to petty ones. Some 3,700 people who committed neither violent nor serious crimes are serving life sentences under California's "three strikes and you're out" law. In Alabama a petty thief called Jerald Sanders was given a life term for pinching a bicycle. Alabama's judges are elected, as are those in 32 other states. This makes them mindful of public opinion: some appear in campaign advertisements waving guns and bragging about how tough they are." The magazine cites the observation that America is conducting "an experiment in imprisoning first-time non-violent offenders for periods of time previously reserved only for those who had killed someone". Moreover, it observes that "badly drafted laws create traps for the unwary" to the point that "innocent defendants may plead guilty in return for a shorter sentence to avoid the risk of a much longer one", with "over 4,000 federal crimes, and many times that number of regulations that carry criminal penalties" inflicted and supported mostly by "tough-on-crime conservatives". Cynics may comment that this is an accurate picture of a criminal justice system as literally *criminal* in Popper's (1973) sense to the point of "murderous" and *injustice* in Durkheim's meaning of gross misfit between crime-sin and Draconian disproportionate punishment, thus an Orwellian totalitarian dystopia, while "true" Christians might only say "Amen."

From a human and individualist perspective, it is difficult to witness a more sinister, tragic form of state terror via government violent repression and severe coercion within modern Western society than American conservatism's primitive Draconian punishments of individuals for their moral sins and their underlying sensual pleasures redefined and so punished as crimes. Specifically, this is imprisoning individuals for life, as by neo-conservative "three strikes laws", or other long sentences because of their non-violent moral sins like repeated drug uses as self-inflicted wounds and potential executions for trade in drugs, as well as innocent persons for such and similar, especially fabricated sexual, offenses. Such government repression effectively ruins or permanently disrupts the lives of individuals literally transformed from human sinners and often inno-cent persons–as proven by DNA evidence about rapes and other sexual offenses–into "dead men walking" for whom being innocent prisoners of ethical conscience and victims of a religiously induced "tough on crime" paranoia is a mere "consolation prize" and "psychic income" or rather, as Americans would say, a "cruel joke".

And the numbers of such human victims of "holy" state terror are staggering and ever-growing. For example, a proxy calculation would yield at the minimum nearly two thirds of almost 2.4 million prisoners punished, often for life thanks to "three strikes" laws and usually by exces-sively, or ridiculously a la 99 and more year, long sentences for drug use and possession and other moral sins at the time of writing these lines. Moreover, this figure could be increased by several millions of former pris-oners whose life the neo-conservative Puritan-style government, espe-cially the "Bible Belt", makes a sort of "living hell" and their settings an "open prison." (As a seemingly trivial yet indicative instance of society as a proxy open prison, in Texas and the "Bible Belt" in parks warning signs about committing certain vices are posted such as "alcoholic beverages are prohibited", thus making these open spaces closed, coercive settings a la prisons or churches. So, those Americans thinking of having a picnic with some beer or wine on a warm day in open spaces in Texas and the South overall definitely should have a second thought about doing so or else and probably feel like being in an open prison or omnipresent church, an Orwellian or Islamic world of state terror via government repression and punishment of sins-vices. In purely theological or Biblical terms, by such and other prohibitions of alcohol a la Prohibition and "dry" counties, as part of its moralistic state terror, the "Bible Belt" violates or contradicts the Bible itself, namely Christ's last supper of wine and bread becoming sacrament in original Christianity. Cynics or comics may comment that in doing so the "Bible Belt" acts as if being more biblical than the Bible itself and US fundamentalists as bigger "Christians" than Christ himself, holier than thou", analogous to some Catholics acting as "bigger Catholic than the Pope.)

Conservative government, notably the "Bible Belt", in America there-fore perpetuates or evokes Puritanism that made society for most humans–minus its self-declared "divines" and "everlasting saints"–"hell in this world" (Tawney 1962). It does by various Puritan-style life-long punishments in society even after serving their legal punishment. For instance, permanent punishments of sinners-as-criminals span from denying them basic political rights like voting (Uggen and Manza 2002) to their actual or potential prohibitions, exclusions, and discriminations in employment, education, and housing (Becky and Western 2004; Pager 2003; Wakefield and Uggen 2010). They are thereby effectively forced to return to sinful-criminal activities and the prison system, or just commit suicide, as they are "advised" to "save" their souls and "return to God" by "holier than thou" evangelical moral crusaders. Such conservative Puritan-style practices eliminating "sinful" individuals as proxy "terrorists" or "enemies of God" make ridicule of glorified American, including Parsons' extolled Puritan theological, "individualism" made hardly worth the paper on which it is legally or otherwise stated. For example, the individual right to "pursuit of happiness" in the Constitution is effectively perverted into the sacred duty to suffer pain, indignity, torment, repentance, expiation, and self-humiliation ("humility") Puritan-style.

In a way, within the modern democratic West nothing appears more or closer to state terror than a government systematically destroying or permanently disrupting humans' lives, thus depreciated, disregarded, or disdained to the extreme, simply, as Americans would say, made "cheap" through long imprisonment and executions as the punishment for their moral sins and so sensual pleasures still remained the "forbidden apple" following Puritanism (Scitovsky 1972). No Western governments do this on the scale and with the intensity, persistence, and fanaticism that the US conservative "godly" government at federal and regional ("Bible Belt") levels does, just as Iran, Taliban, and other Islamic theocracies, instead preferring a "more humane approach" (Reuter 2005) to moral sins like drug uses and the like. Consequently, no other modern Western state so systematically and self-righteously depreciates, disregards, and disdains human life and dignity, thus renders them as "cheap"–a seeming extension of the Wild West "wanted dead or alive" legal norm (Hill 2002)–as does the sanctimonious (Bourdieu 1998) US conservative government and "Bible Belt" and other "red" states, evoking Puritan sanctimony during witch-trials and other "holy" terror, just as do Islamic theocracies.

For example, in 2012 reportedly Britain's High Court "blocked a U.S. government bid to extradite a sex criminal to Minnesota, saying the state's restrictive treatment program for sex offenders was far too draconian [by] the indefinite detention of people found to be 'sexually dangerous'" and that "commitment to the program would be in 'flagrant denial' of [the person's] human rights." Notably, it objected that "in some cases, those placed in the program don't even have to have been convicted of any crime [sic!]." In another case of Draconian treatment, it was reported that in Texas a man "will serve the maximum sentence of 20 years in prison [by] violating the provisions of his civil commitment", though, as his lawyer stated, "a crime has not been committed, yet criminal penalties are at stake", and another "gets 50 years for failing to register as sex offender, a crime with a punishment range of 25 years to life in prison." An outsider, especially from a Western country, may ask life or 50 years in prison "for what?" pointing to the extreme, cynical disrespect, disdain, and depreciation of human liberty, dignity, life and persons thereby rendered the "cheapest" or most "disposable" in the West by these Draconian sentences for sins-crimes (in this case effectively non-crimes). Yet, such questions represent a sort of taboo in the "Bible Belt" and beyond, just as did in its prototype the Puritan "Biblical Commonwealth" and do in its functional equivalents, Islamic theocracies like Iran and Taliban regions, as well as conceivably in an Orwellian dystopia thus more exemplified or approached by this evangelical theocracy than (as usually supposed) "socialism".

The preceding uncovers and predicts a sort of ultimate form or outcome of state terror. For ultimate state terror is the literal and symbolic destruction, based on the depreciation, disregard, and contempt, of human individuals in, as Pareto remarks, the "name of the Divine master", as via executions and life-long imprisonment for criminalized moral sins and so sensual pleasures. These practices are shared by the "godly" US conservative government, notably the theocratic "Bible Belt" (Texas, etc.), and Islamic theocracies, as their joint "favorite pastime", but virtually unknown or rapidly disappearing among modern Western societies from Europe to Canada and Australia. At this juncture, conservative reproduced and celebrated "American exceptionalism" effectively operates and reappears as an Islamic-style repressive aberration from modern Western society (Inglehart 2004) rather than, as in received sociological theory or ethnocentric claims, "libertarian", "democratic", and "individualistic" exceptional outcomes.

Even if such practices of the US conservative, typically theocratic or moralistic government, in particular "Bible Belt" states, are not, as their agents claim and most Americans seemingly believe, acts of state terrorism and not equivalent to and on the scale of those of Nazism and Islamic theocracies as more repressive and lethal, the intended or unintended social effect, i.e., manifest or latent function of "American theocracy"

(Phillips 2006) or "Christian fascism" (Hedges 2006) is identical. This is producing and sustaining the societal climate or ambiance of "terror" (Smelser and Mitchel 2001). The latter involves widespread "ambient fear" (Bauman 2001), the sense of pervasive and total legal insecurity or penal uncertainty in society. This means that humans can at any moment be subjected to "holy" government violent repression and severe coercion, including executions and imprisonment for non-violent sins-as-crimes, only if admittedly "godly" and moralizing prosecutors cum persecutors made "real effort" (Friedman 1997), often regardless of actual innocence, as proven by innocent persons being executed, on death row, and imprisoned, and overly or covertly in dogmatic "original sin" grounds.

The above looks like an Orwellian totalitarian dystopia of "*no* crime, maximal punishment", yet has become a realized condition couched in and rationalized by old "conservative-authoritarian slogans of law and order" (Dahrendorf 1979), "no one is above the law", "tough on crime", and the like. The outcome is making society a total monastery or temple, as the Puritan design, achievement, and legacy, and an open prison in which humans are constantly under the condition of "terror" in the sense of violent repression and the climate of mass fear, i.e., terrorized by physical and symbolic violence (Bourdieu 1989). This is shown by neo-conservatism's use of the death penalty and mass long imprisonment to "terrorize"—either execute and imprison often for life or frighten into panic and submission–lower and even middle classes in the US[28] (Bauman 1997). Hence, even if such repressive and coercive actions of the US neo-conservative government, notably "Bible Belt" states, are not state terror but, as their agents and supporters claim, just "tough on crime" policies based on the "rule of law" and maintaining "law and order", thus not identical to those of Nazism and Islamic theocracies, their ultimate effects are. This is reproducing a pervasive sense of "terror" involving overwhelming fear, intimidation, panic, anxiety, stress, confusion, insecurity, uncertainty, and related negative mental states, simply a sort of collective

---

[28] Bauman (1997:43) comments that in contemporary America "the overwhelming majority of the death row inmates comes from [the] "underclass [so] the spectacle of execution is cynically used by [U.S.] politicians to terrorize a growing underclass. But in demanding the terrorization of the underclass, the silent American majority attempts to terrorize its own inner demons." In general, he proposes that "massive incarceration, spine-chilling stories of the lengthening death-row queues and the systematic, deliberate deterioration of prison conditions [dehumanization] are deployed as the principal means of "terrorization" of the underclass, now presented to public opinion as enemy number one of public safety" (Bauman 1997:60).

madness or hypnosis, in society as the constant aim and outcome of all types of terrorism—i.e., an Orwellian world of state terror.

Of course, the conservative "rule of law" or "law and order" breaks down into a false rationalization or propaganda slogan which even its producers do not believe with executions of innocent people, as the axiomatic instance of state terror or government murder, as well as mass long imprisonment of such persons, as witnessed in the US, especially "Bible Belt" (Texas, etc.) criminal justice system for long. And both punishments intentionally or not tend to recreate the societal climate of terror, namely mass fear, panic, and penal uncertainty among the population ("I can be next") not yet executed or imprisoned, regardless of legal considerations of factual innocence or guilt sacrificed to the dogma of "original sin" and consequently the religious claim of humans' "lost innocence" and "eternal guilt" as per Calvinism, including Puritanism. This ushers in an Orwellian world of people expecting the executor to eventually come and punish, including execute or imprison, them regardless of their real innocence, because, as the old Roman legal principles as well as popular wisdom imply, when the innocent are thus punished, then everyone else (minus rulers) could be as well sooner or later and thus is in lethal danger. (For instance, many young and other ordinary Americans indulging in sins and pleasures like alcohol and drug uses are perhaps in "terror" or panic and fear thinking "I can be next" given that even some celebrities have been harshly punished and constantly tormented by the US moralistic government at various levels because of such sinful conduct. Arguably, when the government thus punishes and torments even young celebrities for their illicit sins and pleasures, then it intentionally or not "terrorizes" others by spreading the climate of "terror" cum fear, panic, and insecurity in society.)

In general, even if, charitably interpreted, the US conservative government, including the "Bible Belt", does not commit state terrorism in the form or on the scale of Nazism and Islamic theocracies, it generates and perpetuates the societal climate of "terror" by spreading like social contagion mass fear, panic, and insecurity in society through its "tough on crime" practices, notably executions and imprisonment of innocent and/ or sinful persons. Such tendencies make, or are likely so, in the process Americans probably the West's most frightened or intimidated people. This means fearing that the criminal justice system could execute or imprison them for life ("three strikes" laws) regardless of factual innocence or for their sins-pleasures not punished or not so severely in modern Western democracies, literally "scared to death" what could happen to them due to the Puritan-rooted conservative government's perennial obsession with and criminalization and severe punishment of sins and vices driven by the "original sin" dogma.

And such seemingly irrational or exaggerated climate and feeling of "ambient fear" or "terror" of execution and imprisonment has a rational objective basis. For the probability of an American being executed and especially imprisoned has increased exponentially during recent times and is by far the highest in the Western world[29] (Beckett and Western 2004; Cooney and Burt 2008; Wakefield and Uggen 2010). This is because of the explosion of the US prison population of which, as noted, non-violent moral sinners like drug users and thus substantively innocent prisoners of ethical conscience make almost two thirds. The lesson and message is hence clear and simple. Most Americans and even more–given the largely nativist or xenophobic anti-foreign bias of the legal system– immigrants or foreigners can hardly ever underestimate with impunity the neo-conservative "godly" government, notably the "Bible Belt" (Texas, etc.), with respect to its seriousness, determination, persistence, and fanaticism in the perpetuation of the climate of "terror" or pervasive fear in society through "law and order" and "tough on crime" practices. Conversely, like those living under fascism in interwar Europe and today's Islamic theocracies, they can do so only at their own peril, sometimes death and usually imprisonment, likely a sort of slow death by physical or mental torture in virtue of their ruined or permanently disrupted human lives, as witnessed by, alongside many innocent persons executed or on death row, many millions of current and former prisoners (Uggen and Manza 2002; Wakefield and Uggen (2010:392–3). Simply, Americans can hardly ever afford to forget that their conservative "godly" government, notably the "Bible Belt", by executions and long imprisonment of inno-cent and sinful persons does make human life and so themselves the "cheapest" or most expendable "commodity" in the Western world, with only Islamic theocracies and Nazism before rivaling this "cheapening", i.e., the depreciation, disregard, and contempt, of humans for the "glory" and in the "name of God" a la Calvin and Puritanism.

---

[29] Wakefield and Uggen (2010:305) observe that "by the first decade of the 21st first cen-tury, the US was incarcerating 1% of its population at any given time, with an additional 2% serving time on probation and parole. Incarceration on this scale is virtually unprece-dented. The US has had the highest incarceration rate in the world since 2002. Although prison populations are growing in many parts of the world, the US dwarfs them all, at jail and prison incarceration levels that are commonly five to seven times larger than those of other nations of similar economic, social or demographic profiles."

In passing, the above striking divergence from the West and the even more "shocking" convergence with the Muslim non-West moves the US neo-conservative government and consequently America under neo-conservatism, at the minimum the "Bible Belt" (and Utah), from the supposed "model" and "leader" of Western civilization (Lipset 1996; Lipset and Marks 2000) into outside of the latter and instead closer to the Islamic world. This uncovers American cum Islamic-style theocratic rather than democratic "exceptionalism" from Western civilization. If one does not know what such divergence and convergence defining American exceptionalism are until and unless seeing them, a sociological comparison would likely reveal that the evangelical "Bible Belt" (or Mormon-ruled Utah) is more sociologically distant from, and even "with pride and joy" opposed to, "post-Christian" Scandinavia and all Western Europe, with minor exceptions like Poland and Ireland (Gorski and Altinordu 2008; Inglehart 2004; Ruiter and Tubergen 2009), than from Iran (Bauman 1997), Saudi Arabia, and Taliban-ruled regions (Mansbach 2006).

In essence, this is conservative ("red") America's, in particular the "Bible Belt," theocratic or fundamentalist divergence from the "old" disdained liberal-secular Europe and the convergence with Islamic theocracies in terms of "holy" state terror by systematic government violent repression and severe coercion through executions and life or long imprisonment of moral sinners-criminals and innocent persons. Simply, by the early 21st century the Western world does not do this anymore, as indicated by the abolition of the death penalty and the non-criminal or humane treatment of moral sinners like drug users and others, and only the US "godly" Puritan-style government or the "Bible Belt" and Islamic theocracies do it. For instance, an uniformed outsider (or Martian) may well conclude, judging from the neo-conservative "tough on crime" policy and the media, that vices like alcohol-drug use and especially non-violent sexual sins such as adultery, prostitution, premarital sex, pornography, etc. are the gravest social problems in modern America, as in contemporaneous Islamic theocracies and New England's Puritan theocracy (adultery, fornication, blasphemy, and witchcraft). On this account, neo-conservatism moves the "leader of the West" closer to the Islamic than the Western world (Inglehart 2004) and historically "freezes" the "new nation" in 17th century Puritanism (Kaufman 2008; Munch 2001) and its "Biblical Commonwealth" as "paradise lost", and often literally so by retaining and enforcing Puritan-era "dumb" or "blue" laws, especially in the "Bible Belt".

Globally, corresponding acts or proxies of "terror" include violent government or extra-government subversions and offensive wars against[30] (Clairmont 1993), including "assassination and extralegal executions" and non-legitimized invasions[31] (Turk 2004), as well as support for dictatorships in, other societies (Lutz and Lutz 2004). In this view, instances of such activities are the US neo-conservative and other government overt or covert support and inciting of counter-state Albanian and other Islamic terrorism in the former Yugoslavia such as Bosnia, Kosovo,

---

[30] Clairmont (1993:1423) states, in apparent reference to the first Iraq war, that "one more crime of US state terrorism against yet another third world country is a grim reminder that indignation is not enough. It must be matched by organised campaigns to ensure that the words of the UN Charter become a binding reality." If this is correct, it holds true even more of the 2003 Iraq second war of aggression that, unlike the first and like the 1999 Yugoslavia war, was not authorized by the UN and consequently unlawful and to that extent an act of inter-state terror (Smelser and Mitchel 2002; Turk 2004). In light of this, then the US, especially conservative, government definition and explication of terrorism as always involving actions of *Other* governments (or groups and societies) seems as trustworthy as—citing a US congressman's statement in reference to "self-regulation" by big corporations, Enron-style–trusting Dracula in charge of a "blood bank."

[31] Turk (2004:280) observes that "political pressures to lessen legal restraints on police, and military responses to terrorism have resulted in the, possibly temporary, erosion in the US and elsewhere of legal protections against intrusive and secret surveillance, arbitrary detention, and hurtful interrogation methods, as well as assassination and extralegal executions." Moreover, in his view, the U.S. neo-conservative government in the wake of September 11, "adopted two fateful [fatal?] policies (1) the decision to dilute or abrogate established legal restraints on governmental power (e.g. indefinite detention along with the suspension of habeas corpus) (2) the decision to invade Iraq without United Nations legitimation [thus] eroding the freedoms being defended in the war against terrorism (Turk 2004:282). Similarly, Béland (2005:33) notes that the US President "discourse following September 11 about so-called rogue states and the 'axis of evil' (Iraq, Iran, and North Korea) illustrates [the] idea that state officials can exaggerate of—or at least exploit—the scope of potential threats to promote their interests at home and abroad [by overdramatizing] the international situation by depicting these countries as manifesting an immediate menace for the rest of the world. The misleading presidential rhetoric about Iraqi 'weapons of mass destruction' and the supposed link between al Qaeda and the Hussein regime that justified the 2003 invasion of Iraq illustrates this ideological logic. [So] the state can protect civil society against threats that state officials themselves can exaggerate or even fabricate. [Hence] the so-called war on terrorism is not an entirely original form |of protection but (a) new expression of the original state-building logic". In this view, the "'war on terrorism' potentially threatens the ability of national states both to protect citizens and to respect individual rights. [For example] the 'USA Patriot Act' has been widely criticized by human rights advocates in the US and abroad. The increase in military spending [is] associated with the 'war on terrorism' divert[ing] resources from other areas of state protection [social policy]" (Béland 2005:34). Béland (2005:35–6) concludes that the "US poses a paradox. In the world's most powerful state, elected officials promoting the economic interests of narrow—and affluent—constituencies have significantly reduced the capacity of the state to raise revenues while increasing military spending and breeding popular fears about terrorism [so] a deepening contradiction between declining extraction powers and rising protection needs."

and Macedonia, and also proxy state terrorism or neo-Nazism in Croatia, as well as other parts of the world, from central and South America to Asia and Africa. The funding, arming, and otherwise supporting the Taliban *mujahideen*, Al-Qaeda, and other Islamic warriors in their "holy" war against "infidels" in Afghanistan—and in part Russia (Chechnya)–is the probably most manifest and paradigmatic historical case of the US and other Western governments sponsoring of counter-state terrorism during recent times.

For instance, displaying a persistent Cold-War syndrome, the US neo-conservative government (the administration, Congress) has tended to characterize and even extol "holy" Islamic warriors in Russia (Chechnya, etc.) as a kind of "freedom fighters" against its old enemy, like those operating before in Afghanistan and Yugoslavia. This Cold War posture has also been typified by the UK and other Western governments within NATO until recently. Namely, following September 11, 2001 the US and other Western governments (or NATO) have finally and reluctantly acknowledged that these anti-Russian Islamic warriors are terrorists like, and often tied with, those committing such terrorist acts against America and the West. Or perhaps this is a premature observation, judging by the conduct of some Western governments almost 10 years after September 11, 2001. Thus, at the time of writing these lines the UK government, while routinely deporting to America suspected Islamic militants wanted by the US government,[32] refuses to deport the very same groups from Britain to Russia and even gives them protection (asylum, citizenship, honors), seemingly continuing the Cold War pattern long after the Cold War officially ended, a double standard also adopted by such former Soviet allies and presently new NATO members as the Polish and other Central European governments. Apparently, for the UK government substantively identical Islamic groups (e.g., with connections to Al-Qaeda) are "terrorists" when committing or planning attacks on the US government, yet "freedom fighters" if they attack the Russian state nearly 10 years after September 11, 2001. To that extent, the UK and other Western effectively incite, support, and perpetuate Islamic terrorism in Chechnya and similar

---

[32] Lutz and Lutz (2004:9) caution that "governments provide definitions, but they are often self-serving. Opponents of the government are defined as terrorists while [its] irregular allies fail to meet the definitional standards as terrorists. Over the years, the US has had a list of countries that have been considered to be state supporters of terrorism (Iran, Iraq, Syria, Libya, Cuba, North Korea, and Sudan). [Yet] it has ignored countries supporting terrorist groups that were [allies], because their inclusion would create problems, or because their actions did not especially concern the US."

regions in Russia, just as they did in Yugoslavia, by bombarding this country on behalf, thus acting through NATO as the air force, of an "ethnic terrorist army" in Kosovo, like Bosnia before. (In Macedonia, NATO reportedly saved its Islamic allies in June of 2001 when they were surrounded by the military forcing the Macedonian government to let them go free to their base in Kosovo and then to return to continue their "holy" war for "liberties" and "human rights".)

Thus, some analysts' (Lutz and Lutz 2004) prediction that the ultimate future goal of this ethnic army in Kosovo and Macedonia may be "union" with Albania" has been, by and large, corroborated since in the form of the persistent, though often hidden, project or dream of the "Greater Albania" uniting "all Albanians" in the Balkans. If so, the US government and NATO cum the "international community" may have destroyed the project of the "Greater Serbia" but in the process objectively recreated, i.e., incited or encouraged, that of "Greater Albania", notably by rewarding its "ally", the "Kosovo Liberation Army" with independence, a sort of perverse military "creative destruction" a la Schumpeter, or political trade-off.

Future historians may register that this political trade-off may well be an irrational choice" or short-sighted decision on the part of the US government and NATO, because (or if) the "Greater Albania" as an Islamic–plus mafia and neo-fascist–state is likely to be a more serious long-term threat, as has been another former "ally" the Taliban government, to the Western world than the Christian "Greater Serbia" ever would be–but this is *not* support for such and any national project–despite its imputed fantasy "Russian connection". In a cost-benefit calculation in terms of terrorism, the cost in actual or prospective terror against the US government and the Western world overall committed by groups or persons from the "Greater Albania" and other Islamic states, including its another Balkan ally, Muslim-dominated Bosnia, is likely to greatly exceed the benefit of disposing with the project of the "Greater Serbia" in the long run of decades or centuries. This future scenario is in part anticipated by the reported terrorist acts or plans in America and Western Europe by Albanians originating from Albania and especially Kosovo and Macedonia as well as by Muslims from Bosnia, but no such terrorists have been detected in the West as descending from Serbia proper despite the US/NATO 1999 unlawful attack and massive sadistic destruction.

But, the US conservative bellicose government and in extension NATO seems to learn only from catastrophes (Habermas 2001),, including

September 11, 2001 and other terrorist attacks by its former "allies", Muslim "holy" warriors against "ungodly" governments in Afghanistan, Yugoslavia, etc. Or rather, US conservatism never learns even from catastrophes, military ones like the near mutual nuclear annihilation during the Cold War, just as, for that matter, catastrophic economic crises such as the 1929–33 Great Depression and the Great Recession of 2008–10, and instead persists in its militarism as well as its "unfettered" authoritarian capitalism as if no catastrophe generated by its militarist-capitalist complex ever happened.

Generally, it appears that Islamic terrorism in these regions and the world overall, including Western Europe and America, would hardly ever reach the present scope and intensity without such Western incitement and support of, including NATO's military alliance with, Muslim "freedom fighters" in their "holy" war against "infidels", from Afghanistan through Bosnia and Kosovo[33] to Chechnya, etc. And, now it seems too late to de-invent or even contain Islamic terrorism. The Pandora Box of Islamic "holy" terror has been opened and tactically a la Machiavelli used by Western powers for protecting their, especially American-British, "values" and "interests" against "enemies" (the Soviet Union, Yugoslavia, Russia, etc.), but in the process has become an anti-Western weapon to the effect of the West, including America, suddenly awakening to the reality of fundamentalist, radical Islam as the "enemy Number 1" (Feldstein 2008). And the latter admittedly appears to be a more serious, persistent, and implacable enemy of Western civilization, including America, than, for example, what Reagan denounced as the "evil empire" of the Soviet Union has ever been (Schelling 2006).

For unlike the latter, Islamic, like all religious, including "Christian", terrorism and fundamentalism overall refuses compromise, convergence, mutual accommodation, or even peaceful co-existence as betrayal of

---

[33] Lutz and Lutz (2004:106) add that "the terrorist activities of the KLA were successful. [And] the Albanians in power in Kosovo have also not acquitted themselves particularly well. They have used violence against the remaining Serbs in Kosovo and the Gypsies who are assumed to be pro-Serbian. The goal has been to drive both groups out of the province. More than 100,000 Gypsies have fled the province as a consequence of the pressure. By 1999 an organized campaign of murder and terror was taking place in an effort to drive out the small number of Serb civilians that had remained in Kosovo [so] if the remaining Serbs are forced out, independence or unity with Albania becomes a much easier proposition to sell [to] Europe. The tactics that worked in Kosovo were apparently being tried again in Macedonia"). They predict that "union with an independent Kosovo or Albania might be a goal for the future, but that is a solution that rewards the dissidents for increasing tensions within Macedonia" (Lutz and Lutz 2004:107).

"God's will" and instead pursues total "cosmic" war and destruction of "infidels" or the "ungodly". For example, the Soviet Union admittedly never used or even contemplated using its vast arsenal of nuclear weapons against the West (Schelling 2006), but Islamic fundamentalist terrorists are evidently willing and ready to use them immediately to "destroy" the "infidel" Western world, including America, only if they had them. In military terms, for the Soviet Union nuclear arms were above all the deterrence mechanism, but for Islamic fundamentalism they are, first and foremost, effective weapons of mass destruction to be used without any qualms and delay or even cost-benefit calculation only if available. This is a moment that Western, especially US and UK, governments have seemingly ignored or underestimated in the past because of their alliances with Muslim "freedom fighters", yet can never underestimate in the present and future with impunity.

The preceding confirms the long-standing experience or proverb that those who conclude a "pact of with the devil" in the non-religious sense to attain their goals and interests ultimately will be devoured or gravely threatened by the latter, as incidentally happened to traditional German conservatism that opted to "ride" the "Nazi tiger" (Blinkhorn 2003) as the potent weapon to attain its anti-liberal, anti-democratic, militarist, and imperial goals, with the effect of Nazism eventually almost devouring its conservative creator or master. Similarly, the Western world, especially US, UK, and German governments, has (re) recreated or incited, from Afghanistan to Yugoslavia and Russia, and used strategically the Islamic terrorist monster, but now the latter, like all such creations after the image of Frankenstein (Friedman 1982), has evidently escaped what Pareto calls the "cage for the insane" and is out of control, and thus threatens to devour the creator, master, and tamer.

In addition, helping overthrow a democratically elected "socialist" government and install a neo-fascist "free market" military dictatorship in Chile, as reportedly the US conservative administration did in the early 1970s, is an instance of supporting state and in part committing inter-state terrorism. But the preceding are not the only cases or things of the past. This is witnessed by such continuing overt or covert subversive activities by the US neo-conservative government (including the CIA and the military), or its support for counter-state terrorism or violence, against certain democratically elected, stigmatized "socialist" and "repressive" in a déjà vu scenario, "unfriendly" governments in Central and South America (Nicaragua, Venezuela, Bolivia, plus undemocratic Cuba, etc.) and elsewhere.

On this account, the US neo-conservative invariably moralistic, repressive and theocratic or theocentric Puritan-style government, notably the "Bible Belt" complex of states, like most Western and non-Western conservative oppressive governments, is hardly viewed as a credible source for adequate definitions and explications of terrorism, including intra-societal violent repression and inter-societal wars. For both activities have been a sort of "favorite pastime" for neo-conservatism with its religiously, including "original-sin", driven "law and order" and "tough on crime" government coercion within society and aggressive "holy" global war against the "evil" world since the 1980s. In a way, to critics for the US neo-conservative and other repressive "godly" governments committing "holy" state terror such as executions and mass imprisonment of innocent or sinful persons on religious grounds, as in the "Bible Belt", to define other governments, non-governmental groups, and societies as "terrorist" appears as almost equivalent to Iranian theocracy and Taliban defining others in terms of state- and counter-state terrorism (or, as a US congressman put it, placing "Dracula in charge of a blood bank").

A disclaimer is in order to preempt misunderstanding or worse. The aforesaid of state and inter-state terror does *not* apply (by most analysts referred to) to the US government as a whole, but only to a certain, though mostly prevalent, ideological type of it. As emphasized, it does apply as a rule to various conservative federal governments and regional "red" states in contemporary America, and exceptionally to their non-conservative opposites (e.g., the 1999 illegal and seemingly Machiavellian attack on Yugoslavia on behalf of an "ethnic terrorist army"[34] by a "liberal" administration). Hence, it is inaccurate and imprecise to state that the US and any other Western government as such commits or supports state and

---

[34] Moreover, the US first female secretary of state reportedly stated "what is the point of having an ethnic [Albanian] terrorist army if you do not use it", presumably in the service of promoting "superior" American values and interests in this region and beyond, specifically the NATO attack on Yugoslavia as a proxy war or war game/rehearsal against Russia. In passing, this war perhaps provoked Russia's own version of a proxy warfare against NATO or the West later in Georgia, showing again that, as is often said, US conservative bellicose foreign policy is its "own worst enemy" since at least the Vietnam War. Yet, US government officials miraculously converted this "terrorist army" into "freedom fighters", with some, like the 2000 vice-presidential Democratic candidate, even proclaiming that they fight for the same goal of "liberty" as did the American revolutionaries! Also, a British soldier commented in the aftermath of the NATO bombardment of Yugoslavia that "we were fed a bad line about Kosovo Liberation Army [as freedom fighters]. They are terrorists and we won their war for them. It's not only Serbs, but the ethnic Albanians as well that are scared of them" (cited in Bauman 2001:207).

inter-state terror. Rather, it is more accurate and precise to say that whenever and wherever conservative, notably evangelical or neo-fascist (Blee and Creasap 2010; Hedges 2006; Owens et al. 2010), forces capture by "word" or "sword" Puritan- and Islamic-style federal government and regional states in America and in part other Western societies, they as a rule tend to commit "holy" state terror through violent repression in society and inter-state terror by global wars against societies. Simply, it is the conservative, notably evangelical-fascist capture and control of power by bullet or ballot, violence or democratic elections, as in Nazi Germany and America over the 1980–2010s, that is terrorist–so ultimately self-destructive and irrational–rather than the US and other Western government as such.

CHAPTER FOUR

ANTI-LIBERALISM AND MODERN TERRORISM

*Antagonism toward Liberal-Democratic
Modernity as the Factor of Modern Terrorism*

This chapter considers and reveals anti-liberalism expressed in the negativity and destructiveness toward liberal-democratic modernity as a salient and persistent factor, predictor, and explanation of modern, notably religiously and ideologically based, terror. Thus, anti-modernity in the first specific dimension of antagonism and revolt against liberal-democratic modernity constitutes a major sociological determinant and predictor of most, though not all, contemporary terrorism, especially the terrorist predominant type committed, advocated, incited, and supported on "sacred" religious grounds. Anti- or counter-modernity typically has been and continues to be primarily expressed as the hostility and opposition to liberal-democratic modernity, in conjunction and mutual reinforcement with opposing secular, rationalistic, notably scientific, and global-cosmopolitan and universalistic modernism in the sociological sense of a social system, including modern capitalism and globalization as its economic structure and process.

The preceding holds true insofar Western modernity is, first and foremost, characterized as a liberal-democratic (Mannheim 1936; Zaret 1989) project, social system, and historical period, not only by its adherents, the moderns (Habermas 2001), but also by its opponents, anti-modern or traditionalist forces within the West, particularly America under conservatism and neo-conservatism, and beyond, especially Islamic settings. Modernism is hence typically defined and analyzed in terms of modern, including classical and contemporary, liberalism, as the principle and social system of liberty (Van Dyke 1995; Mannheim 1986), i.e., the ideal and practice of freedom (Hayek 1941; Mises 1966), thus of liberal democracy and society. Generally, a defining element of modernism is what Smith calls the composite "liberal plan" of liberty, equality, and justice as intertwined components (Mannheim 1986), in interconnection with secularism, scientific rationalism, and cosmopolitanism, globalism and universalism as its other constitutive elements.

Anti-liberalism and consequently, other things equal, anti-democracy in the sense of antagonism to liberal democracy constitutes the ideological, social-systemic, and historical condition of contemporary terrorism in most, again not all, of its forms, including counter-state and state terrorisms. Anti-liberalism and anti-democracy are understood as the ideology, social system, and period arising in adverse reaction against modern liberal democracy and society, aiming to restore or perpetuate pre-liberal and pre-democratic traditionalism such as medievalism, i.e., the *ancien regime* of feudalism in economy, despotism in polity, and theocracy in society. Alternatively, most (though not all) contemporary terrorism is rooted in and derives from the opposition against liberalism as the ideal, social system, and historical era of liberty (Mannheim 1986; Mises 1966), including political and civic liberties, notably its institutionalized form in liberal democracy and civil society. Such anti-liberalism involves the adverse reaction against the processes of political and cultural liberalization, democratization, and modernization generally, including secularization, rationalization, and globalization, since postwar times and also the 1990s through the 2010s (Inglehart and Baker 2000; Inglehart 2004).

In essence, contemporary terrorism is the extreme, ultimate outcome and consummation of anti-liberalism and thus anti-democracy in the form of violent agents and actions aiming to destroy or reverse and subvert modern liberal democracy and civil society, and hence liberalism as its ideological or philosophical foundation and justification (Dahrendorf 1979; Habermas 2001; Mannheim 1986). It results from and manifests the revolt against liberal-democratic modernity in favor of restoring illiberal and pre-democratic or authoritarian (Mannheim 1967) premodernity, particularly despotic medievalist traditionalism. The latter is the "golden past", "paradise lost and found", and the "model" of the "good society" for anti-liberals of all sorts, places and times, specifically religious-political conservatives (Dunn and Woodard 1996; Mannheim 1986; Nisbet 1966), neo-conservatives (Bourdieu 1998), fascists (Blinkhorn 2003), and neo-fascists or conservative extremists (Blee and Creasap 2010; Rydgren 2007a) in Europe and America. Hence, it is anti-liberal and thus anti-democratic "forces of totalitarianism" that primarily, though no solely, commit, advocate, incite, and support contemporary terrorism, including its counter-state and state versions, against "liberal" groups, governments and other social institutions, and societies (Habermas 2001). The latter are typically demonized as "ungodly", specifically "anti-Christian" or "un-American" and "anti-Islamic" by US and Islamic conservative "holy" warriors, respectively (Friedland 2002; Hedges 2006; Juergensmeyer 2003).

In Clausewitz's terms, most contemporary terrorism, including offensive war within society and against other societies as its subtype, is the predictable "continuation" in the form of escalation of the politics of anti-liberalism and so anti-democracy, including anti-liberal and anti-democratic repressive domestic and bellicose foreign policies, by "other means", i.e., force, destruction, severe coercion, and violent repression. In this sense, terrorism, including culture, civil, and offensive military war, is not a random and transient but systemic, methodical, and permanent phenomenon of the "politics" of anti-liberalism and anti-democracy, including anti-liberal and anti-democratic oppressive domestic and bellicose foreign policies. In short, terrorism is intrinsic to anti-liberalism and thus anti-democracy. Conversely, the antagonism and revolt against liberalism and liberal democracy entails built-in terrorist tendencies and outcomes. In this sense, most contemporary terrorism can be analyzed, explained, and predicted in the context of "modern liberty and its discontents" (Manent 1998), i.e., as the extreme form of this discontent with the ideal and social system of liberties, including the "new liberty" (Dahrendorf 1975), defining liberalism and constituting and sustaining liberal democracy, civil society, and culture.

Clausewitz's like definition holds true of counter-state and state terrorisms alike. For both anti-government and government terrorist actions have been and can be predicted to be such continuations or escalations of the "politics" and ideology of anti-liberalism and anti-democracy, as epitomized by fascism, theocracy and fundamentalism, and conservatism in general. Thus, this applies to fascist counter-state subversive *putschist* groups and states in interwar and postwar Europe, theocratic or fundamentalist movements and established theocracies in the Islamic world, past and present, and in evangelical America, from the Puritan "Biblical Commonwealth" to the neo-Puritan "Bible Belt". All these groups and political systems have continued, through their anti-government and government terrorist practices respectively, their typically "godly politics" (Zaret 1989) of anti-liberalism and anti-democracy by violent, warlike, destructive, and coercive-repressive "means".

Alternatively, the fascist and theocratic or fundamentalist "godly politics" of anti-liberalism and anti-democracy in these societies have ultimately escalated or metastasized in counter-state and/or state terrorism. And the outcome in the form of counter-state or state terrorism depends on whether fascism has been in power or opposition, as in interwar and postwar Europe respectively. Such an outcome also hinges on whether theocracy was/will be established, as in Iran, Saudi Arabia, Taliban-ruled regions, as well as Puritan New England and evangelical "Christian America" (Davis and Robinson 2009; Hedges 2006; Owens et al. 2010; Phillips 2006). Conversely, it depends on whether theocracy was/is non-established and disestablished. This is witnessed in officially secular Turkey and Jeffersonian liberal-democratic America (Kloppenberg 1998; Vasi and Strang 2009), yet fragile and constantly condemned and attacked by anti-liberal, anti-democratic forces, especially but not only in the "Bible Belt", with Jefferson himself remaining the prime target of "godly" theocratic "Crusades for Christ" (as some Southern evangelicals sects and cults are named).

For instance, ruling religious conservatives cum "born again" evangelicals in Texas during 2010 reportedly removed (sic!) Jefferson from the public school curriculum like history classes, etc. and replaced him with Calvin and some other "godly" anti-liberal figures as supposedly more important to America, including this state. Apparently, for such conservative groups Jeffersonian ideals of "liberty, equality and justice for all" are less relevant to the "land of freedom", including the "lone star state" and its "true spirit of freedom", than Calvin's theological doctrine of predestination with its, in Weber's view, "extreme inhumanity", and his theocratic design and system of "godly" society, as he conceived it in France and instituted it in Geneva, and his followers did in Holland and via Puritanism in old and New England. Of course, Texas and other "Bible Belt" fundamentalists as would-be theocrats find Jefferson's "mortal crime" in his crucial contribution to building the constitutional "wall of eternal separation of church and state" and the "prohibition of government promotion of religion" (Dayton 1999), notably his and Madison's rejection of the Puritan theocratic vision and rendition of America as "Christian Sparta" (Kloppenberg 1998), and Calvin's supreme virtue in his "Reformed" theocracy as "holy" tyranny and terror (Swidler 1986; Walzer 1965).

Hence, while seemingly shocking and the Orwell-style rewriting of history, this substitution of an "all-American" liberal-democratic founder with a "foreign"—and at that French—theologian and theocrat, is perfectly natural for US religious conservatives, because their perennial ideal has always been and remains theocracy a la "godly" society or the "Bible Garden" and to that extent "holy" tyranny and terror. Simply, if this is their eternal dream, one wonders what else to expect other than erasing Jefferson as the defined main enemy in virtue of his liberal-democratic ideals to fulfilling their theocratic design of "holy" violent repression and global war from American history and schools, and glorifying Calvin as the "Pope of Protestantism" and his prototypical theocracy (in Geneva) as the model and inspiration. On a lighter note, one wonder what invariably nationalistic, xenophobic, and proudly ignorant Texas and other US religious conservatives would do if they knew or were reminded that Jean (not John) Calvin was a *French* Protestant theologian and theocrat born and raised in France (Elwood 199; Heller 1986), notably, of all places, nearby Paris, while they live in or their ideal is the anti-Paris "Bible Belt", like Calvin's Geneva (Garrard 2003)—renaming "French Calvin" into "Freedom Calvin"?

Hence, such anti-liberal and anti-democratic politics by fascism, theocracy and fundamentalism, and conservatism overall can be predicted or expected with almost mathematical precision or a high statistical probability to metastasize in future state and counter-state terrorism according to the respective power constellation in both Europe/America and Islamic countries. This holds true under certain social conditions and historical conjunctures, including economic crises such as the 1929 Great Depression and the 2008 Great Recession, political tensions and changes (e.g., the 2008 US Presidential election and its aftermath), "culture wars" American style, global military war, etc. Specifically, a definite, predictable outcome is likely if neo-fascist or far-right groups in Europe capture or critically influence, via coalitions, as in Italy, Austria, Germany, etc., government, and theocratic-fundamentalist forces in Islamic countries and America, at least the "Bible Belt", establish or perpetuate themselves in political power. This is that neo-fascism and fundamentalism once in proxy absolute power will ultimately resort to state and inter-state terrorism, including intense coercion and violent repression within society and offensive wars against other societies.

Conversely, another also predictable outcome is likely so long as neo-fascism continues to be in the opposite power constellation. Neo-fascism may remain relegated to the opposition against liberal-democratic governments in Western Europe and theocratic-fundamentalist forces in Islamic countries and America fail to reestablish theocracy, as in Turkey and following the 2008 US elections of an "ungodly" and "un-American" President and "liberal" Congress subjected to conservatism's standard "godly" and "patriotic" demonization (Juergensmeyer 2003). Hence, the likely outcome is that neo-fascism and fundamentalism when not in power tends to resort to counter-state terrorism through anti-government subversions, attacks, or treats seeking to destroy or discredit "unpatriotic" and "ungodly" liberal government and replace it by a "patriotic" and "godly" alternative practicing systematic coercion and violent repression and to that extent state terror. This confirms and epitomizes what has been a proxy Michels' like "iron" sociological law or historical pattern. Fascist, fundamentalist, and generally conservative counter-state terrorism or anti-government violence has invariably been and remains the effective instrument and path of actually establishing state terror in the form of systematic government coercion and violent repression once fascism, fundamentalism, and conservatism overall seizes political power either by violence or democratic elections, "bullet or ballot."

On this account, terrorism is constant, a sort of permanent (counter) revolution rather than, as often naively believed or hoped, transient in fascism, fundamentalism, and conservatism in general—counter-state terror or anti-government violence when not in government control, state terror via systematic coercion and violent repression when seizing power either by "bullet or ballot". Simply, terror never ends in fascism, fundamentalism, and conservatism in general. Especially, it does not end if fascist, fundamentalist, and other conservative forces capture[1] government either by force or elections, thus ending their anti-government violence. On the contrary, it changes from counter-state into state terrorism and to that extent actually expands and intensifies rather than disappears and weakens. For while counter-state terrorism attacks only or mostly government and is so relatively limited in scale (Lutz and Lutz 2004), state terrorism, especially its fascist, fundamentalist, and other conservative variant, terrorizes society as a whole and other societies, thus being total and unlimited. This has been witnessed in Puritan "holy" terror in England and New England, Nazism and interwar fascism when in power, contemporary Islamic and "Bible Belt" theocracies, and neo-conservatism's severe coercion and violent repression, including mass imprisonment of "sinners" and executions, not rarely of innocent and invariably of sinful (which is the same) persons, in America since the 1980s through the 2010s.

In turn, the "iron law" or historical pattern of constant fascist, fundamentalist, and other conservative terror casts doubt on not only pacifying neo-fascists in contemporary Europe, as learned from the failed pacification of fascism in interwar times. It also does on pacifying "born again"

---

[1] Echoing Weber and Troeltsch, Maurer (1924:272–3), remarks that the Calvinist aims to "make his law the law of the land" and that the Puritan "sect is bound to capture the secular state in the name of the 'higher law'" [etc.].

Islamic and US fundamentalists by meeting their seemingly "sensible" demands for the greater "public role of religion" (Juergensmeyer 2003) as the supposed way of ending counter-state terrorism or anti-government violence. The greater "public role of religion" is an euphemism that invariably signifies for these fundamentalist groups and ultimately leads to theocracies in the Muslim world, like those resulting from such "godly" demands in Iran, Taliban-ruled regions, and elsewhere such as conceivably Turkey, and America, i.e., "American theocracy [as] Christian fascism" (Hedges 2006; also, Owens et al. 2010; Phillips 2006).

The second scenario of fundamentalist or neo-fascist counter-state terrorism operating as the effective means and path to state terror once fundamentalism or neo-fascism captures power has been already witnessed in America following the 2008 US Presidential Elections, just as before, for example, after the 1992 Election of another "liberal" and so "un-American" President, etc. This is indicated by certain terrorist acts or "hate crimes" and threats against various "ungodly" and "un-American" elements such as abortion[2] doctors or facilities (Juergensmeyer 2003; Lutz and Lutz 2004; also, Blee and Creasap 2010), "liberal" judges and politicians, etc. by fundamentalist/neo-fascist and other neo-conservative groups promising once seizing power to execute, as "Bible Belt" conservatives promise, or otherwise harshly punish offenders and to that extent "holy" state terror in the "name of God."

---

[2] Juergensmeyer (2003:27) remarks that the US Christian anti-abortion movement is "permeated with ideas from Dominion Theology (i.e.) America should "function as a Christian nation" [vs.] such "social moral evils" of secular society as ""abortion on demand, fornication, homosexuality, sexual entertainment, state usurpation of parental rights and God-given liberties [plus] redistribution of their wealth, and evolutionism taught as a monopoly viewpoint in the public schools." Further, for US fundamentalists their "justification of violence against abortion clinics is not the result of a personal vendetta against agencies with which (they) have moral differences, but the consequence of a grand religious vision [i.e.] part of a great crusade conducted by a Christian subculture in America that considers itself at war with the larger society and [even] victimized by it. This subculture sees itself justified in its violent responses to a vast and violent repression waged by secular [etc.] agents of a satanic force [i.e.] engaged in violence not for its own sake but as a response to the institutional violence of what they regard as a repressive secular government. [This] culture did not view [such violence] as an assault on civil liberties or as a vengeful and hateful crime [but] as firing the opening salvos in a great defensive Christian struggle against the secular state, a contest between the forces of spiritual truth and heathen darkness, in which the moral character of America as a righteous nation hangs in the balance" (Juergensmeyer 2003:36). In short, they view "violent abortion clinic protests as part of a "culture war" [i.e.] conflicts between "big and little government, high and low taxation, gun control and no gun control, abortion rights and no abortion rights, rights to sodomy and no sodomy rights" (Juergensmeyer 2003:147).

The scenario is also anticipated by the frantic arming of militia groups cum "Christian warriors" and their declared "godly" armed struggle[3] and "patriotic" threats ("Tea Parties") against the "big" and "ungodly" liberal government. For example, in the spring of 2010, federal prosecutors stated that "nine suspects tied to a Christian militia that was preparing for the Antichrist were charged with conspiring to kill police officers, then attack a funeral using homemade bombs in the hopes of killing more law enforcement personnel." Furthermore, the militia group called *Hutaree* signifying "Christian warrior" and each member wearing cross reportedly "planned to use the attack on police as a catalyst for a larger uprising against the government", i.e., as "part of an armed struggle against the U.S. government." Based on some Bible passages, the group publicly proclaims "we believe that one day, as prophecy says, there will be an Anti-Christ. Jesus wanted us to be ready to defend ourselves using the sword and stay alive using equipment. *The only thing on earth to save the testimony and those who follow it, are the members of the testimony, til* [sic] *the return of Christ in the clouds.*" As the leader's ex-wife said, "it started out as a Christian thing. You go to church. You pray. You take care of your family" and ended as, in the official indictment, as a plan to "levy war" against the U.S. government such that "to incite such a war, the group planned to murder law enforcement officials and then follow up their initial attacks with a separate attack on the fallen officers' funeral[s], where a large number of law enforcement personnel would no doubt be gathered."

Specifically, the target of these and related groups, notably the "Tea Party", is actually the minimal welfare state to be replaced by a maximal yet "small" police-warfare "godly" alternative whose favorite pastime is likely to be, as has been in the past, "holy" state and inter-state terror through government violent repression, including executions and mass imprisonment, and permanent global war on the "evil" world. This was especially witnessed during the health care reform and related reforms such as the economic stimulus tackling the Great Recession, and will likely be so long as fundamentalists, neo-fascists, and other

---

[3] As *Time* commented, "the Hutaree are a symptom of the continuing militia phenomenon, one that seems to have gained impetus since the election of Barack Obama as the first African-American President of the U.S. The Southern Poverty Law Center says that last year alone, the number of patriot and militia groups increased 244%, to 512. Though not necessarily racist, such groups fiercely oppose the federal government. In recent weeks, the health care debate seems to have fueled antigovernment sentiment that is far different from the last noticeable rise in extremist-group activity, after the 1992 election of Bill Clinton."

neo-conservatives remain outside of political power, as during 2008–10 (and 1992–94), notably the Federal government, including the Supreme Court, the total capture and control of which evidently remains their supreme goal, constant dream, and "God-given" commandment, notably for "born again" theocratic evangelicals (Davis and Robinson 2009; Hedges 2006; Keister 2008; King 2008; Lindsey 2008; Owens et al. 2010). For instance, reportedly a likely "Tea Party" member threatened to send snipers to "kill the children of the [Congress] members who voted yes" for the health care reform in 2010. In particular, one of such members was received the following phone message: "You're dead; we know where you live; we'll get you." Moreover, the ultra-conservative House Minority Leader, inciting or flirting with the anti-liberal and anti-welfare state tea party movement, was reported to say to another of those Congress members supporting the health reform something to the effect that he "may be a dead man." Most notoriously, a former Vice-Presidential candidate and would-be-President, following the passage of the health reform law, publicly disclosed locations of and targeted with guns about 20 members of Congress supporting the law, one of whom expressed the concern of being violently attacked and eventually was gravely wounded by an anti-government "lone wolf" in Arizona in January 2011.

The preceding implies that anti-liberalism and thus anti-democracy primarily (though not solely) and most forcefully and persistently assumes the form of conservatism and its inherent or eventual authoritarianism (Blinkhorn 2003; Dahrendorf 1979), as the immediate and perennial antagonist of liberalism and hence liberal democracy and civil society (Mannheim 1986). At this juncture, conservatism forms the anti-liberal, anti-democratic complex of the following fourth components. These are (a) initially authoritarian arch-conservatism born out of despotic medieval traditionalism in adverse reaction to nascent liberalism, (b) subsequently totalitarian fascism like Nazism, and (c) recently revived theocratic fundamentalism, and generally repressive, anti-egalitarian, militarist neo-conservatism, including Reaganism with its sequels and Thatcherism, and its (d) own subtype and product neo-fascism. Hence, anti-liberalism and anti-democracy harbors the initial, continuing, and likely future tendency to be epitomized, first and foremost, by conservatism, from arch-conservatism through fascism to religious fundamentalism, neo-conservatism, and to neo-fascism.

Conversely, conservatism in all its phases, forms, and settings has defined and legitimized itself as the design and social system of overt, uncompromising, and unapologetic anti-liberalism within Western society, especially America (the "Bible Belt", etc.), and beyond, particularly the Islamic world. Consequently, conservatism has operated, first openly and later covertly, as anti-democracy or conservative, including fundamentalist and fascist, illiberal "democracy" or "republic" as what Mises (1966) would call bogus-democracy. This is because without liberalism as the ideal and institutional system of political and all liberty democracy is, in his words, a "shallow form", as shown by Islamic, Southern "Bible Belt" (Dahrendorf 1979), and other religiously determined "democracies" and "republics" as anything but democracies understood as systems of societal liberties, human rights, and individual choices.

As the result of arising and operating in vehement antagonism to liberalism, conservatism categorically demands that, as Michels (1968) observes, liberal democracy "must be eliminated" by any available effective means and tactics a la Machiavelli. Ideally, such elimination is to be conducted by the "democratic way of the popular will" via free elections as a form of Weber's legal-rational legitimation of power charactering Western democracies (Lenski 1994), ultimately by violence and in that sense anti-government terrorist actions. The pattern was exemplified in putsches or subversions by the Nazis, fascists, and "other conservatives"[4] (Lutz and Lutz 2004) in interwar Europe and is continued through their neo-Nazi, neo-fascist, and neo-conservative heirs or the extreme right (Blee and Creasap 2010; Rydgren 2007a) in contemporary European and American societies.

To that extent, the elimination of liberal democracy by using its rules and mechanisms such as free elections and the like (parliamentary procedures, etc.) to ultimately destroy or pervert it beyond recognition is the supreme end that, as Pareto puts it, "justifies the means" in the manner of Machiavellianism, including ultimately a sort of categorical (Goodwin 2006) counter-state terrorism. It thus represents a proxy Pareto-optimum for conservatism in all of its phases, forms, and settings, from medievalist authoritarian paleo-conservatism through totalitarian fascism and theocratic fundamentalism to repressive neo-conservatism and anti-democratic neo-fascism, from the old Europe to the "new nation" of

---

[4] Lutz and Lutz (2004:149) add that "Hitler's abortive attempt in 1923 [the Beer Hall Putsch] to seize power in Bavaria (signaled) a takeover by right-wing groups elsewhere in Germany (and) then chose an electoral approach". Also, they suggest that "fascist ideologies of the right did not die with the defeat of Italy and Germany in WW II or with the deaths of Mussolini and Hitler. (Fascism) did not fall to the same level of disrepute in Italy, and (its) ideas survived defeat in WW II and have continued to be present in the political system (through) a campaign of right-wing terrorism" (Lutz and Lutz 2004:151).

America. It is a "higher cause" that, in the "beautiful minds" of conservatives, in particular fundamentalists and fascists, justifies virtually any anti-liberal and anti-democratic action, including the most egregious acts of anti-government violence, war, destruction, and coercion, simply counter-state terror.

Alternatively, if this optimum is not feasible, as in the presence of countervailing liberal-democratic forces, conservatism pursues the "second best option." This is perverting, exploiting, or manipulating a la Machiavellianism liberal democracy and its rules of the game in order to assure and perpetuate "for generations" (as US neo-conservatives say) the "predominance" (Dahrendorf 1979) of conservative groups, including allied fascists and theocrats or fundamentalists, through severe coercion and violent repression within society and offensive wars against other societies, and to that extent state and inter-state terror. In consequence, most contemporary terrorism can be diagnosed, explicated and predicted in accordance with the above tendency. Namely, anti-liberalism and thus anti-democracy as its major facet tends to manifest and operate as primarily conservatism. Conversely, the latter tends to be vehemently and openly anti-liberal and so, though more covertly, anti-democratic, despite its penchant to have what Michels (1968) calls a "specious democratic mask" when expedient, as during elections and related occasions.

Conservative Anti-Liberalism and Terrorism

Based on the previous considerations, most contemporary terrorism can be analyzed, explicated, and predicted primarily in terms of conservative, including fascist and religiously fundamentalist, anti-liberalism and thus, other things equal, anti-democracy. By assumption, conservative anti-liberalism and anti-democracy reflect ("load on") anti-modernism, and alternatively pre-modernism or traditionalism, specifically medievalism involving medieval feudalism, despotism, and theocracy cum "godly society". Most contemporary terrorism, in particular civil or religious-culture wars within society and aggressive war against other societies, is primarily Clausewitz's style "continuation" through escalation of the "politics" of conservative anti-liberalism and authoritarian anti-democracy, including conservative, fascist, and fundamentalist militant domestic policies and belligerent foreign "policy", by "other means".

Predictably, these "other means" include methodical violence or systematic use of force, destruction, severe coercion, and violent repression.

The latter particularly involves brutal, cruel, and inhumane punishment to the point of the death penalty for actual or imaginary crimes, as in American neo-conservatism and fascism, most egregiously Nazism, as well as sins and vices, as in most world religions, especially Islam and Calvinism and, in Weber's words, its "pure sect" Puritanism. Terrorism, including war, is consequently intrinsic, systemic, and constant rather than random, accidental, and transient in the "extended family" of conservative anti-liberalism and anti-democracy, notably fascism, religious fundamentalism, neo-conservatism, and neo-fascism.

However, conservatism tends to mask (Michels 1968) or embellish counter-state and especially state terror by its slogans of "law and order" (Dahrendorf 1979), particularly in contemporary America (Baumer, Messner and Rosenfeld 2003; Jacobs et al. 2007; Jacobs and Tope 2007). Especially, American neo-conservatism has proven the master of disguise, deception, and Machiavellian manipulation overall through slogans and claims of "freedom", "free enterprise and markets", "individualism", or "small government"–yet in the "all-American" form of anti-welfare, police, and warfare state as the "new [and old] Leviathan" (Bourdieu 1998)–expressing "libertarianism" (Buchanan 1991; Friedman 1982; Lipset and Marks 2000). Although even the most authoritarian conservatives and other anti-liberals like theocratic fundamentalists and totalitarian fascist or extreme-right groups tend to wear "a specious democratic mask" because of their penchant for changing the "disguise" (Michels 1968) within liberal democracy, such masks cannot hide the widely and continuously observed fact. This is that conservatism involves inherent, built-in terror as violent repression due to its intrinsic and intense anti-liberalism and so authoritarianism and even, in its (patho)logical forms fascism and theocracy, totalitarianism.

Notably, terrorism inheres to and derives from, in Michels' words, the "conservative spirit of the old master-caste" to be restored by any effective strategies, tactics, and ways. The latter characterizes conservatism as what Mannheim (1986) calls the "cold-blooded technique of domination" and thus a paradigmatic species of Machiavellianism understood in the sense, as Pareto also observes, of the "ends justifying the means", including violence, destruction, war, physical coercion, and violent repression. As Michels predicts, in virtue of its vehement anti-liberalism, conservatism, including fascism and theocratic fundamentalism, attempts to attain the "noble" end of eliminating liberal democracy ideally through the "democratic way of the popular will" like elections in which anti-liberal conservatives, including fascists and religious fundamentalists, are victorious. For instance, fascists as the self-declared representatives of the "new conservatism" (Blinkhorn 2003) were victorious in Germany's 1933 elections, just as religious fundamentalists have usually been in Iran after the Islamic Revolution and Taliban regions, as well as within the "extended family" or "big tent" of the neo-conservative counter-revolution typically in the US at least since the 1980s through 2010 (except for 1992 and 2008).

However, conservative and other anti-liberalism ultimately, as in electoral defeats and other political failures through non-violent procedures within liberal democracy, resorts to subversive violence and anti-government destruction, thus counter-state terrorism. This characterized the Nazis through their attacks against Germany's Weimar Republic and other fascists via their attempted violent subversion of liberal democracies in interwar Europe, including Italy, Spain, and other countries. Counter-state terrorism also characterizes Islamic fundamentalists by attacking formally secular states in Turkey, Egypt (until recently), etc., as well as "Christian" neo-Nazi militias a la "Sons of the Gestapo", "Dragons of God" (Blee and Creasap 2010; Juergensmeyer 2003; Turk 2004), and "Christian warriors". Like Islamic warriors, the latter declare a "holy" war against liberal democracy. For instance, this war climaxed in the 1995 Oklahoma City bombing and resumed recently, in particular versus the minimalist welfare state (Amenta et al. 2001; Quadagno 1999) construed as "big" government by these anti-liberal groups, during the 1990s, particularly in adverse reaction to the 1992 and 2008 Presidential and Congressional Elections of "liberal" Presidents and Congressmen.

Acts of such a "holy" war range from anti-abortion killings through planed armed anti-government struggle by "godly" militias to ultra-conservative violent or threatening "Tea Parties", etc. In this sense, European fascists and Islamic and US religious conservatives have always been and remain what Americans call "sore losers", virtually never in a dignified manner taking the electoral "No" (defeat) as the answer, just as hardly ever wholeheartedly embracing liberal democracy and its principles and methods, i.e., the democratic "rules of social games" (Dahrendorf 1979). For instance, this is shown in US neo-conservatism's refusal to accept with basic dignity and decency its 2008 (and 1992) electoral defeat and the election of an "un-American" President and "liberal" Congress, resulting in the rise of "Tea Parties" and similar anti-liberal groups immediately after and before the elections couching their acts or threats of anti-government violence and subversion as "American" and "patriotic defense" from "big" government.

In retrospect, by diagnosing the inherent "conservative spirit of the old master-caste" Michels anticipates an underlying source and rationale of conservative, including fascist and fundamentalist, anti-liberalism's tendency for terrorism, in particular counter-state and state and inter-state terror, namely anti-government violence and destruction on one hand and government severe coercion, violent repression, and aggressive war on the other. The factor is conservatism's restoring from the "golden past" pre-liberal and pre-democratic traditionalism in the form of medieval master-servant "godly" society such as feudalism, despotism, and theocracy replacing or perverting modern liberal democracy, thus being "paradise lost and found". Furthermore, Michels implies and predicts an alternative, negative factor of conservative anti-liberalism's tendency to state and counter-state terrorism. This is what he describes as conservatism's and by implication any anti-liberalism's, including fascism's and fundamentalism's, imperative or ultimate end that modern liberal democracy "must be eliminated" by any strategies, tactics, and means according to the Machiavellian recipe. Conservatism attempts to accomplish this goal of elimination ideally in a democratic way by using democracy to actually destroy it, as did Nazism through its victory in free elections and then eliminating them, and as (would) do Islamic and US fundamentalists. It does ultimately by unlawful anti-government violence, subversion, and destruction, and in that sense counter-state terrorism, as the means and path to eventual state terror through exerting systematic government coercion and violent repression once seizing power.

Specifically, in the ideal scenario conservatism eliminates liberal democracy through genuine or proxy state terrorism in the form of systematic government coercion and violent repression (Lutz and Lutz 2004) following an electoral victory according to democratic rules and procedures. This was epitomized by Nazism following its victory in Germany's 1933 Elections, as well as Islamic theocracies and fundamentalists (e.g., formal elections in Iran, the election of an Islamic-rooted government in Turkey, etc.) and to some degree US "born again" evangelicals and other neo-conservatives (Lindsey 2008) after their electoral victories at national and local levels since the 1980s (and before) through the 2010s. In the ultimate scenario, conservatism, notably fascism and religious fundamentalism, effectively eliminates liberal democracy and civil society through counter-state terrorism in the form of anti-government violence, subversion, and destruction. Conservative forces attempted violent elimination of liberal democracy initially through merging with *putschist* Nazism as the "new conservatism" against Germany's Weimar Republics (Blinkhorn 2003), and fully succeeded in this effort by allying with also subversive Italian, Spanish, and other fascism in the rest of inter-war Europe[5] (Lutz and Lutz 2004).

The conservative, specifically fundamentalist, pattern of eliminating democracy or formally secular government through anti-government violence was also witnessed during the Islamic Revolution in Iran, in Taliban-ruled regions, and most other Muslim countries, including even Turkey, transformed or attempted to transform into theocracies by resurgent religious fundamentalism. Similarly, the pattern was demonstrated by revived evangelicalism, embodied in "Christian" militias, and neo-conservatism as a whole in its perpetual violent "crusade" again the "big" government in America culminating in the 1995 Oklahoma City bombing and resuming in adverse reaction to the 2008 elections. The latest enactment of this "crusade" includes murders of or threats against abortion personnel and "liberal" politicians and judges, the frenzied buying of weapons by religious conservatives, violent or threatening hyper-conservative "Tea Parties", planned anti-government attacks by "Christian warriors", etc.

In this sense, terrorism simply inheres in and derives from conservatism's composite of anti-liberalism and consequently anti-democracy, including state, inter-state, and counter-state terrorisms. Specifically, this holds for state terrorism in the form of systematic government coercion and violent repression after conservatism seizes or greatly influences political power through formally democratic procedures like free elections, parliamentary voting, or what Pareto calls Machiavellian "machinations". The latter include conservative-fascist coalitions, as in interwar Europe, notably Germany, and postwar times, for example, neo-conservative-neo-fascist alliances in Italy a la Berlusconi and Mussolini's heirs, in Austria, Holland, some German states, and in part America through the merger or alliance of "born again" evangelicals and other neo-conservatives with neo-fascist groups like "Christian" terrorist anti-government militias (Rydgren 2007a; Turk 2004) since the 1980s through the 2010s, as after the 1992 and 2008 Elections of "liberal"

---

[5] Lutz and Lutz (2004:145) observe that "Mussolini's fascists in Italy took to the streets to do battle with the socialists and the communists [which] helped to promote the fascists as the best alternative available to conservative groups that wanted to prevent the socialists from disrupting the Italian political and economic systems or even of seizing power. It was the socialist agitation that permitted the fascists to organize and gain support from the middle classes and other groups in Italy."

Presidents and Congress. For instance, Comte observes that Puritanism ("Presbyterianism"), following its political victory in societies like Great Britain and America invariably conducts government "violent repression" and to that extent state terrorism, and consequently is "unfit" for governance in a liberal-democratic and rationalistic "positive" polity. Similarly, J. S. Mill notes that whenever and wherever in societal power Puritanism tends to violently suppress individual moral and other liberties, including "amusements" and in that sense to resort to state terrorism.

Comte-Mill's observations are diagnostic and predictive. They are diagnostic in that Puritanism, after the transiently victorious Puritan Revolution of 1640, attempted and in part succeeded to establish the system of state "holy terror", including "local terrorism" (Walzer 1963) in Great Britain, and, following its settlement in the "promised land", installed the "reign of terror" (Merril 1945) in New England. They are also predictive in that Puritan-rooted evangelicalism (Dunn and Woodard 1996; Munch 2001) in America has continued and even escalated and intensified Puritanism's original pattern of "violent repression" and thus state terrorism once seizing political power This is witnessed in a sequence from recreating the "old South" as the "Bible Belt" following the anti-liberal Great Awakenings to the repressive "godly" rule of "born again" fundamentalism and neo-conservatism since the 1980s through the 2010s.

Counter-state terror inheres to it when conservatism fails to seize power through democratic procedures and instead ultimately resorts to undemocratic, violent methods against liberal democracy in order to capture and control government and hence establish an authoritarian or, via fascism and theocracy, a totalitarian and tyrannical political system. This has been a pattern manifest and salient to conservative groups of virtually all types, places, and times. It spans from 18th century arch-conservatives attacking and occasionally reversing nascent liberal democracy (e.g., the temporary Restoration of the *ancien regime* in France after the Revolution) through fascists destroying democratic politics in interwar Europe to Islamic fundamentalists and "born again" evangelicals and other neo-conservatives in America and to European and American neo-fascists, all of them also seeking to violently eliminate or subvert this political system. As observed, while political conflict, including violence, is "normally" solved in liberal democracy through the "standard mix of controlled repression and limited concession", conservative, notably fascist and fundamentalist, counter-state terrorism is typically unwilling of "limited concessions", thus opting out of the democratic process by its "absolute, non-negotiable demands" and its use of violence[6] (Townshend 2002).

As known, interwar Europe provides a paradigmatic, but not isolated, exemplar of conservatism's, including fascism's, resort to anti-government violence and thus counter-state terrorism as the means of eliminating liberal democracy and of seizing power and then creating an authoritarian and even, via fascist rule, totalitarian political system. Recall fascism, including Nazism, was what Mannheim (1936) described as a conservative-based subversive or "putschist" movement seeking to seize power by systematic anti-government violence and exploiting the "crises of modern society", notably the Great Depression and the imputed "crisis" of liberal democracy such as Germany's Weimar Republic.

Not accidentally, this is an anti-liberal imputation shared by US conservatives (Deutsch and Soffer 1987; Dunn and Woodard 1996), including "born again" fundamentalists and neo-fascists, to the point of making "liberal" a pejorative L-word, indicating a striking continuity within the "extended family" of conservatism, with its "family members", totalitarian fascism and theocratic fundamentalism. Reportedly, "fascists and other conservatives" in Italy, Germany, and other European countries during the 1920–30s tried and eventually succeeded to seize power and establish "strong, authoritarian" or totalitarian governments, embodied by Mussolini and Hitler, through right-wing violence as counter-state terrorism (Lutz and Lutz 2004). As observed, counter-state terrorism was used as the effective means of creating a conservative, thus authoritarian, political system replacing liberal democracy by exposing the supposed "weaknesses of the democratic systems" and the need for their "replacement" by their opposite extolling "law and order", thus inventing a "crisis situation"

---

[6] Townshend (2002:36–7) remarks that "interestingly, though, it was a group of liberals who initiated the first modern regime of terror," but admits in the aim to "defend the country"—rather than, as typical of terrorism to attack other countries as well as government institutions within a society—as "the French republic, born with the deposition and execution of King Louis XVI in autumn 1792, was under threat from foreign invasion and internal rebellion." He adds that "the French Revolution's ruthless and systematic use of violence created a model for the application of terrorizing force by the holders of state power over the next couple of centuries. Although the prime exponents of terrorism "from above" were overtly repressive autocracies and despotisms, or radical revolutionary regimes [still], in times of crisis [liberal] constitutional states have also unleashed ferocious repressive action", as in France during the Paris Commune in 1871, as well as America at various historical points (Townshend (2002:38). As regards the latter, Townshend (2002:38) observes that the "USA tolerated (to say no more) the persistent, systematic terrorization of the Southern black community by the Ku Klux Klan, as well as the less dramatic use of intimidatory violence by employers against labour organizations".

(Lutz and Lutz 2004). To that extent, interwar fascist and generally conservative counter-state terrorism in the form of right-wing anti-government violence turned out to be effectively the means of establishing state terror via methodical government coercion and violent repression couched in and justified by "law and order" authoritarian slogans predictably adopted by contemporary conservatism (Dahrendorf 1979) or neo-conservatism, including neo-fascism, in Europe and America.

And Michels' two sources and rationales of terrorism and violence generally within conservative (and other) anti-liberalism are intertwined and mutually reinforcing, effectively blending in a twin, composite source and rationale. Thus, restoring the "conservative spirit of the old master-caste" defining the feudal, despotic, and theocratic *ancien regime* presupposes eliminating modern liberal, egalitarian, and inclusive democracy by any means, ultimately unlawful violence and war, simply counter-state terrorism. Conversely, eliminating liberal democracy is the necessary condition of and the first step toward restoring the "conservative spirit of the old master-caste" as the pre-liberal, pre-democratic or authoritarian, exclusionary, and pre-modern "golden past". Michels' early observations are pertinent and even predictive, for it is difficult, if not impossible, to comprehend and explain such terrorist or violent tendencies within conservative, notably fascist and fundamentalist, anti-liberalism unless considering conservatism's twin imperative. Recall that this is, first, the restoration of a master-servant society as the supreme goal-state and the perennial medieval ideal for conservatism's design of the "good society" (Dunn and Woodard 1996; Nisbet 1966). Second, it is the elimination of liberal democracy as the necessary condition by any means, strategies, and tactics a la Machiavelli, including counter-state terrorism or anti-government violence whenever and wherever expedient and effective.

Now, this may provoke a kind of negative "shock" to sensible conservative souls, especially in America, where conservatism, including neo-conservatism, unlike in Europe, has been construed as almost unmitigated "good", "godly", and so "all-American" by virtue of its anti-liberalism as well as medievalist pre-liberalism or traditionalism rooted in theocratic Puritanism, and liberalism has become "un-American" and a pejorative "L" word. Yet, as the saying goes, the truth can be cruel or brutal so that even such spurious masks and disguises cannot prevent eventually revealing that the "emperor has no cloths" with respect to conservative, notably fundamentalist, and any anti-liberalism and anti-democracy in relation to terrorism. This is demonstrated by the experience of America itself in recent times, as well as Islamic countries and groups, in both of which the intimate link of religious or other anti-liberal and anti-democratic conservatism with counter-state and state terrorisms is observed in what Weber may call its "pure" or even "purest" form.

If modern liberal democracy and civil society has been established or consolidated and legitimated through liberal "bourgeois" revolutions and constitutions (Moore 1993) like the French and American Revolution, then most contemporary terrorism is the ultimate form or initial stage of anti-liberal and anti-democratic counter-revolution as the violent and coercive attempt at restoration of the pre-liberal and pre-democratic, mostly medieval, past. Anti-liberal and anti-democratic counter-revolution is in a way terroristic in its own right due to its usual unlawful violence, aggressive war, destruction, severe coercion, and violent repression in the aim of eliminating or perverting liberal democracy, initially in the form of counter-state terrorism and ultimately, if successful, state terror. To that extent, terrorism only consummates, i.e., escalates and intensifies, such inherent violent, warlike, coercive, and repressive tendencies in anti-liberal and anti-democratic counter-revolutions. At the minimum, the preceding holds true of conservative-fascist counter-revolutions in interwar Europe, notably Nazi Germany, as well as their sequels in neo-conservatism and neo-fascism. This is exemplified by the "Neo-Conservative Revolution" (Bourdieu 1998), including yet another evangelical revival, in America since the 1980s through the 2010s. For example, the "revolution" enfolded and dominated at least until the 2008 Elections, yet resumed through anti-government attacks or threats by "Christian warriors", "Tea Parties", and related adverse counter-revolutionary reactions by what is often called the "crazy right"[7] following these and other political events, including the economic stimulus package, the health care reform, etc.

In essence, both conservative-fascist, notably Nazi, and neo-conservative-evangelical revolutions are more or less violent restorations of the "golden past" or "paradise lost", including, as the Nazis and US neo-conservatives proclaim, restoring "national honor", and thus counter-revolutions, through eliminating or perverting liberal democracy. For instance, "restore [national] honor" through eliminating "big" liberal government in America was the main theme and battle-cry at a meeting of "Tea Party" and related ultra-conservative groups in 2010.

---

[7] A Nobel-prize winning economist (Krugman 2009) and "proud liberal" refers to the "crazy right" and even the fiscally and politically conservative *Economist* describes religious-political conservatives from the US South as "Southern-fried crazies".

To that extent, all conservative revolutions form or generate instances of counter-state terrorism by anti-government violence initially and eventually, when successful and resulting in the seizure of political power, of state terrorism via systematic government coercion and violent repression. They are anti-liberal and anti-democratic counter-revolutions and thus cases of counter-state terrorism in the aim of preventing or reversing social change through liberalization and democratization. Conversely, they intend to restore the pre-liberal and pre-democratic "dead past", notably what Mises (1950) would call the medieval "peace of the cemetery" or the Dark Middle Ages of the feudal master-servant economy, political despotism, and total societal theocracy. In other words, conservative counter-revolutions function as the mechanism of counter-state terrorism in the service of establishing state terrorism in the form of totalitarian or theocratic coercion and violent repression. This is epitomized by Nazism and other fascism in interwar Europe, as well as neo-conservatism, notably "reborn" evangelicalism and neo-Nazism typically in merger or coalition a la "Christian" neo-Nazi militias, etc., in America and Islamic fundamentalism in Muslim countries and beyond. As a paradigmatic, but not sole, instance, the joint conservative-Nazi "revolution of nihilism" (Blinkhorn 2003) in Hitler's Germany was a counter-revolution involving initially counter-state and ultimately state terrorism. It was in virtue of attacking and eventually destroying liberal democracy through totalitarian coercion and repression and returning to "some recent or distant past" as the "golden era"[8] (Lutz and Lutz 2004) like the old "Germanic civilization" supposedly "corrupted" by liberalism (Bourdieu and Haacke 1995).

The above holds true as the general pattern for virtually all conservative, notably fundamentalist or theocratic and fascist or totalitarian, revolutions. Early instances include the fundamentalist Great Awakenings as counter-revolutions, notably "counter-offensives" (Means 1966), against liberalism, secularism, and rationalism, in particular the Enlightenment (Davis and Robinson 2009) as the Age of Reason, in America. Other

---

[8] Lutz and Lutz (2004:144) comment that conservative or right-wing groups aim through coercion and repression "to conserve what exists or seek to return to some recent or distant past situation that they feel should have been conserved. If the golden era is far enough in the past or different enough (Hitler's Germany), the changes being sought can be revolutionary rather than simply conservative. [They] support the existing institutions in society and the ruling elites or to return these elites to power and re-establish institutions." They add that before WW I the "ideologies of the right were in power as the political establishment" and hence through coercion and repression, thus state terrorism, while counter-state terrorism being used by left-wing groups (Lutz and Lutz 2004:144).

examples are the arch-conservative adverse reaction to the French Revolution and the transient restoration of the *ancien regime* and conservative-fascist "revolutionaries" (Blinkhorn 2003) in interwar Germany and Europe. Subsequent cases involve the "Neo-Conservative Revolution" and the new evangelical revival with its "holy" culture and military "warriors" in America, and fundamentalist Islamic revolutionary movements and regimes in Iran, Taliban-ruled regions, and other Muslim countries. At this juncture, the "Neo-Conservative Revolution" in America and to a lesser extent Europe is observed to effectively operate as a counter-revolution. Specifically, it does as the restoration essentially of feudalism and its master-servant regime in the form of capital-labor relations akin to those between feudal masters and servants (Bourdieu 1998) and premised on pro-capital, anti-labor ideology (Fligstein 2001; Hayagreeva et al. 2011; Myles 1994; Piven 2008; Western and Rosenfeld 2011), through state coercion and violent repression and in that sense state terrorism, just as anti-government violence by "Christian warriors" when not in power. Yet, this "revolution" has been remarkably successful in mass deception by replacing "the old Black Forest pastoral of the conservative revolutionaries [renamed "fascists] of the 1930s" with a new of dress of the "signs of modernity" (Bourdieu 1998).

Generally, like anti-liberalism and anti-democracy, anti-liberal and anti-democratic counter-revolution has primarily (though not only) assumed the form of conservative, including fascist and neo-conservative counter-revolutions as restorations of the "golden" past (Bourdieu 1998) and their religious equivalents in fundamentalist, theocratic revivals a la Islamic and evangelical revivalism, such as the "Great Awakenings" and their recent enactments in America. To that extent, this tendency characterizes, explains, and predicts contemporary terrorism accordingly. Contemporary terrorism is mostly, though not always, an ultimate outcome, or the early phase and herald, of conservative anti-liberal and anti-democratic counter-revolution as the restoration of the pre-liberal and pre-democratic past, notably fascist counter-revolutions and fundamentalist, theocratic revivals (Juergensmeyer 2003).

These revolts are terroristic in their own right due to their widespread resort to illegal violence, destruction, and war against liberal-democratic states, and, once in power, systematic government coercion and violent repression of "liberals" and the "ungodly". To that extent, terrorism just escalates and intensifies such violent, warlike, coercive, and repressive attributes and outcome of conservative, especially fascist and fundamentalist, anti-liberal and anti-democratic counter-revolutions. In sum, most contemporary terrorism is the radical outcome and expression of the anti-liberal and anti-democratic conservative reaction and counter-revolution. The latter strives to restore pre-liberalism and despotism, particularly medievalism and its theocracy as "paradise lost", supposedly due to modern liberal democracy as the main culprit, and to be "found" through destroying the latter replaced by pre-liberal "godly society".

Now, perhaps all, including liberal-democratic revolutions, thus the French and American Revolution, are "terrorist" in some description in virtue of involving a certain degree of illegitimate violence or war and coercion, especially from the stance of the *ancien regime* or the powers that be, tending to define the revolutionaries as "terrorists" or "criminals". For instance, some analysts (Lutz and Lutz 2004) include the "Boston Tea Party", as well as other "colonial situations" or anti-colonial revolutions, into "examples of successful terrorism" in virtue of representing a "successful prelude to the American War of Independence". Nevertheless, it is implausible in terms of liberty and democracy to equate, on grounds of shared violence and coercion, liberal-democratic revolutions such as the French and American Revolution with the pre-liberal, pre-democratic despotic *ancien* regime and the imperial power that they destroyed or supplanted, as well as with their attempted reversals through counter-revolutions or restorations, as in the first case, or aggressive military actions, as in the second.

In essence, liberal-democratic revolutions, including the French and American Revolution, initially aimed and eventually succeeded to eliminate unlawful violence, war, severe coercion and violent repression. For the latter are incompatible with their ideals and institutions of liberty and democracy (Townshend 2002), thus their "reign of terror" being transitory as well as defensive in facing destructive and fatal treats from within and outside society (e.g., 1792–5 in France, the 1790s in the US). In stark contrast, conservative, notably fundamentalist and fascist, counter-revolutions typically seek and succeed the exact opposite, namely perpetuating illegitimate, methodical, and widespread violence, war, destruction, severe coercion, and violent repression, thus both initially counter-state and ultimately state terrorism, while eliminating human liberty, including democracy, and eventually life. This indicates that their counter-state and state terrorism, such as severe coercion and violent repression within society and "holy" war against and destruction of other societies, is virtually perpetual and mostly offensive, a sort of "permanent counter-revolution", as witnessed in theocracy or fundamentalism and fascism.

Granted that liberal-democratic revolutions like the French and the American Revolution use counter-state terrorism in some description, i.e., as described by pre-liberal and pre-democratic or imperial powers such as the aristocratic *ancien regime*–of which Burke the putative inventor of the term "terror", alongside de Maistre, was the most vociferous defender (Schmidt 1996)–in France and the British imperial system in America. Even on this assumption, they do not resort to state terrorism during *long dureé* of centuries and even decades simply by virtue of establishing democracy and liberty, so a free open society, in place of pre-liberal despotism, excluding some temporary episodes of the defensive "reign of terror" dictated by internal and external life-threatening counter-attacks mentioned above. In fact, liberal revolutions' successful "counter-state terrorism" through defeating the despotic *ancien regime* or the foreign imperial power proves to be ultimately the instrument of abolishing or minimizing state terrorism in the sense of systematic government unlawful violence, coercion, and violent repression in the long-run. This was witnessed during the decades after the French and American Revolution, such that even Burke et al. would not describe today's liberal-democracies resulting from these revolutions in France, let alone America, as the "reign of terror" by government, as they did their revolutionary aftermath of a few years.

By stark contrast, anti-liberal, notably fascist and fundamentalist, counter-revolutions use counter-state terrorism via anti-government violence and subversion not to abolish or minimize, but rather to establish and perpetuate state terror through unlawful coercion, violent repression, and offensive war. And once established, state terror, including both severe coercion and violent repression within society and offensive war against and destruction of other societies, becomes a constant, a sort of permanent "revolution of nihilism" in the conservative, notably fascist and theocratic or fundamentalist, political systems resulting from these anti-liberal and anti-democratic counter-revolutions.

Thus, while state terrorism in liberal-democratic revolutions and political systems is as a rule temporary lasting only a few years or so (e.g., 1792–5 in France, etc.), it is virtually never-ending or enduring in conservative anti-liberal and anti-democratic counter-revolutions and regimes, notably fascism and theocracy. Recall that Nazism was intended to be the one-thousand-year system effectively of state terrorism, including violent domestic repression and aggressive foreign wars. Moreover, theocracy in general *cum* "God's Kingdom of Earth" has been invariably designed and established as a sort of eternal "holy terror", including severe coercion and violent repression against "infidels" within society and wars against "ungodly" societies, as exemplified by Islamic and Christian theocracies and their internal/external crusades and jihads respectively in the past and present. For instance, England's and New England's Puritan theocracy cum the "Biblical Commonwealth" was created as the eternal or at least millennial reign of "holy terror" (Merril 1945; Walzer 1963) through methodical and permanent government coercion, violent repression, and crusades (Kaufman 2008; Munch 2001), in accordance with Puritanism's millennialism (Kloppenberg 1998). This applies, with secondary modifications or embellishments, to its heir apparent the American "Bible Belt".

In sum, while both liberal-democratic revolutions and anti-liberal and anti-democratic counter-revolutions may share counter-state terrorism in some description through anti-government violence or force, they profoundly differ. The first, even if not immediately, eventually abolish or minimize state terrorism in the sense of systematic unlawful government coercion and violent repression within society and offensive war against other societies, and the second establish and perpetuate terror in its various forms as, in conservative, notably fascist and theocratic designs, an eternal or millennial condition of humanity. A paradigmatic but not isolated exemplar is torture and related practices of state terror in the form of government methodical coercion and violent repression. Liberal-democratic revolutions and societies in long terms have legally abolished and actually minimized torture, just as its correlate the death penalty, primarily due to the influence of Enlightenment liberalism (Einolf 2007). In stark and deadly contrast, their anti-liberal and anti-democratic counterparts continue to use and expand torturing, like executions for sins-crimes, as exemplified by Nazi Germany, Islamic theocracies or fundamentalist movements, the US neo-conservative "godly" government with (two) self-proclaimed "Evangelical Presidents" during 1981–2008.

For instance, Physicians for Human Rights reported that US medical personnel "experimented on terror detainees during CIA-led torture after the September 11 attacks", evoking the specter of Nazi medical experiments on prisoners. According to the report, the medical experimentation has been "performed to provide legal cover for torture" such that "these practices could, in some cases, constitute war crimes and crimes against humanity." Reportedly, medical personnel's "presence and complicity in intentionally harmful interrogation practices were not only apparently intended to enable the routine practice of torture, but also to serve as a potential legal defense against criminal liability for torture." The report suggests that "not only are these alleged acts gross violations of human rights law, they are a grave affront to America's core values". Particularly and hardly surprisingly, "the CIA appears to have broken all accepted legal and ethical standards put in place since the Second World War to protect prisoners from being the subjects of experimentation." Namely, "in their attempt to justify the war crime of torture, the CIA appears to have committed another alleged war crime – illegal experimentation on prisoners [and] Justice Department lawyers appear to never have assessed the lawfulness of the alleged research on detainees in CIA custody, despite how essential it appears to have been to their legal cover for torture." The report also suggests that Congress amend the War Crimes Act "to eliminate changes made to the act in 2006 which weaken the prohibition on biological experimentation on detainees." (Cynics may comment that this is "wishful thinking" so long as Congress is dominated by nationalistic and militaristic conservatives, from both political parties, openly inciting or supporting and even perpetrating, torture, as their seemingly favorite pastime since at least the Vietnam War, of "enemies" and "foreigners".) It concludes that US "health professionals engaged in research on detainees that violates the Geneva Conventions, The Common Rule (on US government research policies), the Nuremberg Code and other international and domestic prohibitions against illegal human subject research and experimentation."

The preceding hence proposes and predicts that the crucial source and rationale of most contemporary terrorism, including counter- and state terrorisms has been and remains conservative, especially fascist and religiously fundamentalist, anti-liberalism and anti-democracy, as a special facet of the general anti-modernism of conservatism, notably fascism and fundamentalism. In its present formulation, this is a relatively novel and seemingly surprising, if not "shocking" proposition ("indecent proposal") and prediction. This may seem so given conservatism's claims, slogans, and public image of "law and order", and even "freedom", "small government", "libertarianism", or "individualism". Such an image/discourse is witnessed especially in America during recent times, just as before, as during McCarthyism and the "red scare" (Smelser and Mitchell 2002; Vasi and Strang 2009), perhaps since the conservative extant source and perennial model, theocratic and aristocratic or oligarchic *cum* "individualistic" Puritanism (Bremer 1995; Dunn and Woodard 1996; Gould 1996; Kaufman 2008; Munch 2001).

Particularly, the above applies to American and British neo-conservatism, represented by Reaganism and Thatcherism, deceptively claiming to be a sort of "libertarianism" and even "modernism" in general

(Bourdieu 1998). Neo-conservative "libertarianism" presents itself as the design and system of unlimited "liberty" in the economy, notably "free enterprise and markets". Yet, this "libertarian paradise" is essentially economic anarchism in the form or the image of the Hobbesian anarchic state of nature, a la the "Wild West" (Hill 2002; Munch 1994) in Reaganism. This is in essence capitalist dictatorship in which capital or plutocracy has the literal or figurative "license to kill" (Desai 2005) with impunity, blended with violent social oppression of, labor and the masses overall, especially political exclusion and moralistic coercion and punishment, including execution and mass imprisonment for sins-crimes as "political terror", just as did pre-capitalist aristocracy of servants in feudalism.

Simply, it is the mix of Anarchy, thus absolute freedom for capitalist plutocracy with Leviathan (Buchanan 1991), i.e., moralistic tyranny, Puritan-style for the populace, notably ever increasing "violent repression" and in that sense state terror, including mass imprisonment and executions, for the American population (Pryor 2002). As has been said often during the 1980s-2010s, in America during neo-conservatism the wealthy and powerful acquire ever more wealth and power becoming ever more plutocracy or "top heavy" (Wolff 2002; also, Keister and Moller 2000; Keister 2008), and the rest of the American people actually or potentially "get prison" for committing sins-crimes like non-violent drug, alcohol, and sexual offenses and other Puritan-style or Orwellian "crimes", thus for being sinners. And since humans, as the Bible itself implies by "who has not sinned", are no moral "saints" or "angels" (Sommers and Block 1995), virtually all Americans face the prospect of getting prison in one form or another for their sins or pleasures such as those mentioned.

This holds true, given American neo-conservatism's "libertarian" Puritan-rooted and Islamic-style "obsession with sin and vice" defined as crime and hence punished with Draconian severity, including executed, through its admittedly "futile" temperance and culture wars a la "tough on crime" paranoia. And in the latter, like any societal madness as in Nazism (Bourdieu 2000) and its "holy" precursor Puritanism (McLaughlin 1996), legal justice is a nuisance or a sort of a luxury US conservative "holy" (and Muslim warriors) cannot afford in their crusade (or jihad) for what Weber would call the "glory of God of Calvinism", i.e., godliness and "purity" (Deutsch and Soffer 1987). For instance, neo-conservatism, namely the conservative Federal government, provides as a possibility the death penalty for such non-violent crimes as drug trade, though it is unknown if anyone has been executed for this activity so far. This makes one wonder what happened to the conservative "libertarian" ideal and protection of "free enterprise" in these "chemical substances" (Friedman 1997) and related "ungodly" goods and services, from alcohol, as during Prohibition, by new federal age restrictions, and in persistent non-alcohol or "dry" counties in the "Bible-Belt" and Utah, to consensual sexual activities (prostitution and the like).

At this juncture, Wall Street is perhaps the symbol and the 2008 Great Recession resulting from its financial excesses and abuses, not to mention the 1929 Great Depression, the outcome of such Hobbesian economic anarchy couched in and rationalized as "all-American", "unfettered" capitalism premised the dogma (Eggertsson 2008) or "fantasy" of laissez-faire (Kloppenberg 1998). The latter tends to eventually degenerate into capitalist dictatorship and/or "mafia capitalism" (Pryor 2002) epitomized by Enronism and related practices of accounting and all imaginable–in this respect, US capitalist entrepreneurs are really the most "innovative" in the world and history–kinds of financial fraud and deception (including fraudulent or deceptive advertising and marketing). These are committed in the function of fulfilling what Merton (1968) describes as the American dream of money "success" as the "sacrosanct goal" consecrating virtually "any means whatsoever", including such "sharp practices" as Veblen observed for the robber barons, to the point of becoming a rule, rather than an exception, in the economy.

By contrast, the prison and generally penal system, including death row, is the emblem of repressive Leviathan for the US population, as the mechanism of severe coercion and violent repression, notably the death penalty and mass long imprisonment for sins-crimes like non-violent drug offenses and related moral sins, and to that extent state terror, typically religiously rationalized and embellished. And the outcome is the explosion of "prisoners of ethical conscience" in virtue of being punished mostly, recall nearly two thirds, for moral sins like non-violent drug offenses (Wakefield and Uggen 2010) admittedly reclassified (Cooney and Burt 2008; Friedman 1997) as "crimes" during the neo-conservative Puritan-style and Islamic-like paranoid obsession with and crusade against sin and vice punished as crime.

In sum, the ever-growing vice-police state after the image of Leviathan is the symbol and product of such growing or continuing repression of the "sinful" population in America during "libertarian" and "godly" neo-conservatism since Reaganism through its sequels. The latter has promised and staged another return to power and eventually violent repression and in that sense state terror following the 2008 Elections and in counter-revolution embodied by neo-fascist "Tea Parties", "Christian warriors", etc.

against the minimalist welfare state–unable to provide health care to all Americans until the reform, for example—construed as big "liberal" government. In particular, American neo-conservative "libertarianism" is with national "pride and joy"—i.e., an invidious distinction from European "collectivism", "statism", and even "liberalism" (Friedman 1982; Lipset and Marks 2000)–self-defined and propagated or perceived in terms of unregulated economic "liberties", notably unrestricted "free-markets", and thus a slightly modified laissez-faire capitalist economy, if ever really existed in a significant degree, except for late 18th and early 19th century England (Habermas 1989). This economy is the type of "free enterprise system" existing prior to the Great Depression when Keynes (also, Popper 1966) and by implication Roosevelt through the New Deal declared the "end of laissez faire" as the rigid dogma with self-destructive outcome (Eggertsson 2008), as well as to the 2008 Great Recession (Stiglitz 2010).

Recall that both economic crises were caused and "generously" spread to and shared with the world through global social contamination or contagion[9] (Diamond and Rajan 2009) by such a "libertarian" and "all-American" brand of "unfettered" capitalism (Fishback 1998). Actually, in some accounts, the latter operates as or eventually degenerates into capitalist dictatorship and mafia-style and ultimately self-destructive (Beck 2000; Habermas 2001) capitalism with a deeply and persistently "inhuman face" (Pryor 2002) in contrast to the admittedly more human facet of European welfare capitalisms epitomized by Scandinavian welfare states, including the "more humane" (Reuter 2005) penal treatment of moral sinners like non-violent drug users in Europe.

Furthermore, neo-conservative "libertarianism" even claims to be the true and only "heir" or "custodian" of classical liberalism, including the idea and practice of free markets and political democracy, both originating in the 18th century Enlightenment (Buchanan and Tullock 1962; also, Davis and Robinson 2009). Yet, its anti-labor and pro-capital agenda (Fligstein 2001; Myles 1994; Piven 2008; Prior 2002), notably labor violent repression, thus a syndrome of state terror or system of capitalist dictatorship, compounded with moralistic severe coercion and political exclusion, makes American as well as British neo-conservatism a sort of polar opposite of true libertarianism such as modern liberalism. Simply, neo-conservatism is far from being "libertarian" and "democratic" (Tilman 2001) in the universalistic sense of Jefferson's "liberty and

---

[9] Diamond and Rajan (2009:608–9) suggest that the 2008 bankruptcy of Lehman Brothers [was] the trigger for a worldwide panic".

justice for all", i.e., liberalism in the classical and contemporary sense. Conversely, it is "libertarian" only for a narrow plutocracy or the "haves" (Dahrendorf 1979), thus oligarchy (Pryor 2002). The latter is generously entrusted with virtually unlimited liberty to the point of literal or figurative "license to kill" laborers and other "un-American" elements after the model or image of "Wild West" capitalism and cowboy "big-gun" capitalists epitomized by Enronism in Texas and beyond, not to mention non-Americans or foreign enemies via offensive wars on the "evil" world.

In general, neo-conservatism, including "libertarianism", like neo-fascism as the neo-conservative extreme, arises, operates, and persists in America and to a lesser extent Europe as strident anti-liberalism and thus, overtly or covertly (Tilman 2001), anti-democracy in counter-revolution to liberalism and democracy, for instance, against the liberalization of the 1960s, just as did arch-conservatism in adverse reaction to liberal-democratic ideology and modernity as its prime "antagonist". For instance, most US "libertarian" politicians, including some affiliated with or endorsed by the "Tea Party" movement, while preaching individual "liberty", oppose various civil liberties and rights, including the personal freedom of choice in birth control and related elements of private life (consensual sexuality, etc.). One wonders what will remain of "libertarianism" if such personal liberties and private choices are denied or restricted by these US "libertarians"–evidently, not much will remain.

Instead, "libertarianism" mutates in coercive and repressive conservatism, including capitalist dictatorship–which actually it has always been since Goldwater and Reagan and remains through the "Tea Party" movement–and to that extent with a built-in tendency for state terror via government coercion and violent repression, including the prohibition and Draconian punishment, in some cases with execution, of the freedom of choice in procreation and related personal liberties and choices, once in power. In short, like before, the latest installment of "libertarianism" in America proves to be a paradoxical or contradictory–yet "logical" for its adherents–mix of capitalist anarchism in economy with government coercion and violent repression in polity and civil society (Tilman 2001), and in that sense with state terror as defined. If the second statement sounds implausible may be illuminating to take a second look at most US self-declared "libertarian" politicians, including those tied with or supported by the ultra-conservative and violent "Tea Party", with their strong penchant for denying or suppressing various civil liberties and personal choices.

The preceding indicates that some things never change, or the "more they change, the more they stay the same", in conservatism, including fascism and fundamentalism, namely anti-liberal and thus anti-democratic antagonism and nihilism. In particular, neo-conservatism, including neo-fascism in postwar Europe and resurrected theocratic fundamentalism in contemporary America and the Islamic world reemerged from the "death" of conservatism (Dunn and Woodard 1996). And it has operated as the anti-Enlightenment (Habermas 1989), just as paleo-conservatism during the 18th and 19th centuries formed the "counter-Enlightenment" (Nisbet 1966) and alternatively the restoration of medievalism as its "model" which, as the Dark Middle Ages, the Enlightenment superseded in the first place.

Against this "libertarian" and "democratic" yet deceptive self-presentation and public-opinion image of neo-conservatism, especially its American version a la Reaganism, the task of this chapter is to eliminate or minimize the surprise or "shock" likely resulting from uncovering a close linkage, affinity, or convergence of conservative, including fascist, fundamentalist, neo-conservative, and neo-fascist, anti-liberalism and anti-democracy with terrorism. The linkage is a sort of sociological rule or historical-empirical pattern by analogy to Michels' "iron" law of oligarchy: "who says conservative, including fascist, fundamentalist, and neo-conservative anti-liberalism/anti-democracy, says terror in the form of illegitimate violence, war, destruction, severe coercion, and violent repression within society and against other societies." Exceptions are generally infrequent, if any, and impertinent that they effectively confirm rather than contradict this sociological law grounded on historical and empirical patterns, especially in long terms like the *long durée* of centuries (Braudel 1979) or Kondratieff's waves of 50–60 years.

Fascism and Terrorism

As indicated, fascism, notably Nazism, in interwar Europe was an ideology and system of initially, when outside government, counter state and subsequently, once in power, state and inter-state terror in its own right. Nazism and all fascism was the extreme form of anti-liberalism and totalitarian anti-democracy (Dahrendorf 1979), born as the monster-child and acting as the standard ally of traditional German and other European conservatism (Blinkhorn 2003). Thus, Nazism and all fascism arose, acted, and defined itself as the "new conservatism" (Blinkhorn 2003) aiming and eventually succeeding to totally implement the old conservative commandment that modern liberal democracy "must be eliminated" by any means, including both counter-state and state terror, thus the Nazis and fascists joining "other conservatives" (Lutz and Lutz 2004). Nazism and all fascism essentially remains extreme anti-liberalism and "new conservatism" through neo-Nazism and neo-fascism overall (the extreme right) in postwar Europe (Rydgren 2007a) and, while assuming a typically "godly" evangelical form or alliance (Hedges 2006) exemplified by "Christian" neo-Nazi militias, contemporary America (Blee and Creasap 2010), i.e., the radical product, subtype, and regular ally of neo-conservatism.

In interwar Europe fascism, notably Nazism, initially operated as, when in opposition to liberal democracy, including Germany's Weimar Republic, counter-state terrorism through anti-government violence, and ultimately once seizing political power, functioned as the total system of state and inter-state terror by systematic government coercion, violent repression, and war. This applies in part to the "all-American" functional substitute or proxy of European fascism, McCarthyism. The difference is that McCarthyism as essentially creation of conservatism (Bourdieu and Haacke 1995; Plotke 2002; Vasi and Strang 2009) operated only in a state or official form through government unlawful coercion and violent repression of "un-American" forces (Lipset 1955; Smelser and Mitchell 2002), no matter how short, as defended by its conservative creators and allies and hyper-patriotic sympathizers, for Nazism also lasted just a decade or so. Nazism was what Mannheim (1936) calls a putschist or subversive, violent conservative movement against the liberal-democratic Weimar Republic until 1933 and the totalitarian political system since then once seizing power, as were Italian and other fascisms in the rest of interwar Europe. Nazi and other fascist putsches epitomize counter-state and state terrorism in virtue of being violent government subversions with the express aim at and the ultimate outcome of destroying liberal-parliamentary democracies[10] (Lutz and Lutz 2004; also, Blinkhorn 2003), thus attaining the perennial conservative goal of elimination of modern democracy by either "bullet or ballot". Totalitarianism, as the total, extremely intense

---

[10] Lutz and Lutz (2004:247) remark that "in the 1930s in Eastern and Central Europe, the fascist parties using violence were successful in preventing the leftist parties from coming to power and aided in destroying parliamentary democracies, even when they did not take power themselves". In their view, for instance, "the fascists in Italy and the Nazis in Germany used street violence and intimidation as a successful adjunct to other political activities in their rise to power even if they could not maintain themselves in power" (Lutz and Lutz 2004:248).

system of government coercion and violent repression (Adorno 2001; Arendt 1951; Bahr 2002), epitomizes state and, by its typical offensive wars, inter-state terror.

The preceding, with minor modifications, holds good for neo-fascism, including neo-Nazism, in postwar Europe and America, embodied by "neo-Nazi" supremacists and militias self-described as "Christian warriors", though remaining in its counter-state phase and failing, as of yet, to reach again its ultimate stage of state terror in the way of total government coercion and violent repression. Still, certain instances and attempts of neo-fascism as state terrorism can be observed or anticipated in contemporary Europe and America alike. For instance, such cases are especially manifest and salient in present times, thus likely for the future, in Italy through neo-conservative-neo-fascist government coalitions (a la Berlusconi and Mussolini's heirs or sympathizers), then in some regional government and cities in Germany through overt alliances or covert sympathies between neo-conservatism (specifically, the Christian Democratic Union) and neo-Nazism, and similar fascist-conservative combinations even in liberal Holland.

Other instances are observed in America through "all-American" variations of the open coalition or "secret admiration" and the effective merger between neo-conservatism, notably resurrected religious fundamentalism cum evangelicalism, and neo-fascism in the form of "Christian" militias and other terrorist or radical groups, including "Tea Party" and similar neo-fascist movements in adverse reaction to liberal "big" and "ungodly" government. These alliances or "flirts" between neo-conservatives and neo-fascists often reach the no-return point of "fatal attraction" on the account of the resulting adverse fate or subversion of liberal democracy in America. Moreover, in some accounts, fundamentalism, especially Calvinist-inspired Dominionism (Juergensmeyer 2003) is considered a theological design and theocratic structure of "Christian fascism" in the form of a new "American theocracy", as in part established in the "Bible Belt"—not to mention Mormon-ruled Utah as the paradigmatic primeval theocratic state since its inception—and "born again" evangelicals are described as "American fascists" (Hedges 2006). To that extent, American, like Islamic, fundamentalism represents the religious vision or perpetual dream when outside government and once in power the effective social system of state and inter-estate terrorism, for established fascism and theocracy are paradigmatic instances of terror in the form of systematic government coercion and violent repression and aggressive war.

Such recent tendencies confirm what was said during the 1930s to the effect that if fascism and to that extent initially counter-state and ultimately state terrorism ever comes to America, it will, if has not already, come wrapped in the American flag and the Christian cross (Paxton 2004) by "Christian," more precisely Protestant evangelical, "warriors" as "all-American fascists" (Hedges 2006). (For instance, the camouflaged members of a Christian militia named Hutaree cum "Christian warrior", arrested and charged by federal authorities for conspiring an "armed struggle against the U.S. government" in 2010, reportedly wear a "patch on the left shoulder with a cross.") This substantively means fascism would come and stay in the composite form of political conservatism and religious fundamentalism, specifically Protestant evangelicalism and sectarianism resurrecting and even expanding with vengeance against liberal democracy and civil society (Munch 2001) condemned and to be destroyed as "ungodly" and "un-American" by "Christian soldiers" in their "Crusade for Christ" within and beyond America.

Fascism would be the compound of political neo-conservatism's invariant aggressive nationalism, militarism, and imperialism striving to build an "empire of liberty" through global offensive wars combined with fundamentalism's inherent moralistic theocratic coercion and violent repression after the perpetual model[11] (Juergensmeyer 2003) of what Weber calls New England's Puritan theocracy (Munch 2001) *cum* the "Biblical Commonwealth" as "unexampled tyranny", yet, to add, "exampled" or resurrected from the "dead past" since its demise through the "Bible Belt" and the like. Hence, if admittedly neo-fascism has effectively come to America in postwar times, notably in the "godly form" of "Christian fascism" (Hedges 2006), during the 1980s–2010s, then it has exactly as predicted for fascism, as indicated by the rise, operation, and remarkable persistence of fundamentalist neo-Nazi and related movements (Friedland 2002; Juergensmeyer 2003; Smith 1994; Turk 2004). This has happened or could happen through the composite of nationalistic, militaristic, and warlike political neo-conservatism and revived theocratic fundamentalism embodied by "born again" evangelicals as self-declared and only "Christian warriors" hence presumably entitled by "Divine Plan" to rule America and the world (Lindsey 2008), wrapping this "foreign"

---

[11] Juergensmeyer (2003:212) observes that the "idea of a nation based on ['Christian law and order', a 'Christian Republic'] is on the minds of Christian religious activists (with) the Protestant governments of the early American colonies (grounding) their constitutions in biblical law (as a model) or precedent for a "new kind of Christian government"."

European product in the "all-American" form of the flag and the cross combined.

However, such a combination of symbols and their underlying substantive elements of nationalism and militarism with religion is hardly an innovation. Fascism, including Nazism, in interwar Europe was more or less "wrapped" in the national flag and the Christian cross, by being the product or ally of traditional nationalistic, militaristic conservatism and theocratic religious orthodoxy alike, including Catholicism, the Orthodox Church, and Protestantism, as exemplified by its alliance with the Vatican Church in Italy, Spain, Croatia, and other Catholic countries. And it remains such through neo-Nazism and neo-fascism as extreme, violent, or right-wing, ultra-conservative movements (Rydgren 2007a).

In this connection, the difference between European fascism and neo-fascism and its American variant is in quasi-statistical "degrees of freedom" with respect to the flag and especially the cross, i.e., conservative nationalism, militarism, and imperialism on one hand and religious fundamentalism and theocracy on the other, not in the substance of these twin elements. Specifically, American neo-Nazism, embodied by "patriotic" and "Christian" militia warriors and related groups committing or threatening anti-government terrorism, while as wrapped in the national flag, thus nationalistic, militaristic, imperialistic, and warlike, as European fascism and neo-fascism, is even more and growingly so in the Christian cross. Thus, it is substantively more theocratic or fundamentalist than European fascism, perhaps excluding Mussolini's, Franco's, and other fascist mergers in Catholic countries with the Vatican Church. Hence, in all places and times within the "old world" and the "new nation" alike, fascism has come and neo-fascism is coming and likely will come wrapped in the national flag and the Christian cross, though somewhat more in the second wrap within "Christian [evangelical] America" than in "post-Christian" (Inglehart 2004; Norris 2004; Ruiter and Tubergen 2009), growingly secular Western Europe, including Scandinavia, Germany, France, even once Puritan England, etc. In general, just as fascism arose and operated within the "extended family" of arch-conservatism, including religious orthodoxy, in interwar Europe and early postwar America, neo-fascism does within that of neo-conservatism in contemporary European societies and, in particular within that of resurrected and expanded fundamentalism, American society.

In sum, the above redefines and reveals fascism, notably Nazism, as fundamentally the arch-conservative anti-liberal and anti-democratic system of counter-state and eventually state and inter-state terror.

Recall Nazism was self-described and self-extolled as the true or "new conservatism" (Blinkhorn 2003), with the Nazis and all fascists in interwar Europe behaving as or merging and allying with "other conservatives" (Lutz and Lutz 2004). In turn, neo-fascism, including neo-Nazism, is the system of the neo-conservative, in particular, as in America, revived fundamentalist, campaign of mostly oppositional terror in view of its failure so far to completely seize either by "bullet or ballot" political power in the manner that Nazism and fascism did in interwar Europe. Generally, neo-Nazism and all neo-fascism explicitly or explicitly presents and extols itself as the "true" neo-conservatism, including the "new" religious conservatism. This is especially witnessed in America, as neo-Nazi militias and other radical Christina Right groups a la "Tea Parties", etc. declare themselves as the genuine and only "conservatives", "Christians"—for example, "Christian identity", "Christian warriors", "Crusaders for Christ", or "Dragons of God" embodied by McVeigh[12] et al.–and so "Americans", a pattern of which the proto-fascist model and inspiration is undoubtedly the "godly" terrorist KKK in the "Bible Belt" (Bailey and Snedker 2011; Blee and Creasap 2010; Jacobs et al. 2005; Messner et al. 2005; Townshend 2002; Owens et al. 2010; Turk 2004).

Religious Fundamentalism and Terrorism

In addition to and conjunction with fascism, religious conservatism or fundamentalism arises, reinvents, and revives itself and functions as the "holy" form of anti-liberalism and thus theocratic anti-democracy. Religious fundamentalism has become the most relevant, persistent, and intense agent, source, and rationale of terrorism in Western and non-Western societies, including America, Europe, and Islamic and other developing countries (Friedland 2002; Juergensmeyer 2003). Fundamentalism operates as the prime mover of terrorism and generally experiences revival primarily in the form of persistent Islamic radicalism in Muslim environments and resurrected Christian, typically Protestant evangelicalism and sectarianism in Western societies, first and foremost,

---

[12] Juergensmeyer (2003:127) notes that "McVeigh and Nichols were fighting a quasi-religious war against the [US] government, and they chose a building that symbolized what they regarded as an oppressive government force". Also, "Sons of the Gestapo" "specified retaliation for the federal government's brutality at Waco [etc.] as the reason for the attack" on an Amtrak train in October 1995, Phoenix (Juergensmeyer (2003:130).

America, as well as other secondary forms like Catholic, Hindu, Buddhist, Judaic, etc. (Juergensmeyer[13] 2003).

Predictably and proudly or self-consciously, Islamic fundamentalism and "Christian" evangelicalism are paradigmatic exemplars of conservative anti-liberalism and theocratic anti-democracy. This is epitomized by the fundamentalist "integrisme" in Iran and the "evangelist churches of the Bible Belt" in America, belonging to the same category of anti-liberal, proto-totalitarian "solutions" Bauman 1997) to the supposed evil or danger of individual liberty and choice. Yet, they represent the type of solution that performs a "splendid" surgery (Mannheim 1986) or cures the disease (Keynes 1960), i.e., relieving the "burden" of individual liberty or the "agony of choice" (Bauman 1997, 2001; Crabtree and Pelham 2009), by killing the patient. They do so by eliminating human liberties, choices, and rights, and eventually humans and their lives (Bauman 2001) via the shared and functionally equivalent (Jacobs et al. 2005), notably religiously sanctified by Biblical and Koran law, system of death penalty for sins-as-crimes and offensive wars a la proxy crusades and jihads (Juergensmeyer 2003; Turner 2002), and to that extent state and inter-state terrorism as defined.

As noted, religious fundamentalism is difficult to disentangle or substantively distinguish from neo-fascism given the latter's typical godliness in the form of, especially in America, "Christian" neo-fascist groups, designing and creating "Christian fascism" through "American theocracy" (Hedges 2006; Phillips 2006), and to lesser or decreasing in European societies. Like its twin apparent or "close cousin" neo-fascism, the new religious fundamentalism arises, self-locates, and operates in the "extended family" of neo-conservatism, especially in America (e.g., the "big tent" of the Republican Party) since at least Reagan's "I am one of you [evangelicals]" infamous yet Machiavellian proclamation assuring his two

---

[13] Juergensmeyer (2003:205) finds that the US Christian militia's "attitudes toward modern liberal government (are) similar to those of neo-conservative Hindu (and Islamic) nationalists (agreeing) that liberal government expects an obedience that is "feminine" and "infantile." In turn, Christian militia groups disdain "liberal Protestantism" (Juergensmeyer 2003:219). Generally, according to Juergensmeyer (2003:221) "Christian, Jewish, Muslim (and other radical movements) have in common [a] reject[ing] the compromises with liberal values and secular institutions that were made by most mainstream religious leaders and organizations; [b] refus[ing] to observe the boundaries that secular society has imposed around religion—keeping it private rather than allowing it to intrude into public spaces; [c] replac[ing] what they regard as weak modern substitutes with the more vibrant and demanding forms of religion that they imagine to be a part of their tradition's beginnings."

electoral victories, a pattern followed also with success by another self-proclaimed "Evangelical President" in 2000–04.

The above redefines and reveals, like neo-fascism, revived religious fundamentalism, including both Islamic radicalism and Protestant evangelicalism, as essentially the neo-conservative extremely anti-liberal and consequently anti-democratic "holy" system, source, and sanctification of terrorism. The latter operates especially in Muslim countries or is committed by Islamic fundamentalists, as well as in Western societies, secondarily in Europe except for official terror, primarily in "evangelical America", i.e., the "Bible Belt" and other would-be theocratic ultra-conservative ("red") states. It incorporates both counter-state and state terrorism depending on what Weber would call specific "power constellations", i.e., whether fundamentalist and other conservative forces are outside of political power and in opposition to a liberal-secular government, as in Turkey and Egypt during recent times, the US during the 1960s and the 1990s and after the 2008 elections, *or* in total and other theocratic dominance, as in Iran, Saudi Arabia, Taliban-ruled regions, the "Bible Belt", Utah, etc.

For instance, the vast majority of major terrorist acts and threats in America since the late 1960s through the 2010s have been advocated, incited, committed, and supported, including but not limited to, the 1995 Oklahoma City[14] (Habermas et al. 1998) and 1996 Atlanta Olympics bombings, by "born again" religious fundamentalists and other conservative "right-wing" groups. These actions form part of their anti-liberal and anti-democratic "holy" war seeking to destroy forever "big" and "ungodly" liberal- government[15] (Blee and Creasap 2010; Juergensmeyer 2003;

---

[14] Habermas et al. (1998:118) comment that the "rising tide of fundamentalism and even terrorism (as witnessed by the Oklahoma bombing) [in the US] represent a warning signal. [The US and other] multicultural societies can be held together by a political culture, however much it has proven itself, only if democratic citizenship pays off not only in terms of liberal individual rights and rights of political participation, but also in the enjoyment of social and cultural rights."

[15] Juergensmeyer (2003:152) registers that a "Christian Identity novel (*The Turner Diaries*) imagines a scenario that begins with a liberal-dominated Congress enacting a law abolishing private ownership of firearms." In this account, US fundamentalists advocate a "biblically based religious politics to replace the secular government [based] on the conservative Dominion Theology [i.e.] that Christianity must reassert the dominion of God over all things, including secular politics and society [Falwell and Robertson] lead[ing] to a burst of social and political activism in the Christian right (the 1980–90s)" (Juergensmeyer 2003:26). Thus, *The Turner Diaries* describes an apocalyptic battle between freedom fighters and a dictatorial American government. Such [bombings] were necessary because of the mindset of dictatorial secularism that had been imposed on American

Smith 1994; Turk 2004). And judging by government reports, they are committed or planned and attempted by "holy" neo-conservative warriors a la "Christian warriors" at the time of writing these lines, especially following the 2008 Presidential election of a "liberal" and "un-American" President. A case in point is murdering or threatening and attacking abortion physicians, as well as non-conservative judges and politicians, etc. For instance, in June 2009, the media reported that "abortion providers say that threats of more slayings from [the person] accused in the shooting death of a high-profile Kansas abortion doctor [murdered in his church] proves the existence of a "violent, terrorist movement" coalescing around the issue", citing his statement "I know there are many other similar events planned around the country as long as abortion remains legal." Also, a physician commented that "I don't believe he is an isolated terrorist. There is more than one lunatic running loose in this country that can be influenced by the religious rhetoric". Another physician remarked that "it is exactly the same as the Taliban, but the Taliban is 8,000 miles away and the Taliban is too civilized to assassinate people in mosques."

In sum, by the time of writing these pages, terrorism in Western and non-Western societies has primarily become an "intimate affair" and "affirmative action" of revived religious, notably Islamic and Protestant cum "Christian" fundamentalism and/or neo-fascism, and hence rooted in and predicted by neo-conservative anti-liberalism and anti-democracy. At least such a tendency justifies and necessitates assuming and predicting conservative anti-liberalism and anti-democracy as the critical sociological determinant of most modern terrorism. Minimally, this holds true of counter-state and state religiously grounded or sanctified terrorism as the dominant or growing violent and destructive feature and threat, "plague", "curse", or "cancer" of modern society. Alternatively, it is difficult to understand and explain these "right-wing" forms of terrorism without considering conservative, notably revived fundamentalist and neo-fascist, anti-liberalism and anti-democracy and situating them within the latter as their overarching societal source, setting, and rationale and their concrete historical constellation, thus their explanatory, predictive, and justifying factor.

---

society as the result of an elaborate conspiracy orchestrated by liberals [etc.] hell-bent on depriving Christian society of its freedom and its spiritual moorings" (Juergensmeyer 2003:32).

Opposition to Liberal Democracy and Terrorism

As indicated, most contemporary terrorism can be either directly attributed or indirectly traced to the antagonistic reaction against modern liberal, including pluralist, democracy, and diverse civil society, and culture (Munch 2001), in particular "liberal-democratic polities" (Townshend 2002), as sociological theory posits and research documents. In this sense, it is mostly anti-liberal and thus anti-democratic terror, specifically counter-state terrorism initially and, if successful in seizing political power, state and inter-state terror ultimately. This holds true of most terrorist types, especially religiously based or sanctified counter-state and state terrorisms (Friedland 2002; Juergensmeyer 2003; Smith 1994) and other actions and agents of collective and individual violence, destruction, severe coercion, and violent repression mostly representing anti-liberal or anti-democratic terror (Habermas et al. 1998; Habermas 2001). In 20th-21st century society, instances of such terrorism include lynching in the post-bellum U.S. South (Bailey and Snedker 2011; Messner et al. 2005) and other forms of counter- and extra-state vigilante violence in America (Jacobs et al. 2005; also, Roche 2004) up to the 2010s, including racially motivated and xenophobic or anti-immigration vigilantism in ultra-conservative "red" states like Arizona, Texas, etc. Another instance is what recently have been officially designated by the US government as "hate crimes"—a designation which would include most of these acts–as the "close cousin" of terrorism proper (Krueger and Maleckova 2003; also, King et al. 2009).

Other instances of anti-liberal or anti-democratic terrorism are fascist *coups d'état* as violent counter-state attacks and attempted and often successful destructions of liberal democracy in interwar Europe, notably Nazi putsches in interwar Germany (Beck 2000) and Austria (Barnett and Woywode 2004). Their postwar and recent sequels or variations involve neo-fascist, including neo-Nazi, anti-government violence against liberal democracy in European and American societies, in the second assuming the "all-American" religious form of fundamentalist terrorist militias called "Crusaders for Christ", "Dragons of God", "Christian Identity", "Christian solders", and the like, combined with hyper-patriotic and "revolutionary" forms a la "Tea Party" and similar movements. Related cases of anti-liberal or anti-democratic terrorism are religiously driven and sanctified forms of terrorist agents and actions, especially those induced and justified by Islamic fundamentalism within non-Western and Western settings and Protestant evangelicalism and sectarianism in Western societies primarily America, as well as by other world religions (Juergensmeyer 2003). In turn, recall in modern America religiously grounded terrorism is typically fused or linked with neo-fascist anti-government violence, just as conversely. This fusion makes it difficult to disentangle or differentiate the two, as shown by "Christian" neo-Nazi terrorist militias and warriors fusing the new theocratic fundamentalism and destructive neo-fascism, notably using the design for "Christian America" as effective theocracy (Phillips 2006) to sanctify their fascist-style destruction, coercion, and violent repression, including domestic culture and global military wars, as "godly" activity and part of a cosmic war[16] (Juergensmeyer 2003).

As implied, the above is a variation on the theme that fascism in America has typically assumed or is likely to assume the "all-American" form of "Christian" fundamentalism, mostly Protestant evangelicalism and sectarianism. The latter perpetuates "vigorous Puritan hypocrisy" (Gould 1996) by not being, especially its theological design and social system of "American theocracy", called "Christian fascism", although it reportedly represents a "godly" proxy fascist order (Friedland 2002; Hedges 2006). Instead, it is named something more pleasing to and perhaps demanded by most deeply religious, mainly and ever-growingly and power-seeking (Lindsay 2008) evangelical, Americans, viz., "godly" or "faith-based" politics and society, "Christian" liberty, justice, and America, and the like such as "Christian science" and education, including "medicine" through the Bible and prayer, as exceptional and superior in relation to European fascism, specifically "ungodly" Nazism.

---

[16] Juergensmeyer (2003:217) comments that "religious concepts of cosmic war are ultimately beyond historical control, [although] they are identified with this-world struggles. A satanic enemy cannot be transformed; it can only be destroyed. The vast time lines of religious struggles also set them apart from secular conflicts. In spiritualizing violence, therefore, religion has given terrorism a remarkable power." Alternatively, in his view, "terrorism has given religion power as well [i.e.,] the political potency of religious ideology (Juergensmeyer 2003:218). Also, Lutz and Lutz (2004:72) observe that "religious groups that resort to terrorism [are] more willing to inflict mass casualties with their attacks, especially when the population is composed of unbelievers. Over half of the attacks (resulting in 25+ fatalities in the 1980s-90s) were undertaken by groups with religious motivations. Religious terrorists [too] see themselves as following a higher law [superseding] normal rules or behavior [i.e.,] in a struggle between good and evil, and any outsider is evil. Religious [terrorists] call for the purification of their society. The rites of purification necessary to re-establish the ideal society may lead to actions (causing) a large number of casualties as part of the process of purification. Such apocalyptical views may require massive rather than selective casualties."

At this juncture, it is sobering and potentially frightening that no less than around 70 percent of Americans at the start of the third millennium still continue to hold a sort of evangelicalism or Biblicism by believing that the Bible is "the actual word of God and is to be taken literally" (Edelman 2009) as Biblical inerrancy (Darnell and Sherkat 1997), just as they did in the early 18th century during the Puritan theocracy of New England (Kaufman 2008; Minch 2001). This is sobering and potentially frightening because such beliefs may cause and predict committing or at least advocating, inciting, supporting, and justifying both counter-state terrorism through anti-"big" liberal government violence and state "holy" terror in the form of government theocratic coercion and violent repression of the "ungodly" on a mass scale, including culture and global wars, perpetrated, advocated, incited, and sanctified as crusades for the "glory of God" by "crusaders for Christ". This was exemplified and prefigured by the 1995 Oklahoma City and 1996 Atlanta Olympics bombings incited, perpetrated, and supported openly by many, and perhaps covertly by most, US evangelicals (Juergensmeyer 2003), as well as neo-conservatives overall with their Reagan-style "godly" anti- "big" liberal government ideology and rhetoric.

In comparative terms, such prevalent evangelical beliefs, including the belief in and practice of "Crusades and Crusaders for Christ" broadly understood, in "Christian" America are functionally equivalent, in terms of their source or potential for anti-government and government terrorism, to Muslim societies' virtually universal belief in the Koran as the "word of Allah" and its literal application, notably jihad, like crusade, both in the sense of domestic culture and global military "holy" wars and warriors (Friedland 2002; Mansbach 2006; Turner 2002). No wonder that the two main types of contemporary terrorism in recent times have been those based on or sanctified by continuing Islamic fundamentalism and resurrected and expanded American evangelicalism, as in essence, despite some rationalizing or sympathetic accounts (Emerson and Hartman 2006; Lindsay 2008; Smith 2000), the "godly", "all-American" form that fascism takes on or is likely to take in America (Friedland 2002; Hedges 2006) in contrast to "ungodly" liberal Europe. Thus, the 70 percent of actual or potential evangelicalism seems frightening and likely will be fatal for Jeffersonian "liberty and justice for all" and even human happiness and life in America in the long *durée* of decades or centuries.

For this type of, like Islamic, fundamentalism can be expected with almost mathematical precision or high probability to ultimately result when outside government in mass-scale counter-state terrorism by "godly" anti-government violence cum "revolution" a la "Tea-Party" or other style. And once in political power it is likely to generate "holy" state terror through government systematic coercion and violent repression, as well as global war, both terrorist types being sanctified as a "crusade for Christ," just as it has done in the past and does in the present. As persons, the authors sincerely hope that this "irrational expectation" will not be fulfilled but nothing in the past and present of American, like Islamic, fundamentalism grounds and justifies such a hope. And there is no rational and realistic element to suggest that the latter will change and so end "as we know it", just as it is unrealistic that its twin neo-fascism will ever alter its nature and outcomes. Hence, on the account of its prospective and in part current consequences for both counter-state and state and inter-terror, the figure of the 70 percent of US evangelicals is perhaps functionally equivalent to the same percent of, say, neo-Nazis in Germany, not to mention Islamic fundamentalists in Turkey or Egypt, if the evangelical design or dream is "American theocracy" and thus "Christian fascism" (Hedges 2006).

The aforesaid may sound "outrageous" and "offensive" but is a logical derivation from the theological premise of fundamentalism and more importantly an historical-empirical generalization from its past and present theocratic practices or tendencies; after all, as is often said, the truth can be painful. Simply, religious fundamentalism perpetrated or advocated so many "unthinkable" acts of "holy" terror in American history and presently, from Puritanism's "witch trials" and proxy genocide of the Native Americans through Puritanical Prohibition and fundamentalist lynching and "Monkey Trials" to revived evangelicalism's violent culture wars, "tough" on sin-as-crime paranoia, executions, mass incarceration for sins-crimes, etc., that there is no "rational expectation" that it will miraculously desist in committing or advocating such actions in the future. And distinguishing, as recently done, "fundamentalism" from "evangelicalism" is a sort of distinction without difference, first, because evangelicalism or Biblicism is by definition the Christian type of fundamentalism. Second, it is trying to make the old and admittedly discredited US fundamentalists following the 1925 "Monkey Trial", etc. look better and more acceptable (Lindsey 2008; Smith 2000) by renaming them "born again evangelicals" cum the only and true "Christians", a change which is analogous to renaming "fascists" into "new conservatives", "nationalists", "true patriots", and the like (Rydgren 2007a).

Comparatively, however, the evangelical design of America as "godly" society vs. "ungodly" fascist Europe involves an incorrect distinction and thus false religious American "exceptionalism", because all fascism in interwar Europe was self-proclaimed "Christian", either "Catholic" (fascist Italy, Spain, Croatia, etc.) or "Protestant" or mixed (Nazi Germany, etc.), as has been neo-fascism, including neo-Nazism, in post-war European societies (Rydgren 2007a) and Latin American dictatorships during the 1970s-80s. This indicates that virtually always and everywhere, from interwar to postwar Europe and Latin America, fascism, including Nazism, tend to merge or ally and "flirt" with theocratic religion, thus to become "godly" or "Christian", not just in "exceptional" America as US fascist groups, from proto-fascist KKK to neo-Nazi "Christian" militias, did and do claim.

Antagonism to Political Pluralism and Culture Diversity and Terrorism

As implied, the hostility and opposition to modern Western liberal-pluralist democracy and society, as well as diverse culture and civil society, tends to cause and explain most contemporary terrorism. In other words, the antagonism to political pluralism, as well as to cultural diversity and civil-society diverse lifestyles, generates and predicts contemporary terrorism in its various forms, including counter-state and state terror, especially religiously based and sanctified anti-government violence and government violent repression. At this juncture, terrorism emerges and operates as the violent, destructive, warlike, coercive, and repressive form of adverse reaction to political pluralism, cultural and civil diversity, and generally liberal democracy and society, a kind of nihilism resulting from, expressing, thus predicted or anticipated by anti-pluralist, anti-diversity, and overall anti-liberal and anti-democratic antagonism. In short, terrorism arises as the extreme, violent form of the revolt against social pluralism and diversity in modern liberal-democratic society.

Hence, terrorism can be linked with, first, the opposition to modern liberal-pluralist democracy (Munch 2001) or political pluralism and, second, with the hostility to cultural diversity or multiculturalism defining multicultural societies (Habermas et al. 1998), as sociological theory posits and empirical research documents. For instance, in America anti-"big" government, mostly religiously based and sanctified, terrorism perpetrated, incited, advocated, or supported by individuals and groups is reportedly rooted in and explained by the hostility to "increasing pluralism" in politics, culture, and civil society, especially growing "pluralist cultural values" as "un-American" and "ungodly" elements, in American society[17] (Edgell et al. 2006; Juergensmeyer 2003; also, Bauman 2001; Friedland 2002; Habermas et al. 1998; Turk 2004).

In consequence, terrorism and related forms of violence and destruction are more likely to be advocated, committed, and supported by those individuals, social groups, states, and societies that are hostile and opposed toward modern Western pluralistic democracy and diverse culture/civil society, including increasing political pluralism and cultural-civic diversity, than are by others. As before, while not all individuals, social groups, states, and societies hostile to and opposing political pluralism and multiculturalism invariably perpetrate or defend terrorism, they typically tend to do so more persistently and intensively than others. Simply, politically anti-pluralist and culturally anti-diversity, so mostly conservative, individual and collective agents exhibit a stronger and more persistent tendency for perpetrating or defending terrorism and related forms of violence such as hate crimes than do others. This holds for most types of terrorism, including anti-government and government, religious, conservative, domestic and transnational, within- and inter-society terrorisms, as well as individual and collective agents, notably terrorist organizations *and* violent governments and societies. In general, much of terrorism develops as a violent form or extreme expression of culture wars and symbolic violence. In this sense, terrorism operates as a kind of revolt against modern culture, notably cultural liberalization and diversity, through violence, destruction, war, coercion, and violent repression, which especially applies to religiously motivated terrorist actions and agents in contemporary America and the Islamic world[18] (Juergensmeyer 2003; also, Alexander 2004).

---

[17] In Juergensmeyer's (2003:135) account, US "Christian" terrorists "wanted to proclaim freedom of white Americans from the increasing pluralism of American society." Namely, they "saw evidence of an antireligious governmental pogrom in what they regarded as a pandering to pluralist cultural values in a society with no single set of religious moorings" (Juergensmeyer 2003:226).

[18] Juergensmeyer (2003:13) suggests that a "cultural approach to analyzing terrorist movements (aims) at reconstructing the terrorists" world views from within [i.e.] a comparative cultural study of religious terrorism. "In this view, religious terrorism [is] *performance* [symbolic] *violence*. Public ritual [is] the province of religion, and this is one of the reasons that performance violence comes so naturally to activists from a religious background. [Just as] there is a violent streak in the history of religion [so] terrorist acts have a symbolic side and [thus] mimic religious rites. When [observers take] these acts seriously—are disgusted and repelled by them, and begin to distrust the peacefulness of the world around us—the purposes of [religious terrorism as theater] are achieved" (Juergensmeyer 2003:124–6). For instance, often the "symbolism of the locale was specific: the abortion clinics in the US that were bombed by religious pro-life activists or the tourist boats and hotels in Egypt that were attacked by Islamic activists who regarded them as

Summary: Anti-Liberalism and Modern Terrorism

Most contemporary terrorism can be explained and predicted as an expression and outcome of antagonism or counterrevolution by anti-liberalism, specifically extreme, reactionary conservatism, against modern liberalism as an ideological and social system and historical period in the form of violent rebellion against the latter. Previous sociological theory and research suggest this explanation and prediction of contemporary terrorism. In general, they indicate that conservatism originally identified and attacked liberalism, including its project of liberal democracy and society, as the "immediate antagonist" (Mannheim 1986; also, Nisbet 1966), thus defining itself in terms of counter-liberal antagonism or anti-liberalism (Dahrendorf 1979). Notably, conservative and related anti-liberalism (Dahrendorf 1979; Mannheim[19] 1986), including neo-conservative antagonism and counterrevolution against modern liberalism (Beck 2000; Bourdieu 1998; Giddens 2000; Habermas 1989), are observed to be effectively or potentially associated with contemporary terrorism, including its counter-state and state, religious and non-religious forms.

In particular, fascism as the extreme subtype of conservatism and of anti-liberalism (Blinkhorn 2003; Dahrendorf 1979; Paxton 2004) is identified as the salient source and predictor of counter-state and state, religious and non-religious, intra- and inter-society terrorism (Habermas 2001). Also, research identifies extreme theological-religious conservatism or cultural anti-liberalism as the source and rationale of counter-state terrorism and related violence by certain groups in historical and contemporary America,[20] as well as by Islamic (Feldstein 2008) and other conservative religious or theocratic forces (Juergensmeyer 2003). For instance,

---

impositions from a foreign culture" (Juergensmeyer 2003:131). In this context, "what makes an act terrorism is that it terrifies [i.e.] a social event with both real and symbolic aspects. These rites of violence [bring] an alternative view of public reality—not just a single society in transition, but a world challenged by strident religious visions of transforming change" (Juergensmeyer 2003:139–44). Juergensmeyer (2003:185) concludes that "for those in cultures of violence who experience both despair and defiance over what they perceive to be hopeless situations, religion provides a solution: cosmic war. As opponents become satanized and regarded as "forces of evil" or "black-coated bachelors from hell," the world begins to make sense".

[19] Mannheim (1986) observes that conservatism was born out of medieval traditionalism, in adverse, including violent, reaction to modern liberalism defined and attacked as the "immediate antagonist".

[20] For instance, Juergensmeyer (2003) identifies the "conservative Dominion Theology" in America as the theological-religious ground or rationale for terrorist and other violent activities by "Christian" militias and allied groups.

conservative religious and other social groups are found to be the prime perpetrators and/or supporters of lynching as a form of "terroristic social control" (Messner et al. 2005; also, Bailey and Snedker 2011) and other collective vigilante violence (Jacobs et al. 2005; Roche 2004) and hate crimes as a proxy of terrorism in the South and elsewhere in America during the past and present (King et al. 2009).

Hence, terrorism and related forms of violence and destruction are more likely to be advocated, committed, and supported by those individuals, social groups, states, and societies that espouse, practice, and institute conservatism, including religious fundamentalism or theocracy and fascism, and anti-liberalism overall than are by others. This leads to a qualification and a specification. The qualification is that not all individuals, social groups, states, and societies espousing conservatism and generally anti-liberalism necessarily advocate, commit and support terrorism, but they typically have a tendency to do more than do others. The specification is that virtually all individuals, social groups, states, and societies with religiously fundamentalist or theocratic and fascist ideas, practices, and institutions tend to advocate, incite, commit, and support terrorist and other violent actions more than do others, because theocracy premised on religious fundamentalism and fascism are designs and systems of terror in their own right, specifically, once established in power, of state and inter-societal terror via government violent repression and global wars. The above helps to account for and anticipate most types of contemporary terrorism, including anti-government and government, religious and quasi-religious, conservative and other anti-liberal, domestic and transnational, within- and across-society terror, just as individuals, groups, governments, and societies of violence.

As a variation on the previous, terrorism can be explained and predicted as an expression and outcome of the antagonism by absolutism and monism, as the typical attributes of anti-liberalism, in particular conservatism and fascism, to social pluralism and relativism through violent rebellion against the latter. Previous theory and research suggest that absolutism and monism, or anti-relativism and anti-pluralism, identified as typical conservative, notably fascist and theocratic, properties, is likely linked with terrorism and related forms of violence and coercion overall. These include fascism's, notably Nazism's, totalitarian counter-state "putschist" and state terrorism (Adorno 2001; Arendt 1951; Bahr 2002; Dahrendorf 1959; Habermas 2001; Mannheim 1986; Mises 1966), past and present theocracies' oppositional when not established or disestablished, and official "holy" terror or repression and war (Bauman 1997;

Juergensmeyer 1994; Stivers 1994; Walzer 1963; Zaret 1989). In particular, religious absolutism is observed to be the source or "sacred" rationale of counter-state and intra-society, as well as counter-state and inter-society, terrorism and related forms of violence, from past and present violent vigilantism and hate crimes (Jacobs et al. 2005; King et al. 2009) Krueger and Maleckova 2003; Roche 2004) to "holy" culture and military wars in contemporary societies, including America and Islamic countries (Friedland 2001; Juergensmeyer 2003; Smelser and Mitchell 2002; Turner 2002).

As a result, terrorism and related forms of violence and destruction are more likely to be advocated, committed, and supported by those individuals, social groups, states, and societies that espouse, practice, and institute absolutism and monism by claiming absolute and exclusive truths and values than are by others. As before, this does not mean that all absolutist and monistic or monopolistic–in Weber's general sense of "monocratic"–individuals, groups, states, and societies engage in, advocate, and support terrorist and related violent activities, but they tend to do so more than others. And the above can explain and predict most types of contemporary terrorism, particularly counter-state and state, domestic and transnational, religious and non- or quasi-religious, including Nazi-fascist, intra- and inter-society terrorisms, thus terrorist or violent social groups, governments and societies.

CHAPTER FIVE

ANTI-SECULARISM AND MODERN TERRORISM

Antagonism toward Secular Modernity as the Factor of Modern Terrorism

This chapter argues and demonstrates that anti-secularism, i.e., the antagonism to and reversal of secular modernity, is a major factor and predictor of modern, notably religious, terror. Most contemporary, especially religiously founded and rationalized, terrorism has been and is likely to be the product and expression of the hostility and revolt against secular, conjoined and mutually reinforced with the antagonism to liberal-democratic, Western modernity. Simply, it follows from and reflects anti-secularism as another facet, alongside and in interconnection with anti-liberalism and anti-democracy, of anti-modernism as the principal, overarching determinant and predictor of contemporary terrorism.

Contemporary terrorism mostly can be attributed to and hence explained and predicted by the adverse reaction toward modern Western secular society, politics, and culture, in conjunction and mutual reinforcement with the opposition to the project and system of liberal democracy and modernity. This reaction includes opposing and eventually reversing the process of secularization, as part of the composite and intertwined processes of liberalization, democratization, and rationalization, as well as of economic, political, and cultural globalization, in contemporary societies (Gorski and Altinordu 2008; Juergensmeyer 2003; Inglehart 2004; Norris and Inglehart 2004; Ruiter and Tubergen 2009). Comparatively, the process of secularization or the institutional condition of secularism as the target of religiously sanctified terrorism, has been especially manifest, salient, and probably irreversible in Western Europe, notably Scandinavia becoming a sort of "post-Christian" (Inglehart 2004) society during recent times, and to a lesser extent and in more complex and ambivalent ways in America.

In particular, while remaining the most religious, "godly," and fundamentalist or evangelical Western society (Edgell et al. 2006; Inglehart 2004; Lindsay 2008; Lipset 1996), notably the last Puritan nation (Munch 2001) and in that sense the "only remaining primitive society" (Baudrillard 1999) within the Western world, America has also experienced the process of increased, though relatively secondary and limited, secularization during recent years. For instance, this is indicated by the growing numbers of Americans (around 20 percentage) without formal religious affiliation, yet unlike in the "old world", along with and partly in response to the revival of fundamentalism cum evangelicalism or the "religious right" with extreme theocratic and generally anti-democratic coercive-repressive political ambitions and actions (Davis and Robinson 2009; Hedges 2006; Hout and Fischer 2002; Owens et al. 2010). Contrary to rational choice and neo-conservative vehement denials of and assaults on secularization as, like liberalization and implicitly democratization, "foreign", "European", and un-American", by the early 21st century Americans with "no religion" have become the fastest growing (non) religious category. This has occurred in addition and counter-balance to rapidly expanding extreme evangelical sects and cults, including "Christian warriors", challenging and supplanting mainline Protestantism (Hout and Fischer 2002; Madsen 2009; Martin 2002; Vaisey 2009) to become the dominant religious denomination in contemporary America. The above indicates increasing liberal-democratic secularism even in America and as a sort of oasis or island in the "desert" (Baudrillard 1999) or "paradise" of a "godly" growingly evangelical society, including evangelicals' aspiration for and penetration into the "power elite" (Lindsay 2008) in the theocratic "Bible Belt" and beyond.

No doubt, secularization in contemporary America finds itself in the midst of and as the secondary alternative to revived and expanded primary evangelicalism and sectarianism. Thus, it faces the anti-democratic compound of Puritan-inspired theocratic anti-secularism and anti-liberalism (Juergensmeyer 1994; Kaufman 2008; Munch 2001) with its design and partly realized system of "American theocracy" (Phillips 2006), i.e., "Christian fascism" (Hedges 2006) cum "faith-based" society, as explicitly designed and almost fully implemented in the "Bible Belt" and beyond (theocratic Mormon-ruled Utah, etc.). In passing, estimates for the share of evangelicalism and thus Protestant cum "Christian" fundamentalism (Davis and Robinson 2009; Hicks 2006; King 2008; Somers and Block 2006) in America today range from at the minimum one quarter or third based on formal affiliation (Keister 2008; Hout and Fischer 2002; Lindsey 2008; Madsen 2009) to no less than almost three quarters on the basis of expressed personal religious views of the Bible as the "actual word of God and is to be taken literally" (Edelman 2009; Edgell et al. 2006) and conceivably Bible-inspired individual actions, "words and deeds". The second estimate of evangelicalism and thus anti-secularism[1] (Edgell et al. 2006; Lichterman 2008) as well as anti-liberalism, anti-individualism, anti-rationalism or counter-Enlightenment, and counter-modernism overall (Davis and Robinson 2009; also, Evans and Evans 2008) in today's America seems more plausible in virtue of being based on substantive rather than formal criteria, on beliefs and implicitly actions, and not merely nominal, often passive membership. Such dominance of Puritan-inspired evangelicalism in American society does and will likely have corresponding implications for both counter-state terrorism when evangelical anti-secularists are in opposition to secular government and state terror once they seize political power by "ballot or bullet". And seizing power is what they fanatically or persistently attempt to do at the total federal level (Davis and Robinson 2009; Hedges 2006; Lindsey 2008; Owens et al. 2010) and succeed at partial regional levels (King 2008), as in the "Bible Belt" (Bauman 1997; Hicks 2006) and beyond, evidently emulating (Friedland 2001; Turner 2002) and reportedly admiring (Juergensmeyer 2003) Taliban and other Islamic fundamentalists in their equivalent theocratic attempts and successes.

In turn, as a manifest and salient determinant and predictor of terrorism, anti-secularism exists and operates in reciprocal relationship and reinforcement with anti-liberalism and anti-democracy as another such factor considered earlier. Consequently, anti-secularism and anti-liberalism/anti-democracy form a truly twin, composite determinant and predictor of terrorism in the shape of antagonism toward modern liberal-democratic and secular modernity, i.e., liberal-secular democracy and society. Hence, intertwined and mutually reinforcing with anti-liberalism and anti-democracy, anti-secularism through its hostility to and its attempted reversal of modern increasingly secularized society, including politics, the civil sphere, and culture alike, generates or exacerbates, endorses, and exploits terror in its various types, especially religiously grounded and sanctified counter-state and state terrorisms.

---

[1] Edgell et al. (2006:225) find that evangelicalism in the form of conservative Protestantism in America rejects the "possibility of a secular basis for the good society". In particular, Lichterman (2007:253) observes that US "evangelical Protestant congregations are less likely than others to run government-funded social services" and (hence) the "symbolic politics of the faith-based initiatives enterprise matters at least to white evangelicals for reasons apart from any strong interest in proselytizing clients". Relatedly, Ruiter and Graaf (2006:194) refer to the finding that "conservative Protestant denominations discourage secular volunteering".

As implied and expected, anti-secularism primarily has assumed and will likely assume the form of the survival and even revival of religious fundamentalism (Darnell and Sherkat 1997; Eisenstadt 1999; Emerson and Hartman 2006; Lutz and Lutz 2004; Townshend 2002), including religiously sanctified nationalism (Friedland 2001), especially, though not only, in Islamic settings and America during recent times. In turn, such survival and notably revival of Islamic, Protestant cum "Christian", and other fundamentalism seems "quite puzzling" according to the "long-standing liberal assumption" that the process of secularization and generally cultural rationalization, just as liberalization and democratization, is "irreversible"[2] (Townshend 2002). And the process has essentially been irreversible, contradicting rational choice and other conservative denials of and assaults on secularization, within Western modernity in its *long durée* of centuries or decades, which especially holds true of Europe (excepting, for example, post-communist Catholic Poland descending into a proxy theocratic system during recent times).

On the other hand, historical and contemporary America, with some qualifications such as the dramatic rise of people with no religious affiliation recently, is a "deviant case" (Baker and Inglehart 2000) manifesting the "phenomenon of American exceptionalism" (Inglehart 2004), thus confirming rather than contradicting the sociological rule or historical pattern of secularization and rationalization overall within Western society (Gorski and Altinordu 2008; Norris and Inglehart 2004; Ruiter and Tubergen 2009). At this juncture, the revival of religious, particularly Islamic and Protestant "Christian", fundamentalism represents the anti-secular radical revolt against the seemingly irreversible process of secularization, just as rationalization, liberalization, and democratization, within Western liberal modernity, including partly or eventually in "godly" America. Such revolt tends to reach the point of what fundamentalist "Christian warriors" construe as the cosmic "war between religious and secular authority"[3] (Juergensmeyer 2003). This "holy" warfare aims at devaluation and eventually elimination of secular politics in favor of a

---

[2] Townshend (2002:96) adds that the "long-standing liberal assumption that the rise of modern society and the decay of religion were two sides of the same coin was suddenly thrown into doubt (with) religion (being) consigned to the margins of terrorist motivation". Also, Townshend (2002:101) comments that "religious violence [may be] 'terror'; but it remains important to maintain a distinction between terror and terrorism [i.e.] fanaticism rather than terrorism", subscribing to the view that "where religion has been the principal justification for contemporary terror, the results have been more deadly".

[3] According to Juergensmeyer (2003:133), "in the war between religious and secular authority, the loss of a secular government's ability to control and secure public spaces,

theocratic or equivalent government (Blee and Creasap 2010; Hedges 2006; Juergensmeyer 2003; Owens et al. 2010) and to that extent "holy" systematic state terror after the perennial model of the old Puritan theocracy (Juergensmeyer 1994; Kaufman 2008; Munch 2001) and its "reign of terror" (Merril 1945) and in admiration for or affinity with contemporary Islamic theocracies (Friedland 2001; Turner 2002).

And most contemporary terrorism, at least in Muslim environments and America, has been the violent expression and result of the anti-secular revolt or "cosmic war" by Islamic, Protestant, and other religious fundamentalism against the process of secularization and rationalization and the resulting secularized and rationalistic state, culture, and civil society, as well as liberalization and democratization and the ensuing political system of liberal democracy. Reportedly, the "explosion of religious terror" in contemporary societies, in particular America and Islamic countries, forms a "linked set" with fundamentalist anti-secularism, seeking the "desacralization of the modern nation-state" and the "return of religion to the public sphere" (Friedland 2001) as the effective way of dispensing with the secular state in separation from church and reestablishing a theocratic government with its intrinsic "holy" state terror and war.

In this context, contemporary terrorism arises and functions as a type of violent, destructive, warlike, coercive and repressive revolt and thus radical adverse reaction against secular modernism as an ideal, social system, and historical period manifested in a secularized state, culture, and civil society. Simply, terrorism, especially its religious form, is the result of anti-secularism becoming anti-secular nihilism, thus "turned mad" (Habermas 2001) and making the social world "mad and arbitrary" (Bourdieu 2000), a social stage of "madness" through anti-government warfare as well as government violent repression, severe, coercion, and culture wars within society and a global "holy" war of extermination and destruction against other societies. In particular, such intra- and inter-societal violence and wars are exemplified by domestic and foreign crusades and jihads by Protestant evangelicalism in America and Islamic fundamentalism in Muslim settings.

As observed, these two forms of religious fundamentalism and theocratic anti-secularism, and consequently of counter-state and state

---

even for a terrible moment, is ground gained for religion's side". In his view, "lurking in the background of much of religion's unrest and the occasion for its political revival is the devaluation of secular authority" (Juergensmeyer (2003:15).

"godly" terrorism, while nominally enemies, share varying commonalities (Friedland 2002), affinities (Turner 2002), and even respect and admiration (Juergensmeyer 2003). Especially US would-be-theocratic or power-ambitious (Davis and Robinson 2009; Edgell et al. 2006; Hedges 2006; Hout and Fischer 202; Keister 2008; Lindsey 2008; Owens et al. 2010) evangelicals in the "Bible Belt," from the "deep South" and Texas and Oklahoma to Idaho, Montana, and Nebraska, emulate and even openly or secretly admire Muslim effective, strict theocrats in Islamic states (Juergensmeyer 2003; also, Oberschall 2004). Notably, US "born again" evangelicals seek and even succeed, as in the "Bible Belt" and its death penalty and penal system (Texas, etc.), to reestablish—after the old Puritan formally disestablished model—Biblical Law cum the "law of the land" as a Christian functional equivalent of Koran Sharia law in Islamic theocracies Iran, Saudi Arabia, Taliban regions, etc.

For instance, sociological analyses detect the "commonalities between Iranian and American fundamentalism" (Friedland 2002) with respect to theocratic anti-secularism. The latter is manifested in the shared opposition to and attempted destruction of the modern secular state as "ungodly", i.e., "anti-Christian" and "anti-Islamic", and "religious terror" in the form of both counter-state and state terrorisms depending on the specific power constellation–i.e., outside of or in political power (Juergensmeyer 2003). Moreover, US fundamentalist groups reportedly admire or envy the "attempts of Muslims" in Islamic theocracies like Iran, Sudan, and Taliban-ruled regions at creating political systems based on "Islamic law"[4] (Juergensmeyer 2003). They do so, precisely because they attempt to reconstruct American society as theocracy or its equivalent (Davis and Robinson 2009; Hedges 2006; Owens et al. 2010; Phillips 2006) on the basis of "Christian law" from the Bible and thus as "Christian America" or another, after its Puritan prototype, "Biblical Garden". In virtue of such admiration or envy for their Islamic theocratic "brothers in arms"–yet enemies in the contest for global military dominance and religious conversion via missions–conceivably, US fundamentalists seek and even, as

---

[4] Juergensmeyer (2003:12) reports that "in mountain towns in Idaho and Montana religious and individual freedoms are thought to be imperiled by an enormous governmental conspiracy, and in pious Muslim communities around the world where Islam is felt to be at war with the surrounding secular forces of modern society." Juergensmeyer (2003:30) cites the case of the 1996 Atlanta Olympics bomber as being "concerned about the permissiveness of secular authorities in the US and "atheistic internationalism", concerns shared by "Christian Identity" and related fundamentalist groups usually merged or allied with neo-Nazi militias. Similarly, Islamic and Hindu fundamentalists claim the "corruption of secular governments in Egypt and India" (Juergensmeyer 2003:184–5).

in the "Bible Belt", succeed to remake America, as outside observers and domestic critics object, a sort of "Christian Taliban" (Mansbach 2006) or "Christian Iran" (Bauman 1997) in substantive terms (even though not formally).

Substantively, this signifies a primitive Puritan-rooted evangelical theocracy (Munch 2001) functionally equivalent to atavistic Taliban-style and other Islamic theocracies, including a shared fundamentalist Draconian death-penalty and penal system (as in Texas and other Southern states and Taliban-ruled regions) abolished and humanized in modern Western secular states. Admittedly, terrorist activities by fundamentalist groups in America such as the 1995 Oklahoma and 1996 Atlanta Olympics bombings and related acts, including anti-government attacks and threats, continuing murders and destructions of abortion personnel and facilities, and the like, demonstrate the "destructive potential of Christian fundamentalism in the West itself"[5] (Townshend 2002), just as that of fundamentalist Islam (Feldstein 2008). In turn, certain continuing tendencies by these and related groups anticipate acts of counter-state terror and destruction for the future. These include the frantic arming of "Christian" militias and warriors in preparation for the final act of "cosmic war" against the secular state and "revolutionary" anti-government hyperconservative "Tea Parties" exemplifying the "crazy right" in a predictable adverse reaction to the 2008 Elections of "un-American" forces and the ensuing "big" liberal government and its reforms (health care reform, economic stimulus, etc.).

In comparative terms, US evangelicalism's condemnation and attempted theocratic seizure of—sanctified as "godly" influence (Lindsey 2008) on or "sacralizing" (Davis and Robinson 2009; Friedland 2001)–the secular government and the legal separation of church and state are unknown or unparalleled among modern Western democracies, while only paralleled by Islamic fundamentalism's equivalent practices in Muslim and other countries (Oberschall 2004). Consequently, evangelical anti-secularism explains and predicts why counter-state religious terrorism has been and will likely continue to be more manifest, salient, and intense in America than in other Western societies, just as Islamic fundamentalism does

---

5 Townshend (2002:97–103) comments that "it is undoubtedly Islam in particular rather than religion in general that engrosses Western attention", and that "much of Islam's negative image in the West is surely due to its apparent propensity to encourage sacrificial or suicidal action by *mujahideen*, holy warriors –including children". However, Townshend (2002:101) suggests that "in the wake of the Oklahoma bombing–until September 11 the most murderous "terrorist" act of all time–we can hardly mistake the destructive potential of Christian fundamentalism in the West itself".

explain such terrorist activities in Muslim and non-Muslim countries alike. For instance, a Southern religious neo-conservative, former history professor/Speaker of the House of Representatives, as well as self-admitted adulterer, etc., and putative Presidential candidate declared in a speech to "Tea Party" activists in 2010 that "what we're up against is unlike we've ever seen in America. This is a secular, socialist machine" referring to the US federal government formed after the 2008 Presidential elections. As typical of US as well as Islamic fundamentalism, such condemning declarations form the "sacred" rationale and prelude for anti-government violent attacks, as undertaken or attempted and threatened by "Tea Party" activists and other extreme neo-conservatives, and thus counter-state terrorism. In retrospect, even a history professor apparently overlooks or "forgets" that the conservative-fundamentalist condemnation of and attack on the US government as "secular, socialist" have been as "American as apple pie" during America's history, from Jeffersonian ideas condemned as "ungodly" by theocratic Puritans and their "Federalist" supporters to the New Deal denounced as "socialist" or "even "communist" by arch-conservatives. Apparently, what is problematic and "un-American" for this and related neo-conservative anti-secularism is the Jeffersonian con-stitutional separation of church and state defining the modern "secular" government; no wonder, Jefferson was removed from the public school curriculum by Texas "born again" evangelicals and replaced by Calvin. Notably, such evangelical demonization of the constitutional separation of church and state (covertly) or the "secular" government (openly) has generated, as exemplified by "Christian" militia and other terrorist attacks and plans, and is likely to generated anti-government violence or counter-state terrorism thus driven and sanctified by anti-secularism.

In historical terms, it is striking that these US religious forces condemn and seek to eliminate the formally secular government, hence the consti-tutional separation of church and state and the "prohibition of govern-ment promotion of religion" as the "established law of the land", in America ushering in the 21st century. Thus, they do so more than two cen-turies after its Jeffersonian Enlightenment-based (Davis and Robinson 2009) formulation and institutionalization made appear as if never happened (Dayton 1999), just as Islamic fundamentalism has historically never accepted its proxies in Muslim countries (Turkey, Egypt, etc.). Consequently, "die-hard" evangelical anti-secularism explains and pre-dicts why counter-state religious terror has historically been and is likely to remain remarkably persistent in America by the early 21st century and beyond and more so than in all other Western societies, just as Islamic fundamentalism does explain such persisting terrorist activities in Muslim and in extension non-Muslim countries.

Generally, in contemporary society, anti-secularism assumes, first and foremost, the form of conservatism, in particular, alongside typically "godly" fascism, including Nazism, religious traditionalism or orthodoxy. Notably, religious conservatism is manifested in fundamentalism especially observed in Islam, Christianity, and to some extent and in proxy forms in other world religions (orthodox Judaism, traditional Hinduism and Buddhism, etc.). Within Christianity it is manifest and salient primarily in Protestantism such as French-born Calvinism and its sectarian English-American transplant Puritanism in the form of evangelicalism or Biblicism (Bloom 1988) as well as in part Lutheranism, and secondarily Catholicism and the Christian Orthodox Church. To that extent, anti-secular conservatism in the form of Islamic, Protestant, and related religious fundamentalism is the prime source, explanation, and predictor as well as sanctification of contemporary terrorism within the setting of anti-secularism and anti-liberalism in general, as sociological theory suggests and empirical research evidences.

Thus, sociological theory suggests and empirical research confirms that religious fundamentalism and even religion as such is inherently violent, destructive, coercive, and repressive, notably warlike due to its doctrine and practice of "cosmic war" and/or "holy" revolution[6] (Adorno 2001; Davis and Robinson 2009; Edgell et al. 2006; Friedland 2001; Juergensmeyer 2003; Townshend 2002) by "good" against "evil", effectively by its adherents or believers as incarnations of the first versus outsiders or infidels as emanations of the second. This is a type of total and eternal warfare waged both within society through theocratic coercion, violent repression, and extermination and also against other societies via offensive "holy" wars after the model or image of Islamic jihads and Puritan crusades. To that extent, religious fundamentalism is effectively

---

[6] Juergensmeyer (2003:217) identifies the "notion of cosmic war" shared by Christian and Islamic fundamentalism. In this view, the solution in which "religion returns to its privatization in the post-Enlightenment world is unlikely. Few religious activists are willing to retreat to the time when secular authorities ran the public arena and religion remained safely within the confines of churches [etc.]. [They] regard the social manifestation of cosmic struggle to be at the very heart of their faith and dream of restoring religion to what they regard as its rightful position at the center of public consciousness" (Juergensmeyer 2003:235). Similarly, Townshend (2002:99) registers that the shared aim of Christian and Islamic fundamentalism "is a kind of cosmic revolution" in that the "practitioners of religious violence do not" operate on the premise of social change by peaceful human agency.

or potentially the theological design and the theocratic system of "holy" terror, notably the "practice of public terrorism"[7] (Juergensmeyer 2003), as Calvinism and its offspring Puritanism as well as Islam are often described (Mansbach 2006; Merrill 1945; Turner 2002; Walzer 1963), just as "godly" fascism is terror in its own right epitomized by "Nazi terrorism". Recall terrorism as defined constitutes just a specific—illegitimate, indiscriminate, methodical, and strategic—type of violence, destruction, war, coercion, and repression. Alternatively, the kind of violence, destruction, war, coercion, and repression used by religious fundamentalism and its inexorable outcome or perennial ideal theocracy, just as in "godly" fascism, is invariably the type that defines and identifies terrorism: illegitimate, indiscriminate, methodical, and strategic.

The preceding restates and confirms that religious fundamentalism in the form of either established theocracy or theocratic opposition against an "ungodly" secular government and fascism are blueprints and systems of terrorism in their own right, including both state and counter-state terrorism depending on whether they are in political power or not, respectively. Since religious fundamentalism or theocracy and fascism alike invariably have been and are likely to be creations, integral elements, or regular allies of–both simply "load on"–of anti-secular and anti-liberal conservatism, the latter reemerges and operates as the design and system of state and counter-state terrorism. Conservatism does so at least in the dual and usually intertwined and mutually reinforced form of, as in inter-war Europe and contemporary America, fundamentalist or theocratic and fascist "holy" terror, i.e., anti-secular and anti-liberal violence, destruction, war, coercion, and repression.

Conversely, the "children" or parts such as theocracy and fascism reproduce or reveal their parent or the "extended family", namely religious-political conservatism, as a design and system of anti-secular and anti-liberal terrorism. Not surprisingly, religious, especially Islamic and Protestant "Christian" fundamentalism either in the form of established theocracy or theocratic rebellion and fascism have been the main, though not sole, advocates, perpetrators, and supporter of counter-state and state and inter-state terrorism in contemporary Western societies, as especially applies to America during last several decades (Juergensmeyer 2003; Smith 1994).

---

[7] Juergensmeyer (2003:216) remarks that Christian and Islamic anti-secular extremists or fundamentalists "would do virtually anything if they thought it had been sanctioned by divine mandate or conceived in the mind of God. Religion has given an extraordinary twist to the practice of public terrorism".

In the latter, this is exemplified by such intertwined and even basically fused fundamentalist-fascist terrorist groups and acts embodying "Christian fascism" such as "Christian Identity", "Christian warriors", "Crusaders for Christ", and other "godly" neo-Nazi militias ("Dragons of God", etc.) committing or conspiring in the Oklahoma and Atlanta Olympics bombings, abortion clinics destructions and murders, anti-government attacks, and the like (Blee and Creasap 2010; Emerson and Hartman[8] 2006; Juergensmeyer 2003; Turk 2004). The persistence and even growing intensity of fundamentalist, fascist, and other neo-conservative anti-secularism is the likely determinant and predictor of such acts and agents of terrorism in the present and foreseeable future. For instance, the anti-secular conservative reaction to the 2008 US Elections involved murders of or attacks on abortion physicians, liberal politicians and judges, and other terrorist acts and threats, including various hate crimes and threatening anti-government and anti-secular "Tea Parties", "Christian warriors" condemning and attacking "secular" and "big" government, and other elements of the violent "crazy [Christian] right" (Blee and Creasap 2010; Owens et al. 2010).

Theocratic Revolt and Terrorism

The preceding indicates that most types and cases of contemporary terrorism, particularly religious violence through theocentric (Wall 1998) violent repression and anti-government attacks by state and counter-state agents respectively, are rooted in and justified and predicted by anti-secularism, specifically anti-secular and anti-liberal conservatism and its integral element religious fundamentalism. Notably, religious terrorism is the result, expression, and even the ultimate, though desperate, act of anti-secular theocratic revolt against liberal-secular modernity in contemporary Western and non-Western societies, especially America and Islamic countries. In Western societies, above all America during

---

[8] Emerson and Hartman (2006:137) propose that sociological analyses should address the question of "why fundamentalism leads to or condones violence in some cases but not in others." In their view, "violent acts perpetuated by U.S. Protestant fundamentalists, such as abortion clinic bombings, underlie political agendas but do not characterize their overall strategy of creating political and social change" (Emerson and Hartman 2006:138). They infer that "not all religiously based violence is done by fundamentalists. Sometimes, in fact, religion is used as a justification for violence by people and groups not specifically religious. Not all fundamentalist groups are violent. Yet much religious violence is committed by extremist fundamentalist groups" (Emerson and Hartman 2006:136).

conservatism, the above applies to Protestant "Christian" fundamentalism (Darnell and Sherkat 1997; Edgell et al. 2006; Emerson and Hartman 2006; Hout and Fischer 2002; King 2008; Lutz and Lutz[9] 2004). The latter invariably arises and operates in the axiomatic form of evangelicalism or Biblicism as the dominant form of anti-secularism, namely of anti-secular, anti-rationalistic, and anti-liberal and anti-democratic neo-conservatism. This holds despite recent distinctions between "fundamentalism" and "evangelicalism" in which the latter appears as virtually non-theocratic and "democratic" or politically activist (Lindsey 2008; Madsen 2009; Smith 2000) in contrast to the former's self-imposed political isolation following its discredit in the wake of its infamous 1925 "Monkey Trial" against evolution theory (Davis and Robinson 2009; Martin 2002).

This form of "Christian" fundamentalism qua evangelicalism, like neo-conservatism generally, is historically rooted in, inspired by, and perpetuates the venerable "tradition" of Puritanism (Dunn and Woodard 1996) and in extension its theological parent and dogmatic basis, Calvinism. To that extent, such "parentage" (Dunn and Woodard 1996) reveals Puritanism (Juergensmeyer 1994; Kaufman 2008; Munch 2001; Tiryakian 2002) and in extension its own parent Calvinism (Gorski 1993; Mansbach 2006; Munch 1981; Walzer 1965) as the extant indirect source and inspiration, at least precursor, of contemporary religiously grounded and sanctified terrorism. The latter includes both violence, severe coercion, and violent repression within society and global "holy" wars, as committed, advocated, and supported by evangelical or "godly" fascist groups ("Christian" neo-Nazi militias, etc.) outside of and in political power alike, in America and to a lesser extent other historically Puritan and generally Calvinist Western societies such as Great Britain, Holland, and in part Germany. At this juncture, sociological observations suggest that Calvinism via the agency of Puritanism as its English-American "agent" performed the same "sociological function" (McLaughlin 1996) in Anglo-Saxon societies, above all America, as fascism, specifically Nazism in Germany. This is that of violence, systematic violent repression, and severe coercion within society

---

[9] Lutz and Lutz (2004:65–6) note that US "fundamentalist groups opposed to a variety of practices and modern attitudes (are) within the Christian community. Some of these groups have been willing to use violence to reach their objectives. Many Christian groups have supported anti-abortion protests in the US. [Yet] the violence has escalated to assaults on individuals. Doctors and other clinic workers have been attacked or murdered. [Those] involved in such attacks or murders have frequently been difficult to capture, even when they have been identified. It has been apparent in the US that there have been groups that have been willing to aid the activists in escaping from punishment for the assaults and murders [such as] the Army of God".

and aggressive war or militarism against other societies and to that extent state, inter-state, and counter-state terrorism.

At first sight, the above is a shocking proposition ("indecent proposal"). Yet upon a careful, detailed inspection it appears less so, namely a logical inference and, more importantly, an empirically grounded generalization derived from the theological dogmas and theocratic actions of Puritanism and in extension Calvinism, notably the dogma of predestination and Calvinist-Puritan theocracies or theocratic rebellions in Europe, Great Britain, and America. The authors are also "shocked" when making this "rediscovery". For in the conventional wisdom Puritanism and in extension Calvinism is the historical source of democracy, individualism, and freedom, alongside modern capitalism, in America and comparable societies, as Weber in part implies and Parsons et al. explicitly argue.

To make the above "shocking" proposition less so, recall Weber registers Calvinism's, in particular Puritanism's "fundamental antagonism" to secular "sensuous" or "emotional" culture as the underlying cultural source and rationale of what he and Edward Ross call Puritan "tyranny". This tyranny, like all tyrannies, was the system of state terror in the form of, in Comte's words, "violent repression" and thus proto-totalitarian violence, coercion, and intolerance (Bauman 1997; Kaufman 2008, Stivers 1994), just as when not in political power counter-state terrorism through anti-government attacks and warfare. Also, recollect historical research reports a "kind of local terrorism" in 17th century England under Puritanism traced to its anti-secularism and anti-liberalism to the point of eventuating in or threatening to become the national "Puritan terror" (Walzer 1963) as well as the "reign of terror" in New England's Puritan "theocracy" (Merrill 1945).

Notably, as mentioned, sociological studies identify Puritanism on the account of its "theocratic revolt" against "increasing secularism" in 17th century English politics and society as the model or precursor of "modern antisecular radicals" like theocrats or fundamentalists (Juergensmeyer 1994; also, Goldstone 1986; Gorski 2000; Zaret 1989). The latter are identified in two predictable main forms in a mutual convergence and affinity such as "born again" US evangelicals and revived Islamic fundamentalists (Friedland 2002; Juergensmeyer 2003; Mansbach 2006; Turner 2002). Also, some analysts identify Calvinism due to its combined sadism-masochism and related violent, repressive, and inhumane properties as the historical source or precursor of fascism, specifically Nazism in Germany (Adorno 2001; Fromm 1941; Harrold 1936; McLaughlin 1996) and thus of Nazi terror and perversions (Arendt 1951; Barnes 2000). Furthermore, other sociologists identity Puritanism as the continuing primary source and justification of a complex of intertwined violent and coercive outcomes. This involves offensive global war, militarism, and imperialism in America and in part Great Britain, where Puritanism was reincorporated under and moderated by Anglicanism, and to that extent inter-societal terrorism, plus the observed lack of institutional compassion, caritas, and so of a generous welfare state (Tiryakian 2002), as the "dark side of the [Puritan] Protestant Ethic" (Hudson and Coukos 2005) in these societies.

As indicated, a paradigmatic instance or precursor of religious terrorism in Western history is Puritan "holy" terror in 17th century England and New England from its settlement to the middle 19th century. Hume in his classical historical analysis suggests that Puritanism with its "wild" and "wretched fanaticism" was a theocratic design and system of terror (while not using the term) in the form of violence against non-Puritan (i.e., Anglican and royal) institutions and of violent repression and coercion once established as the claimed "only true" religion and church, thus counter-state and state terrorism. On this account, Hume implicitly and in retrospect, given subsequent Puritan developments or ramifications in contemporary Protestant fundamentalism and conservatism overall (Adorno 2001; Juergensmeyer 1994; Kaufman 2008; Munch 2001), prophetically warns about the violent, repressive, militarist, coercive, and in that sense terrorist "spectre of Puritanism" (Seed 2005). Recall Comte evoking Hume registers that Puritanism (Presbyterianism) once in government resorts to "violent repression" and in that sense state terror, thus being "unsuitable" for democratic governance. Mill similarly observes that whenever Puritans are in power, as in England briefly and New England for long time, they tend to coercively suppress individual liberties and pleasures or "amusements" and to that extent terrorize, including execute and imprison, "sinful" humans.

Also, historical research shows that after its temporarily victorious anti-secular Calvinist revolution Puritanism in England designed and eventually established theocracy cum the "Holy Commonwealth" that was governed, as Hume classically recounts, by one hundred or so self-proclaimed "divines" forming the Parliament of Saints and enacting and representing "the Puritan terror" (Walzer 1963). In particular, various Puritan congregations during this time were pervaded by "a kind of local terrorism" enforced by the "godly elders" just as the "national" terror or discipline was (to be) imposed by an "elite of saints" such as Cromwell and Baxter intent on converting "all England into a land of the saints" (Walzer 1963). This infers that, contrary to received views, Puritanism's achievement in England and beyond was not freedom but "the terror" it committed through creating a theocratic "Holy Commonwealth" and forcing people to be "godly" (Walzer 1963). In essence, the creation and thus legacy of Puritanism is what a sociological analysis calls "coercive theocracy" cum "godly politics" (Zaret 1989) as a theological design when Puritans are outside government or as a social system once in power, and to that extent counter- and state-terrorism. Furthermore, in virtue of their "theocratic revolt against the increasing secularism of 17th century English politics" through "godly" terror or violence against established political and religious institutions, recall Puritans were reportedly proto-types of "modern antisecular radicals" resorting to anti-government terrorism such as "born again" Protestant evangelicals in America directly and indirectly Islamic fundamentalists (Juergensmeyer 1994).

In addition, historical research describes New England's theocracy as the "Puritan Babel tower" containing the "germs of its own destruction" due to the "reign of terror", "suspicion and martyrdom of innocent people in the deplorable witchcraft delusion at Salem" (Merrill 1945). A particular element or agent of this "reign of terror", specifically state terrorism, was the "Puritan policeman" (Merrill 1945). The latter embodies or prefigures what sociologists observe as the contemporary ever-growing policing or penal repressive state in America under Puritan-rooted conservatism (Bourdieu 1998; Cable et al. 2008; Cooney and Burt 2008; Harris et al. 2011; Miliband 1969; Vasi and Strang 2009; Wacquant 2002), notably a sort of religious-vice police (Hill 2002; Infantino 2003; Wagner 1997). The latter, given the theocratic and moralistic nature of Puritanism and its heir evangelicalism, forms the natural and major element of the police state, especially in the evangelical "Bible Belt" from the "deep South" to Texas and Oklahoma, etc. and its analogues (e.g., Utah). In turn, Puritanism did and in extension contemporary evangelicalism in America does perpetuate and rationalize its vice-police state and thus state terror by claiming to be "God's [anti] vice regent" (Zaret 1989). For instance, Oklahoma's ultra-conservative "godly" legislature invented around 30 new felonies and thus more potential criminals and prisoners in its 2010 session, while the state of Texas has cumulatively created no less than a total of 2,000 felonies in the "books." This is a typical "method in the madness "of "Bible Belt" states, from South Carolina, Alabama, Georgia, and Tennessee to Texas and Oklahoma, whose "favorite pastime" seems to be the political-institutional reproduction (Sutton 2004) of crime, imprisonment, and executions and thus "holy" state terror, as was of their model the Puritan "Biblical Commonwealth" and is of Islamic theocracies like Iran and Taliban regions.

The above claim expresses the perpetual "obsession with vice and sin" (Wagner 1997) and results in moralistic culture wars (Bell 2002; Hill 2002) in American history since the early Puritans through their heirs "reborn" Protestant sectarians and fundamentalists (also, Jenness 2004; Lipset 1996; Munch 2001). As noted, the probably most manifest, enduring, and intense is Puritanism's and evangelicalism's striking obsession with "Sex [and God]" (Friedland 2002) as a genuine or proxy crime, shared especially with Islamic fundamentalism as the main contestant in this field, and providing the religious, moralistic, or psychological (psychiatric?) basis for the vice-police state and so state terror. At this juncture, the evangelical vice-police state and the resulting moralistic state terror or repression in America, minimally the "Bible Belt", is the patho-logical outcome of the Puritan-rooted morbid obsession with moral sins and vices, above all "sexual mores" (Bauman 1997) and all private life of the hated Other (Habermas et al. 1998), and thus "normal pathology" (Gouldner 1970) of neo-conservatism, as is in Islamic theocracies the result of fundamentalist Islam's identical feature.

Thus, the Puritan-style conservative perpetual obsession with "Sex" as a crime and thus by implication "original sin" makes, together with the mass media, especially television, non-violent sexual sins like premarital sex, adultery, prostitution, pornography, etc. (let alone rapes and related violent offenses) the "gravest" crimes and "most serious" social problems, alongside drug and alcohol use, in America. Historically, this is what Puritanism precisely did in its "Biblical Commonwealth", and comparatively what Islamic fundamentalism does in theocracies such as Iran, Saudi Arabia, and Taliban regions. For instance, "Bible Belt" states (e.g., Texas, etc.) seem so obsessed with adultery to the point of exonerating murderers of adulterous wives as if the latter committed a graver crime than the former ("crimes of passion") and killing for adulteries were a justified "God-commanded" punishment, just as New England's Puritan "Biblical Commonwealth" did punish such sexual offenses simply with death, and Islamic "Republics" do (stoning). Similarly, the Puritan-rooted arch-conservative obsession with other vices like alcohol use made the latter the "biggest" and "gravest" social problem in early 20th century America requiring for its "solution" no less than changing the Constitution—an act unknown in modern Western history–to enforce "thou shall not drink" Prohibition and even wine, part of Christ's last supper, or else, including life in prison for vices as an instance of moralistic state terror.

In spite of the dismal failure of Prohibition, the puritanical conservative obsession with related vices like drug use persists and makes the latter among the "most serious" crimes or social problems in post-1960s America necessitating a military-like "war on drugs" (Hill 2002). As known, this has caused such an explosion of the prison population and executions, above all in the "Bible Belt", that is unparalleled in modern Western society and only rivaled by Islamic theocracies like Iran and Nazi-fascist dictatorships in interwar Europe. Recall, due to neo-conservatism's obsession with and war on drugs and related vices and sins, including alcohol and sexuality, the US has really become "Number 1" in the world in terms of prison population–nearly 2.4 million of whom almost two third are non-violent drug users and similar sinners by the 2010s–thus outnumbering and outdoing every other country, including even far more populous China.

In aggregate, US conservatism's "obsession" with sins and vices, notably sexual and all private life, renders them the "gravest" crimes usually punished or condemned, as in the "Bible Belt", more severely than others, including murders, or among "most serious" social problems to be solved by religious-moralistic "solutions" a la Prohibition and "war on drugs" in America, just as did Puritanism in New England and does Islamic fundamentalism in Iran and Taliban regions. In doing so it renders human sensual and all pleasures the supreme "crimes" and the gravest "social problems" in America, precisely as Puritanism did by, as Pareto notes, equating pleasure (and so sin) with crime, and fundamentalist Islam does in Iran or Taliban regions. Recall some Americans capture this Puritan- and Islamic-style neo-conservative equation of pleasure with crime saying (referring to illicit drugs and the like) that the US government credo is "if it feels good, then it must be prohibited and punished."

As noted, the police state in general, including its Puritan-Islamic theocratic and Nazi-fascist variants, is a special subtype or instrument of government institutionalized terrorism and totalitarianism generally which is a total social system of terror in its own right. While the police state is the type or agent of terror once Puritanism or evangelicalism and Islam, like Nazism or fascism, is established in political power, Puritan-evangelical, just as Nazi-fascist, forces resort to counter-state terrorism when being in opposition to existing institutions. The latter tendency is witnessed in the used or threatened violence by evangelical sects, neo-Nazi militias a la Christian warriors" and "Crusaders for Christ", and other neo-conservatives ("Tea Parties", etc.) against "big" secular government as the minimal welfare state, in America following the 2008 Elections and before, as well as Islamic fundamentalist attacks on "infidel" governments in countries like Turkey and Egypt (until the victory of Islamists and their control of government).

As indicated, the first major group of "modern antisecular radicals" or theocratic extremists whose prototypes and models (Dunn and Woodard 1996; Juergensmeyer 2003; Munch 2001) were early English Puritans includes "Christian", mainly Protestant "born again", fundamentalist and sectarian cum evangelical denominations, sects, and cults in America, especially, though not only, the Southern and other "Bible Belt". For instance, some analysis classify most US religious and political neo-conservatives like Reaganites into the category of "rigid and uncompro-mising extremists" (Blomberg and Harrington 2000); also, recall Reagan's own open proclamation "I am one of you [reborn evangelicals]" as likely, given his Calvinist Presbyterianism, genuine, though strategically used a la Machiavelli in the function of pursuit of political power and discredit of and assault on "un-American" liberalism and secularism.

While differing in certain theological terms, including the strict adher-ence to or relaxation of the Calvinist dogma of predestination, these fun-damentalist groups share the commonalty of being more or less inspired by and seeking to revive from the dead past the revered Puritan theocratic, intolerant, repressive, moralistic, anti-egalitarian or aristocratic, and mili-tarist heritage (Bremer 1995; Juergensmeyer 2003; Kaufman 2008; Munch 2001) via culture and military wars as new "crusades" within society and against other societies, respectively. They incorporate or are naturally allied as "brothers in arms with neo-Nazi "Christian" militias and related "Christian Right" groups (Blee and Creasap 2010; Owens et al. 2010; Turk 2004). These perpetrate, support, incite, and threaten terrorist acts against "big" secular government in contemporary America (Friedman 1982; Smith 1994), as during the 1990s culminating in the 1995 Oklahoma bomb-ing by "Dragons of God" as well as following the 2008 Election by attacks on "ungodly" abortion and other facilities and persons or anti-government threats by Christian warriors" and counter-revolutionary "Tea Parties", etc. An identified instance of "modern antisecular radicals" within American evangelicalism is Calvinist-inspired "Dominion Theology",[10] including

---

[10] According to Juergensmeyer (2003:27–8), the Dominion Theology "trace[s] [its] ideas ['theonomy'] to Cornelius Van Til, a 20th century Presbyterian professor of theology (Princeton) who took seriously [Calvin's] 16th century ideas [for] the necessity for presup-posing the authority of God in all worldly matters." This curious case confirms that, first,

"Reconstruction Theology", in the "Bible Belt" (Virginia, etc.) and beyond, aiming to reconstruct America once again, after the model of New England's Puritan disestablished theocracy cum "paradise lost", as a "Christian theocratic state"[11] (Juergensmeyer 2003; also, Friedland 2002; Hedges 2006). In this account, the overriding and permanent end of this and other forms of evangelicalism is eliminating the "separation of church and state" in America and merging "religion and state" to create a "new society" ruled and sanctified by "religious [Biblical] law" through "a Christian revolution" or a "righteous rebellion" against "big" and secular "ungodly" government as the most effective means of redeeming this paradise (Juergensmeyer 2003).

Historically, this is a design and path inspired by theocratic Puritanism and in extension Calvinism (Clemens 2007; Hedges 2006; Munch 1981), while comparatively shared with Islamic fundamentalism and theocracies. The major evangelical imperative is summed in that the "moral obligation of Christians", specifically Protestant fundamentalists, in America and beyond is recapturing and reconstructing "every institution for Jesus Christ" even if with the "currency of violence", warfare, coercion, and repression (Juergensmeyer 2003). To that extent, this involves initially counter-state and ultimately state and inter-state terrorism justified and sanctified as "Crusade for Christ" (as the first author was told in Texas during the 2000s). These evangelical sects and cults, particularly Baptism as the largest US Protestant denomination, monopolizing the "Christian" name and branding all other, non-evangelical Christian denominations (especially Catholics) "non-Christian", use the Biblical concept of "dominion" to proclaim themselves as the only true "Christians" cum "the new chosen people of God" with a Divine right to rule America and the entire world. They do so in the belief that establishing a "Christian kingdom" on Earth shall precede "Christ's return" through "a form of religious politics" enforcing the Biblical commandments as the "law of the land" (Juergensmeyer 2003). They thus tend to commit, advocate, incite, or support a composite of counter-state and state and inter-state terror as

---

the "rumors of the death" of Calvin and his theocratic ideas of "holy" tyranny and thus state terror, are "grossly exaggerated", and second, moderate Calvinist Presbyterianism (and generally Calvinism or Puritanism) may well be what Weber calls an "impossible contradiction" (or oxymoron), despite being typically classified under "mainline" and even "liberal" Protestantism (Martin 2002).

[11] Juergensmeyer (2003:32) adds that "this is why so many (Christian) Identity groups live together in theocratic societies" such as Elohim City, Freeman Compound, Aryan Nations compound, etc..

the effective means of attaining and retaining of such a "holy" cause. And they reportedly hate the comparatively minimal welfare state cum "big" secular government in America with an "almost transcendent passion", as seen déjà vu in the rise of the "Tea Party", while planning, preparing for, or dreaming of a religious revolution or civil war (Juergensmeyer 2003). For them the latter is the optimal instrument of reestablishing a "godly social order" in the "rubble" of what they condemn and aim to destroy as "modern, egalitarian democracies" as "ungodly" and "un-American", as do Islamists whom they openly or secretly admire[12] (Juergensmeyer 2003).

As noted, the second group of contemporary theocratic extremists or "modern antisecular radicals" of whom early Calvinist Puritans were precursors–though as "pure" Christians not direct prototypes or models–comprises Islamic fundamentalists (summarized in Table 4.1). Like Protestant evangelicals in America, they seek to reconstruct or reproduce Muslim nations as theocracies (Oberschall 2004) through counter-state and state and inter-state terrorism when not in government and once in power, respectively, including a renewed jihad or "holy" war in the broadest sense against non-Islamic "infidel" individuals, groups, and societies as well as not "truly Islamic" believers in Islamic settings (Friedland 2002; Juergensmeyer 2003; Mansbach 2006; Turner 2002). While fundamentalist Islam particularly, as distinct from religion generally, has apparently captured "Western attention" (Townshend 2002; also, Feldstein 2008) during recent times, especially since September 11, 2001, its overarching and constant end of a "kind of cosmic revolution" as the means of reestablishing and expanding theocracy is admittedly shared (Juergensmeyer 2003; Smelser and Mitchell 2002; Turk 2004) with Protestant fundamentalism cum evangelicalism in America and beyond.

This is a commonality which objectively makes the two religious systems a sort of "brothers in arms" in the sense of objective allies in their shared vision and pursuit of theocracy, driven by what analysts call

---

[12] Juergensmeyer (2003:212) comments that to US fundamentalists "freedom of religion means freedom to live under religious law. Since America's secular government has denied (them) this freedom, (they regard) it as hypocritical. (US fundamentalists) feel it necessary to 'reconstruct' Christian society by turning to the Bible as the basis for a nation's law and social order. [They view] secular law as construed by the Supreme Court and defended by liberal politicians (as) moving in a decidedly un-Christian direction (abortion). [They] ultimately want [even] more than the rejection of secularism." Juergensmeyer (2003:228) concludes that militant religiosity's challenge [is] profound for it (contains) a fundamental critique of the world's post-Enlightenment secular culture and politics [i.e.] attempts to purchase public recognition of the legitimacy of religious world-views with the currency of violence."

"jihadic politics", i.e., crusades and jihads in the broad sense of culture and military wars (Turner 2002), even if remaining mortal enemies in other respects, notably the pursuit of world domination. As also observed, a shared design or outcome of Protestant and Islamic fundamentalism is the "new terror" (Friedland 2001), including counter-state and state and inter-state terrorism alike. Notably, state and inter-state terror is attained or designed and exercised through reconstructing theocracy in the form of a state endowed with "powers of the divine", thus making God "once again" descend to human society and sanctify violence, war, destruction, and generally violent repression, and replacing the "fear of a godless state" imputed to liberal-secular democracy (Friedland 2001; also, Davis and Robinson 2009).

Hence, contemporary terrorism, especially counter-state and "holy" religious terror, in Western and non-Western societies, in particular America and the Islamic world, is grounded in and predicted by the adverse reaction via theocratic counter-revolution against modern secular society or institutionalized secularism, including the renewed global process of secularization (Friedland 2002; Juergensmeyer 2003; Ruiter and Tubergen 2009; Smelser and Mitchell 2002; Smith[13] 1994; Townshend 2002, Turk 2004; also, Emerson and Hartman 2006). Anti-secularism in the main shape of religious conservatism or fundamentalism, notably the anti-secular theocratic conservative or fundamentalist counter-revolution, is the driving force as well as the societal setting ("extended family") of terrorism in its "holy" forms against secular government, social forces, and societies, i.e., of counter-state, state, and inter-state terror for the "glory of God". It is useful to emphasize that anti-secularism as the factor of terrorism operates in conjunction and mutual reinforcement with anti-liberalism, including anti-pluralism, and anti-democracy, as well as anti-rationalism and anti-globalism and anti-cosmopolitanism.

---

[13] Smith (1994:32) observes that "of the 170 individuals [indicted] for domestic terrorism or terrorism-related activities [in the US] during the 1980s, 103 were members of or associated with a loose coalition of right-wing groups frequently referred to as being part of the Christian Identity." In his view, "the right-wing groups are easiest to label since most are tied together by the Christian Identity Movement. While left-wing terrorist groups in America have adopted primarily a political focus, most right-wing terrorists are ideologically bound by religious beliefs. Similar to Shiite terrorism in its justification of violence, right-wing religious extremists in America advocate the use of terrorism as a prelude to war—the Armageddon, which will establish Christ's kingdom (36). The evidence suggests a move toward more indiscriminate violence by right-wing terrorists (Smith 1994:45). Notably, he concludes that since the 1980s "the number of right-wing extremists indicted for terrorism-related activities far exceeds the number of left-wing extremists" (Smith 1994:193–4).

Table 4.1. Main forms of anti-secularism before and during liberal-secular modernity.

Original Calvinism in Europe (France, Geneva, Holland, Prussia)
    Early Calvinist Puritanism in England (and Scotland) and America (New England)
Puritan-rooted revived theocratic evangelicalism and sectarianism in the USA and in part the UK
Other forms of Christianity: official Catholicism (the Vatican), Orthodox Christian Church (Eastern and Southern Europe, Russia, etc.)
Islamic fundamentalism or radicalism in Muslim countries
    Islamic fundamentalism in non-Muslim liberal-secular or Christian societies (Europe, Russia, the US, etc.)
Others: other world religions (traditional Hinduism, orthodox Judaism, etc.)

Furthermore, like virtually all conservative counter-revolutions against liberal modernity (Infantino 2003), the theocratic or fundamentalist counter-revolution is when successful and seizing power a kind of state terrorism in its own right in virtue of its systematic severe coercion and violent repression of forces of "ungodliness". And if unsuccessful, such counter-revolution is counter-state terrorism in itself through subversive violence against an "ungodly", i.e., "anti-Christian", "anti-Islamic", etc., government and by a path of escalation inter-state terror via offensive wars on "evil" societies. As noted, this pattern was exemplified by Calvinism's theocratic counter-revolution or "disciplinary" revolution in Europe (Gorski 2003; Loveman 2005; Walzer 1965), including Puritanism's "theocratic revolt" (Juergensmeyer 1994) against actual or perceived secularism in England. Puritanism manifested this pattern even more extensively and enduringly in America from the 17th to the 21st century, displaying a remarkable sociological continuity and historical sequence.

The pattern starts with New England's Puritan "reign of terror" involving persecution of dissenters (Kaufman 2008) and war of extermination against the Native Americans (Gould 1996; Munch 2001) as prototypical genocide (Mann 2005) and thus state or inter-estate terror, expanding through the "Great Awakenings" expressing Calvinist revivalism (Clemens 2007; German 1995) and operating as anti-secular, anti-liberal, and anti-rationalistic "counteroffensives" (Means 1967; also, Archer 2001; Rossel

1970). And it continues through the new fundamentalist revival embodied by "born again" Puritan-inspired evangelicals fervently seeking political power (Lindsey 2008; Owens et al. 2010) to implement their theocratic design (Hedges 2006; Phillips 2006) of a "godly" government typified by systematic coercion and violent repression of the "ungodly" and thus "holy" state terror "sweetened" (Beck 2000) by the "apple pie of authoritarianism" (Wagner 1997) a la "one nation indivisible under God" (Giddens 2000) and the like.

Another paradigmatic exemplar involves Islamic counter-revolutions against Western secularism and liberalism, as exemplified by successful fundamentalist revolutions in Iran, Taliban-ruled regions, and other Muslim countries, and those attempted and partly realized in Turkey, Egypt, etc. In turn, such revolutions, as Weber suggests, function as the functional equivalent to the Calvinist-Puritan revolution in virtue of, as he emphasizes, Calvinism, in particular Puritanism, and Islam sharing the idea and practice of religious revolution and "holy" war to the point of extermination of "infidels" or the "ungodly" (also, Harrold 1936; Mansbach 2006; Turner 2002). Recall whenever and wherever successful or, as Mill puts it, in power, Calvinist and Puritan counter-revolutions against secularism establish a sort of government system of "holy terror" or what Comte prophetically identifies as "violent repression" by suppressing virtually all liberties, including, as Mill registers, the arts and "amusements".

These tendencies span from Calvin's Geneva and attempted in France's Huguenot-ruled parts through Holland under Calvinism's theocratic rule to England during the Puritan "Holy Commonwealth" (Goldstone 1986; Gorski 2000; Hillmann 2008a; Walzer 1963; Zaret 1989) to New England's "Biblical Garden" (Brener 1995; Gould 1996; Kaufman 2008; Munch 2001) and the Southern "Bible Belt" ruled by what Mencken (1982) prophetically diagnosed as evangelical theocratic "barbarism" or proto-totalitarianism (Bauman 1997). In the latter instance, such a system has recently assumed or rather resumed the form of a Puritan-rooted neo-conservative Draconian penal code. As noted, this code involves the fundamentalist-grounded death penalty as a "selective terror" (Jacobs et al. 2005), systematically "terrorizing" (Bauman 2000), through both direct and indirect coercion, namely actual and potential executions, especially the low class and powerless, not to mention immigrants or foreigners (e.g., Mexicans and others in Texas and other parts of the "Bible Belt"), in America during recent times. Such a system perpetuates or evokes the venerable tradition of Puritanism as the perennial model and its long-lived New England theocracy. Recall the latter became the "reign of terror" (Merrill 1945) and death against "ungodly" dissenting groups (Quakers, "witches", etc.) within society (Kaufman 2008) and of war of extermination and so genocide of "heathen" peoples like Native Americans, both activities sanctified as Divinely commanded, namely, as cited by Tocqueville, "in the name of God Amen" (Gould 1996; Mann 2005; Munch 2001).

Conversely, whenever and wherever unsuccessful or not in power, but in what Comte and Weber call "fanatical opposition" and Simmel "protest" against existing religious-political institutions and powers, Calvinist-Puritan counter-revolutions commit or incite and advocate counter-state terrorist acts. They do so for the "higher" cause of establishing theocracy a la the "Kingdom of God on Earth"–as stipulated by original Calvinism in Europe and the Calvinist-inspired Dominion theology in America— through "Crusades and Crusaders for Christ". Such outcomes are proto-typically epitomized in Puritanism's violent theocratic revolt against the Anglican Church and the Monarchy culminating in the transiently successful Puritan Revolution of 1640–60. They climax or persist in the anti-government terror of fundamentalism merged with fascism to become "Christian fascism" (Friedland 2002; Hedges 2006) or extreme "Christian Right" (Blee and Creasap 2010; Hout and Fischer 2002; Owens et al. 2010, embodied and to be enforced by "Christian" neo-Nazi militias, in America, especially since the 1990s through 2010s in reaction to the elections of "liberal" and so "un-American" Presidents (1992 and 2008).

The exactly identical pattern of state terrorism once the counter-revolution succeeds and captures government and of counter-state terrorism when outside power has been also witnessed in Islamic funda-mentalism, as in more or less "godly" fascism, including Nazism, in Europe as well as America during interwar and postwar times. For instance, whenever and wherever Islamic anti-secular counter-revolutions have been victorious and seized power, they have established the theocratic system of "holy terror", as in Iran, Sudan, Saudi Arabia, Taliban-ruled regions, and other Muslim theocracies (Oberschall 2004), and apparently or likely in Egypt, Turkey, etc. Conversely, in the opposite scenario, they have resorted to systematic and persistent or "chronic" (Spilerman and Stecklov 2009) anti-government terrorism, as witnessed in Turkey (prior to the Islamic-rooted government of the 2000–10s), Egypt (before the elec-toral victories of Islamists in the 2010s), and other nominally secular "ungodly" states. Additionally, they commit terrorist acts against Western liberal-secular governments, including the US government, though not because of its supposed secularism and liberalism defamed and rendered by anti-liberal neo-conservatism since Reaganism into "un-American" (yet Western?) values for most Americans as of its perceived "anti-Islamic" and so in a sense anti-secular and "imperialistic" foreign policy.

Also, more or less "godly" fascism, including Nazism, conforms to the pattern of state and counter-state terrorism typical for anti-secular and generally anti-liberal counter-revolutions depending on their victory or defeat and thus concrete power configurations. For instance, victorious fascist counter-revolutions, notably the Nazi "revolution of nihilism" (Blinkhorn 2003), immediately upon seizing power installed and conducted the totalitarian reign of state terror, including war of extermination against "objective enemies" (Bahr 2002), in interwar Europe, most egregiously Germany, as did in part their versions or proxies like McCarthyism as a conservative type (Bourdieu and Haacke 1995; Plotke 2002) of violent repression leaving "ugly scars" (Smelser and Mitchell 2002; Vasi and Strang 2009) in postwar America. In turn, Nazism and all fascism resorted to counter-state terrorism when in opposition or temporary failure against liberal institutions such as the German Weimar Republic, and still do through counter-revolutionary neo-Nazism and neo-fascism in contemporary European and American societies (Rydgren 2007a). These cases confirm and exemplify a sort of Michels' like "iron law" of the link of conservative, in particular fundamentalist and fascist, counter-revolution and terrorism. To paraphrase his statement of the "iron" law of oligarchy, "who says conservative-fundamentalist and fascist counter-revolution, says state terror whenever and wherever being successful by capturing government, and counter-state terror if unsuccessful or in early stages."

In sum, virtually all religious, notably fundamentalist, including Calvinist-Puritan cum "Christian", Islamic, and other, counter-revolutions or revivals, just as their fascist counterparts, have been and remain designs and systems of "holy terror" in—as New England Puritans claimed cited by Tocqueville—the "name [and the mind] of God" (Juergensmeyer 2003). For instance, they are for the glory of what Weber calls the "absolutely transcendental", non-understanding, and even merciless or "capricious" "God of Calvinism" after the image of, as he puts it, a "hard king" and "arbitrary despot" a la an Oriental sultan (also, Artz 1998) in the case of their early Puritan and recent evangelical versions. In particular, these religious counter-revolutions, like their fascist versions, represent or generate state or counter-state terrorism, depending on their success or failure, thus what Weber call concrete power constellations favorable or unfavorable to such religious revolutionaries or "holy warriors" such as "Christian"

Protestant crusaders and Islamic jihadists (Turner 2002), as to fascist-Nazi counter-revolutionaries.

The aforesaid of anti-secularism, in particular anti-secular theocratic revolt or counter-revolution, as the factor and predictor of "holy" terrorism also applies to its role in certain terrorist functional substitutes or proxies in historical and contemporary societies. As before, anti-secularism in this role naturally and primarily implicates anti-secular religious conservatism. Thus, anti-secular religiously conservative or fundamentalist persons and groups, alongside with "godly" fascists from whom they hardly detachable or distinguishable (Hedges 2006), despite "democratic" disguises, particularly of U.S. evangelicals (Lindsey 2008), have especially tended and are likely to perpetrate, advocate, and support a special case of these substitutes or proxies of terrorism. This involves individual and collective contemporary hate crimes (King et al. 2009) as a functional equivalent or proxy of terror and mostly committed, advocated, incited, or supported by religious conservatives or fundamentalists in virtually all past and present, Western and non-Western societies, notably America and Islamic countries.

In particular, a sort of "favorite pastime" of religious conservatives in America, especially "Christian" racist, xenophobic, and exclusionary "clans" and militias in the South (Bailey and Snedker 2011; Jacobs et al. 2005; Messner et al. 2005), has been and partly still is violent vigilantism as an American historical and in part continuing exemplar of hate crimes (King et al. 2009) and to that extent actual or proxy terror. As known, vigilantism ranges from lynching in post-bellum times to anti-immigration vigilante "justice", including murders, torture, and other mistreatment of illegal and even legal immigrants, during the 2010s. This applies to another softer or less visible case of hate crimes that American conservative anti-secularism also probably commits or supports the most extensively and persistently among Western liberal-secular democracies. It involves conservative anti-secular and anti-liberal persistent and extensive culture or ideological and religious wars. These wars commit or incite hate crimes in virtue of using symbolic soft and often physical brutal violence and coercion (Bourdieu 1988) by excluding, discriminating, and attacking or otherwise mistreating, either through vigilantism when not in power or via government control and violent repression, secularists, unbelievers, and liberals as supremely "un-American" (Edgell et al. 2006).

No wonder that the main targets of terrorist agents and actions in America since the 1990s through the 2010s have been and are likely to continue to be well-defined secular-liberal "ungodly" and so "un-American" persons and institutions, from abortion doctors and "infidel" scientists, teachers, lawyers, and politicians to "big" government agencies and objects. This was manifested in the Oklahoma and Atlanta Olympics bombings, and similar acts of counter-state terrorism before and after, especially following the 1992 and 2008 Elections. In Clausewitz's terms, in America during conservative anti-secularism and Islamic societies under theocracy terrorism, including domestic hate crimes or culture wars and offensive foreign war, can be defined as the continuation or escalation of the anti-secular politics of exclusion, discrimination, and other mistreatment of "ungodly" secularists, and of bellicose foreign policy by other violent and destructive means. In short, it is the continuation of the ideology and politics, including the foreign policy, of "symbolic", "soft" violence against secular "ungodly" elements within society and in other societies by the means of force and destruction.

Consequently, terrorism has been and is likely to be more advocated, committed and supported by individuals, social groups, states, and societies that are hostile to and oppose secular modernity or the process of secularization, including secularized politics and culture, than by others. While this does not imply that all individuals, social groups, states, and societies opposing modern secular society or institutionalized secularism invariably commit and justify terrorism, they show a tendency for doing so more than do others. The above is potentially explanatory and predictive of the most prevalent types of terrorism, notably that with religious bases and justifications and its various, counter-state and state, domestic and transnational, within- and inter-society manifestations. It hence encompasses all effective or potential terrorist agents, individuals, groups, states, and societies of violence.

From Theological Orthodoxy to Terrorism through Theocratic Revolt

Generally, the antagonism by religious or theological orthodoxy against secular modernism as a social system and time period to the point of anti-secular theocratic revolt or counter-revolution against the latter causes, explains, and predicts most of modern terrorism, as especially witnessed in America and Islamic settings. Previous sociological theory and research suggest that religious orthodoxy, expressing strictness (McBride 2008) or traditionalism in religion, including theological dogmatism, is directly or indirectly implicated in or associated with terrorism and related collective or individual violence (Angel 1994; Emerson and Hartman 2006; Friedland 2001; Habermas 2001; Inglehart 2004; Juergensmeyer 2003; Smelser and Mitchell 2002; Turk 2004). This is found to include counter-state as well as state religiously-grounded terror and related violent actions and wars, as exemplified by what sociologists (Bauman 1997, 2001) identify as ruling Iranian Islamic fundamentalism and dominant "Bible Belt" evangelicalism with their shared "proto-totalitarian" solution to the "burden" of individual liberty and the "agony of choice" by eliminating liberties and choices. These violent actions comprise within-society culture wars or repression and military wars or aggression against other societies, specifically domestic and global "crusades" and "jihads" literally or figuratively in reciprocal affinity (Turner 2002).

Hence, individuals, social groups, states, and societies that hold religious orthodoxy or rigid theological dogmas are likely more to advocate, commit and support terrorism than are others. While not all religiously orthodox or theologically dogmatic individuals, social groups, states, and societies engage in or justify terrorism, they tend to do so more than do others. Specifically, fundamentalism in religion as a case of religious orthodoxy or traditionalism, including theological dogmatism, by its antagonism and revolt against secular modernism causes explains, and predicts terrorism, including both counter- and state terror pursued and sanctified as anti-modern "godly" revolution and "holy" war in the shared manner, as Weber proposes, of Islam and Calvinism. Sociological theory and research suggest and document that religious fundamentalism, including its Christian, mainly Protestant, version of evangelicalism and its Islamic and other non-Christian forms, is instrumental in and/or instrumentalized by terrorism, including variations or proxies of crusades and jihads (Eliasoph and Lichterman 2003; Emerson and Hartman 2006; Friedland 2002, Habermas et al. 1998; Juergensmeyer 2003; Smelser and Mitchell 2002; Turk 2004; Townshend 2002; Turner 2002).

A special observed case is Biblical literalism or inerancy characterizing evangelicalism or Biblicism within Christianity, especially Protestantism, with almost two thirds of Americans holding the belief that the Bible is the "actual word of God and is to be taken literally" (Edelman 2009) and thus by implication "Biblical law" applied almost totally as the "law of the land", as it is apparently in the "Bible Belt" death penalty and legal system– or else. The latter outcome involves at least exclusion from and discrimination within American society (Edgell et al. 2006), notably political power, if not extermination or execution and persecution and so "holy" terror, as in New England's Puritan Biblical theocracy ordering "whosoever shall worship any other God than the Lord shall surely be put to death", as cited by Tocqueville.

Another analogous case is the strict interpretation and implementation of the Koran and its Sharia law as the Islamic legal code that typifies fundamentalist or radical Islam (Davis and Robinson 2006; Feldstein 2008; Juergensmeyer 2003; Oberschall 2004; Turner 2002). Comparatively, what is Koran Sharia Law for Islamic fundamentalism is Biblical Law for US evangelicalism, and in that sense the criminal justice, notably death penalty, systems premised on each of these religious laws are functionally equivalent (Jacobs et al. 2005) or comparable, as shown by those of Iran or Taliban regions and the "Bible Belt". No wonder that Iranian theocracy and the evangelical "Bible Belt" (Texas) are the world leaders in executions as well as imprisonment for sins-as-crimes, alongside other Islamic theocracies (Saudi Arabia, Sudan, Taliban regions, etc.) and dictatorships (North Korea, China). If executions, above all of innocent persons, sinners, and dissenters, and mass long imprisonment for sins-as-crimes in the form of "less crime, more punishment" belong to the scale of political terrorism noted above, then Islamic fundamentalist theocracies and "Bible Belt" evangelical theocracy (ab)use Sharia Law and Biblical Law respectively as "sacred" legal mechanisms and instruments of state "holy" terror and tyranny overall, replicating or evoking the uses of these laws for the purpose of genocide, war, and other violence in earlier times (Angel 1994).

Hence, individuals, social groups, states, and societies that adopt and practice religious fundamentalism, in particular literalism about interpreting and implementing" holy" writings, have been and are more likely advocate, commit, and support terrorism than are others. With respect to Christian and Islamic individuals, groups, states or political organizations, and societies, this can be stated accordingly, as suggested by sociological and related theory and research (Feldstein 2008; Friedland 2002; Juergensmeyer 2003; Munch 2001; Oberschall 2004; Townshend 2002; Turner 2002). Christian and Islamic individuals, groups, states or political organizations, and societies that adhere to evangelicalism or Biblicism and strictly follow the Koran, specifically Biblical Law and Sharia Law, are more likely to advocate, commit and support terrorism than are others. To be sure, not all fundamentalist, in particular literalist evangelical and strictly Koran-following Islamic, individuals, groups, states, and societies commit or advocate terrorist activities, and yet they tend to do so more than do others.

As implied, terrorism can particularly be analyzed, explained, and predicted as an expression and outcome of theocratic counter-revolution or opposition against secular democracy and society in the form of anti-secular radical revolt or violent rebellion. Thus, Pareto implies that the Protestant Reformation was effectively a theocratic counter-revolution rather than, as in conventional wisdom, a sort of liberal-democratic and individualistic revolution or minimally reform. Pareto does so observing that the Protestant Reformation (alongside the revolution founding the Roman Empire) was a type of revolution "against" innovation (or "speculators" in a general sense). To that extent, it was a counter-revolution, since revolution is axiomatically defined by a set of innovations, as Schumpeter suggests with his conception of a "constant revolution of industrial and commercial methods" or "creative destruction" propelled by inventions in modern capitalism.

Especially, Pareto suggests that the Protestant Reformation arose as a counter-revolution against artistic, cultural, humanistic, modernist, and implicitly secular and liberal-democratic innovation, specifically against the Renaissance as such an invention par excellence, as Simmel also registers. Pareto observes that the Renaissance was "halted too soon" in "rough" Northern Europe, though not in "refined" Italy, by this religious anti-secular "revolution" as the counter-Renaissance and in that sense effectively an anti-artistic, anti-humanistic, and extremely anti-secular counter-revolution. Curiously, even Parsons (1967), while extolling the Protestant Reformation as the innovation and source of individualism and democracy, unwittingly admits that it was a counter-revolution by contrasting Puritan Protestants with the "men of the humanistic Renaissance" in that the two could agree only a few points (e.g., the rejection of ritual) while disagreeing on most others. In particular, the Puritan Revolution in 17th century England was reportedly the compound of a "defense of traditional English ways" and "an attack on all innovations" (Goldstone 1986) in politics and society, notably on secular institutions (Zaret 1989), amounting to a "theocratic revolt" against growing secularism in the polity and society (Juergensmeyer 1994).

Sociological theory and research posit and demonstrate that theocratic or theocentric ideas and practices seeking to merge religion and polity into "godly politics" are strongly related to religious terrorism, including its state and counter-state variants, and related forms of collective violence such as domestic and transnational wars of religion (Friedland 2001; Juergensmeyer 2003; Merrill 1945; Munch 2001; Oberschall 2004; Turner 2002; Wall 1998; Walzer 1963; Zaret 1989). In particular, this is suggested and predicted for Islamic and Christian, mainly Protestant, theocratic or fundamentalist groups, states, and societies (Friedland 2002; Turner 2002), as well as virtually all world religions as inherently representing or supporting "cultures of violence" (Juergensmeyer 2003).

Historical and contemporary instances of the osmosis of theocracy as "holy" tyranny with terrorism and related forms of religious violence reportedly abound in virtually all world religions, from Judaism, Hinduism, and Buddhism to traditional Christianity and Islam (Juergensmeyer 2003). For instance, within English-American Protestantism such instances are identified in Puritan "godly politics" (Zaret 1989) and "holy" wars (Gorski 2000) in England, the Puritan "godly community" (German 1995) or "Biblical Commonwealth" (Gould 1996) as what Weber calls the "theocracy of New England" (Kaufman 2008; Munch 2001) and its revivals or proxies such as the design for "Christian America" (Lindsay 2008; Owens et al. 2010; Smith 2000) and the "Bible Belt" (Bauman 1997), regarded as functional equivalents of theocracies and religious violence in Islam and other world religions (Juergensmeyer 2003). Moreover, as noted, Puritanism is identified as the prototype or precursor of modern anti-secular extremists such as Protestant and Islamic fundamentalists and terrorists, owing to its theocratic counter-revolution against growingly secular institutions and political innovations in 17th century England (Goldstone 1986; Gorski 2000; Juergensmeyer 1994; Munch 2001).

In consequence, individuals, social groups, states, and societies that are theocratic or theocentric through merging or linking religion and politics into theocracy and related social systems have been and are more likely to advocate, commit and support terrorism than are others. Moreover, in contrast to the previous, this requires no qualification or disclaimer so long as virtually all theocratic individuals, social groups, states, and societies tend to commit or advocate and justify terrorism in various forms, at least significantly more so than do others, simply are intrinsically or ultimately terrorist or violent on "sacred" grounds. The hypothesis could be a proxy Michels-like "iron" sociological law of theocracy: "who says theocracy as holy tyranny, says terrorism in various forms", including counter- and state, domestic and global, intra- and inter-society (except for secular) terrorisms. In sum, once established theocracy is the design and system of "holy" state and in extension through wars inter-state terror in its own right and if not instituted but a mere plan, dream, fantasy, or disestablished ("gone with the wind") one of counter-state terror, as is "godly" fascism, though somewhat less "sacred" terrorism, as shown by Nazism.

Closely related, terrorism is caused, explained, and predicted by the antagonism toward modern secular humanism, simply of anti-humanism, through violent revolt against humanistic Western modernity. Sociological theory and research suggest that anti-humanism in the form of antagonism toward modern secular-humanistic society are in some ways and degrees associated with terrorism and related forms of violence. In particular, it is suggested that terrorism and other violence are linked with religious conservatism's and fascism's repugnance (Comte's word) or abhorrence for secular Western humanism (Van Dyke 1995) as a perceived threat to both Divine and secular authority (Darnell and Sherkat 1997; also, Angel 1994; Bauman 2001; Friedland 2001, Juergensmeyer 2003; Smelser and Mitchell 2002).

The preceding therefore suggests that individuals, social, in particular religious, groups, states, and societies that are anti-humanistic by opposing or abhorring secular humanism have been and are more likely to advocate, commit and support terrorism than are others. The disclaimer is that not all anti-humanistic individuals, social, including religious, groups, states, and societies commit or support terrorist activities, but they tend to do so more than do others.

World Religions and Terrorism Revisited

Moreover, sociological analysis suggests and historical and present evidence indicates that in a way elements or syndromes and embryos of terror, namely violence, destruction, war of extermination or genocide, systematic coercion and violent repression, are probably inherent in religion (Angel 1994). Especially this applies to what Weber calls the great world religions such as Hinduism, Buddhism, Confucianism, Judaism, Christianity, and Islam, and within them his student Jaspers' "axial-age" religions and religiously determined civilizations, namely Judaic and Christian strictly speaking and Islamic in a broader interpretation (Eisenstadt 1986; Hamilton 1994; Lenski 1994). In sociological terms, this is likely because religion tends or claims to be the design and realm of sacred principles, human practices, and social institutions in Durkheim's sense, including actually or potentially "holy" violence, war and genocide, destruction, severe coercion and violent repression directed against the "profane" and "infidels" and in that sense "terror" in, as Pareto puts it, the "name of the Divine master." At the minimum, all religion or faith is, as

Weber, Pareto, and Simmel suggest, exclusive[14] with respect to outsiders or non-believers and thus potentially violent, militant or militarist, coercive, and repressive, with the effect that what Tönnies describes as the "free will of mankind" is "lost".[15] In particular, all the world religions, as Weber and other sociologists demonstrate, have been and remain systems of "restraint" (Bell 1977), control, coercion, and repression within society and religious wars of extermination or genocide against "infidel" societies. To that extent, they develop, contain, and perpetuate components or embryos of "holy" terror, war, and tyranny overall, as especially, though not solely, reportedly epitomized in past times by Islam and parts of Christianity (Angel 1994), including Protestantism (Juergensmeyer 2003), and in contemporary societies by Islamic fundamentalism and Protestant evangelicalism (Bauman 1997; Friedland 2002; Hedges 2006; Turner 2002; Turk 2004).

In particular, Calvinism, including Puritanism, and Islam have always been and remain, the first through revived Protestant evangelicalism in America and second via contemporary Islamic fundamentalism, what Weber characterizes as designs and systems of religious revolution[16] within society and "holy" war against "infidel" societies a la crusade and jihad. To that extent, they are complexes of mostly illegitimate, indiscriminate, systematic or continuous, and strategic violence, destruction, and severe coercion and violent repression as a "Divine" commandment and for the "glory of God", and to that extent intrinsically of state and counter-state terror and tyranny overall. Notably, such "holy" terror in Calvinism, Islam, and other religions manifests itself, as Pareto puts it referring the Christian God, in the tendency to "kill in the name of the divine master".

At this juncture, Calvinism originally represented, in Weber's words, the "Church Militant" in the sense of both intra-societal religious revolution and inter-societal "holy" wars, just as did early Islam as its functional

---

[14] Weber observes that historically the "formation of a political association entails subordination to its corresponding god. When fully developed, this god was altogether exclusive with respect to outsiders".

[15] Tönnies observes that "once the world and all its destinies are put into the hands of one single God, who created them from noting, sustains them according to his good pleasure and gives them laws and ordinances which make their entire development seem regular and necessary, all subordinate wills and freedoms in nature are lost, even the free will of mankind."

[16] Following Weber, Tawney (1923:804) observes that "Calvinism, assuming different shapes in different countries, became an international movement, which brought not peace but a sword, and the path of which was strewn with revolutions."

equivalent or main contestant (Harrold 1936; Mansbach 2006). On this account, Puritan-rooted resurrected and expanding evangelicalism in America can be so designated in virtue of its proto-Calvinist composite of religious revolution or culture wars within society cum "sacralizing" or "influencing" politics (Davis and Robinson 2009; Bell 2002; Friedland 2001; Juergensmeyer 2003; Lindsay 2008; Munch 2001; Owens et al. 2010; Wagner 1997) and "holy" global war against other "evil" societies (Turk 2004; Turner 2002). In so doing, it operates as functionally equivalent to or emulates and competes with Islamic fundamentalism also defined, driven, and sustained by dual militancy expressed in the concept of jihad in the broad sense, as is also understood crusade, of a total struggle (Friedland 2002; Juergensmeyer 2003; Mansbach 2006; Turner 2002).

In essence, if religion intrinsically constitutes a design and eventually becomes a system of "holy terror", as do notably most world religions, then the underlying causes are certain common religious properties or outcomes. They are anti-humanism, anti-egalitarianism and anti-universalism, anti- or pre-liberalism and thus anti- or pre-democracy, militant radicalism and militarism, anti-progressivism and anti-modernism, and anti-rationalism or anti-scientism, in conjunction and mutual reinforcement (as elaborated later). Alternatively, such causes are the repugnance or abhorrence for secular "ungodly" humanism, the substitution or subversion of secular egalitarianism and universalism through its religious particularistic or non-universalistic, including sectarian or factional, and thus "deceptive" (Dahrendorf 1979) variants, the opposition to liberalism both as an ideal of individual and all liberty and an institutional system of liberal-secular democracy. They also comprise the rejection or suspicion of pacifism or peaceful conflict resolution within society and across societies, the antagonism to modernism and social progress, and the hostility to scientific and other rationalism.

The preceding hence yields the following empirical generalization and prediction of the reasons why elements of terrorism, namely violence, destruction, war, and coercion and violent repression, are inherent to religion as Diderot-Durkheim's sacred sphere, notably Weber's world religions. Namely, anti-humanistic, anti-egalitarian and anti-universalistic, anti-liberal, militant and militarist, anti-progressive and anti-modern, and irrational and anti-rational religious individuals, organizations, governments, and societies are more likely to advocate, commit, and support terrorism than are others. This does not mean that all such religious individuals, organizations, governments, and societies resort and endorse terrorism, yet they tend to do so more than others.

Relaxing the previous statement, *insofar* as elements of terrorism, including violent repression within society and aggressive war against other societies, are inherent to religion, notably most world religions, then this is primarily because of the composite of factors. To summarize, these are religious anti-humanism, anti-egalitarianism and anti-universalism, anti-liberalism, militancy and militarism, anti-progressivism and anti-modernism, and irrationalism or anti-rationalism. In short, these variables form the sources or correlates of terror within religion, including most world religions (summarized in Table 4.2). Simply, *if* religion as such is, notably most world religions are, violent and warlike in the form or proxy of terror, this is mostly due to being anti-humanistic, anti-egalitarian and anti-universalistic, anti-liberal, militant and militarist, anti-progressive and anti-modern, and irrational and anti-rational.

The above is thus a conditional proposition, namely these six interconnected and mutually reinforcing factors are explanatory and predictive on the condition or likelihood that religion is, notably most world religions are, inherently or ultimately violent and warlike. If it is (they are) not, then these causes do not apply. This is perhaps an overly charitable assumption, as suggested by a long line of observers, from Diderot, Hume, Voltaire, and other Enlightenment philosophers through in part Weber to many contemporary sociologists, but preempts potential allegations or imputations of "anti-religion", usually made by US and other religious conservatives, fascists, and rational choice theorists of religious "capital", "economies", "free markets", and the like characterizing the "economics of religion".

In passing, with its concepts of religious "capital", "markets", "economies", etc., the "economics of religion" usually, as one would expect, appears so economistic or mechanistic and in that sense grotesque or artificial, like perhaps all rational choice theory cum the economics of society, that even some of its exponents do not take it very seriously or literally (Frey 1997). Especially it does so when expounded by "rational choice" sociologists thus acting as "second rate" economists. In addition, the economics of religion, especially in the US, represents a sort of scientific rationalization (cover) for religious values and beliefs, typically anti-secularism and evangelicalism, as indicated by the rational choice model's rejection of the near-universal or classical sociological treatment of religion as the realm of irrationalism and of the theory and process of secularization in modern society. And such non-scientific values violate the ideal of value-free social science in Weber's sense and make the rational choice model of religion a sort of anti-secularization—so, if one wishes,

Table 4.2. Sources or correlates of terror in religion.

I Religious anti-humanism
II Religious anti-egalitarianism and anti-universalism
III Religious anti-liberalism
IV Religious militancy and militarism
V Religious anti-progressivism and anti-modernism
VI Religious irrationalism or anti-rationalism

anti-liberation–theology mixed with trivial, incongruous economics applied to a paradigmatically non-economic and irrational domain.

As implied, the observation that elements of terror, i.e., violence, destruction, war, coercion and repression, are inherent to religion especially holds true of theocratic world (and local) religions defined by what Tocqueville and Weber calls an alliance or unity and Dahrendorf (1979) merger between religion and political power, sacred and secular powers, simply church and state (also, Dombrowski 2001). This is because, as Tocqueville classically admonishes, Weber implies, and Dahrendorf (1979) states, such an alliance or merger between religion and political power whenever and wherever established has never done "any good" to society, despite usually professed "good intentions" by theocratic and other religious groups. The typical condition has been instead the exact opposite, including government "holy" violence, destruction, war, coercion and repression against the "unholy", thus state and inter-state terror as defined.

Conversely, the outcome is counter-state terrorism whenever and wherever such theocratic alliance or merger of religion and political power is formally disestablished, as in Puritan New England during the 1820–30s primarily due to Jeffersonian secularism and liberalism (Dayton 1999, Gould 1996; Hillmann 2008b) and Turkey in the 1920s. The outcome is also likely when the theocratic merger is prevented from being completely realized or reinstituted by countervailing religious or non-religious social forces, as in America since the 1960s through the 2010s (despite the "Bible Belt"), and Turkey until recent times, not to mention Western Europe, notably Scandinavian countries as "post-Christian" societies (Norris and Inglehart 2004). In short, theocratic religions through allying and ultimately merging with political power are the composite of what Tocqueville calls state "terror and faith", and when failing to do so the same compound of terrorism and religious belief in a counter-state or anti-government form.

Both outcomes—state and counter-state "terror and faith" when in merger with or exclusion from political power—have historically been manifested in such paradigmatic theocratic religions as Calvinism, particularly its Anglo-Saxon "pure sect" (Weber's term) Puritanism, and Islam, including their survivals or revivals in contemporary American and Islamic fundamentalism. Thus, whenever and wherever Calvinism/Puritanism and Islam ally or merge with political power they both establish or reinstitute systems of genuine or proxy state and inter-state terror, including violence and coercion or, as Mill registers, the suppression of virtually all liberties and "amusements" within society and "holy" wars against "unholy" societies. As indicated, this was exemplified by the "reign of terror" (Merril 1945; Walzer 1963) in old and New England's Puritan "coercive theocracy" (Zaret 1989) and their Islamic equivalents in the past and present.

Alternatively, if Puritanism and Islam, like any theocratic religions, fail in their alliance or merger with government, they both resort to anti-government violence, destruction, and, as Weber observes, a religious revolution or civil war and in that sense counter-state terror. This is what Puritanism did in its "theocratic revolt" against increasing secularism (Juergensmeyer 1994) as well as Anglicanism and the monarchy, in England (Goldstone 1986; Gorski 2000; Hillmann 2008a; Zaret 1989) and in part the "ungodly" Episcopal Church in the old South through the Puritan-incited Great Awakenings as partly violent anti-secular counter-revolutions or "counteroffensives" (Archer 2001; Means 1963; Rossel 1970). It is also what its heir evangelicalism commits against secular democracy condemned and attacked as "big" and "ungodly" government in contemporary America (Adorno 2001; Davis and Robinson 2009; Friedland 2001; Lindsay 2008; Munch 2001), as well as Islamic fundamentalism did and does through counter-state terrorist attacks against "infidel" governments and societies.

For instance, Tocqueville observes that "religions intimately united with [government] exercise sovereign power founded on terror and faith; but when a religion contracts an alliance of this nature [then] it commits the same error as a man who should sacrifice his future to his present welfare; and in obtaining a power to which it has no claim, it risks that authority which is rightfully its own. When a religion founds its empire only upon the desire of immortality that lives in every human heart, it may aspire to universal dominion; but when it connects itself with a government, it must adopt maxims which are applicable only to certain nations. Thus, in forming an alliance with a political power, religion augments its authority over a few and forfeits the hope of reigning over all." If this is correct, then any theocratic religion as defined by its unity with political power is intrinsically or ultimately the system of "holy" state terror, and conversely, non-theocratic religions not seeking such merger do not form systems of that sort.

In particular, Tocqueville's is not only a diagnostic observation, with apparent reference to the original and persistent theocratic tendencies of Puritanism as what he calls "the destiny" of America, just as–and perhaps in virtue of–being its pre-revolutionary genesis. It is also an almost prophetic prediction in light of Puritan-rooted evangelicalism's revived theological design and partly realized social system of theocracy or its "Christian Right" equivalent (Hedges 2006; Hout and Fischer 2002; Owens 20010; Phillips 2006) a la "Christian [evangelical] America", including the Southern and other "Bible Belt" since his visit during the 1830s through the early 21st century.

After all, theocracy is intrinsically the design and social system of "holy" terror, including "holy" war a la crusades and jihads, and tyranny or despotism overall prefiguring and in part inspiring contemporary totalitarianism and militarism such as, in the case of Calvinist theocracies, fascism, including Nazism (Adorno 2001; Fromm 1944; McLaughlin 1996). For instance, recall in Anglo-Saxon societies, in particular America, reportedly theocratic and militant French-born Calvinism in the English-American shape and name of Puritanism fulfilled the identical "sociological function" as did fascism in Europe, notably Nazism in Germany (McLaughlin 1996). This is the "function" of severe coercion and what Comte identifies and predicts as "violent repression" and thus tyranny within society as well as of aggressive war of extermination or destruction against "evil" societies, and to that extent terror, including both its government and anti-government variants, as defined in this work. No wonder that in virtue of its "theocratic revolt" against growing secularism in early England and establishing a "coercive theocracy" (Zaret 1989) pervaded by the reign of "holy terror" by what Comte sarcastically calls Puritan "saints" and Weber (and curiously Marx) "religious virtuosi", Puritanism is considered the prototype or precursor of modern anti-secular extremists committing or advocating terrorism such as Protestant and Islamic fundamentalists. Generally, it remains the perennial model of American religious and political conservatism continually and proudly standing in the venerable violent, coercive, repressive, and warlike "tradition of the Puritans" (Dunn and Woodard 1996).

In general, so long as religion is intrinsically a theological design, or eventually becomes a social system, of theocracy it is inherently or ultimately the "reign of terror" both in its state and counter-state forms depending on the victory or failure of theocratic plans, in the "name and mind of God". It is the design and system of brute force, severe coercion, and violent repression within society for the sake of establishing "God's Kingdom on Earth"–as envisioned by Calvinist-inspired Dominion theology within American evangelicalism–and "holy" total war of extermination and destruction against other societies in the aim of eliminating "infidels" as "enemies of God". Conversely, if religion is not theocratic, if ever, then it is not such reign of terror, i.e., of systematic coercion and violent repression via permanent religious revolution in society and "holy" total war against other societies. These properties of "holy" terror especially, as in Weber's and other sociological accounts, typify Calvinism/Puritanism and Islam, and consequently contemporary Protestant and Islamic fundamentalism operating as functional equivalents or major competitors (Friedland 2001; Hedges 2006; Mansbach 2006; Turner 2002), in part Hinduism (Archer 2001), and to a lesser extent other world religions like Buddhism (Juergensmeyer 2003), with Confucianism as a type of secularized, non-transcendental or proxy religion being the sole or main exception. The latter thus confirms rather than refutes the sociological rule or historical pattern of an inner link between transcendental, true religion and violence, war, coercion, and repression.

On this condition, Michels' like "iron" sociological law can be both generalized from experience and predicted for the future to the effect that "who says theocratic religion says reign of holy terror, including brute force, coercion, and violent repression within society and wars of extermination and destruction against other societies." Evidently, this is a strong and seemingly dubious argument. The argument is conditional on that religion intrinsically aims or eventually succeeds to establish theocracy as a special "holy" type of state terror and tyranny overall in its own right, and, if disestablished or the theocratic design fails, of counter-state terrorism against non-theocratic or secular—or, in the limiting case, other theocratic–powers and institutions. This is paradigmatically exemplified by Islam and Calvinism/Puritanism and their contemporary ramifications in Islamic fundamentalism and Protestant evangelicalism.

Conversely, so long as the condition of religion or theology cum theocracy is not always found, as Tocqueville and Weber imply, not all, including world, religions, can be considered the "reign of terror" in the sense of religiously determined violence, destruction, war, coercion, and repression. Rather, *only* their specifically theocratic design and outcome can be deemed inherently and invariably terrorist, i.e., violent, coercive, repressive, warlike, or militarist. At this juncture, terrorism arises and functions as a theocratic type of collective political action aiming at eliminating what "born again" American and Islamic religious conservatives construe as the "crisis" or failure of liberal-secular democracy (Deutsch and Soffer 1987; Dunn and Woodard 1996; Emerson and Hartman 2006; Lindsay 2008) and reconstructing America and some more or less democratic Muslim societies (e.g., Turkey, Egypt) as theocracies cum "Christian" and "Islamic" states and nations (Friedland 2002; Hedges 2006; Juergensmeyer 2003). As observed, it does as "an extreme, violent response", with a theocratic ground and rationale, to what is perceived as fragile (Eisenstadt 1998) and "failed" secular politics to the effect of involving "political regimes and ethnic and ideological adversaries over fundamental governance issues" (Oberschall 2004). In particular, Islamist and other religiously grounded terrorism reportedly results from considering theocracy the "only answer" to political and all societal problems, in spite of the "internal contradictions of theocratic states" (Oberschall 2004) in the Muslim world like Iran, Saudi Arabia, Taliban-ruled regions, etc., as well as their "Christian" Protestant emulations in America (Hedges 2006; Juergensmeyer 2003), especially the fundamentalist "Bible Belt", and to a lesser extent other Western societies, such as post-communist Catholic Poland and in part Ireland (Inglehart 2004).

Hence, the above strong argument can be relaxed insofar as not all religions or theologies design, become, or establish theocracies, at least within Tocqueville's and Weber's framework. This yields the weaker thesis that only those types of religion that design and establish theocracy constitute the designs and systems of state "holy" terror, namely brute force, destruction, war, severe coercion, and violent repression within society and against other societies. Conversely, non-theocratic religions are less likely to be terrorist, i.e., violent and warlike, in this sense. For instance, Islam and Calvinism/Puritanism have been, as Weber suggests, and remain, through Islamic and Protestant fundamentalism, paradigmatic types of religion as theocracy. Consequently, they have been and remain exemplary theological designs and political systems of state and inter-state, just as when disestablished or not yet established, and counter-state terror, through their shared notion and practice of religious revolution within society and "holy" war against "infidel" societies. Reverse instances are Confucianism and Buddhism as non- or less theocratic and consequently, other things equal, less terrorist, i.e., less violent, coercive, militarist, or warlike, though with some qualifications for the latter (Juergensmeyer 2003).

Alternatively, the preceding implies the underlying reason why Islam and Calvinism have been and Islamic and Protestant fundamentalism are the two major forces of state and inter-state as well as when outside of political power, counter-state terror, in particular intra-societal coercion and "holy" global wars. This is that they are inherently the theological designs and, as Mill observed for Puritanism, whenever and wherever feasible become, the institutional systems of theocracy as "sacred" tyranny. In turn, the probable reason why Confucianism, Buddhism, and similar world or local religions have not or less been forces of state and inter-state and counter-state terrorism, at least so far, may be simply that they are non- or less theocratic than fundamentalist Islam and evangelical Protestantism. Thus, Tocqueville's quoted statement suggests that only those religions that establish theocracy through being "united" with political power form the double composite of state "terror and faith". And conversely, those not seeking such unity do not, though he implies the reverse outcome as a hypothetical possibility or desideratum and less as an historical-empirical reality.

Skeptics may also object that a non-theocratic and thus non-terrorist or non-violent religion (even Buddhism according to Juergensmeyer 2003) has historically been and remains what Weber calls an "impossible contradiction" ("impossibility theorem"). Arguably, this is so if all religions aim to unite or ally, though in different degrees, with political power in order to promote their "sacred" goals in Durkheim's sense in opposition to and elimination of "profane" secular non-religious forces and other religious groups. Of course, among these goals, the paramount and ultimate is the victory in a "holy" cosmic war against "evil" and the "ungodly" (Juergensmeyer 2003), involving religious revolution or culture wars American-style within society and global crusades or jihads against other societies, through superior physical and symbolic force, repression, and coercion, including military power, and to that extent terror in its counter- and state, intra- and inter-state, forms.

Still, Weber's sociological framework allows for the possibility that not all world religions are theocratic to the same degree by design and equally willing or capable of instituting and sustaining theocracy. Consequently, they would not be all a system of state and inter-state–and, if outside of government, counter-state–terror within society via religious revolution and violent repression and against other societies through offensive wars. Specifically, those religions that seek passive adaptation or "mere accommodation" to the world, namely existing secular or non-secular political powers and institutions would be non- or less theocratic and consequently would not establish the reign of terror exerted by Comte's saints or Weber's religious virtuosi Puritan- and Islamic-style for the "glory of God". In Weber's view, all the world religions, including both the "Oriental" and traditional pre-Protestant Christianity like Catholicism and the Orthodox Church, belong to this category, with the sole and salient exception of Protestantism, more precisely Calvinism, including Puritanism. Conversely, those world religions aiming at and succeeding in what Weber calls the total "mastery of the world", including economy, politics, culture, and civil society, tend to be theocratic. In this connection, theocracy represents the only or most effective instrument to attain this aim of the "domination over the sinful world by religious virtuosi belonging to the 'pure' church'" such as Calvinists, notably Puritans, and consequently the design and system of "holy" state as well as when not in power counter-state terror.

As implied, Calvinism, including Puritanism, is Weber's exemplar of the world religions seeking and attaining the absolute mastery of the social world, alongside fundamentalist Islam which he ironically classified under those of "passive adaptation". In retrospect, this is an apparent contradiction and perhaps even an error in view of what he emphasizes as the shared Calvinist-Islamic concept and systematic practice of religious revolution and "holy" war operating as evidently the exact opposite of "passive adaptation" or "mere accommodation" to the "sinful" world. This is likely because contemporary Islamic fundamentalism, like power-aspiring Protestant evangelicalism (Friedland 2001; Hedges 2006; Lindsey 2008; Owens et al. 2010 can be considered anything but "passive adaptation" to modern society, including secular government and civil society. At least, radical Islam through its revived or intensified theocratic fundamentalism has moved since Weber's time from a religion of "passive adaptation" to the socio-political world to one of "mastery" or domination of politics and society (Feldstein 2008; Smelser and Mitchell 2002; Oberschall 2004; Turk 2004), including economy and culture, in a manner analogous, though not identical, to Calvinism, including Puritanism and its heir revived evangelicalism in America and elsewhere.

Thus, Weber implies that Calvinism and Islam are equivalent or comparable in terms of mastery or domination of the social world in the following remarks. He first remarks that Islam "makes obligatory the violent propagation of the true prophecy which consciously eschews universal conversion and enjoins the subjugation of unbelievers under the dominion of a ruling order dedicated to the religious war as one of the basic postulates of its faith". By assumption, Islamic-style and any religious war is an endeavor and practice of literal, military or violent "mastery of the world". Then, Weber suggests that, as paradigmatic "inner-worldly asceticism", radical Calvinism and consequently Puritanism "reached a similar solution [to Islam in that] it represented as God's will the domination over the sinful world by religious virtuosi belonging to the 'pure' church". In this connection, it would seem that the only or major difference is that Calvinism/Puritanism pursues and attains total, both military and economic, political, and cultural, "domination over the sinful world", and Islam solely or mostly the first via "holy" war cum jihad. Yet, this is more apparent than factual difference, given that Islamic fundamentalism precisely seeks and, if victorious, reaches such Calvinist-style total mastery or dominance of society, as witnessed in Iran, Saudi Arabia, Taliban-ruled regions, etc. After all, Islamic "jihad" signifies both military war against "infidel" societies and what US fundamentalists call and conduct as "culture wars" against "infidels" within society, simply a "struggle" for the "true faith" and "Allah" in the broadest sense (Juergensmeyer 2003), as does, for that matter, Christian "crusade [for faith and Christ]" (Turner 2002).

Generally, one wonders what is Islamic and any theocracy and tyranny overall if not the supreme political, i.e., violent, coercive, repressive, and militarist, form of mastery, control, or domination over the social world. In sociological retrospect, this is a moment that Weber surprisingly overlooks because he emphasizes intrinsic theocratic and militarist outcomes in Islam and still categorizes it under the religions of "mere accommodation" to politics and society. He does perhaps because of his thesis of an "elective affinity" or "intimate relationship" between Calvinism and modern capitalism, for the latter is just the economic and so not the only form or outcome of the Calvinist total "mastery of the world". Hence, in Weber's framework the likely underlying cause and explanation why Islamic and Protestant fundamentalism are the major perpetrators of both state and counter-state terrorism in contemporary societies is that Calvinism originally was and Islam since his times has become the religious systems of the "mastery of the world", specifically the political and all social system, through their shared design and activity of religious revolution and "holy" war. Alternatively, their "mastery of the world" through the shared religious revolution and "holy" war, i.e., crusades and jihads in the broadest sense, likely explains and predicts their state, inter-state, and counter-state terror.

In turn, Weber's framework implies that a reason why non-Protestant Christianity such as Catholicism and the Orthodox Church, Confucianism, and Buddhism are less manifest or salient agents of state and counter-state terrorism is that they are the religions of "passive adaptation" or "mere accommodation" to the world" of politics, economy and culture. If the above is correct, then from the stance of the relationship between religion/theocracy and terror, notably the policy of counter-terrorism, the "passive adaptation" or "mere accommodation" to the secular "sinful" world of politics and society may prove to be a blessing and virtue, a sort of antidote to terrorist agents and actions. However, the Calvinist-Puritan and analogous Islamic total mastery of the political and social world may prove to be a self-destructive "curse" and theocratic totalitarian poison of liberal-secular democracy.

Such mastery could thus ultimately generate what Weber would call "adverse fate" for those contemporary societies dominated or over-determined by Puritanism and Islam such as, via Puritan- and generally Calvinist-rooted evangelicalism (Hedges 2006; Munch 2001), "Christian America" and Muslim theocracies. Consequently, it would do so for the world as a whole through their shared idea and practice of "holy" global war with a MAD outcome (mutually assured destruction) (Habermas 2000) in the form or image of a nuclear or other devastating military catastrophe (Schelling 2006). Conversely, the "mastery of the world" is far from being, as Weber implies and Parsons et al. celebrate by the assumed "elective affinity" of Calvinism and modern capitalism, an "unmitigated blessing" in an invidious distinction from non-Protestantism, including Catholicism and Oriental religions, supposedly failing to generate the capitalist economy due to their "passive adaptation".

CHAPTER SIX

ANTI-RATIONALISM AND MODERN TERRORISM

Antagonism toward Rationalistic Modernity as the Factor of Modern Terrorism

Another related effective or potential sociological factor of contemporary terrorism is the antagonism toward modern rationalistic society and culture, or the process of societal rationalization and the resulting condition of socio-cultural rationalism. The antagonism to social-cultural rationalism and generally what Schumpeter (1991) calls "rationalist civilizations", primarily originating in and typifying the Western world since at least the "Enlightenment West" (Angel 1994), also causes, explains, and predicts terrorism. Terrorism hence becomes an expression and outcome of anti-rationalism in the form of a radical adverse reaction, i.e., violent, destructive, and militant revolt, against rationalistic Western modernity as an ideal, social system, and period. Anti-rationalism as the pertinent factor of terrorism operates in conjunction and mutual reinforcement with the previous sociological factors, viz., anti-liberalism and anti-democracy and anti-secularism, being, like these, the integral dimension of anti-modernism.

Especially the antagonism toward scientific rationalism or scientism (Habermas 1971) operates as a determinant and predictor of terrorism. In turn, such antagonism is likely linked to and justified by scientific rationalism's, in Schumpeter's[1] words, "aversion to extra-empirical [transcendental theological] cognition". It is also related to, as classical economist Ricardo remarks, the fact that "interests of science" necessitate unrestricted individual liberty in the form of academic freedom yet condemned and eliminated as "ungodly" (e.g., "anti-Christian" and "anti-Islamic") by anti-liberal, anti-rationalistic, and generally anti-modern

---

[1] Schumpeter (1991:317) remarks that "the scientific attitude and that aversion to extra-empirical cognition are, of course, sociologically related. They are both products of rationalist civilizations" as the subject of the "sociology of *geist* [spirit, knowledge]".

forces, particularly "religious and political fundamentalists"[2] (Bendix 1970). Terrorism hence is the reflection and outcome of anti-rationalism, notably anti-scientism, through violent, destructive revolt against scientific rationalism, i.e., modern rational and secular science, education, technology, and medicine, and the concomitant scientific-technological, medical, and societal progress. In essence, whenever and wherever anti-scientism and anti-rationalism overall emerges and prevails so does terrorism through radical adverse reaction, i.e., violence, destruction, war, and coercion and violent repression, against scientific and other cultural rationalism. Anti-scientism, like anti-rationalism, tends to be total and uncompromising encompassing antagonism to physical and social science. It is antagonistic especially to "ungodly" evolutionary biology as the "eternal" enemy for "Christian", especially Protestant, evangelicalism in America (Martin 2002) and Islamic fundamentalism, and even aspects of modern medicine such as birth control, vaccinations, and other medical treatments, as often condemned by US fundamentalists on "godly" grounds, and climate science, notably global warming theory, as a recent target of (only) American religious conservatism.

Religious, conservative anti-scientism is also antagonistic to critical "un-American" economics, sociology, and other social sciences since at least economist-sociologist Veblen, not to mention Marx's writings as a proxy taboo in America until recently. Veblen's ordeal typifies the conservative, religiously rationalized, hostility or suspicion to scientists and intellectuals and anti-intellectualism in America, i.e., as the "just desert" for his "crime" of scientific critique–that conservatives construe as equivalent to blasphemy–of American society, thus branded as one of the "saboteurs of the Status Quo" (Levi 1998), compounded with personal sins offending pervasive Puritanical sensibilities disdainful

---

2 Bendix (1970:95) observes that "a modern university has its common basis in the liberal idea of independent inquiry, free discussion, and academic self-government. Like other tenets of liberalism, this idea is subject to attack from the right and left. We are all familiar with outside attacks of religious and political fundamentalists upon the inherent radicalism of free inquiry."

3 Richard Ely, a contemporary of Veblen, upon visiting Germany's university system during the late 19th century reported "a new and exhilarating atmosphere of freedom" that was non-existent at American universities at the time (King 2004) and, with certain qualifications, later times, especially during national crises or emergencies like the "red scare", McCarthyism, the Cold War, and the "war on terror", etc. And, under conservatism America has been almost invariably placed under some sort of state of emergency in the form of domestic anti-liberal culture wars a la Prohibition and the war on drugs and other sins and vices (sexuality, abortion, Internet content, etc.) or offensive "patriotic" or "holy" wars

and repressive of academic freedom[3] (King 2004) at universities then and now.[4] Primarily owing to anti-scientific and anti-rationalistic conservatism, academic freedom as the chief prerequisite of scientific rationalism and hence technological and social progress, in America has reportedly "never been the rule", with scientists being the "principal victims of public attacks" (Coats 1967) a la "Monkey Trials", but a random irrelevant exception to be routinely dispensed with during crises, wars, or states of emergency, from Veblen's predicament to the "war on terror" a century later. America during revived religious and political neo-conservatism, like in any previous period under conservative dominance such as the "red scare" and the Cold War (Smelser and Mitchell 2002), has been placed in a sort of permanent state of emergency (Habermas et al 1998; Turner 2002). Predictably, the latter has assumed the dual form of domestic anti-rational or futile (Bell 2002) anti-liberal culture, temperance wars against "vice and sin" and "ungodliness" *and* offensive self-destructive and thus irrational "holy" war against "evil" societies, with the consequent destructive effects on academic freedom and scientific rationalism for, as Ricardo again admonishes and "every schoolboy knows", "interests of science" necessitate liberty.

As often observed, with respect to scientific rationalism and progress, the "first casualty" of temperance and military wars or states of emergency, including the "war on terror", in America, like elsewhere, has always been truth in the sense of science and knowledge, just as human liberty and life, while the outcome being resurrected or reinforced irrationalism through fundamentalist anti-rationalism, including religious superstition. No wonder, some U.S. physical scientists lament that solutions to global warming and related problems in America are "greatly retarded" because of the "lack of scientific and technological awareness" or rationalism in society to the point of invariably fundamentalist "superstitions"

---

against "evil" societies, including the 2000s war on the "axis of evil" (Iraq, etc.)—or typically, both in interconnection and mutual reinforcement, as with the linked "war on drugs" and "war on terror".

[4] ACADEME (2009) reports that "U.S. professors feel less powerful [in relation to administrative and political powers that be] than their colleagues abroad." Reportedly "U.S. academics are (or perceive themselves to be) among the least powerful, especially compared with academics in other countries with mature higher education systems, such as Japan, Germany Italy, and Norway." Many non-US academics are likely to be surprised by this finding of a comparatively lower degree of academic freedom in the "promised land of freedom" as the "only truly free" society, following neo-conservative claims (Lipset and Marks 2000) and perhaps for most Americans, than in other supposedly "less" free and democratic Western societies, notably the "old" Europe.

and usually conservative "political passions" overwhelming "sound reasoning", science, and secular knowledge as "ungodly" and "un-American". In addition to global warming, the lack or weakness of scientific rationalism and the force of religious "superstitions" and conservative "political passions" retard and often preclude sensible solutions to a variety of social problems in American society, spanning from poverty and welfare and extreme economic disparities, universal health care and medical treatments (vaccinations, radiation, preventive medicine, etc.) to political liberties (voting, etc.) and human rights and choices (privacy, birth control, etc.). The fact that even such a meteorological, non-political phenomenon as global warming, namely climate science documenting its human causes and proposing solutions, can revive religious "superstitions" and arose conservative "political passions", simply is, like virtually all other sciences, demonized and politicized, in America is remarkable and unknown in modern Western society.

The above indicates the remarkable depth, intensity, and magnitude of anti-rationalism in American fundamentalism and neo-conservatism overall, a type of anti-rationalistic revolt unparalleled within modern Western society and only rivaled by Islamic theocracies like Taliban-ruled regions, Iran, and Saudi Arabia. Evidently, the opposition to scientific theory and evidence of global warming is not an exception but a rule within American conservative anti-rationalism induced by religious "superstitions" and "political passions" and characterized with deep, intense, and comprehensive antagonism to scientific rationalism in general as "foreign" (European), "ungodly", and so "un-American".

As a consequence of comprehensive religiously grounded anti-rationalism, terrorism tends to be correspondingly total by anti-government and government agents through targeting, attacking, and destroying both physical and social science subjects, resources, and institutions. For example, such terrorism driven by anti-rationalism involves assaulting or threatening evolutionary biologists and teachers, killing "ungodly" physicians, similarly targeting or menacing (black-listing) sociologists, economists, and other social scientists, bombing medical and other facilities (abortion clinics, etc.), burning and banning libraries and books, as witnessed in America and Muslim countries in the past and present, etc.

Not surprisingly, anti-scientific and generally anti-rationalist groups like US "born again" evangelicals and Islamic fundamentalists have become the two major agents and/or sources of terrorism in contemporary societies. For instance, among many commonalities (Friedland 2002) of these two versions of religious fundamentalism or radicalism, both vehemently reject scientific biological evolutionism, by contrast accepted by or resigned to by official Catholicism, and attack or mistreat its scientists through "Monkey Trials" in the generic sense of anti-scientism, as "ungodly" and so "un-American" and "anti-Islamic" ideas, respectively, in favor of their versions of creationism (including "intelligent design" as in US evangelicalism). In another instance, US evangelicals and Islamic fundamentalists both maintain the primitive pre-scientific medieval belief in Satan, as the paradigmatic exemplar (the "mother") of all superstitions and prejudices (Popper 1973), and implicitly in the associated "witches" (Byrne 1997), as do in consequence no less than 71 percent of Americans (Glaeser 2004) and probably virtually all Muslims, compared to a small fraction of Europeans (11 percent in Denmark and 18 percent in France). On these two and most accounts, US evangelicalism and Islamic fundamentalism have become and solidified as the two most intense and comprehensive forms of anti-rationalism, just as in conjunction and mutual reinforcement of anti-liberalism, anti-democracy, and anti-secularism, in contemporary society (Norris and Inglehart 2004).

Thus, comparative sociological studies identify America primarily due to the revival of religious fundamentalism or traditional religion as the striking "deviant case" within modern Western society from the prevailing global process of rationalization as well as liberalization, democratization, and secularization to the point of ranking on the rationalist dimension alongside Islamic and other third-world traditionalist countries (Inglehart 2004). What is crucial in the present context is that US evangelicalism and Islamic fundamentalism are the two major agents, sources, and rationales of contemporary terrorism, because they are the two strongest forces of anti-rationalism, just as of intertwined and mutually reinforced anti-liberalism, anti-democracy and anti-secularism, and anti-globalism and anti-cosmopolitanism in modern society. Alternatively, their operating as the global "leaders" of anti-rationalism, as well as anti-liberalism, anti-democracy and anti-secularism, anti-globalism and anti-cosmopolitanism explains and predicts their acting as the world's major perpetrators or supporters of terrorism, including violent repression and coercion within society and aggressive "holy" wars against other societies. The underlying reason why anti-rationalistic American and Islamic fundamentalism are the two main agents or sanctifications of terrorism is that the latter as defined and generally radicalism or extremism is probably intrinsic to religious and other anti-rationalism, as well as to anti-liberalism, anti-democracy and (perhaps) anti-secularism, anti-globalism and anti-cosmopolitanism, just as conversely, as Popper (1966) implies, anti-rationalism is "inherent in radicalism." In short, it is because anti-rationalism has a "built-in" tendency to and practice of terror or violence.

Reportedly, contemporary terrorism and cognate violent activities are often connected to and explained by anti-rationalism, including anti-intellectualism, i.e., the antagonism toward the evolutionary process of societal rationalization, including the expansion of science and education (Schofer and Meyer 2005), and the resulting cultural system of rationalism (Dahrendorf 1979; Habermas 1989; Mannheim 1986; Popper 1973). Notably, various terrorist agents and activities reflect and derive from anti-scientism, i.e., the antagonism to rational and secular science, theory, method, research, education, and technology, including biology, medicine, stem-cell research, climate science, critical economics and sociology, etc., and to scientific-technological, medical, and other societal progress (Habermas 1989; Mannheim 1986; Juergensmeyer 2003). A paradigmatic example are religious schools ("madrasahs") in some Islamic countries in that they provide immediate inspiration to terrorists and are implicated with terrorist organizations (Krueger and Maleckova 2003; Turk 2004) in virtue of their opposition and suspicion to and depreciation and neglect of secular rational physical and social science substituted by "religious indoctrination", notably the explicitly or implicitly stated duty of "holy war" (jihad) against the broadly defined enemies of Islam, viz., "infidel" dissenting or different domestic and foreign persons and groups as well as governments and societies. Another, similar paradigmatic exemplar involves US conservative Protestantism's long-standing and continuing antagonism and attack against rational science (Martin 2002) and secular education, including medicine and by implication technology, perceived as a threat to sacred and political powers, and hence replaced or perverted by private and home-based religious schools and even "no" schooling as "better" than any secular instruction and knowledge as a sort of truly "forbidden apple" (Darnell and Sherkat 1997).

In turn, this curious commonality in anti-scientism reflects the general convergence or affinity between Protestant and Islamic fundamentalism, i.e., Calvinism, including its Anglo-Saxon "pure sect" Puritanism, and Islam, in terms of systematic violence, permanent religious war, and theocratic coercion and tyranny against the "ungodly" and "impure", as classically detected and analyzed by Weber. Reportedly, many terrorist (Juergensmeyer 2003) agents and acts, including vigilantes and vigilante violence, "professional" haters and hate crimes against "ungodly" scientists, teachers of evolution, etc., and medical personnel and facilities like abortion doctors and clinics in America, are traced to and explained by such shared fundamentalist enmity and opposition toward scientific and other cultural rationalism, notably the progress of science, technology and medicine, simply anti-scientism.

In consequence, one can infer and predict that those individuals, social groups, states, and societies opposed to cultural rationalism, including intellectualism, rational science, technology, and medicine, especially to scientific, technological, and medical progress, are more likely to commit, advocate, and support terrorism than are others. This needs to be qualified in that not all individuals, social groups, states, and societies antagonistic to rationalism, including rational science and technology and their progress, practice or preach terrorism, and yet they display a stronger and more persistent tendency for doing so than do others. The preceding holds true of contemporary terrorism in most of its forms, in particular counter-state and state, religious and quasi-religious, within- and across-society, including fundamentalist and fascist oppositional and official, domestic and global, terrorisms.

Irrationalism and Terrorism

Alternatively, terrorism expresses and results from the revival of irrationalism, including the pre- and anti-Enlightenment, in counterrevolution or opposition against modern rationalism, in particular the rationalistic Enlightenment, through violent revolt against the latter. In a sense, terrorism, like radicalism in general, is intrinsic to irrationalism, just as conversely, irrationalism being "inherent" in extremism, including terrorist violence. To the extent that, as Popper (1973) observes, irrationalism tends to "engender criminality" in the broadest sense, including government committed or sponsored crimes such as murders and executions, then it also does terrorism in its state and counter-state forms. Thus, the belief in witches, as the axiomatic instance of irrationalism, notably of religious superstition, during medieval and earlier times engendered certain types of criminality mostly in the form of government and other witch-hunts and trials (Byrne 1997) and to that extent state terror, and still does, as observed in some primitive societies today (as in Africa, India, etc.).

For instance, Puritanism's superstitious primitive belief in witches in 17th century England (Harley 1996) produced the "reign" of state terror (Merril 1945) by Puritan self-proclaimed saints through official witch-trials and the resulting execution of "witches" and in extension the "exorcism" of their assumed "master" Satan, in reality innocent humans. And the even more widespread and enduring belief in Satan, as the related paradigmatic case of religious superstition and irrationalism, did, does, and will likely continue to engender criminality, including both government committed crimes and vigilante violence against the Devil and his "allies", of course innocent humans, and in that sense state and counter-state terrorism. As noted, the belief in Satan remains most widespread and enduring in American evangelicalism and Islamic fundamentalism, and, given their respective societal dominance, consequently in "Christian" America in which almost three quarters of the population (71 percent) hold such admittedly primitive superstitious and irrational beliefs (Glaeser 2004), just as apparently virtually everyone does in most Muslim countries (perhaps excluding Turkey).

   As sociological analyses and observations indicate, American evangelicalism and Islamic fundamentalism as exemplary instances of religious irrationalism are also the two major operating, supporting, or rationalizing forces of religious and other terrorism. At this juncture, the perverted logic of "holy terror", including both state and counter-state terrorism, in American and Islamic fundamentalism operates through defining rationalistic, as well as liberal-democratic and secular modernity, as the Devil incarnate and its representatives as "witches" to be exorcised and exterminated by any means, i.e., violent repression and coercion within society and aggressive wars a la jihads and crusades against other societies, for the "glory of God" (Allah, Christ, etc.). In this sense, the demonization of scientific rationalism, as well as liberalism and liberal democracy and secularism, explains and predicts "holy" state, inter-state, and counter-state terror committed, advocated, or sanctified as "in the name and mind of God" by American evangelicalism and Islamic fundamentalism (Juergensmeyer 2003). If rationalistic, as well as liberal-democratic and secular, society is the creation of Satan and its adherents are "witches", then "holy" terror against and ultimately the destruction of these "evil" forces by the "godly", "virtuous", and "good"[5] (Smelser and Mitchell 2002) is the logical outcome, even the supreme commandment in American and Islamic fundamentalism, thus their shared "normal pathology" (Gouldner 1970).

---

   [5] According to Smelser and Mitchell (2002:12), "the contemporary terrorist mentality and culture, which are rooted in absolutist, either-or, good-and-evil world views, resist efforts to negotiate, because accommodation, bargaining, and mutually acceptable compromise are not envisioned as possibilities within many terrorists' mental framework. A corollary of terrorism based on absolute religious principles is that it is resistant to mechanisms of peaceful influence and persuasion, to say nothing of conversion, because of the strength and rigidity of these principles."

In general, religious and other irrationalism, including pre- and anti-Enlightenment prejudice, superstition, and fanaticism, is directly or indirectly associated with terrorism and related forms of violence, as sociological theory suggests and empirical research documents. In modern times, terrorism and related violence that is attributed to and justified by irrationalism ranges from Nazi and other fascist counter-state putsches (Beck 2000; Mannheim 1986) and state and inter-society terrorism via mass murder and wars of extermination (Arendt 1951; Bahr 2002; Barnes 2000; Eisenstadt 1999; Habermas 2001; also, Popper 1973) to oppositional terrorist attacks by extreme religious and other social groups (Juergensmeyer 2003; Smelser and Mitchell 2002; Turk 2004).

Hence, one can argue and predict that those individuals, social groups, states, and societies that systematically favor irrationalism over modern rationalism, in particular pre- and anti-Enlightenment over the Enlightenment, are more likely commit, advocate, and support terrorism than are others. The argument is qualified in that not all individuals, social groups, states, and societies favoring irrationalism over rationalism and intellectualism, including pre- and anti-Enlightenment superstition and fanaticism over the Enlightenment rule of reason, conduct and endorse terrorism, but they tend to do more than others. A specification of this argument is that terrorism expresses and results from a rebellion or revival of pre-scientific irrationalism, including religious and other superstition and fanaticism, against scientific-technological rationalism (Juergensmeyer 2003) or simply scientism (Habermas 1971) through violent revolt against the latter. Consequently, one can contend and expect that individuals, social groups, states, and societies that systematically prefer pre-scientific irrationalism over scientific and technological rationalism are more likely to commit, advocate, and support terrorism than are others. This contention is relaxed in that not all individuals, social groups, states, and societies favoring pre-scientific irrationalism over scientific and technological rationalism conduct and endorse terrorism, yet they tend to do more than others.

In this connection, terrorism arises and operates as the violent, destructive irrational "holy" war against rationalistic as well as liberal-democratic and secular modernity, in particular as "a form of psychological warfare" seeking to destroy or capture "ungodly" governments as well as influence or manipulate the general public (Lutz and Lutz 2004). For instance, the "godly" anti-government and anti-rationalistic terrorists by the Oklahoma City bombing not only produced a physical effect by killing as many persons as dying in homicides in three days in the entire country, but also generated a major "psychological impact" through a "combination of fear and fascination" (Heymann[6] 1999). The first included a kind of "collective alarmism" (Townshend 2002), and the second open or tacit support and the elevation of martyrdom[7] (Smelser and Mitchell 2002) of these "Christian warriors" among many "born again" US evangelicals (Juergensmeyer 2003). This also holds true of the September 11 2001 attacks by Islamic terrorists, with generating a stronger sense of "collective alarmism" and fear, from the White House to American "peasant villages" (Townshend 2002; also, Cragin and Chalk 2003), though no open fascination or support among US evangelicals, though the most extreme among them (e.g., televangelists and/or advocates of Dominion theology, etc.) describe these terrorist acts as "God's punishment" for America's "sins" and the like.

Superstition, Fanaticism and Terrorism

The previous argument is further specified in that terrorism expresses and results from a rebellion or revival of religious superstition, prejudice, fanaticism, dogma, and other pre-scientific beliefs against rational science, knowledge, and education, including their technological and medical applications, through violent revolt against scientism. Religious superstition, ignorance, prejudice, fanaticism, dogma, and other pre-scientific beliefs and practices are directly or indirectly linked to terrorism and related forms of violence, as sociological theory suggests and empirical research evidences. As noted, terrorism can in particular be directly or indirectly linked to the beliefs in "Satan" or the devil (Glaser 2004), including "witches" and witch-trials (Byrne 1997; Harley 1996), and "evil" cosmic forces overall (Juergensmeyer 2003), then in creationism, "godly" medicine (prayer, "holy" books), and the like.

---

[6] Heymann (1999:16) observes that, for instance, "for the US [government], terrorism does not pose any great national security threat to our stability or well-being as a nation—unless the traditional reluctance of terrorists to use weapons of mass destruction changes. With a single bomb, the terrorists in Oklahoma City killed as many people as die in homicides in three ordinary days in the entire US".

[7] Smelser and Mitchell (2002:32) suggest that "glorification of and personal salvation through violence is not limited to Islamic terrorists. Salvation as a voluntary martyr to violence or suffering has a religious history with roots in the theology of Christianity, Judaism, and Islam, as well as analogs in Buddhism. Self-fulfillment through perpetration of violence also has a history, going back at least to 19th century anarchists, early elements of Soviet communism, and some elements of the cowboy culture. Similarly, utopian visions achieved through apocryphal transformation are not limited to Islam but are common both in mainstream and sectarian aspects of Christianity and Judaism."

Alternatively, terrorism can be associated with vehement attacks on evolutionary biology and other secular science and medicine, including vaccination, radiation, birth control, etc., to be substituted with creationism or "intelligent design", the medical "efficacy of prayer" (Evans and Evans 2008), and the like (Darnell and Sherkat 1997; Goldstone 2000; Martin 2002). These pre-scientific religious beliefs and practices and their attacks on science are particularly (but not solely) observed among Islamic and U.S. fundamentalists and terrorists and their educational institutions (Juergensmeyer 2003). As indicated, the latter include "madrasahs" in some Muslim countries (Krueger and Maleckova 2003; Turk 2004) and fundamentalist private and home-based schools in America, especially, though not only, in the South, in opposition to secular public schooling, including, but not confined to, evolutionism (Darnell and Sherkat 1997; Juergensmeyer 2003; Martin 2002). And, as noted and documented by sociological and other studies, the two major forces or sources of religiously grounded terrorism are precisely Islamic and American religious fundamentalism.

The preceding yields the argument and expectation that individuals, social groups, states, and societies that maintain superstitious, fanatical, and other pre-scientific beliefs and practices in opposition to scientific ideas and values are more likely to commit, advocate, and support terrorism than are others. The argument is qualified that not all individuals, social groups, states, and societies maintaining superstitious religious and other pre-scientific beliefs (witches, Satan, "evil" cosmic forces, flat-earth theory, creationism, etc.) and practices (witch-trials, exorcism, ritual sacrifices of humans or animals to Divine powers) versus science conduct and endorse terrorism, yet they tend to do so more than others.

The above argument and expectation is specified for Islamic and Christian persons, groups, states, and societies with respect to the belief in "evil" cosmic forces (Juergensmeyer 2003), notably Satan (Glaser 2004) and the associated "witches", and corresponding practices like the exorcism of the "devil" and other ritual sacrifices of humans and witch-trials. Namely, Islamic and Christian persons, groups, states, and societies that maintain the beliefs in Satan and the associated witches and corresponding practices against the latter are more likely to commit, advocate and support terrorism than are others. This is also qualified in that not all Islamic and Christian and other religious groups, states, and societies maintaining the belief in "Satan" and "witches" and corresponding practices conduct and endorse terrorists, but they tend to do so more than others. This argument could potentially explain and predict most forms of religious, viz., Islamic, Christian, and other terrorism (Juergensmeyer 2003), its counter-state and state, domestic and global, within- and across-society forms, such as "holy" wars a la "crusades" and "jihads" against "ungodly" governments, social groups, and persons at home and abroad, just as other "infidel" or "evil" societies.

The Anti-Enlightenment and Terrorism

In particular, much of terrorism expresses and results from the antagonism to the Western European Enlightenment or the "Age of Reason" and its rationalistic and intellectualist, notably scientific, as well as liberal-democratic, pluralist, and secular, values and legacies. Notably, it is a violent expression and result of the opposition to scientific rationalism, as well as, in conjunction and mutual reinforcement, to the separation of religion and politics, as the Enlightenment value and legacy. In short, terrorism is often the violent child of the anti-Enlightenment in the form of a radical, destructive revolt against Enlightenment values and legacies. Particularly, religiously grounded and sanctified terrorism represents an extreme expression and outcome, thus a sort of ultimate act, of anti-Enlightenment revolt.

The latter typified and justified religious and other conservatism since its birth out of medieval traditionalism after the image of the Dark Middle Ages, become "self-reflective" in facing the Enlightenment and its political outcome the French Revolution and nascent liberalism (Mannheim 1986; also, Acemoglu et al. 2011; Dahrendorf 1979). Namely, during the late 18th and early 19th centuries conservatism represented the original and paradigmatic "anti-Enlightenment", as conservative sociologists approvingly register (Nisbet 1966; also, Dunn and Woodard 1996). Especially, religious conservatism declared a "holy" war, ultimately a "mindless" ineffective battle, against the "evil" liberal-democratic, secular, and rationalistic Enlightenment (Habermas 2001), as exemplified by the "Papal struggles" with liberalism (Burns 1990) and their Protestant versions in, as Weber observes, Lutheranism and especially Calvinism (Dombrowski 2001), including the evangelical Great Awakenings as the anti-Enlightenment revivals or "counteroffensives" (Archer 2001; German 1995; Means 1967; Rossel 1970). For instance, religious conservatives attacked the Enlightenment "values of secular morality in 18th century France" (Juergensmeyer 2003). And religious and other conservatism has basically continued to present and justify itself as "anti-Enlightenment" and anti-liberalism since, as through its extreme offspring fascism in interwar and postwar times and its revival neo-conservatism, including its own product neo-fascism, in recent years (Berman 2000; Habermas 1989).

Thus, sociological theory and research suggest that a particular covariate or rationale of contemporary, especially counter-state, religious and fascist, terrorism is counter-Enlightenment antagonism. Notably, this antagonism includes the opposition to the Enlightenment's "comprehensive liberalism" (Dombrowski 2001) and democratic, secular, and rationalistic ideals, including the separation of religion and politics, scientific rationalism, and "universalist morality" (Habermas 1989). Predictably, such a counter-Enlightenment posture is especially observed in conservatism (Angel 1994; Berman 2000; Juergensmeyer 2003; Mannheim 1986) as the original and perennial counter-Enlightenment (Nisbet 1966), including neo-conservatism[8] as a sort of new anti-Enlightenment (Habermas 1989), and also fascism and neo-fascism (Habermas 2001). As observed and expected, two contemporary religious systems tend to be "especially" opposed to and "unhappy" with the "Enlightenment formulation of church-state separation"[9] in the polity, just as to the "temper of

---

[8] Habermas (1989:41) comments that a universalist Enlightenment morality "recognizes no limits; it subjects even political action to moral scrutiny, although not so directly as our personal relationships. In an extreme case this kind of moralization can even encourage terrorist actions—so runs an old anti-Enlightenment theme. Even the terrorist, who sees himself as a last, lonely advocate of justice, could try to realize the freedom he is struggling for through direct violent action in the name of universal principles. It (is) not be difficult to demonstrate the inconsistency or the error in the imaginary moral reflections of the individual terrorist. In particular, he (Habermas 1989, 42) suggests that "neoconservatives present this extreme case [because] they want to minimize the burdens of moral justification on the political system" by instead resorting to Machiavellian amoral strategies of the ends justifying the means a la, as U.S. conservatives like say, "whatever it takes" to attain and maintain power, including anti-government violence, coercion and violent repression or culture wars and global "holy" war on the "evil" world and to that extent counter-state, state, and inter-state terrorism.

[9] Juergensmeyer (2003:28) registers that US "born again" fundamentalists "regard the history of Protestant politics since the early years of the Reformation as having taken a bad turn, and they are especially unhappy with the Enlightenment formulation of church-state separation." Juergensmeyer (2003:224–5) adds that "by its nature, the secular state is opposed to the idea that religion (has) a role in public life. From the time that modern secular nationalism emerged in the 18th century as a product of the European Enlightenment's political values, it has assumed a distinctly antireligious, or at least anticlerical, posture [while] religious "enemies of the Enlightenment" protested religion's public demise." In this account, "but their views were submerged in a wave of approval for a new view of social order in which secular nationalism was thought to be virtually a natural law, universally applicable and morally right. Enlightenment modernity proclaimed the death of religion. (It) signaled not only the demise of the Church's institutional authority and clerical control, but also the loosening of religion's ideological and intellectual grip on society. Scientific reasoning and the moral claims of the secular social contract replaced theology and the Church as the bases for truth and social identity" (Juergensmeyer 2003:225).

rationality" (and "fair play") in civil society stemming from Enlightenment values (Juergensmeyer 2003), Islamic fundamentalism and Protestant evangelicalism in America. In consequence, they seek to eliminate or reverse such Enlightenment secular legacy in favor of merging politics and religion and thus creating theocracy a la "Islamic republics" and "Christian America" through both anti-government violence and counter-revolutions *and* government theocratic or religiously sanctified coercion and repression once established in power, as well as "holy" culture and military wars against "ungodly" societies, and to that extent counter-state, state, and inter-state terrorism.

In this respect, the moment that Islamic fundamentalism and American evangelicalism are "especially unhappy" with the Enlightenment-based separation of religion and politics state as well as with scientific rationalism and related Enlightenment values helps, at least in part, to explain the observation and predict the prospect that two major "modern anti-secular radicals" (Juergensmeyer 1994) cum terrorist or violent and militarist groups are Muslim and US fundamentalists. Alternatively, in order to fully understand, explain, and predict how and why these two groups have become and will likely remain major theocratic extremists or terrorists it is instructive to take into consideration their shared "unhappiness" with the Enlightenment-rooted separation of church and state in the polity as well as rationalism in civil society and culture.

Hence, at least for these two religious groups, their shared anti-Enlightenment generates, explains, and predicts their common anti-secular terrorism or extremism, including anti-government violence when not in governance and state theocratic coercion and violent repression once established in power. Such anti-Enlightenment assumes the form of anti-liberalism and thus anti-democracy, anti-secularism, anti-rationalism, and generally anti-modernism opposing and reversing through terrorism or extremism liberalism, secularism, rationalism, and modernism, including the "ideology of individualism and skepticism", as emerging from the "European Enlightenment" and spreading beyond, including Jeffersonian America, since the 18th century through the 21st century (Juergensmeyer 2003). In essence, the shared battle-cry of Islamic and American fundamentalism is the "death of Enlightenment-based secularism, democracy, and rationalism, long live anti-secularism, theocracy and superstition"[10]

---

[10] Juergensmeyer (2003:225) observes that "in countering this disintegration, resurgent religious activists (proclaim) the death of secularism. The moral leadership of the secular state has become increasingly challenged in the (late) 20th century following the end of

(Juergensmeyer 2003), a composite of anti-secular and anti-rationalistic "dead wish" and theocratic and superstitious revival to be attained through their resort to counter-state, state, and inter-state terrorism.

An implied special case of counter-Enlightenment irrationalism includes anti- and pre-Enlightenment superstitions, prejudices, ignorance, and fanaticism, for example, the belief in "Satan" and similar "evil" cosmic forces (Juergensmeyer 2003), and corresponding practices like exorcism and ritual sacrifices, including "witches" and witch-trials to end, just as did torture (Einolf 2007), at least in the Western world, primarily because of the Enlightenment (Byrne 1997). These and related anti- and pre-Enlightenment beliefs and practices, notably the opposition to the Enlightenment's separation of religion and politics, especially typify extreme religious groups (Juergensmeyer 2003) and pervasive in America in contrast to Western Europe, while near-universal in Islamic countries. Recall more than 70 percent of Americans and all US evangelicals, who in turn comprise theologically, in virtue of treating the Bible as the "word of God", no less than three quarters of the US population, hold the primitive medieval belief in Satan or the Devil, as also virtually all people in Islamic countries, but only 11 percent of Danes and 18 percent of the French believe so (Glaeser 2004).

Therefore, individuals, social groups, states, and societies antagonistic to Enlightenment values and legacies, in particular the separation of religion and politics, have been and are likely more to advocate, commit, and support terrorism than are others. This is qualified in that not all anti- and pre-Enlightenment social groups, states, and societies, including those maintaining superstitious religious beliefs and practices, engage in or endorse terrorist activities, but they tend to do so more than others. The preceding helps to explain and predict counter-state and state, domestic and transnational, and within- and inter-society terrorism, particularly their conservative, religious, and fascist forms, thus terrorist or violent individuals, groups, states, and societies.

---

the Cold War and the rise of a global economy. Both Christian and Enlightenment values were left behind." Juergensmeyer (2003:239) comments that "it is poignant that [modern] governments [are] so often perceived as being morally corrupt and spiritually vacuous since the Enlightenment concepts that launched the modern nation-state were characterized by a fair amount of moralistic fervor (Rousseau's civil religion). Despite the noble rhetoric of [the] Enlightenment [it's early] opponents belittled the secularists' morality just as their modern critics have done".

Religious Anti-Rationalism and Terrorism—Factors of "Holy" Terror

The question arises as to the reasons why religious anti-rationalism or religion itself as, if Hume, Diderot, and other Enlightenment thinkers are correct, a paradigmatic species of irrationalism, in particular the polar opposite of Enlightenment rationalism, generates, explains, and predicts terrorism. This is the question of, paraphrasing Weber, reproduction and "justification of violence" in its various forms through religion, in particular religious irrationalism or anti-rationalism in the sense of opposition to or distrust for the Enlightenment's ideal of human reason condemned as "blasphemous" or "ungodly" in favor of Providential intelligence ("intelligent design"), as observed in most world religions (Angel 1994), excluding Confucianism and including "rationalistic" Calvinism and its sectarian derivative Puritanism. In short, one wonders about "reasons why acts of extreme, norm-transgressing" terrorist atrocities and destruction are engendered as well as sanctified by "religious conviction" (Townshend 2002). Sociological theory since especially the Enlightenment, historical evidence, and present tendencies suggest a set of interconnected and mutually reinforcing reasons why religious irrationalism and even religion as such inherently represents the design and justification and ultimately develops into the system and practice of "holy" terror in the "name and mind of God"[11] (Juergensmeyer 2003). This in particular holds true for Weber's virtually all world religions, though to a greater extent for some of them such as Protestant Christianity and Islam (and perhaps Hinduism and Judaism) than for others like Confucianism and Buddhism (Juergensmeyer 2003; Turk[12] 2004).

These factors operate in interconnection and mutual reinforcement and for the sake of this work can be classified into six broad categories as follows (also, Bittner 1996; Townshend 2002). They hence explain and

---

[11] Juergensmeyer (2003:5) uses the expression "terror in the mind of God" to indicate the religious practice and justification of contemporary terrorism by registering that "religion has supplied not only the ideology but also the motivation and the organizational structure for the perpetrators". In this comparative account, religion, either in combination with other factors or as the primary motivation, has mostly "incited terrorist acts [i.e.] a rise in religious violence around the world" during recent times to the effect that religious terrorism involves "public acts of violence for which religion has provided the motivation, the justification, the organization, and the world view [i.e. committed] by pious people dedicated to a moral vision of the world" (Juergensmeyer 2003:6–7).

[12] Turk (2004:277) infers that "Christianity, Judaism, Islam, Sikhism, and Buddhism permit, and may even require, violence in defense of the faith (as) interpretations of sacred texts foster "cultures of violence" in the name of creating or restoring a true moral order."

predict how and why religion and thus religious anti-rationalism has established itself as the prime force and rationale of terrorism, especially in Islamic settings and evangelical America, during recent times (Juergensmeyer 2003; Smelser and Mitchell 2002; Townshend 2002; Turk 2004). Simply, they help solve the widespread puzzle, bewilderment, or consternation, especially among non-academic circles, of "how in the world" religion or faith, including Christianity and Islam, as supposedly peaceful or non-violent, can operate as (Turk[13] 2004), or be harnessed in the service of (Eliasoph and Lichterman[14] 2003), "holy" terror, including counter-state, state, and inter-state terrorism.

Total and Unconditional Submission of Humans to "God's Kingdom on Earth"

The first reason why religion generates or sanctifies "holy" terror is the total and unconditional submission or subjection, humiliation, and eventually physical and other sacrifice of humans and their liberty and ultimately life to supra-human sacred, Divine causes and entities, effectively to their self-assigned agents or representatives claiming to establish "God's Kingdom on Earth." This is a defining property of religion as such, as in Durkheim's definition in terms of the sacred versus the profane world. Ultimately, it is expressed in the conviction that "death in a sacred cause" constitutes the most appropriate and dignified "end of life" (Townshend 2002). It is also a common element of most world religions, especially Islam and Christianity, particularly Protestantism and within it Calvinism and Puritanism (Juergensmeyer 2003), as well as Hinduism (Archer 2001), and to a lesser extent of Confucianism and Buddhism (remember a religion without a formal god but still characterized by the sacred).

Weber registers "every conceivable self-humiliation" and in extension humiliation of other humans, and to that extent composite of

---

[13] Turk (2004:277) notices that "nationalist and material concerns receded (still significant in the Balkan conflicts), while ideological, especially religious, and wider geopolitical concerns were in the ascendant (the India-Pakistan conflict). Most recently, religious fundamentalism has propelled the recruitment and organization of multitudes into loose networks of terrorist groups acting more or less on their own with encouragement and logistical assistance from facilitators with resources (al Qaeda, etc.). For most contemporary terrorists fundamentalist religious themes justify their deeds. Religiously motivated terrorists see themselves as "holy warriors" in a "cosmic war" between good and evil. All are creatures of cosmic evil who are to be annihilated."

[14] In the view of Eliasoph and Lichterman (2003), "Christianity and Islam [and other religions] can be used by terrorists and pacifists, fanatics and contemplative scholars, and casual observers alike."

sadism-masochism (Adorno 2001; Fromm 1941; McLaughlin 1996), for the "glory of God [of Calvinism]" within Puritanism that is invariably characterized with "unexampled tyranny", as epitomized in the "theocracy of New England" and briefly in England (Munch 2001). For instance, immediately upon arriving in the "promised land" during the 1630s, the supreme Puritan master and the role model for theocrats and conservatives of all kinds and times in America, including Reagan et al. (Dunn and Woodard 1996), Winthrop expressed his "austere Calvinism" (Kloppenberg 1998) by declaring a la Calvin that few "must be rich" and "high and eminent in power and dignity" and the rest "poor", "mean" and "in subjection", thus humiliation, sacrifice, and sadistic torment for the "glory of God", as the "Divinely ordained and irremediable" state of society (Gould 1996).

In turn, following the successful Puritan Revolution of the 1640s in England Cromwell proclaimed himself the "Lord of the Domain" and stated "I was a chief of sinners [but now] I may honor my God either by doing or suffering", thus masochistic sacrifice, especially by inflicting sadistic suffering on "infidels" through "holy" war cum crusade within society (Goldstone 1986; Gorski 2000). This was exemplified by what Simmel describes as the "cruel suppression of the Irish Catholics" involving their persecution and massacres by, in Weber's words, Cromwell's "unconquerable Puritan army", thus intensifying the prior less violent anti-Catholic practices of the Church of England[15] (Lutz and Lutz 2004). Also, Pareto remarks that such Puritans as Scottish Presbyterians "experience great delight in tormenting [and sacrificing] themselves and others" in accordance with their code that "all the natural affections, all the pleasures of society, all the pastimes, all the guy instincts of the human heart were so many sins [and so crimes]", and comments that "long before, the monks had carried this kind of insanity to the utmost limit." Notably, recent comparative sociological analyses find that religious notions of "martyrdom and sacrifice" (Juergensmeyer 2003) are especially salient in Islamic fundamentalism and Puritan-rooted American evangelicalism, and serve as the sacred reason or rationale for terrorism, especially anti-government violent attacks and destruction, by Muslim and evangelical "Christian" "martyrs" and "soldiers" (also, Townshend 2002; Turk 2004).

---

[15] Lutz and Lutz (2004:64) observe that "in England after the establishment of the Church of England, Catholics were viewed as an untrustworthy group likely to serve foreign (i.e. papal) interests and re-establish the former dominant religion".

Hence, the first cause of why religion generates or sanctifies "holy" terror can be deemed theological or transcendental anti-humanism depreciating humans versus supra-human entities and causes, and in consequence religiously justified or theocratic inhumanity, cruelty, and brutality against human subjects for the "glory of God". Such anti-humanism ultimately reaches the no-return point of, as Pareto sarcastically remarks, sadistically tormenting and eventually killing humans "in the name of the Divine master," including the "acceptability of genocidal campaigns [in] the Hebrew Bible" (Angel 1994; also, Juergensmeyer 2003). Theological anti-humanism and consequently religiously sanctified inhumanity is shared by most world religions as systems of depreciation, humiliation, and constraint of humans (Bell 1977) in favor of supra-human entities and causes, particularly Protestant and partly Catholic and Orthodox Christianity, notably Calvinism and Puritanism, and Islam, as well as Hinduism, and to a lesser extent Confucianism and Buddhism. For instance, Weber identifies Calvinist anti-humanism in registering that for Calvinism, including Puritanism, "humans exist for the sake of God", not conversely (also, Bendix 1977). Moreover, he diagnoses the "extreme inhumanity" of Calvinism's cardinal dogma of predestination due to the "the unjust (according to human standards) [salvation] of only a few" and damnation of most humans, and in extension "Calvinistic state churches" sanctified by the doctrine, including what he calls the "unexampled tyranny of Puritanism" as exerted through the "theocracy of New England" for two centuries and of England for two decades.

Curiously, none other than Parsons (1967) with his "Puritan heritage" (Alexander 1983) is particularly relevant at this juncture in that he unwittingly identifies theological anti-humanism and implicitly religiously justified inhumanity, as well as Machiavellianism, in Puritanism. He does so by noting that Protestantism's extolled "immediacy of the individual soul to God" resulted in the "corresponding devaluation of his attachment to his fellows, above all the tendency to reduce them to impersonal, unsentimental terms and to consider others not so much from the point of their value in themselves as of their usefulness, ultimately to the purposes of God, more immediately to his own ends". Apparently, the phrase "ultimately to the purposes of God" and effectively the latter's self-declared agents or representatives on earth with Divine Rights a la Calvin, Winthrop and Cromwell implies theological anti-humanism and theocratic inhumanity respectively. In turn, "more immediately to his own ends" implies Machiavellianism classically defined, as Pareto puts it, by the "ends justifying the means" (also, Bowles, Gintis and Osborne 2001; Merton 1968) and thus a sort of non-transcendental non-humanism or amorality and brutality, and egoism or utilitarianism (Mayway 1984) generally.

Negatively, both expressions reveal Puritanism's polar opposite and destruction of Enlightenment (and Renaissance) humanism (Delanty 2000; Habermas 2001) epitomized in Kant's humanistic principle (categorical imperative) of considering humans as the within the "kingdom of ends" and never as the means to other ends, be they "the purposes of God" or "own ends." Notably, what Parsons was unable or unwilling to envision but has been observed since his times is that considering other humans as the means "ultimately to the purposes of God" can often result in and justify killing them in the "name of the Divine master" and generally in "terror for the glory and in the mind of God", as especially witnessed in Puritan-rooted American evangelicalism and Islamic fundamentalism. For within these two types of religious fundamentalism, virtually all terrorist agents and acts have been driven and justified by some variation on the theme of "the purposes of God", a sort of "love and glory God, hate and kill ungodly humans" bumper-sticker (as a Texas country song goes "God is great, people are crazy", reminiscent of "Allah Akbar" in Islam). These terrorist tendencies, especially those within Puritan-inspired American evangelicalism, would likely surprise and even shock "godly" and patriotic Parsons, but not more neutral Weber who implies such violent actions, as by characterizing Calvinism as the "Church Militant" sharing the concept and practice of religious revolution and "holy" war with Islam. This lack of surprise especially applies to irreverent and skeptical Pareto who actually predicts such actions, as by registering that Puritan-style and other temperance groups are "ready to kill a person only to keep him healthy" and thus commit vigilante terrorism, as well as that the US government "tries to enforce morality by law" with resulting "gross abuses that are not observable in countries where there are no such restrictions", thus committing moralistic coercion and repression, including execution and incarceration for moral sins and by implication "original sin", and in that sense genuine or proxy state terror.

In a way, unlike Parsons et al., by these and related observations Weber and Pareto prophetically imply that Puritanism and Calvinism in general, with its "theocratic revolt" against rising secularism in England and Europe, would become the model or "precursor" of contemporary anti-secular extremists or terrorists such as "born again" US and Islamic fundamentalists (Juergensmeyer 1994). Notably, Weber effectively envisions such an outcome by observing and emphasizing that Calvinism, including Puritanism, adopts the "essentially same solution" to the problem of the "sinful world" as does Islam. The solution is the composite of religious revolution against "infidels" in the function of establishing theocratic coercion and repression within society and of "holy" wars against "infidel" societies in the service of global domination, in short crusade and jihad in the broadest intra- and inter-societal meanings[16] (Juergensmeyer 2003; Turner 2002).

And the composite of religious revolution or theocratic coercion and repression and of "holy" wars is what in essence Puritan-rooted American evangelicalism and Islamic fundamentalism design and practice, thus exhibiting their elective affinity (Turner 2002) or commonalities (Friedland 2002) and confirming Weber's as well as Pareto's nearly prescient observations. In short, Parsons et al. overlook that theological, like any other, anti-humanism, extolled as "individualism" (Mayway 1984) through the individual "immediacy to God", can generate and sanctify "holy" terror, including counter-state, state, and inter-state terrorism. In turn, as implied by defining theocracy as a design and system of state terrorism, theocratic, or religiously justified inhumanity, notably cruelty, torture, and murder, is an act or type of terror in its own right[17] (Lutz and Lutz 2004).

Alternatively, the cause of why religion generates or justifies 'holy" terror can be described as what Comte calls the "repugnance" for human emancipation and thus for secular humanism as "ungodly", and considers to be as characteristic especially of Protestantism more than even of the "most degenerate" Catholicism. Generally, religious conservatism, especially its Islamic fundamentalist and American evangelical version, reportedly "abhors" secular humanism, as well as in conjunction and mutual reinforcement, liberalism, democracy, secularism, and rationalism (Van Dyke 1995). And, as indicated, theological anti-humanism and religiously justified inhumanity in the form of depreciation, submission, humiliation, and sacrifice, including death, of humans for Divine causes and entities displays what Weber would call an "elective affinity"

---

[16] Juergensmeyer (2003:147–8) refers to the Muslim concept of struggle—jihad", commenting that "jihad is fundamentally a concept of struggle, an image that abounds in the rhetoric of violent religious activists in [all] faiths", including its Christian equivalent or counterpart of crusade usually understood in almost identical terms, viz. as a composite of culture wars on "sin and vice" within society and global military war against the "evil" world within revived American fundamentalism (Turner 2002).

[17] Lutz and Lutz (2004:64) suggest that "terrorism can also involve groups that are part of the dominant or majority religion in a country. They [can] seek to create a theocratic state where religious leaders have the final word on what is permissible and possible within the country".

or "intimate connection" and Parsons "convergence" with "holy" terror, including counter-state, state, and inter-state terrorism, as especially witnessed in Islamic and American fundamentalism (Friedland 2002; Turner 2002).

In Clausewitz's context, "holy" terror, including violent repression within society and aggressive religious war a la crusade and jihad against other societies, is the logical "continuation" or the ultimate escalation of the "politics" of theological anti-humanism and religiously justified inhumanity by "other [violent] means". Moreover, in Michels' terms the above represents a sort of" "iron law" of "holy" terror: "who says theological anti-humanism and religiously justified inhumanity, says 'holy' terror, including counter-state, state, and inter-state terrorism." The "law" posits and predicts that theologically anti-humanistic or inhumane religious individuals, organizations, religiously-based governments, and societies are more likely to advocate, commit, and support terrorism, i.e., violence, destruction, war, and coercion or repression, than are others. The "law" can be relaxed in that not all anti-humanistic religious individuals, organizations, religiously-based governments, and societies resort and endorse terrorism, but they as a rule tend to do so more than others.

"True Believers" Versus "Infidels"

The second cause of why religion generates and/or rationalizes "holy" terror is the invidious division of humans, groups and societies into "true believers" and "infidels" or the "ungodly" representing the "sacred" and the "profane" in Durkheim's sense respectively, thus "good" insiders and "evil" outsiders to be ultimately eliminated as "enemies of God", simply "us" versus "them". As Pareto observes, religion "by its very nature is exclusive", consequently anti-egalitarian and intolerant and ultimately violent, coercive, and repressive toward those excluded that are condemned and punished, ideally exterminated, as "ungodly" Satanic forces, including "witches", opposing God and bent on destroying or perverting the "true" faith and "pure" church, as virtually all local and global religions, churches, sects, and cults present themselves or claim to be. Such division or exclusiveness is also a defining trait of religion, notably an element shared by virtually all world religions, though with different degrees of consistency, intensity, and application via religious revolution and "holy war", namely the highest in Islam and Calvinism and its revival, evangelical Protestantism, intermediate in Judaism and Hinduism, the lowest in Confucianism and Buddhism, as implied in Weber's account. For instance,

Calvinism claimed to be the only, exclusive "true" Reformed and thus "Christian" faith and church, and its Anglo-Saxon derivative Puritanism defined itself as a "pure church", in an invidious distinction from and exclusion and ultimately persecution and elimination of other Christian and even Protestant churches, notably Catholicism as well as Lutheranism, Anglicanism, Quakerism, etc., not to mention non-Christians (e.g. Native Americans in New England) and non-believers or secularists in general.

As regards the latter, sociological analyses indicate that primarily owing to predominant Puritan-rooted Protestant sectarianism and evangelicalism (Jenness 2004; Lipset 1996), non-believers in religious terms have been systematically and persistently excluded from civil society, especially government, and even economic opportunities during most of American history, up to the 21st century (Edgell et al. 2006). Predictably, such exclusion and discrimination on "godly" grounds is especially perpetual and pervasive in the fundamentalist "Bible Belt" (e.g., Alabama, Tennessee, Texas, etc.) in which, based on the legal mandate of recognizing "the existence of Divinity", judged unconstitutional in the 1960s yet still somehow illegally enforced, simply "infidels need not apply" for political office and other public employment (state schools and other agencies). If anything, these remarkably methodical and long-standing exclusionary practices by primarily Puritan-based prevailing sectarianism of non-believers or "non-Christians" as supremely "un-American" forces in the "promised land" of "liberty and justice for all" regardless of their personal beliefs confirm classical sociological insights and predictions. In particular, the latter involve Pareto's and previous Enlightenment's observations of the inherently exclusive and consequently intolerant and coercive and repressive tendency of most world religions, as well as denominations or sects within them[18] (Cragin and Chalk 2003), each religion and sect claiming to the "only and true" faith and church and condemning all others as "false" and "evil".

Hence, within most global religions, particularly fundamentalist Islam and sectarian Protestantism, exclusion and discrimination, thus intolerance of "infidels" in religious and non-religious terms is the first step of or prelude to violence, coercion and repression, and war directed against

---

[18] Cragin and Chalk (2003:5) remark that Northern Ireland's "contemporary conflict has essentially focused on the conflicting ambitions of militant extremists in both Catholic and Protestant communities. The onset of [its] present "Troubles" dates back to the late 1960s and the outbreak of sectarian riots following Protestant mob attacks against Catholic civil rights marches".

them and in that sense "holy" terror, ranging from counter-state vigilante to state theocratic and inter-state militarist terrorism. In this sense, the composite of religious exclusion, discrimination, and intolerance generates, explains, and predicts religiously grounded and justified terrorism by anti-government and government agents. For instance, what sociological analyses observe as the exclusion of non-believers (Edgell et al. 2006) and even "sadistic intolerance of cultural otherness widespread in American society" (Bauman 1997), especially the "Bible Belt", by primarily "born again" and growingly powerful or politically ambitious theocratic evangelicalism (Keister 2008; Lindsey 2008) generates and justifies agents and acts of "holy" terror. These include first anti-government groups and attacks like the 1995 Oklahoma bombing by "Christian solders" and vigilante violence against "un-American" groups (sexual deviants, minorities, immigrants, etc.) as actions of counter-state terror. Second, they comprise government religiously grounded coercion and repression, at least in the "Bible Belt" (e.g., Texas) with its fundamentalist death penalty and penal system, including the execution and imprisonment of moral sinners (drug offenders, etc.) comprising nearly two thirds of the prison population, as well as "aggressive "holy" crusade-like wars on the "evil world", thus practices of state, and inter-state terrorism respectively.

In Clausewitz's setting, then "holy" terror, including religiously based intra-societal coercion and repression *and* inter-societal war and extermination, represents the logical continuation or ultimate escalation of the "politics" of religious exclusion, discrimination, and intolerance, as the inherent attribute or outcome of most world religions and perhaps religion as such, by "other, violent means." In this sense, Michels' like "iron law" of "holy" terror and religious exclusion is that "who says religious exclusion, discrimination, and intolerance, says holy terror, including counter-state, state, and inter-state terrorism."

Hence, the second cause for religion generating and sanctifying "holy" terror is anti-egalitarianism and anti-universalism as axiomatically exclusionary and intolerant through the opposition to secular egalitarianism and universalism, and their substitution or subversion by religious, inherently particularistic, sectarian or factional, thus deceptive forms, as what Simmel calls their "compensatory substitutes" and Mises ersatz alternatives. For instance, Dahrendorf (1979) implies this substitution and deception by pointing to "deceptive Christian egalitarianism" from the prism of secular egalitarianism and universalism. The latter originated in the Enlightenment and liberalism generally (Habermas et al. 1998) and considers all humans regardless of their religious ascription or affiliation, not only or mostly "Christians", to be equal before social institutions like the law and included in society. Notably, Enlightenment universalism or egalitarianism places humans within Kant's "kingdom of ends" (Habermas 2001) rather the means to other goals, notably Parsons' "purposes of God" (and one's own aims) as a common element of virtually all world and local religions, though he seemingly extols that "godly" component as the comparative advantage of Protestantism like Puritanism.

A paradigmatic instance of exclusion, discrimination, and intolerance, thus anti-egalitarianism and anti-universalism in Christianity, specifically Protestantism, is Calvinism's dogma of predestination postulating what Weber calls the "particularism of grace" to the point of sectarianism in heaven, and eventually in society, through the "double decree" of election of only a few as the "spiritual aristocracy of salvation" or "heavenly" oligarchy (Zaret 1989) and damnation of the "remainder of humanity." Moreover, insofar as original Christianity is, as Weber and other analysts imply, the religion of egalitarian and universal salvation conditional on "good" intentions and works, then Calvinism, including Puritanism, is not only anti-egalitarianism and anti-universalism in a secular sense. It is, contrary to its claims as the only and true "Christian" church, anti- or quasi-Christian and generally anti-brotherly (Symonds and Pudsey 2006) in Christian terms (also, Tawney 1962), while being a functional equivalent to Islam as also, in Weber's view, a non-universalistic religion of salvation in this respect, like most respects, including theocracy, fundamentalism, religious revolution, and "holy" war. And, as indicated, exclusionary, intolerant, anti-egalitarian and anti-universalistic or sectarian religious individuals, organizations, governments, and societies are more likely to advocate, commit, and support terrorism, i.e., violence, destruction, war, and coercion, than are others. No doubt, not all exclusionary, intolerant, anti-egalitarian and anti-universalistic or sectarian religious individuals, organizations, religiously-based governments, and societies resort and endorse terrorism, but they tend to do so more than others.

Denial and Suppression of Individual Liberties

The third cause, largely a corollary of the first, of why religion generates or sanctifies "holy" terror is the denial and suppression of individual liberty, especially personal moral liberties and choices, in favor of collective religious as well as political constraint, control, and repression, simply church and state. This is also a defining characteristic of religion in general in which invariably or typically individual moral and related liberties and choices are denied and suppressed or constrained for the cause of the sacred, as Durkheim implies, notably Divine purpose, causing the loss of what Tönnies calls the "free will of mankind." The loss of human freedom is an element common to virtually all world religions as systems of "restraint" (Bell 1977) and ultimately suppression of individual liberties and choices, though with different pseudo-statistical "degrees of un-freedom".

As implied in Weber's and other sociological accounts (Archer 2001; Juergensmeyer 2003; Mansbach 2006; Turner 2002; Van Dyke 1995), these "degrees of un-freedom" range from the highest in Islam and Calvinism, notably Puritanism and its revival in evangelical Protestantism, as well as Hinduism, through intermediate in Judaism, and to the lowest in Confucianism and Buddhism. Among world religions especially Islam and Calvinism did, and Islamic and Puritan-rooted American fundamentalism do, deny and suppress or restrain human liberties and choices, claiming to solve the "agony of choice" or the "burden" of individual liberty by eliminating the choice and liberty itself (Bauman 1997). And, they both do so for, as Weber and Parsons remarked referring to Calvinism or Protestantism, putatively the "glory" and "purposes of God", effectively for the latter's self-designated agents as theocratic rulers with Divine rights to rule and destroy the "sinful world", as exemplified by Calvin's "aristocracy of predestined salvation" and its Islamic variation.

For instance, English-American Puritanism declared to be God's anti-sin agent or "[anti] vice "regent" (Zaret 1989), as does American revived evangelicalism standing in the venerable theocratic Puritan tradition (Dunn and Woodard 1996), as well as did early and still does contemporary Islam. Then Puritanism and Islam used this self-assigned status as the sacred rationale for their shared denial and suppression or restraint of individual liberties and choices, especially moral-religious liberty and choice, with Cromwell proclaiming himself the "Lord of the Domain", and similar proclamations are also found in his Islamic counterparts.

Recall that Weber characterizes the "rule of Calvinism" as the "most absolutely unbearable" type of theocratic or ecclesiastical control realized and even "imaginable", notably using the expression the "unexampled tyranny of Puritanism", by implication only equated or emulated by Islam, as implied by his detection of their shared composite of religious revolution and "holy" war. In particular, he observes that Calvinism, including Baptism, once established in power denies "freedom of conscience" to non-Calvinist others more than do Catholicism and Lutheranism, consequently that religious toleration and hence liberty was actually "least strong" in those societies dominated by Puritanism, such as New England, thus contradicting the Parsonian "naïve assumptions" (Coffey 1998) or the "liberal mythology" (Gould 1996) of Puritan "tolerance", "freedom of conscience", and "pluralism". For instance, ruling Calvinists in early Holland displayed the lack of "liberality" by refusing to grant to others what they had so vehemently and righteously demanded for themselves when not in power, namely religious liberty and tolerance only to be fully recognized and established in this country and Western Europe overall, just as torture was abolished (Einoff 2007), because of the Enlightenment (Kaplan 2002). Further, most early Calvinists, including Puritans, reportedly condemned or suspected religious tolerance, liberty, and pluralism as a "catastrophe" for their only "true" Reformed and so "Christian" Church, rather than a liberal-democratic value to be established and nurtured (Sprunger 1982).

Generally, what Weber identifies as the shared composite concept and practice of intra-societal religious revolution as the path to theocratic coercion and inter-societal "holy" war as the means of global domination, crusade and jihad in the broadest sense, essentially caused the greatest "degrees of un-freedom" in Islam and Calvinism, thus Islamic and Puritan-inspired American fundamentalism (Turner 2002). Alternatively, this theocratic and militarist composite rendered individual liberty and choice in these religious systems what Weber would call an "impossible contradiction" and contemporary social-choice theorists an "impossibility theorem" (Arrow 1950), typically denied and destroyed, at most restrained and perverted or subverted. For, as often said, the first casualty of these shared Calvinist/evangelical and Islamic, like any other, theocratic revolutions or rather counter-revolutions in the sense of restoration of theocracy as "sacred" tyranny, and "holy" wars is human liberty and choice, as well as truth and life, as at least in part witnessed during the neo-conservative "war on terror" *cum* crusade against "evil" (Turner 2002) as well as before (the Cold War, the Vietnam War, etc.).

And, the world religions that have the greatest "degrees of un-freedom" also feature the highest magnitude and intensity of "holy" terror, and conversely. Namely, those world religions that are the strongest and persistent systems of denial and suppression or restraint of individual liberties and choices tend to most strongly and persistently generate and sanctify "holy" terror, and the other way round. As implied, this is epitomized by Islam and Calvinism, in particular contemporary Islamic and Puritan-rooted American fundamentalism. As seen, these two global religions are characterized with both the greatest "degrees of un-freedom" and the highest magnitude and intensity of "holy" terror, namely the strongest denial and suppression or restraint of human liberties and choices *and* the most intense intra-societal violence or coercion and inter-societal destruction and war. Hence, to better understand and explain why Islamic and American fundamentalism have established themselves as the two main agents or supporters of contemporary terrorism requires taking into consideration the fact that they represent the most systematic and persistent religious systems of denial and suppression or restraint of individual liberties and choices, notably personal moral liberty and choice and privacy through their shared "obsession with sin and vice" (Wagner 1997) redefined and severely punished as crimes (e.g., adultery and other sexual sins, birth control, alcohol use, non-violent, drug offenses, etc.).

Conversely, it is difficult to fully understand and explain Islamic and evangelical joint global "leadership" in terrorism without considering their shared "championing" of the practices, institutions and symbols of illiberty (Dahrendorf 1979). For instance, sociological observations indicate that the ruling evangelical forces of the "Bible Belt" and the Islamic fundamentalists of Iran are the main contemporary proto-totalitarian "solutions" to the supposed "evil" or "burden" of individual liberty and the "agony" of personal choice by eliminating such liberties and choices (Bauman 1997; 2001), thus the types of solution that, as Keynes would put it, "cures the disease by killing the patient". This proto-totalitarian, more precisely theocratic or fundamentalist, convergence and commonality helps to understand, explain, and perhaps predict how and why "Bible Belt" and other US evangelicals and Islamic fundamentalists have acted, act, and will likely continue to act as the two major forces of "holy" terror, including counter-state, state and inter-state terrorisms. In Clausewitz's context, "holy" terror, including intra-societal violent coercion and inter-societal aggressive war, is the logical continuation or eventual escalation of the religious "politics" of denial and suppression or restraint of human liberties and choice for the sacred and higher "purposes of God" by "other means." To that extent, this yields Michels' like "iron law" of "holy" terror in relation to the religious denial and suppression of human liberties and choices. Namely, the "law" states "who says the religious denial and suppression of human liberties and choices for the glory of God, says 'holy' terror, including violent coercion and repression within society and aggressive war against other societies."

In short, the third cause of why world and other religions generate and sanctify terror can be designated as anti- and/or pre-liberalism. The latter is understood in the sense of antagonism to and predating (not knowing), respectively, modern liberalism as the ideal and social system of individual moral-civil liberties and choices as well as political freedom, both institutionalized in contemporary liberal-secular democracy and civil society in the Western world and beyond. Given the inherent and factual or eventual symbiosis of liberalism and democracy, and conversely of anti-liberalism and authoritarianism, in virtually all societies and historical times (Dahrendorf 1979; Dombrowski 2001; Mises 1957), the present cause is what Mannheim (1967) would call anti- or "pre-democratic authoritarian" ideology ("mind").

The latter originated in medieval traditionalism and opposed or predated liberal-democratic ideology (Zaret 1989), and often generating, advocating, or supporting terrorist agents and actions in the form of "political violence in or against true democracies"[19] (Heymann 1999) or "normal" democratic politics[20] (Friedland 2001) as a rule premised on liberalism. And as indicated, anti- or pre-liberal religious individuals, organizations, governments, and societies denying and suppressing or restraining human liberties and rights are more likely to advocate, commit, and support terrorism in the form of violence, destruction, war, and coercion, than are others. No doubt, not all anti- or pre-liberal religious individuals, organizations, religiously-based governments, and societies destructive to liberty resort and endorse terrorism, but they tend to do so more than others.

Religious Revolution and "Holy" War

As intimated, the fourth cause, logically and empirically derived from the second, of why religion generates and justifies "holy" terror is what Weber identifies as the concept and practice of religious revolution within society and a "holy" total or cosmic war against other societies. In Weber's account, the composite of intra-societal and ultimately global religious revolution and of inter-societal war is used as the violent, yet most effective instrument of, positively, establishing "God's Kingdom on Earth" and,

---

[19] Generally, Heymann (1999:9) considers terrorism, including implicitly that religiously motivated, as a "form of violent domestic politics" directed at liberal-democratic political systems.

[20] Friedland (2001:130) comments that "religious terrorism is not primarily an instrument to transform government policy as much as it is a ritual drama designed to be noticed, typically targeted at symbolically charged sites (public places). Religious terrorism represents a symbolic order more than it produces a profanely practical result. It is a theatre of war. Terror signals the immorality of one's foe [or] of the other's evil. Terror is not normal politics by scandalous means but a declaration that normal politics are not possible".

negatively, eliminating "infidels" as "enemies of God"—i.e., as Pareto puts it, killing "in the name of the divine master." In short, religious revolution is in the service of theocratic coercion and violent repression within society and "holy" war against other societies in the function of global rule and domination.

As indicated, theocratic and any coercion and violent repression is a paradigmatic, classic type of state as well as, when used by anti-governmental or vigilante groups, counter-state terrorism on its own right, thus making religious revolution in its service an effective instrument of "sacred" terror, as is "holy" and other aggressive war an axiomatic form of inter-state terrorism. At least, religious revolutions and "holy" wars generate and justify terror, including counter-state, state, and inter-state terrorism, as the integral element and the effective mechanism for achieving victory *within* human society and history in these eternal or perpetual transcendental struggles subsumed under the notion of a "cosmic", divine" war[21] between "good and evil" (Friedland 2001; Juergensmeyer 2003). Alternatively, "holy" terror, including counter-state, state, and inter-state terrorism, represents just an act and enactment, directed against rationalistic as well as liberal-democratic, secular, and globalized modernity, of such a "cosmic war", thus of the composite of permanent religious revolution within society and "holy" offensive wars against other societies.

The preceding is also an overt or covert defining trait of religion in virtue of being defined a la Durkheim by the sacred and "good" versus the profane and "evil", especially its most anti-humanistic, exclusive, repressive, and radical or militant types. Arguably, religion tends to "naturally" revolves around the "language and postures of war" because the latter and

---

[21] Juergensmeyer (2003:146) suggests that the "images of divine warfare (are) behind contemporary acts of performance violence. What makes religious violence particularly savage and relentless is that its perpetrators have placed such religious images of divine struggle—cosmic war—in the service of worldly political battles. For this reason, acts of religious terror serve not only as tactics in a political strategy but also as evocations of a much larger spiritual confrontation. The script of cosmic war is central to virtually all of the incidents of performance violence", as exemplified by "Christian movements' images of warfare". As regards the latter, admittedly "in addition to "just war" ("why the Christian church is not pacifist"), there are other, less legitimate examples of religious violence from Christianity's heritage, including the Inquisitions and Crusades" (Juergensmeyer 2003:26). Generally, in this view, the "notion of cosmic war provides the script being played out in the violent performances of militant religious activists and is linked to notions of conquest and failure, martyrdom and sacrifice" (Juergensmeyer 2003:148). Juergensmeyer (2003:242–3) infers that terrorism "has much to do with the nature of the religious imagination, which always has had the propensity to absolutize and to project images of cosmic war" and that "in the wake of secularism religion has made its reappearance as an ideology of social order in a dramatic fashion: violently."

other violence represents an ultimate stage and opportunity for the "display and adjudication of absolute, non-negotiable differences", namely the "incommensurable divide between the sacred and the profane" in Durkheim's sense, consequently "an absolute partitioning into good and evil" respectively represented as "us and them" (Friedland 2001).

In this sense, the "capacity" for and eventually the practice of warfare and violence overall is "ultimately" the hallmark of religion cum the sacred, as especially epitomized by Islamic and American fundamentalism and their common "holy" war against liberal and rationalistic modernity, notably liberal-secular democracy "without God" as a "profane state" whose "profanity" is proven by their shared "sacred" violence against it (Friedland 2001) and in that sense counter-state terrorism. Consequently, warfare and other violence and destruction for the "sacred" has reportedly always been manifestly or latently present in religion revealing its "darker, more mysterious symbols" to the point of acts or "images of death" virtually being at the "heart of religion's power" of arousing and acting on the religious imagination, with the effect of terror becoming imagined "in the mind of God"[22] (Juergensmeyer 2003). And, divine warfare is not merely the "glorious" past recounted in "religion's legendary histories" but rather "intricately" linked with its "contemporary symbols"[23] (Juergensmeyer 2003), specifically with those of modern world religions.

Hence, at least Weber's intertwined composite of religious revolution and "holy" war is a common element of virtually all world religions, including Christianity as well as even supposedly pacifist Buddhism[24] (Juergensmeyer 2003; Turk 2004), to a greater or less extent characterized with "sacred" violence and militancy, including wars and overall militarism for the "glory of God". Thus, echoing Weber contemporary sociologists observe that the concepts and practices or "images of divine warfare",

---

[22] Juergensmeyer (2003:10) adds that "religion does make a difference [e.g.] transcendent moralism (as justification) and (terrorism's) ritual intensity (and) the very heart of religion (i.e.) concepts of cosmic war. When these cosmic battles are conceived as occurring on the human plane, they result in real acts of violence (though) religion does not ordinarily lead to violence. That happens only with the coalescence of a peculiar set of circumstances—political, social, and ideological—when religion becomes fused with violent expressions of social aspirations, personal pride, and movements for political change".

[23] Juergensmeyer (2003:160–1) infers that the "symbiosis between symbolic and real violence is profound and goes to the very heart of the religious imagination. Extremism in religion has led to violence at the same time that violent conflicts have cried out for religious validation".

[24] According to Juergensmeyer (2003:156–7), the "Muslim notion of *jihad* is the most notable example, but even in Buddhist legends great wars are to be found".

as "persistent features" of contemporary religious terrorism or radical
anti-secular and anti-rationalistic activism, far from being new form "part
of the heritage" of most world religions (Juergensmeyer 2003; also
Friedland 2001). In this account, the practice and idea of divine warfare
has typically been in an "intimate relationship" to world religions and religion as such, with Western and world history being inflicted with "overtly"
religious wars, including "the Crusades, the Muslim conquests, and the
Wars of Religion" between Calvinist Protestants and Catholics in the 16th
century France (Juergensmeyer 2003).

   In particular, like most world religions, reportedly Christianity "always"
entailed a "violent side", mixed with and in spite of its ideals of Christian
"love and peace" (also, Sorokin 1970) with "violent conflict" or warfare
between "good" and "evil" being "vividly" depicted and even sanctified in
"both the Old and New Testaments of the Bible" (Juergensmeyer 2003;
Friedland 2001), as exemplified by the "acceptability of genocidal campaigns [in] the Hebrew Bible" (Angel 1994). With regards the latter, for
example, "whole books of the Hebrew Bible" glorify the "military exploits
of great kings" and depict their warfare in "gory detail" (Juergensmeyer
2003). Admittedly the "later history" of the Christian Church furnished
Christianity with a "bloody record of crusades and religious wars"
(Juergensmeyer 2003). Moreover, in this account, the "bloody history" of
Christianity contains "images as disturbing as those" contained in Islam,
spanning from "biblical wars to crusading ventures and great acts of martyrdom" revealing violence in manifest or "shadowy presence", such that
"religious warfare" persists in the "most modern of 20th century" Western
societies through terrorist agents and acts sanctified by "Christian principles" (Juergensmeyer 2003).

   In particular, such "history" and various "biblical images" continue to
serve as the "raw material for theologically justifying the violence of contemporary Christian groups" in America, especially their "attacks on abortion clinics" construed as "skirmishes in a grand confrontation between
forces of evil and good" with critical social-political "implications", such
that fundamentalism serving as the main "ideological support for militia
movements" tragically personified by McVeigh et al. (Juergensmeyer[25] 2003;

---

[25] Juergensmeyer (2003:31) adds that fundamentalist theology is "based on racial
supremacy and biblical law (and) popular in many militia movements (and its) ideas were
most likely part of the thinking of McVeigh [whose] favorite author (Pierce) once served as
a writer for the American Nazi Party." In another example, "Christian Identity minister
Robert Millar and former Nazi Party member Glenn Miller established Elohim City. It was

Turk[26] 2004). Notably, "Christian" terrorists in America reportedly strongly believe that attacking abortion clinics and murdering their personnel is "justified" by the "tenets of the just-war theory in Christian theology" to the effect that a "small act of violence" is necessary and justifiable for the sake of preventing or stopping a "much greater violent assault" (Juergensmeyer 2003), a sort of mere "collateral damage", so not really a "big deal", a la McVeigh in discharging "military duty" (Turk 2004). As noted, Weber especially attributes the composite of societal religious revolution as the instrument of establishing theocratic repression and of "holy" war as the means of attaining world dominance to Calvinism, including Puritanism, within Christianity and to Islam among other world religions, in the respective forms of crusade and jihad in the broad meanings of domestic and global wars or struggles (Juergensmeyer 2003; Turner 2002; Turk 2004).

(Recall that Weber states that "the concept of a religious revolution was consistent most with inner-worldly ascetic rationalism which oriented to the holy orders of God" commandments within the world. Within Christianity this was true in Calvinism, which made it a religious obligation to defend the faith against tyranny by the use of force. The duty of religious revolution for the cause of faith was naturally taught by the religions that engaged in wars of missionary enterprise and by their derivative sects (in Islam). The employment of force by the state can have moral sanction only when the force is used for the control of sins, for the glory of God, and for combating religious injustice –in short, only for religious purposes.")

---

this Christian Identity encampment that McVeigh contacted shortly before the Oklahoma City federal building blast. This obsession with gun control has made many Christian Identity followers natural allies with the NRA (whose rhetoric) has played a significant role in legitimizing Christian Identity members' fears of the evil intentions behind governmental gun control and has provided a public voice for their paranoid views" (Juergensmeyer (2003:34–5).

[26] Turk (2004:277) observes that US racist-xenophobic groups have transformed from "easily identifiable secret societies" a la the Ku Klux Klan to "congeries of individuals", such as McVeigh and "sundry antigovernment rightists responsible for the 1995 Oklahoma City bombing", all "sharing Christian identity or some other extremist worldview. [They] have moved from explicit organizations to movements of like-minded people willing to encourage and support terrorists such as Rudolph (the racist Atlanta Olympics and antiabortion bomber), even if they themselves do not commit violent acts". In his view, their "terrorist attacks were inspired by ideological zealotry and encouraged by sympathizers (and) exemplify the increasing shift, especially among violent extremists within the US, from organized to individual terrorism" (Turk 2004:278).

And Puritan-rooted Protestant evangelicalism in America, as Weber would expect, continues to represent the major form of "Christian militancy in the West" (Juergensmeyer 2003), just as does Islamic fundamentalism in the world as whole. Reportedly, "Protestant Christianity" provides a paradigmatic "example" of the concept and practice of cosmic divine war, with "Protestant preachers everywhere" imploring and encouraging their flocks to start and endure in "war against the forces of evil" and singing "hymns about 'Christian soldiers,'" enjoying "the good fight," and battling "manfully onward" (Juergensmeyer 2003). Thus, the "model of warfare" in the broadest sense involving intra-social religious revolution or culture wars and inter-societal military war is "one of the most enduring" ideas and practice within "modern Protestant Christianity" in America and elsewhere (Juergensmeyer 2003). Simply, for contemporary, like historical, Protestantism, notably Protestant sectarianism and evangelicalism in the Calvinist-Puritan tradition[27] (Dunn and Woodard 1996), "Christian living *is* war" as a "literal fact", with the "images of warfare" placing the "true" believers cum "born again" fundamentalists in a "religious cosmos" with a supposedly superior "moral valence"[28] (Juergensmeyer 2003), as is the life of a "true" Muslim to modern Islamic fundamentalism. In short, the "Lord God is a man of War" and the Bible rendered into "a book of war [and] hate" commanding the "Christian Army of God" in contemporary American fundamentalist Protestantism a la "Christian Identity" (Juergensmeyer 2003). In sum, for US Protestant evangelicals exemplified by "Christian Identity" and "Reconstruction" theology contemporary society, including America, a "world at war", i.e., a "hidden albeit "cosmic" war between the forces of darkness and the forces of light"

---

[27] Coincidentally or rather expectedly, the "dean" of the fundamentalist "Christian Identity" movement is Richard Butler, "an 80-year-old former Presbyterian [Calvinist-Puritan] minister [i.e.] "the elder statesman of American hate", at its "extreme fringes" being "rogue terrorists (Juergensmeyer 2003:35).

[28] Juergensmeyer (2003:151–2) adds that the US fundamentalists' "scenario of cosmic war is also something of a self-fulfilling prophecy (as) contemporary social struggles can be traced back to a conflict as old as the creation of the universe", namely Lucifer vs. God and "pure white Protestant Christians", which makes "Christian militias" in America "defensive responses to an ancient and ongoing war." In his view (Juergensmeyer 2003:151–2), "one of the reasons a state of war is preferable to peace is that it gives moral justification to acts of violence (which) offers the illusion of power. (US fundamentalists) argue that public executions are appropriate in a time of warfare, implying that they, rather than the state, can mete out punitive judgments." In general, Juergensmeyer (2003:155) registers that "in the images of cosmic war this victorious triumph is a grand moment of social and personal transformation, transcending all worldly limitations. One does not easily abandon such expectations. To be without such images of war is almost to be without hope itself."

(Juergensmeyer 2003). Specifically, this involves a "secret war between colossal evil forces allied with the UN, the US, and other government powers, and a small band of the enlightened few" unmasking courageously fighting these "invisible enemies" as "satanic powers" (Juergensmeyer 2003) through crusade-style warfare and ultimately "apocalyptic confrontation"[29] to be followed by Christ's "return to earth", as do their Islamic counterpart through jihad (Turner 2002).

On this account, Weber and other sociological analyses (Mansbach 2006; Turner 2002; Van Dyke 1996) suggest that Calvinism and Islam, notably contemporary Puritan-inspired evangelicalism and Islamic fundamentalism, are functional equivalents. In this sense, they often act as a sort of "brothers in arms" evincing mutual admiration or respect (Juergensmeyer 2003) and occasionally tacit cooperation, as often witnessed at international conferences on human liberties and rights (notably birth control) by joining their "hands" against these "ungodly" liberal choices, even if warring with each other to the point of war of attrition for world religious and military domination. In general, as observed "virtually all the major religions in the world" did and do supply the "justification for terrorist violence" by their members, in particular the "justification for many (religious) wars over the centuries" (Lutz and Lutz 2004).

Hence, the above yields Michels' proxy "iron law" of "holy" terror in relation to the composite concept and practice of religious revolution and war. The "law" posits "who says religious revolution and war, says 'holy' terror, including counter-state, state, and inter-state terrorism." Almost axiomatically radical or militant and militarist or anti-pacifist religious individuals, organizations, governments, and societies are more likely to advocate, commit, and support terrorism through violence, destruction, war, and coercion than are others. The "law" is relaxed in that not all radical, militant, and militarist religious individuals, organizations, religiously-based governments, and societies resort and endorse terrorism, but they tend to do so more than others.

In a sense, the present cause of why religion generates or justifies "holy" terror can be considered radicalism within society and militarism against other societies, negatively anti-pacifism in both intra- and inter-societal

---

[29] Juergensmeyer (2003:138) presents the case of US "Concerned Christians" who went to Jerusalem "with the expectation that the end of the millennium would be the occasion for the apocalyptic confrontation (Armageddon) after which Christ would return to earth (and) charged with planning to instigate a series of terrorist acts in order to precipitate Armageddon, and perhaps to kill themselves in an act of mass suicide in the process".

terms, thus a sort of overarching militancy, including effective or potential, physical or symbolic violence. In short, most contemporary terrorism is an expression and implementation of "holy war" and terrorists act as or claim to be "holy warriors." For instance, in addition to observing that Calvinism shares with Islam the concept and systematic practice of religious revolution and "holy" war, Weber describes the former as the "Church Militant" and thus effectively or potentially violent and in that sense "terrorist, namely, if Calvinist violence conforms to the definition of terrorism, as it, like its Islamic variant, typically does. Also, Puritan-rooted evangelicalism especially in America continues and expands original Calvinist militancy and militarism to the point of becoming, as Calvinism has been, the most intensively militant or radical and militarist or anti-pacifist branch of contemporary Christianity (Juergensmeyer 2003), just as resolutely nationalistic (Friedland 2002), though some strands of supposedly pacifist Catholicism are not immune to the temptations of anti-pacifism a la preemptive "just" war (Heurbach 1992). In consequence, what is called "Christian" terrorism and militancy is as a rule, especially in America, Protestant, more precisely committed or supported by Puritan-rooted evangelical or fundamentalist groups within contemporary American Protestantism (Juergensmeyer 2003) and only exceptionally non-Protestant (Catholic, etc.).

Perhaps religion in itself make humans anti-human or inhumane and hateful creatures, sort of human-looking monsters and beasts a la Hobbes "wolves" (*homo homini lupus*) through its commandment and justification of religious revolution as the instrument of theocracy within society and/or holy war against "infidel" societies as the means of global dominance, and generally via what Hume identified and deplored as its intrinsic zealotry and violent fanaticism. Notably, the above seems to apply to most world religions, although in varying degrees. As indicated, it especially holds true of Calvinism, including Puritanism and its survival or revival through "born again" evangelicalism in America, and fundamentalist Islam, as the two most militant and warlike religious and social systems, driven by the shared concept and practice of religious revolution and "cosmic war", in Weber's and other sociological accounts (Friedland 2001; Juergensmeyer 2003; Mansbach 2006; Turner 2002).

It often seems as if Calvinism, notably Puritanism or its heir evangelicalism, and fundamentalist Islam through their militant, warlike commandments and practices convert normal, reasonable, and decent, even compassionate, human beings into genuine monsters, beasts, and wild fanatics or lunatics willing and ready to perpetrate all imaginable kinds and acts of terror, including, as Pareto diagnosed and predicted, to kill others and themselves "for the divine master", as does fascism, notably Nazism for nearly identical or similar causes (Adorno 2001; Fromm 1941; McLaughlin 1998). For instance, Calvin is in some accounts classified into the "greatest haters of humanity" and the religious prototype of the fascist-type sadistic-masochistic character structure (Fromm 1941) and thus the authoritarian personality (Adorno 2001), notably the Protestant model of "holy" state terror and theocratic tyranny (Mansbach 2006).

In this connection, Hume in his classical historical study portrayed early Puritans in England (and Scotland), following Calvin's "discipline and worship of Geneva", as unreasonable, hateful, intolerant, and militant "sectaries" guided by "religious zeal", "wild" and "wretched" fanaticism, "uncharitableness", and "unreasonable obstinacy". Even sympathetic Tawney (1962) describes English-Americans Puritans as "strange monsters" driven in their economic, religious, and military activities by "demonic energy" and in the process becoming prototypes of modern anti-secular extremists like US Protestant "Christian" evangelicals, whose perennial model and inspiration remains theocratic Puritanism (Dunn and Woodard 1996; Munch 2001), and Islamic fundamentalists (Juergensmeyer 1994). Recall Puritans were described as "iron Protestants", epitomized in England by Cromwell whose political activities were "holy" wars or crusades against "infidels" (Goldstone 1986; Gorski 2000), and in early America by Winthrop et al. characterized by "austere Calvinism" and acting as "stodgy, orthodox Calvinists" (Gould 1996) in their equivalent militant and repressive practices.

Conversely, it appears as though the most certain and effective way to transform humans defined by humanity into anti-human agents after the image of Hobbes' wolves and other wild beasts or monsters in an universal hatred and war against each other and perpetrating any form of inhumanity, cruelty, brutality, and murder is to make or convert them into Calvinists-Puritans or evangelicals and Islamic fundamentalists, just as (neo) fascists, including (neo) Nazis. Thus, Tawney (1962) in describing early Puritans in England and America as "strange monsters" driven by "demonic energy" implies that they were so motivated into committing corresponding monstrous acts of terror. Recall the latter involved Puritan "holy" terror in England (Walzer 1963) and the "reign of terror" by Puritans in New England (Merril 1945), including the persecution of Quakers and witch trials, and "holy" wars against other societies, such as the genocide or war of extermination against Native Americans, for supra-human Divine "causes" such as what Weber calls the glorification of the "God of

Calvinism." In this connection, cynics may comment that the Puritan pilgrims' solemn, ultimate form of "thanksgiving" to the Native Americans for their initial generosity and helping them survive was genocide or war of extermination against the latter as "heathen" (Gould 1996; Mann 2005; Munch 2001). Generally, it is striking that "Thanksgiving" has become a major national holiday in America but in a sort of collective amnesia it is hardly ever mentioned how the Puritan pilgrims "reciprocated" these admittedly life-saving acts of the Native Americans by, to put it mildly, such an ultimate form of ingratitude. Yet, Hume would suggest that the American Puritans could not truly reciprocate, minimally, to paraphrase Schumpeter, "live and let [Native Americans] live", because they were, like their English predecessors, zealous "sectaries" driven by "wild" and "wretched fanaticism", i.e., what Tocqueville calls "religious passions", striving to purge the "ungodly" and "impure" in the "name of God." So, when Mencken (1982) says "show me a Puritan and I will show you son of a [B]", this evokes the early Puritans' "thanksgiving" to their admitted saviors by exterminating them via a "holy" war.

Hume and Tawney would have likely depicted in identical or comparable terms Puritan-inspired evangelicalism and its "born again" members in America, just as Islamic fundamentalism and fundamentalists, as some contemporary sociological analyses explicitly or implicitly suggest (Juergensmeyer 2003; Turner 2002). For instance, the 2008 Vice-Presidential candidate, a self-described "born again" evangelical, said after an ultra-conservative candidate was defeated in an Congressional election, the evangelical and generally conservative "cause continues". Given the evangelical and neo-conservative militant and warlike pattern and method, this "cause" implies culture wars as the means of coercion within society and global war against the "evil" world. It this involves "holy" counter-state and state terror–depending on whether evangelicalism or neo-conservatism is in what Comte calls "fanatical opposition" against the "big" liberal-secular government as after the 2008 Presidential election, or in political power, as during the 1980s-2010s—all in the "name of God (and nation)", as Tocqueville's "Puritan fathers" stated in their "Statutes of [Christian] Liberty" evidently not worth the paper on which were written for non-Puritans, including Native American, Quakers, etc.

If not religion as such in a charitable yet disputable assumption, apparently there is "something" at least in most world religions, notably Calvinist Puritanism and its revived form, American evangelicalism as well as in fundamentalist Islam, just as in Nazism and other fascism, that tends to ultimately make humans Hobbes' wolves. This thus makes humans the polar opposite of what is understood by "human" within liberal-secular modernity, in particular the Enlightenment's humanism exemplified by Kant's humanistic principle of placing human subjects within the "kingdom of ends", and even Christianity like the "golden rule". If this is correct, such inhumanity or anti-humanism contradicts early Puritans' and contemporary US evangelicals' (notably, Southern Baptists') claims to be the "only and true" Christians vs. non-evangelicals (Catholics, mainline Protestants, etc.) branded as "non-Christian" and the "Anti-Christ" (the Vatican Church), and instead it exposes them, as Tawney and Weber imply, as anti- or quasi-Christians.

However, this is an internal theological or sectarian dispute belonging to what Pareto calls, referring to the early "disputes of the Christian sects", a "cage for the insane" and not relevant for sociological and other scientific analysis. And, the above "something" is evidently the commandment and practice of "religious revolution" as the instrument of theocracy and "holy war", and in this sense "holy terror" within society and against other societies, which Puritanism or Puritan-rooted evangelicalism shares with fundamentalist Islam (and fascism). They thus become "brothers in arms" when facing their common enemy, liberal-secular modernity, in accordance with the old rule of, as Simmel puts it, "my enemy's enemy is my friend", even if remaining mortal enemies in other respects like global religious, cultural, political, and military dominance through their contest in conversions (missionary work, etc.) and violent conflicts.

Anti-Modernism and Anti-Progressivism

The fifth cause of why religion generates and/or justifies "holy" terror is that itself, notably the world religions, represent or claim to be what Weber calls "sacred tradition" and thus traditionalism. As such, it is directly or indirectly opposed or suspicious to modernization or modernism and to social progress or progressivism in favor of conservation of the present state of society as Divinely ordained and so immutable and eternal or, if changed and reformed, the restoration of the "golden past" as "paradise lost". As before, this is a defining attribute of religion as the "sacred" phenomenon in Durkheim's sense and a common element of virtually all Weber's world religions, including both those characterized with "passive adaptation" to and those seeking total "mastery" of the social and physical world. Weber observes that initially Protestantism, including Calvinism, had "precious little" with social progress and even was "directly opposed" to most aspects of liberal-secular modernity, thus admonishing against presuming, as Parsons et al. tend to do, some "Protestant progressivism" and "modernism" in an invidious distinction from putatively regressive and anti-modernist pre-Protestantism, like Catholicism and the Orthodox Church, in Christianity and other world religions, including Hinduism, Confucianism, Buddhism, Islam, and in part Judaism. Consequently, he implies that Protestantism, despite its "elective affinity" with modern capitalism, just as pre-Protestant Christianity and other world religions, was a species of societal, especially cultural and political, traditionalism or orthodoxy, more precisely medievalism or feudalism, thus pre-modernism and in that sense what Comte calls primitivism and barbarism. Comte explicitly suggests this by observing that Protestantism attempts and often succeeds to restore the "dream of the primitive [Christian] church", including the "most barbarous part of Scripture [Hebrew antiquity]" as a sort of "paradise lost and found".

In Protestantism, like Christianity overall and other world religions, notably Islam, this primitivism or barbarism as a rule assumes the form of fundamentalism, i.e., a return to the supposed first origins of a religion and church (Turner 2002), in this case Biblical societies and times, hence Biblicism or evangelicalism, despite some formal distinctions between "fundamentalism" and "evangelicalism" in America. For instance, Mencken (1982) uses the expression "Methodist and Baptist barbarism" ruling for long through systematic coercion and violent repression and in that sense "holy" state terror and turning the post-bellum US South into a primitive fundamentalist "Bible Belt." Also, when Mises registers that the Middle Ages and other primitive societies and pre-modern times in Europe and beyond were "petrified" he implicates in this institutional petrification not only, as Parsons et al. do, early medieval Catholicism and its Vatican theocracy but also high-medieval Protestantism and what Weber calls despotic "Calvinist state churches" in European societies as well as tyrannical Puritan theocracies in England (and Scotland) and New England.

In a sense, the fifth cause can be designated anti- or pre-progressivism and anti- or pre-modernism typifying religion in general, notably virtually all the world religions, including, contrary to received theory and popular opinion, supposedly "progressive" and "modernist" Protestantism, specifically Calvinism and its English-American derivative Puritanism. A paradigmatic instance of religious primitivism, including fanaticism, is messianism, the "expectation of imminent transformation" or destruction cum "rapture" of the world, including its secular proxies (Townshend 2002). For instance, some US evangelicals prophesized and propagated the "second coming of Christ" and the resulting "end of the world" and their own journey to heaven ("rapture") on May 21, 2011 (then postponed for 6 months later and so on). And primitive or traditionalist, anti-progressive and anti-modernist religious individuals, organizations, governments, and societies are more likely to advocate, commit, and support terrorism from violence and coercion within society to aggressive war and destruction against other societies, than are others. To be sure, not all anti-progressive and anti-modernist religious individuals, organizations, religiously-based governments, and societies resort and endorse terrorism, but they tend to do so more than others.

Religious Irrationalism—Fanaticism and "Holy" Madness

The sixth cause of why religion generates and justifies "holy "terror is, as indicated, its intrinsic irrationalism or pre- and anti-rationalism. This is expressed in excessive enthusiasm and fervor, zealotry, fanaticism, absurdities, absolutism, superstition, and prejudice, anti- and pre-scientific errors, myths, and fables, and eventually some sort of "holy" madness or hysteria, opposing or predating and ultimately destroying scientific and other cultural rationalism. Again, this is a defining attribute of religion as the irrational or non- and pre-rational realm of the sacred, as Durkheim implies, including what he calls "collective effervescence" or mass "enthusiasm", notably Weber's world religions. Before Durkheim, Enlightenment philosopher Diderot explicitly identifies and emphasizes such an attribute by characterizing religion as mass "sacred contagion" and hence societal irrationalism. Diderot's colleague Voltaire specifically points to the "childish absurdities" ("Noah's Ark", the six-day "creation" of the world, "original sin", etc.), including, as Pareto puts it later, the "scientific errors" of the Christian religion presented in the Bible. Also, another Enlightenment philosopher Montesquieu suggests that religion intrinsically entails irrationalism stating that theology is "doubly intelligible by the matter which is treated and by manner of treating it", which Pareto approvingly quotes. Furthermore, Hume, the leader of the Scottish Enlightenment, identifies and emphasizes "religious fanaticism", including "madness with religious ecstasies", in early England and implicitly virtually all societies and times. Similarly, his admirer, classical economist Adam Smith, also the member of the Scottish Enlightenment, implies that virtually all existing religions are a "mixture of absurdity, imposture, or fanaticism", observing and predicting that what he calls "pure and rational religion" always has been and will be a sort of non-entity or impossibility[30] contrary to the economics or rational choice model of religion.

On the account of Diderot's idea of "sacred contagion", Voltaire's of "childish absurdities", Hume's of "madness with religious ecstasies", Durkheim's of "collective effervescence", and related irrational states of mass extremely intense and uncontrollable emotions, perhaps religion as such constitutes a design or becomes a system of societal madness (in a value-neutral sense) and contagion. This is incidentally (or not) implied in the expression "method in the madness" often (Smith 2000) used with respect to contemporary fundamentalism and/or evangelicalism in America. A system of societal madness also characterizes fascism, notably Nazism making through its methodical madness of absolute power the world "mad" (Bourdieu 2000), and any totalitarianism premised on either hyper-emotional religion, as were most fascisms and also neo-fascism or neo-Nazism in Europe and America, or on non-religious ideology (political nationalism, communism, etc.). Generally, Weber observes that "the religious experience as such is of course irrational" and in that sense genuine or proxy "madness", including what he refers to as "childishness" associated with religion, while Tönnies proposes that "spirit as a special entity [typifying religion] exists in the world of ghosts".[31]

And Weber implies that virtually all the world religions represent or generate theological designs and social systems of severe or mild societal madness or insanity and contagion in Diderot's sense of "sacred contagion" and Durkheim's of "collective effervescence". Hence, these religions include not only, as usually supposed, the Oriental ones and pre-Protestant Christianity resigned to "mere accommodation" to the world but also Calvinism and its sect Puritanism and Protestantism overall seeking total theocratic "mastery" of society. Weber uses such terms as the "hysterical condition", "mass hysteria", and the like to describe Puritanism, specifically Pietism in Europe, Baptism and Methodism in America. For instance, he registers the "often definitely pathological character of Methodist emotionalism" as particularly witnessed in

---

[30] Smith refers to "that pure and rational religion, free from every mixture of absurdity, imposture, or fanaticism, such as wise men have in all ages of the world wished to see established; but such as positive law has perhaps never yet established, and probably never will establish, in any country: because, with regard to religion, positive law always has been, and probably always will be, more or less influenced by popular superstition and enthusiasm."

[31] Tönnies states that "a Messianic hope [for community] based on the 'spirit' alone [is not enough], for spirit as a special entity exists in the world of ghosts."

America, and comments that "only a neurologist [or psychiatrist?] could decide" on the connection between such religious irrationalism and "the greater ascetic penetration of life" by Methodism and Calvinism or Protestant asceticism generally. He adds that initially Calvinist or Puritan Methodism assumed "a strongly emotional character, especially in America" to the effect that "the attainment of repentance under certain circumstances involved an emotional struggle of such intensity as to lead to the most terrible ecstasies, which in America often took place in a public meeting." Similarly, he observes that Baptism, specifically "the idea of expectant waiting for the Spirit to descend", produces "hysterical conditions", thus assuming, alongside Pietism, a "positively hysterical character" which is "neuropathologically understandable" and involving "half-conscious states of religious ecstasy with periods of nervous exhaustion."[32]

Moreover, Pareto effectively considers Calvinism, specifically Puritanism, to be a "kind of insanity" on the account of the tendency for Puritans (e.g., Scottish Presbyterians) to "experience great delight in tormenting themselves and others". Generally, Pareto depicts Christianity (e.g., early "Christian sects") after the image of a "cage for the insane". Preceding Weber and Pareto, Hume classically portrays early Puritanism in England as well as New England in terms of "wretched" and "wild fanaticism" and by implication collective madness or hysteria and generally societal irrationalism, "preemptively" contradicting the Weberian (and Parsonian) rationalistic thesis of an "elective affinity" between the Puritan religion or its parent Calvinism and modern capitalism, with his successor Smith describing Puritans as the "sect no doubt of very wild enthusiasts." And Hume (and Smith) implies that Puritanism, including Puritan-rooted "born again" evangelicalism, and any religious fanaticism or zealotry is a sort of "holy" madness or insanity and thus ultimate irrationalism, as does Diderot's expression "sacred contagion", through the "capacity of religious belief" for inspiring fanatical "commitment" and its "resistance to compromise"[33] (Townshend 2002). Thus, in what at least Hume, Diderot, and

---

[32] Weber's full statement is that in Pietism, "moreover, the emotion (of mystic union with God) was capable of such intensity, that religion took on a positively hysterical character, resulting in the alternation which is familiar from examples without number and neuropathologically understandable, of half-conscious states of religious ecstasy with periods of nervous exhaustion, which were felt as abandonment by God.

[33] Townshend (2002:16) adds that "the ethical mechanism by which ordinary people have been able to set aside pity and remorse in order to kill other(s) has been symbolic generalization–the smothering of the victims' individual human qualities by

other Enlightenment thinkers, as well as Pareto and perhaps Weber, would consider a syndrome of religiously induced madness or fanaticism, one of the founders of "reborn" US evangelicalism (or "televangelism") claimed "I become anointed with God's word, and the spirit of the Lord builds up in me like a coiled spring. By the time I'm ready to go on, my mind is razor-sharp. I know exactly what I'm going to say and I'm feeling like a lion." Perhaps, it is rather a mixture of religious madness/fanaticism with a sort of profitable con-artistry, as revealed for many televangelists preaching their "Prosperity Gospel" in the service of methodical extortion of money from their flocks, including the abjectly poor, in the tradition of admittedly Puritan "pure hypocrisy" (Weber's word), perhaps the only kind of "purity" in Puritanism.

Furthermore, some contemporary sociologists (Grossman 2006), explicitly rejecting the Weberian and Parsonian rationalistic thesis, treat original Calvinism as an exemplar of religious "irrationalism", due to its irrational as well as non-universalistic and exclusionary theological dogma of predestination, which Weber himself described as "harsh" and "extremely inhumane" (also, Fourcade and Healy 2007) and to its theocratic system of tyrannical repression alike. Prima facie, a manifest syndrome of such madness or irrationalism is what social psychologists identify as the sadistic-masochistic character structure, and thus the totalitarian or authoritarian personality, in early Calvinism and inherited or shared by fascism, notably Nazism (Fromm 1941; also, Adorno 2001; McLaughlin 1996). In this account, Calvinism in virtue of its irrational and inhumane tendencies or outcomes performed, as a sort of principal, through its Anglo-Saxon "agent" Puritanism, the "same sociological function" of violent repression, systematic coercion, and offensive war in English-American contexts as did Nazism in Germany (McLaughlin 1996). In this respect, Calvinism, notably Puritanism, reveals itself as the functional equivalent of fascism, just as of Islam, in terms of religiously or

---

their collective identity (religion, class, race, ethnicity). [Such] stereotyping powered most, if not all, of the wars, genocide, and violent revolutionary struggles of the 20th century and remains the common currency of nationalis(m) and the motor of ethnic cleansing. If terrorists are "fanatics of simplicity", so are all too many good citizens". Particularly, in this view, superterrorism is an irresistible topic. Religious extremists could find exemplars in the behaviour of gods like Jehovah, who visited his enemies with massive destruction, or holy men like Phineas (the myth for the white supremacist Christian Patriots), who "purified" the community by murdering the chief of his tribe. Millenarianism likewise can be impelled to demonstrative rather than instrumental violence. In the secular sphere, emulation of Hitler might well validate the use of mass destruction by neo-Nazi groups" (Townshend 2002:34).

ideologically grounded and sanctified irrationalism and in that sense genuine or proxy collective madness or insanity exemplified by the composite of sadism and masochism in the service, as Puritan Cromwell solemnly proclaimed, of "honoring God". And, masochistic or "suffering", let alone sadistic, individuals and groups usually direct their "aggressions" against others through, alongside non-violent cynicism, terrorism (Olick 1999).

Alternatively, the sixth cause can be designated as anti- or prerationalism, including absolutism, in the sense of either opposing or historically predating rationalism, notably its scientific version or scientism with its underlying relativism (Habermas 2001). In particular, since the absolutism and generally self-destructive irrationalism of most religion, notably such world religions as Islam and Protestant Christianity, especially manifests itself in the "notion of cosmic war" (Juergensmeyer 2003), the latter and thus terrorism can be characterized a la Clausewitz as the continuation of the absolutist, irrational religious, specifically Islamic and evangelical, politics as well as morality by other, violent means. Generally, irrational or anti-rational, including fanatic, superstitious, and absolutist, religious individuals, organizations, governments, and societies are more likely to advocate, commit, and support terrorism, such as domestic violence and coercion and aggressive wars and destruction against other societies, than are others. While not all irrational or anti-rational religious individuals, organizations, governments, and societies resort and endorse terrorism, still they tend to do so more than others. (The causes of why religion generates or sanctifies terror are summarized in Table 6.1.)

Table 6.1. Causes of "Holy" Terror.

1. Submission, humiliation, and sacrifice of humans, their liberty and life to Divine causes
2. Division of humans, groups and societies into "true believers" and "infidels" ("us" versus "them")
3. Denial and suppression of individual liberties in favor of collective religious constraint
4. Concept and practice of religious revolution within society and a "holy" total war against other societies.
5. Religion as "sacred tradition" in opposition to social modernism and progressivism
6. Religious irrationalism, including fanaticism, superstition, and prejudice, madness versus scientific rationalism

CHAPTER SEVEN

ANTI-GLOBALISM AND MODERN TERRORISM

Antagonism toward Global-Cosmopolitan Modernity as the Factor of Modern Terrorism

Yet another interrelated effective or potential sociological determinant and predictor of contemporary terrorism is the antagonism toward global-cosmopolitan and thus universalistic and humanistic modernity. The hostility and adverse reaction to modern globalized, open, cosmopolitan, and universalistic and humanistic society generates and predicts terrorism in interconnection and mutual reinforcement with the antagonism to liberal-democratic, secularized, and rationalistic modernity. At this juncture, terrorism represents a radical, violent form and expression of the composite of anti-globalism, anti-cosmopolitanism, anti-universalism, and anti-humanism as a vehement revolt against and attempted reversal of global-cosmopolitan and humanistic modernity, just as of anti-liberalism and anti-democracy, anti-secularism, and anti-rationalism revolting against and seeking to reverse liberalism and democracy, secularism, and scientific rationalism, respectively.

In particular, anti-globalism and anti-cosmopolitanism include the opposition to the renewed and accelerating trend to economic, political, and cultural globalization (Bartley 2007; Benson and Saguy 2005; Brady, Beckfield, and Zhao 2007; Fiss and Hirsch 2005; Guillen 2001; Janssen, Kuipers, and Verboord 2008; Romer 2010) as the integral element or "new face" of the general and continuing process of societal modernization, including liberalization and democratization, secularization, and rationalization. Notably, to the extent that globalization enhances, sustains, or promises mostly (Acemoglu and Yared 2010; Fischer 2003; Giddens 2000; Habermas 2001; Samuelson 2004)–though not invariably (as critics object, cf., Bauman 2001; Beck 2000)–societal liberalization and democratization, as well as prosperity, diversity and choice, thus liberation and human emancipation, the opposition toward the first process expresses and originates in the adverse reaction to the second and modernization.

Alternatively, the adverse reaction to societal modernization, particularly liberalization and democratization, political pluralism and culture diversity, secularization, and rationalization, harbors or generates the opposition toward globalization, so long as the former process assumes worldwide dimensions during recent times as the "second era of globalization" (Hummels 2007), as well as the end of the 19th and early 20th centuries and before (Chase-Dunn, Kawano and Brewer 2000). Especially, to the degree that liberalization and democratization, political pluralism and multiculturalism, secularization, and rationalization have or are like to become prevalent global trends (Alesina and Ferrara 2005; Gorski and Altınordu 2008; Habermas et al. 1998; Inglehart and Baker 2000; Inglehart 2004; Munch 2001; Norris and Inglehart 2004), the opposition to the process of globalization is implied in and predicted from the adverse reaction toward these modernizing processes expressing originally Western liberal modernity and spreading to and shaping subsequently non-Western settings (Japan, Turkey, South Korea, Taiwan, China, South America, etc.).

More specifically, the compound of anti-globalism and anti-cosmopolitanism and in extension anti-universalism and anti-humanism entails a two-fold revolt or opposition. First, it involves the revolt against modern global, open, cosmopolitan, universalistic, and humanistic society as an emerging societal reality (Inglehart 2004; Munch 2001) and the historical time of the "new liberty" (Dahrendorf 1975), especially since the 1960s and perhaps post-war times through the 2000s. Second, it entails also the revolt against this model of society, if not yet realized to the full extent, as an enduring Western ideal or dream since the Enlightenment and liberalism generally (Beck 2001; Dahrendorf 1979; Dombrowski 2001; Habermas 2001), as well as perhaps the artistic and humanistic Renaissance (Eisenstadt 1998) and classical democracy and civilization before (Manent 1998; Popper 1973).

Global-Cosmopolitan "Utopia", Anti-Globalism, and Terrorism

In aggregate terms, then the composite of anti-globalism, anti-cosmopolitanism, anti-universalism, and anti-humanism contains a dual antagonism in the form of deep-seated hostility and concerted opposition toward modern open, global-cosmopolitan, universalistic, and humanistic society. This entails negativity and ultimately nihilism toward the latter in a double sense. This means first an established social system, as in the modern Western world and its extensions or emulations, for example, America, Canada, Australia, New Zealand, Japan, South Korea, post-communist Eastern and Central Europe, parts of South America, etc.

It means, second, a vision and search of such a society of the "new liberty" (Dahrendorf 1975), equality, and justice, just as in Adam Smith's classical "liberal plan" involving this trinity of ideals rather than only the first as in "libertarian" reductive interpretations a la Hayek (1948) et al. (As an illustration of such invalid yet influential "libertarian" reductionism, Hayek [1948:7] suggests that what he calls the "true individualism"– somewhat invidiously reminiscent of claims to "true" religion or church by virtually all religions or churches–"achieved its stature for the first time in the works of Adam Smith" (plus Tucker and Ferguson), but fails to consider and even mention Smith's "liberal plan" involving equality and justice alongside liberty. Moreover, Hayek [1948:30] claims that the "main principle" of Smithian and other "true individualism" is that "no man or group should have power to decide what another man's status ought to be, and it regards this as a condition of freedom so essential that it must not be sacrificed to the gratification of our sense of justice or envy." Prima facie, this is a gross misrepresentation of Smith because evidently his "true individualism" or liberalism includes not only individual liberty but also *justice* and equality. Similarly, other "libertarian" economists [Buchanan 1991:4] propose that "the challenge is one of [re]constructing a political order that will channel the self-serving behavior of participants towards the common goal in a manner close to that described by Adam Smith with respect to the economic order" and generally extols the latter as the "father" of economic science, but does not even mention Smith's "liberal plan" combining liberty with equality and justice.)

Simply, anti-globalism opposes global-cosmopolitan modernity both as a reality and a utopia in Mannheim's (1936) sense of transcending the present societal condition, and not necessarily a totally unrealizable project, as conservative, fascist, and other anti-Enlightenment and anti-liberal forces allege finding in pre-Enlightenment and pre-liberal medieval despotism and theocracy the model for their "vision of the good society" (Nisbet 1966). Like any societal projects seeking to transcend the petrified status quo of society after the image of what Mises (1950) calls the "peace of cemetery"[1] typifying medievalism and its heir conservatism, the project of global-cosmopolitan, liberal-democratic, secular, and rationalistic, simply open modernity has been a utopia before (Popper 1973), including the Enlightenment and the subsequent French and American Revolutions.

---

[1] Mises (1950) uses the expression the "peace of cemetery" explicitly in reference to "socialism" or rather "communism" and implicitly to "despotic government" and "conservatism" or "traditionalism" usually characterized with despotism.

And perhaps still it is such a utopia, dream, or quest of the future "good" society.

Yet, this global-cosmopolitan, thus universalistic, inclusive utopia may well become an institutionalized social reality in the near or distant future, and even, in some sociological accounts, has already reached or approximated this stage of realization within the modern Western world (Giddens 2000; Habermas 2001), especially liberal-secular "post-Christian" (Inglehart 2004) Scandinavian societies also globalized, economically and politically and culturally alike. Scandinavian and related societies like Sweden and others are both paradigmatic modernist welfare states, thus egalitarian social democracies, *and* (among) the most globalized modern economies, notably more[2] so (Brady, Beckfield, and Seeleib-Kaiser 2005), contrary to "libertarian" economic allegations, than American traditionalist laissez-faire, "unfettered capitalism" (Fishback 1998). Incidentally or rather not, these societies, for example, Denmark, Finland, Norway, Austria, Holland, Belgium, Switzerland, Germany, etc., are also found to be the "happiest" nations and the "best places to live" in the world primarily owing to their "welfare capitalism" (Esping-Andersen 1994; Korpi 1978; Quadagno 1984)–not "socialism" contrary to what US "libertarians" and other neo-conservatives allege and perhaps most Americans think– and implicitly to their increasingly globalized economies, politics, and cultures.

Instead, American conservative-reproduced and glorified "unfettered capitalism" is typified by a minimal welfare (Amenta, Bonastia and Caren 2001; Moller; Alderson, and Nielsen 2009; Quadagno 1999; Steensland 2006)–or rather a maximal anti-welfare police-warfare, i.e., repressive-militarist (Bourdieu 1998; Wacquant 2002)—state. Hence, this social-economic system is characterized with salient and, within the Western world, strongest and most persistent anti-egalitarianism, authoritarianism, and militarism driven by nationalism[3] (Acemoglu and Yared 2010) and metastasizing in the "new imperialism" (Steinmetz 2005). For instance, such outcomes are manifested in the greatest wealth-income inequality and poverty in the Western world and the most severe repression (Pryor 2002) as well, including the biggest prisoner and, along

---

[2] Brady et al. (2005:924) suggest "consider that Sweden has a generous welfare state and is highly globalized, while the United States is less globalized and has a minimal welfare state."

[3] Acemoglu and Jared (2010: 83) observe that "despite the increasing reach of globalization, anecdotal evidence suggests that nationalism and militarism [defined as the doctrine or policy of "aggressive military preparedness"] are strong around the world, in countries ranging from the United States to China, Russia, and India."

with Islamic theocracies, executed population in the world, and also the highest military spending reaching no less than half of its global level and constant or recurring "imperial wars" (Abott 2005). "Unfettered capitalism" is also observed to be a less globalized, historically (Chase-Dunn, Kawano, and Brewer 2000) and presently (Brady et al. 2005), and a "relatively closed" economic system (Leijonhufvud 2004), evoking Fichte's "closed commercial state", compared to Scandinavian and other European welfare capitalisms, just as in consequence, especially of the anti-welfare, anti-egalitarian, and thus non- or quasi-democratic (Acemoglu 2005) element, "less happy" than the latter.

For instance, a US leading economist effectively anticipated this superficially, if following anarchic and dogmatic "libertarian" economics and ideology, unexpected outcome in observing that "egalitarian and regimented Scandinavia was freer than my [free-enterprise] America" during postwar times (Samuelson cited in Tilman 2001). By implication, this was and still is, because American "unfettered capitalism" mixed, and still does, Anarchy or unlimited liberty for capitalist plutocracy or oligarchy with Leviathan or systematic oppression of labor (Hayagreeva et al. 2011; Pryor 2002). And the latter is conjoined and mutually reinforced with conservatism's political suppression of "un-American" groups and its rigid social control[4] (Jacobs and Tope 2007; King 2008) via Puritan-style fundamentalist moralistic repression and Draconian punishment ("moral fascism"), including executions (Cunningham and Phillips 2007; Jacobs et al. 2005) and long imprisonment (Matsueda, Kreager, and Huizinga 2006), of sinners cum criminals for alcohol and drug use, sexual sins, etc. For instance, the predicament, including imprisonment, etc., of a young Hollywood actress during the 2010s, because of her sins and thus pleasures like alcohol and drug use, reveals a symptom of moralistic state terror and generally Puritan-rooted moralistic fascism under American neo-conservatism, for in modern Western democracy such sinners are not criminalized and to that extent are truly innocent prisoners of ethical conscience. Virtually nowhere in Western Europe and other liberal democracies (Canada, Australia, etc.) would a 20 or so year old person be imprisoned for alcohol use and so harshly punished for drug possession

---

[4] King (2008:1354) remarks that "two varieties of conservatism, political and religious, are independently predictive of state social control" in contemporary America. In this account, "the increase in government social control since the 1970s aligns with a simultaneous movement toward political conservatism in the US. Political conservatism shares an affinity with Christian fundamentalism and both inform ideas on punishment and civil rights. Conservative political candidates increasingly draw support from Christian fundamentalists in the US, who generally favor harsher criminal sanctions" (King 2008:1355).

but "only in [conservative] America" and Islamic theocracies. Evidently, such sins and pleasures are just "too much" important to be left unpunished or unrestrained for the Puritan-style US government, even in "liberal" California, just as Islamic theocracies, but innocuous or insignificant to Western liberal democracies.

At this juncture, recall Mill's classical liberal statement that "these intrusively pious members of society" such as like English-American Puritans ("stricter Calvinists and Methodists") should "mind their own business" and that "this is precisely what should be said to every government and every public, who have the pretension that no person shall enjoy any pleasure which they think wrong." Hence, Mill would propose the US Puritan-rooted conservative government has no "business" in prohibiting and punishing such moral sins and pleasures of individuals, if it is to be democratic; and if it pretends that it shall do so for the "glory of God", then it perpetrates "holy" state terror. Mill would thus wonder what "business" the US moralistic government has in interfering with, disrupting, and even psychologically or otherwise ruining the private life of this and any other individuals in America by harshly punishing and tormenting them because of their moral sins and pleasures? However, this is a sort of unrealistic proposition or suggestion because Puritan and Islamic governments or groups never have done what Mill proposes, "mind your own business" and respect individual liberty and privacy, simply leave individuals alone, but instead decreeing that "no person shall enjoy any pleasure which they think wrong" and punishing harshly such pleasures and sins, thus committing "holy" state terror. And never will they likely do in the foreseeable future.

In other accounts, Scandinavian and other welfare capitalism is observed to be "both economically and [especially] socially more efficient" (Trigilia 2002) than American unregulated capitalism, minimally the latter does not show "economic superiority", contrary to conventional wisdom in economics and conservative "American ethnocentrism" (Beck 2001). This is demonstrated by unregulated capitalism's built-in tendency, due to its archaic laissez-faire dogmas (the dogma against government regulation, consumption, and investment, for balance budgets, etc.), to self-destruction through generating and spreading via global contagion catastrophic crises, from the 1929 Great Depression[5] (Eggertsson 2008) to

---

[5] Eggertsson (2008:1476) observes that with its New Deal "Roosevelt eliminated several policy dogmas that Hoover had subscribed to: the gold standard, a balanced budget, and

the 2008 Great Recession (Stiglitz 2010). Simply, it was American conservative "unfettered" capitalism in alliance with an ultra-conservative government, not Scandinavian and other liberal, welfare, regulated capitalism, that engendered and then generously "imported" to the world both the Great Depression (as Keynes showed) and the Great Recession. It thus displayed its intrinsic self-destructive tendency and outcome when left to its own devices and dogmas, notably the anachronistic laissez-faire dogma, defining market fundamentalism (Stiglitz 2010), against government regulation, expenditure, and investment, and the like (Eggertsson 2008).

At any rate, the project or utopia of modern global-cosmopolitan society, including a globalized economy, appears to be, contrary to US "libertarian" allegations and received views, more wholeheartedly and fully realized or approached in European, notably Scandinavian, modernized welfare, egalitarian and regulated capitalism than in American conservative-reproduced anti-egalitarian and unregulated ("Wild West") mafia capitalism (Pryor 2002), epitomized by what can be described as Enronism in the generic sense (Prechel and Morris 2010), as near-total capitalist dictatorship.

In general, the global-cosmopolitan and thus universalistic, like any, utopia likely "is tomorrow's [or today's] truth" (Hugo cited in Bauman 2001), and thus the present or the future. This is what at least modern Scandinavian and related Western liberal-democratic, open, and globalized societies (Holland, Canada, Australia, etc.) indicate at present or augur for the foreseeable future. In turn, anti-global and anti-cosmopolitan forces, raising in adverse reaction or vehement revolt against global-cosmopolitan and universalistic modernity, attempt to prevent making its utopia or vision a societal reality through radical, violent actions in the form of counter-state terrorism via anti-government violence, when deprived of government control, and, once seizing political power, state and inter-state terror through violent repression and inter-state war, respectively.

---

small government" or the dogma against "government consumption and investment", which, especially the latter, caused or perpetuated the Great Depression (as Keynes also emphasized). Moreover, it is estimated that "the elimination of these policy dogmas [explains] about 70–80 percent of the recovery of output and prices in the data from 1933 to 1937. In the absence of the regime change, however, the economy would have continued its free fall in 1933, and output would have been 30 percent lower in 1937 than in 1933, instead of increasing 39 percent in this period" (Eggertsson 2008:1479–80).

In sum, the antagonism toward what, for the lack of a better term, can be called modern globalism in the sense of a complex of economic, political, and cultural globalization, openness, cosmopolitanism, and universalism, including multiculturalism and pacifism, tends to generate, explain, and predict contemporary terrorism. And, one cannot emphasize enough that the composite of anti-globalism and anti-cosmopolitanism and anti-universalism does so in interrelation and mutual reinforcement with its close correlates anti-liberalism and anti-democracy, anti-secularism, and anti-rationalism, in turn all of them expressing ("loading on") anti-modernism as their synthesis or aggregate. The connection of anti-globalism and anti-cosmopolitanism, including anti-multiculturalism and anti-pacifism, with terrorism especially holds true for non-Western agents and settings such as fundamentalist Islamic groups and theocracies, as exemplified by Al-Qaeda, Taliban-ruled regions, and associated terrorist organizations and theocratic forces. These fundamentalist Islamic terrorist forces and established theocratic powers are as a rule anti-global, anti-cosmopolitan, and anti-universalistic, including anti-multicultural and anti-pacifist, just as, in interaction and mutual reinforcement, anti-liberal and anti-democratic, anti-secular, and anti-rationalistic, and generally anti-modernist.

However, the link of anti-globalism and anti-cosmopolitanism, including overt or implied anti-multiculturalism and anti-pacifism, with contemporary terrorism is also witnessed in some fringe or "exceptional" elements and regions of modern Western societies. Among these fringe Western elements particularly manifest and salient are the ultra-conservative, nativist, xenophobic, and evangelical segments of the US (Inglehart 2004), epitomized by the Southern "Bible Belt" and its extensions in other "red" (or rather, as often self-described, "redneck") regions. These regions represent the probably American and Western world "leader" in nativism or aggressive nationalism, hysterical xenophobia in the form of anti-immigration paranoia to the point of criminalizing immigration[6] (Collins 2010), as well as consequently militarism and

---

[6] Collins (2010:13) remarks that the "shift toward local, rather than national, immigration policies is a Homeland Security strategy to rid the country of undocumented, illegal immigrants who have become socially constructed as criminals by recent immigration policies [in Southern and other US states]. These examples pivot on fear and risk catalyzed by ideas about the "enemy without" as well as the "enemy within". Also, Collins (2010:13) observes "the Office of Homeland Security's preoccupation with protecting individuals within U.S. borders from foreigners and foreign terrorists" rather than from home-grown terrorist groups or individuals like those involved in the 1995 Oklahoma bombing and similar acts.

renewed imperialism (Acemoglu and Yared 2010; Steinmetz 2005), including imperial-style hegemony (Smelser and Mitchell 2002) and wars[7] (Abbott 2005). For instance, the highest percentage of support for an apparently xenophobic law against illegal immigration passed by Arizona's ruling ultraconservatives in the 2010s was reported in the Southern "Bible Belt" and other "red" regions emulating or surpassing it in severity and even sheer economic irrationality (e.g., Alabama reportedly lost billions of dollars due to the enforcement of its own "tough" version, plus South Carolina, etc.); cynics may comment "where else" than in "sweet home Alabama [South]" and "red" America overall.

Like terrorist and theocratic Islamic fundamentalists, US fundamentalist anti-government terrorists and, when in power, theocrats cum self-described "holy" culture and military warriors are almost invariably anti-global, anti-cosmopolitan, and anti-universalistic, including anti-multiculturalist and anti-pacifist, as well as, in mutual relation and reinforcement, anti-liberal and anti-democratic, anti-secular, and anti-rationalistic, and anti-modernist in general. In particular, US fundamentalist or neo-fascist "Christian" terrorist militias and other neo-conservative extremists are obsessed with and vehemently attack the project of the "new world order", ironically inaugurated by none other than a relatively moderate conservative US president in the aftermath of the collapse of the Soviet Union. And admittedly, the intended or implied meaning of the "new world order" is renewed and expanded American global military, economic, political, and cultural hegemony (Smelser and Mitchell 2002) or yet another "American century" through the further "Americanization" of the world (Habermas 2001) as the experience or perception of globalization in most non-Western and some Western countries. On this account, US fundamentalists' and most other conservatives' "fears of globalization"[8] (Ceobanu and Escandell 2010) as, especially in its economic

---

[7] According to Abbott (2005:270), "in the current imperial situation, the U.S. military must maintain a complex set of strategic outputs ranging from nuclear deterrence to preparedness for major conventional war to the long list of quasi-warfare activities characteristic of imperial militaries: counterterrorism and reprisals against terrorism, police actions involving conflicts over race, property, and the like in places where policymakers decide that the US has interests, protection of American nationals working worldwide, guaranteeing of the free trade that keeps the US hegemonic [etc.]." Also, Steinmetz (2005:350) notes that "although the CIA abducts criminal suspects from Italian streets for interrogation, the US does not claim jurisdiction over Italy but only the right to punctually violate its sovereignty in the interests of its global war on terrorism."

[8] Ceobanu and Escandell (2010) refer to 'fears of globalization and terrorism' but from the stance of this analysis it is more accurate to say fears of anti-globalization and

and cultural forms or perceptions, "Americanization" and their terrorist acts or hostile stance against it are both illogical and empirically ungrounded, uninformed, and thus irrational. In a way (to cite the Biblical passage), "they do not know what they are doing" by not knowing that globalization is *not* really, as they accuse, the process of expansion and domination of the UN as the favorite global object of their hatred and violence but, as at least perceived in most other societies, of "Americanization" and generally "Westernization" in Max Weber's sense.

The "fatal attraction" or link of the compound of anti-globalism and anti-cosmopolitanism, in extension anti-universalism and anti-humanism, to terrorism was exemplified indirectly by the 1995 Oklahoma destruction and directly the 1996 Atlanta Olympics bombing. They were attacks, implicit and explicit, on globalism and cosmopolitanism, including openly or implicitly "foreign" multiculturalism or culture diversity within America, by US fundamentalist groups or the religious right a la "Christian Identity" (Turk 2004), "Crusaders for Christ", and other self-proclaimed "Christian warriors" described as "American fascists"[9] or theocrats by some analysts (Hedges 2006; Phillips 2006). For example, the Atlanta Olympics bomber was a member of "Christian identity" and justified the terrorist act as a patriotic duty in response to what these groups construe as "atheistic internationalism" and "international socialism" attributed to the "new world order", as well as the "permissiveness" of the American secular federal government, regarded as the "evil" enemy or the Anti-Christ[10] in what religious fundamentalists, neo-fascists, and other neo-conservatives declare and wage as a "cosmic" war in America and the entire world as the stage of operations (Juergensmeyer 2003).

Coincidentally or perhaps not, a Georgia neo-conservative and a former Speaker of the House of Representatives and potential Presidential candidate used during the 2010s virtually the same words in denouncing the federal government formed after the 2008 Presidential Elections—the "secular, socialist machine"—as the Atlanta Olympic bomber had in 1996

---

terrorism because anti-globalization, and not globalization, causes or results in terrorist tendencies and actions.

[9] Hedges (2006) uses the term "American Fascists" to describe US "born again" religious fundamentalists such as "Dominionists" and related evangelicals seeking to establish Christian "Dominion" in America and the world as a whole in the form of "American theocracy" or "Christian fascism", thus "theocratic tyranny" or totalitarianism.

[10] Exemplifying the typical pattern and rhetoric of "Christian" anti-government militia in America, one of them self-described as the "Christian warrior" following the 2008 Presidential election reportedly condemned and planned to attack the US "big government" as the Anti-Christ.

in justifying his terrorist actions. Apparently, within the "extended family" or "big tent" of neo-conservatism, the distance from "godly" words of condemnation to "holy" deeds of terror or the Biblical "sword" is usually short and quick, as "mainstream" neo-conservatives with their anti-liberal, anti-secular, anti-rationalist, and anti-global or nationalistic declarations usually influence and often even incite or encourage "born again" fundamentalists and/or neo-fascists such as "Christian" militias to perpetrate terrorist actions against "big" liberal-secular and "socialist" government. Alongside the 1996 Atlanta Olympic attack, the even more destructive 1995 Oklahoma bombing was a paradigmatic instance of the path from neo-conservative anti-liberal manifest discourse and latent incitement to terrorist attacks against "big" liberal government to fundamentalist or neo-fascist counter-state terrorism, as is (likely to be) "Tea Party" committed, attempted, or planned anti-government violence either through militias or by "lone wolves", in order to "take America back." For instance, the House conservatives reportedly incited or encouraged "Tea Party" members of the "crazy right" to revolt to the point of near-riot at Capitol Hill during the health care reform vote, which is symptomatic and perhaps predictive of the future, as is the movement's de facto leader's notorious gun-targeting of some members of Congress supporting the law, one of whom being eventually attacked by an anti-government lunatic.

In a more recent episode evoking the 1996 Atlanta attack, the violent or threatening "Tea Party" movement has officially denounced multiculturalism in America as a "myth", just as did and do other radical, "revolutionary" ultra-conservative "anti-government groups such as "Christian" neo-Nazi militias, as well as most neo-conservatives. For example, the first 2010 convention of the "Tea Party" movement featured a topic entitled "the myth of multiculturalism". Generally, for the "Tea Party" and other US conservatism globalism, universalism, cosmopolitanism, humanism, just as liberalism, including liberal democracy, secularism, in particular the separation of church, rationalism, particularly rational science (not just biology) and academic freedom—all these defining elements of Western modernity are "myths", "lies", "conspiracies", "foreign", and anti- or un-American. This indicates that the admittedly conservative "politics of unreason" (Lipset and Rau 1978) has reached in the "Tea Party" and other US neo-conservatism the ultimate (patho)logical magnitude and intensity of proxy ideologically and religiously induced madness (the "crazy right"). Comparatively, the "Tea Party" and US neo-conservatism overall shares such anti-modernity with Islamic fundamentalism, and historically with Nazism, thus all these being "brothers in arms" in terms of their antagonism and eventually terrorism or violent nihilism against Western liberal-secular-rationalistic-globalized modernity.

Generally, like all US ultra-conservative movements, the "Tea Party" movement openly or otherwise opposes universal inclusion, cosmopolitanism, and openness in favor of exclusion, nativism, and closure, and "promises" to develop in a genuine or proxy terrorist group apparently determined to "take America back" through not only by the "ballot" of electoral and other political victories (as in the 2010 elections), but also by the "bullet" of terrorist violence against cum "defense" from "big" liberal and "socialist" federal government. If the latter scenario appears overstated consider the following indicative episode mentioned earlier. In the Spring of 2010, hardly one year after the "Tea Party" founding by extreme neo-conservatives (former ultra-conservative congressmen, extreme lobbyists, talk hosts, etc.) immediately following the 2008 elections, media reported that "tea parties and lawmakers envision militia". Specifically, reportedly "frustrated by recent political setbacks such as the economic stimulus package, the health care reform, etc., "Tea Party" leaders and some conservative members of the Oklahoma Legislature say they would like to create a new volunteer militia to help defend against what they believe are improper federal infringements on state sovereignty". And the state "Tea Party" leader started recruitment to a state militia by a call to "buy more guns, more bullets" in the movement newsletter.

Apparently, for "Tea Parties" electoral ballot is not enough to attain their supreme goal of "taking America [and government] back" to conservative state terror but has to be replaced by lethal "bullet" against "un-American" persons and groups whenever necessary cum "patriotic" and expedient in terms of power and money (e.g., guns targeting, in a map drawn by the informal leader of the movement, 20 members of Congress voting in favor of the health reform law, one of whom publicly expressed fear of violent attack and eventually was attacked by an anti-government deranged warrior). The "Tea Party" and allied or similar movements' rejection of multiculturalism and universal inclusion hence exemplifies and confirms religious-political conservatism's typical antagonism to cultural diversity and exclusion of minorities as "un-American" and the threat to American culture in denial of the reality or idea of America as a multicultural society, just as, closely related, to ideological, political, and other social pluralisms.

At this juncture, those observers unimpressed by "Tea Party" revolutionary claims ("do not tread on me") may comment that these and related neo-fascist or fundamentalist and other neo-conservative groups attacking liberal "big" government in America after the 2008 Elections are the strongest and most enduring economic masochists in the Western world. This is so in the light of Western economies, including the US, just experiencing and overcoming the most severe economic crisis since the Great Depression, namely the Great Recession generated and then "exported", like the first, by the anachronistic laissez-faire dogmas and activities of American "unfettered capitalism", exemplified by Wall Street (Stiglitz 2010). "Tea Party" and other US neo-conservatives appear economically masochistic in seemingly preferring and enjoying a sort of self-inflicted medical and so financial hardship and generally economic "pain" to reforms enhancing material and non-material welfare, such as universal and more efficient health care, sensible and necessary anti-recession measures via government demand stimulus effectively ending the Great Recession in America and Western Europe, regulation of criminal, predatory, and economically dangerous financial actions on Wall Street and beyond, and so forth.

Seemingly, these patriotic "All-American" and neo-Puritan "godly" groups prefer what analysts call the "natural Puritanism of a 'pain economy'" (Calhoun 1925) or the Puritan "masochistic ecstasy of pain" (Woodard 1938) to the economy of pleasure or what Weber calls referring to the Enlightenment "joy of life" (also, Phelps 2007), with pleasures condemned by such ascetic religions as sins and hence punished as crimes, as Pareto observes, to the point of executions of sinners and thus "holy" state terror. In passing, Pareto observes that such masochistic–and sadistic–"insanity" torturing or tormenting selves and others alike has been a constant in religious asceticism, from medieval monasticism to Puritanism and apparently to Puritan-rooted American evangelicalism as well as Islamic fundamentalism. In addition to such a mix of economic and other sadism and masochism, "Tea Party" and other fundamentalist and neo-conservative groups in America are even more driven by Puritan-inspired religious and ideological "wretched fanaticism" (Hume's expression) directed against "big" liberal-secular government in the form of a minimal welfare state, as well as intense hatred and fanatical intolerance of the Other, including a "liberal" and so "un-American" President, reaching the point of "holy" war or counter-state terror against both secular democracy and cultural diversity.

In general, conservatism typically condemns and often violently attacks both types and institutions of pluralism, especially and growingly multiculturalism, as "foreign" liberal "conspiracies" and "lies", starting with the

1996 Olympic bombing to various hate crimes perpetrated or incited and condoned by US fundamentalists and other neo-conservatives driven by religious, ethnic-racial, and other bigotry (King 2008), prejudice or intolerance (Edgell et al. 2006; Jacobs and Tope 2007), against cultural and other "un-American" minorities. Even if not perpetrating hate crimes against cultural and other minorities as the bearers of detested and feared multiculturalism or culture diversity, US religious-political conservatism openly or implicitly reproduces, incites, or condones such terrorist or criminal acts.

Thus, neo-conservatives reportedly tend to find virtually no or less "malfeasance" in violent and other actions targeting various minority groups (King 2008) construed as "un-American", including "foreign", and "ungodly", and thereby as almost legitimate targets of "patriotic" and "godly" terror and abuse, let alone exclusion and discrimination (Edgell et al. 2006). As particularly observed, "influential fundamentalists" oppose or dismiss hate crimes legislation in America at federal and state levels on the grounds that such laws grant "special protection" to certain minority culture groups, including racial-ethnic, religious, and sexual minorities. Furthermore, US fundamentalist groups in and outside government tend to resist or suspend crime law enforcement with respect to hate crimes, thus terrorist attacks, against religious, ethnic, and other cultural minorities for the reason that such legislation explicitly protects their cultural characteristics corresponding to "contentious civil rights" (King 2008). These observations yield the inference that US religious-political conservatism's characteristic slogans and practices of "law and order", "tough on crime", and severe "criminal sanctioning" are confined to laws and policies negatively affecting cultural minorities, but not to hate crimes and thus genuine or proxy terrorist acts against these groups (King 2008).

Specifically, those US states, mostly from the Southern "Bible Belt" and other conservative regions, that are "punitive" against cultural (especially sexual, religious, and ethnic-racial) minorities are not likely to protect the latter from hate crimes such that "hate crime prosecutions" are less frequent in those jurisdictions in which both "political conservatism" and "Christian [Protestant] fundamentalism",[11] intertwined and mutually

---

[11] For instance, King (2008:1356) registers that "historically, Christian fundamentalist leaders have been ambivalent about, if not in opposition to, much civil rights legislation. Influential fundamentalists have been leery of hate crimes legislation because the laws have purportedly granted some groups special protection. In particular, "sexual orientation is less often a protected category where the Christian Right is stronger' and generally

reinforcing,[12] are stronger (King 2008). Hence, "conservative political dominance" and Protestant "fundamentalism" pervasive in these regions are observed and predicted to result in suppressing the "state sanctioning of bigotry" motivating hate crimes or terrorist acts against certain "un-American" groups, as well as various "civil rights violations" (King 2008).

Anti-Cosmopolitanism and Terrorism

Moreover, US fundamentalist-fascist terrorist groups and neo-conservatives overall appear more vehement and obstinate in their anti-globalism, anti-cosmopolitanism, and anti-universalism, including anti-multiculturalism and anti-pacifism, than their Islamic enemies and contestants for global religious and military dominance yet "brothers in arms" in counter-state "godly" terrorism and theocratic "holy" state terror. More specifically, the former do so in a manifest and salient dimension missing or impertinent in the latter and other religious extremists and terrorists in non-American settings.

This is American fundamentalism-fascism's and generally neo-conservatism's comparatively unrivaled antagonism toward and condemnation of the United Nations (UN). The latter are demonized as the supreme "evil" anti-American force, simply the" Anti-Christ", accused of promoting "atheistic internationalism", pacifism, "foreign" multiculturalism, and establishing a "world government" or "new world order" as the presumed denial of or threat to America's "sovereignty, liberty, and democracy", religious "heart and soul" (Lichterman 2007), including "law and order" (King 2008; Jacobs and Tope 2007), of which they are self-anointed guardians cum "Christian warriors" (Edgell et al. 2006; Friedland 2002; Juergensmeyer 2003; Turk 2004). Recall that it was a relatively moderate US neo-conservative President who precisely coined the term the "new world order" during the late 1980s and the early 1990s in the aftermath of the collapse of the Soviet Union and Eastern European communism generally.

Conversely, no other contemporary, including Islamic fundamentalist, terrorist groups and governments in the Western and even entire world

US "conservatives are less apt to see malfeasance in behavior that disproportionately affects minorities" (King 2008:1356).

[12] King (2008:1355) adds the "proclivity" of political conservatism and "Christian" fundamentalism in America for harsh punishment "may not extend to laws that sanction bigotry and civil rights violations."

are more antagonistic and actively opposed to the UN, ironically a project of the postwar US government, as the agency and symbol of cosmopolitanism or internationalism, including pluralism, multiculturalism, and pacifism, than is revived American religious fundamentalism, neo-fascism, and generally neo-conservatism, thus evangelical-conservative ("red") America and the "Bible Belt" within it.

On this account, religious fundamentalism, neo-fascism, and American neo-conservatism overall is the most intense and persistent anti-global, anti-cosmopolitan or anti-international, anti-universalistic, and anti-pacifist force among contemporary Western and even non-Western societies, a sort of truly "world leader" in this respect, particularly in anti-UN antagonism and nihilism. Thus, more than even for Islamic fundamentalist and any other terrorist groups and governments in the Western and entire world, this anti-UN antagonism has often provided an "all-American" or "patriotic" justification for various terrorist agents and acts within American religious fundamentalism, neo-fascism, and neo-conservatism in general. For instance, this was witnessed in the 1995 Oklahoma City and 1996 Atlanta Olympics bombings by the members or sympathizers of merged fundamentalist-fascist terrorist militia like "Christian Identity" with its admittedly "paranoid views" about the UN as belonging, alongside the US Democratic Party, to "accomplices" in a liberal international "conspiracy" for ruling the world and depriving Americans of their "freedom"[13] (Juergensmeyer 2003). "Christian Identity", "Christian Warriors", and related fundamentalist and/or neo-fascist groups comprising the "religious right" and neo-conservatism generally as their "extended family" (or "big tent") reportedly portray themselves as America's "small band" of "courageous" saviors fighting a "secret war" against "invisible enemies" in the form of "colossal evil forces" such as the UN as well as the US secular "big" government as "liberal conspirators" condemned and therefore to be destroyed, in the "name and mind of God", as "satanic powers"[14] (Juergensmeyer 2003).

Furthermore, US "reborn" fundamentalist-fascist and other neo-conservative terrorist groups, as manifested in these two and other

---

[13] Juergensmeyer (2003:34) remarks that "the American incarnation of Christian Identity incorporated many of the British movement's paranoid views, updated to suit the social anxieties of many contemporary Americans."

[14] Juergensmeyer (2003:226) adds that during the late 1990s "when Michael Bray and other members of the religious right cast aspersions at "the new world order" allegedly promoted by President Bill Clinton and the United Nations, what he and his colleagues feared was the imposition of a reign of order that was not just tyrannical but atheist."

related acts, are in a way probably the only major agents of contemporary terrorism motivated and self-justified by anti-UN obsessive hatred and vehement antagonism. This reveals the unparalleled depth, magnitude, and intensity of American religious fundamentalism's, neo-fascism's, and generally neo-conservatism's anti-cosmopolitanism or anti-internationalism, including anti-pluralism, anti-multiculturalism, and anti-pacifism, in particular anti-UN antagonism, within the Western and entire world.

In general, anti-multiculturalism has been a virtually universal attribute or outcome of conservatism, from arch-conservatism to neo-conservatism, everywhere, including both Europe and America. For instance, like all European and US conservatives, the conservative (female) German chancellor alleged during the 2010s that multiculturalism in Germany "utterly field", thus evoking the anti-multiculturalism of traditional German conservatism and neo-conservatism, including the anti-multicultural and anti-pluralist ghost of Nazism and neo-Nazism, just as the neo-conservative British Prime Minister branded its version in Great Britain "failure" in 2011. Conversely, this implies that an alternative to multiculturalism in Germany would be Nazi-style totalitarian and generally conservative enforced cultural uniformity based on the idea of "blood and soil", with some "softer" neo-conservative alternatives in Great Britain. Such neo-conservative, including neo-fascist, assaults deny or overlook that multiculturalism and generally societal pluralism, thus a multi-cultural and plural liberal society has become an objective reality (Munch 2001) in both Europe and America and beyond during late modernity, thus that culture and other diversity constitutes a necessary condition of modern inclusive democracy and liberty overall (Hirschman 1982; Van Dyke 1995). Curiously, the German and other conservative Western governments, while condemning multiculturalism or diversity at home, have defended and supported it beyond their borders, as in the Balkans, for example, justifying their attack, via NATO, on Yugoslavia in 1999 by the project of a "multicultural" society, including "protection of human rights", in Kosovo (and Bosnia before and Macedonia later) in defense of their Albanian and other Islamic allies' "cultural identity".

In particular, hardly any major terrorist groups and governments have consistently perpetrated or advocated, incited, and supported acts of terrorism directly or indirectly motivated and rationalized specifically by the hostility and opposition toward the UN as a legitimate international organization, except for US "born again" fundamentalists, neo-fascists, and other neo-conservatives (Juergensmeyer 2003; Turk 2004). To that extent, such a manifest and salient exception reveals a sort of fundamentalist and overall neo-conservative "American exceptionalism" in terrorism in the sense that terrorist agents and acts driven by anti-UN antagonism appear "only in evangelical America" embarked on a "crusade for Christ and nation" against the "ungodly", cosmopolitan or transnational, and pacifist, as by virtue of its prohibition of wars of aggression, UN (Habermas 2001).

Furthermore, virtually nowhere else in the modern world, from advanced Western European societies to most remote and backward third-world countries, including even Taliban-ruled regions, Iran, and other Islamic theocracies, is observed such intense and persistent anti-UN antagonism as is witnessed in America during religious fundamentalism and neo-conservatism overall, notably the Southern "Bible Belt" and the "Wild West." For illustration, revived US religious fundamentalism alleges the "falsity of the UN", conjoined with its "apocalyptic"[15] vision and expectation of a "global conflagration of good versus evil" and the "materialization of a European [sic] anti-Christ" and the "perfidy of the French" (and "French fries"?) (Phillips 2006). In turn, within the "Bible Belt" and perhaps America overall, Texas is the probably most antagonistic state versus the UN and its agencies like World Court of Justice whose various rulings about "unfair" executions of foreigners like Mexicans and others and in that sense acts of "selective terror" in this state Texan theocentric "godly" powers routinely reject as "foreign interference", just as do, for that matter, Iranian, Taliban, and other Islamic death-penalty systems as the functional equivalents of its religiously grounded penal system of execution and imprisonment.

As a result of this unparalleled anti-UN hostility, US fundamentalist or conservative regions and forces are more willing and ready than virtually any others in the Western world and perhaps beyond to commit, advocate, incite, and support terrorist acts, like the 1996 Atlanta Olympics bombing, against the UN's underlying "ungodly" and so "anti-American" ideals and agencies of cosmopolitanism or internationalism, pluralism, multiculturalism, pacifism, and related values and conventions, such as those about universal human liberties and rights. For instance, seemingly more than even Taliban-Islamic and any fundamentalists, theocrats, and terrorists, American religious fundamentalism and consequently its

---

[15] Phillips (2006:6) comments that "according to these apocalyptic scenarios, the faithful can expect: wars on a worldwide scale, economic crashes, earthquakes, diseases and virtually every other calamity imaginable. Given the pervasiveness of such thinking, it is no wonder that upwards of 70 percent of the American people believed Saddam was "the evil one" who was in on the 9/11 plot."

religiously sanctified terrorism has evidently defined and attacked the UN with its imputed "atheistic internationalism" as well as "foreign" multiculturalism as the "demonic" power and the "evil" enemy of the shared theocratic design and system of "godly" society (Hedges 2006; Phillips 2006).

This exceptional anti-UN antagonism and "patriotic" terrorism by US fundamentalists a la "Christian warriors" on grounds of UN "ungodly" and "anti-American" internationalism and multiculturalism is striking and seemingly perplexing–yet less so considering religious conservatism's exceptionally intense nationalism (Friedland 2001) in the form of obsessive "Americanism" (Lipset 1996)–even when compared to their Taliban and other Islamic terrorist functional equivalents. While such exceptionality is virtually unnoticed and unanalyzed in the sociological and related literature, it is anticipated by the observation of the "phenomenon of American exceptionalism" (Inglehart 2004) in the form of a salient deviation from the global, minimally Western, prevalent processes of renewed and reinforced secularization, liberalization, rationalization, and modernization overall. Especially, such observations find that the degree of nationalism ("national pride") in America during religious-political neo-conservatism, while the highest in the Western world, is equal or comparable to those found in Islamic and other Third-World societies (Inglehart 2004), and implicitly even higher than in the latter judging by the antagonism to UN-associated internationalism and multiculturalism.

What is relevant within the present context is not such hostility to and demonization per se of the UN and its values, rules, and agencies in contemporary America, specifically by religious fundamentalism, neo-fascism, and neo-conservatism overall. Rather it is the actual or potential inducement and rationalization of terrorism by anti-UN antagonism. Exceptional anti-UN antagonism did, does, and will likely act as a stronger and more persistent source or justification for terrorism, including both domestic terrorist acts and offensive illegal wars, in American religious fundamentalism, neo-fascism, and neo-conservatism as a whole than in Islamic fundamentalist and any other extreme religious forces in the world. To that extent, such antagonism reveals a more profound and persistent, as well as more concrete, basis and rationale for terrorism in the first type of religious fundamentalism or extremism than in any other types among modern societies. Simply, so long as the UN exists and is demonized, as done primarily by US religious fundamentalists, neo-fascists, and other neo-conservatives, anti-UN antagonism operates and will likely operate as the self-perpetuating and potent force or rationalization of terrorism in its intra- and inter-societal forms for these "super-patriotic" groups intent and embarking on reconstructing and "saving" their "Christian America" from "atheist internationalism", even more than for their Islamic and any other counterparts in which such hostility is absent or weaker. (This holds unless the world organization, especially the Security Council, is exploited by the US government, as perceived in most of the world, for promoting "American values and interests" and "godly" purposes like crusade-style wars against "evil" countries.)

The preceding yields the probably surprising, if not "shocking", inference that US religious fundamentalism, neo-fascism, and all neo-conservatism is likely to remain the most persistent and strongest force or advocate of anti-cosmopolitan or anti-international, including anti-multicultural and anti-pacifist, terrorism within society and across societies in virtue of its unique anti-UN antagonism as the driving force and justification of its terrorist agents and actions. Comparatively, this expectation holds so long as Islamic and other fundamentalist forces are not driven and self-justified by such hatred for the UN to the extent that their American mortal enemies cum theocratic "brothers in arms" or "closest allies"[16] (Hedges 2006) have been, are, and likely will be.

In retrospect, the fundamentalist-fascist and generally neo-conservative demonization of and direct or indirect violence against the UN and its ideals and institutions are somewhat mystifying or contradictory. For the UN was more or less a project and creation of the American postwar government and, as many critics object, has typically been used, particularly the Security Council (e.g., during the Korea War, the Yugoslavia War, the Iraq War II, etc.), in the service of admittedly American and generally Western "hegemony" (Smelser and Mitchell 2002), as US neo-conservatives state by saying that the UN is "only good" if promoting "American values and interests". But such are apparently what Merton's (1968) would call the "perversities" of the theocratic and anti-cosmopolitan or anti-international "social logic" of US religious fundamentalism, fascism, and conservatism overall in its unique

---

[16] Hedges (2008:24) observes that "it is perhaps telling that our [US] closest allies in the UN on issues dealing with reproductive rights, one of the few issues where we cooperate with other nations, are Islamic states such as Iran. But then the Christian Right and radical Islamists, while locked in a holy war, increasingly mirror each other. They share the same obsessions. They do not tolerate other forms of belief or disbelief. They are at war with artistic and cultural expression. They promote severe sexual repression and they seek to express themselves through violence", thus including counter-state, state, and inter-state terrorism.

anti-UN antagonism often turned terrorism, reproducing another form of "American exceptionalism" as admittedly a "double-edged sword" (Lipset 1996), though this statement is neither defense nor disapproval of the UN, but just an historical and factual observation.

A related, more recent perversity in this sense is, as implied, that US "Christian warriors" and most other neo-conservatives are obsessed with, fear, and attack by terrorist acts the "new world order" that was proposed by none other than a President from the "extended family" (or "big tent") of conservatism and admittedly to be dominated by American power, values, and interests (Smelser and Mitchell 2002). It is remarkable that virtually all states and peoples in the world, including both the West and especially beyond, experience or perceive "the new world order" in terms of renewed or continuing "American hegemony" (Smelser and Mitchell 2002) or the "Americanization" of the global economy, politics, and culture (Habermas 2001), but not these ultra-conservative groups and regions in America itself. Conceivably, if they somehow realize what virtually "every schoolboy knows" of the "new world order", including the UN (especially the Security Council, the IMF, the World Bank, etc.), as expressing and serving mostly "American values and interests", or more than those of any other particular member-state, then they would perhaps stop demonizing and hence desist seeking to destroy via terrorist activities this global system.

In sum, Islamic and American religious fundamentalism and ultra-conservatism overall share anti-globalism, anti-cosmopolitanism or anti-internationalism, and anti-universalism, including anti-pluralism, anti-multiculturalism, and anti-pacifism, as the composite source and justification for terrorism, including anti-government violence, state violent repression, and "holy" wars a la crusades and jihads, respectively. In turn, it is to reemphasized that this composite factor of terrorism operates in interaction and mutual reinforcement with such other factors as anti-liberalism and anti-democracy, anti-secularism, and anti-rationalism considered before, while, like all these, indicating ("loading on") anti-modernism. Hence, the above reveals shared Islamic and "Christian" Protestant fundamentalist affinity (Turner 2002) or commonality (Friedland 2002) in terror driven and rationalized by anti-globalism and anti-cosmopolitanism, including anti-multiculturalism and anti-pacifism, spanning from violent repression within society to "holy" cosmic wars. However, American religious fundamentalism, neo-fascism, and neo-conservatism overall is truly and seemingly "proudly" exceptional or unique with respect to a specific dimension of its general negativism toward global-cosmopolitan modernity. As noted, US fundamentalists, fascists, and other neo-conservatives are the probably only or major group in the Western and entire world that is induced by anti-UN antagonism into committing or advocating and supporting terrorism, such as counter-state attacks like the 1996 Atlanta Olympics bombing, violent theocentric repression and Draconian punishment for sins-crimes, including executions of innocent persons, in the "Bible Belt" and beyond, and offensive "holy" wars or "crusades" against "evil" countries.

To that extent, the above reveals a sort of fundamentalist-conservative reproduced "American exceptionalism" in anti-UN antagonism and nihilism. This exceptionalism consists, first, in demonizing the UN as the agent of "ungodly" and "anti-American" internationalism promoting culture diversity or "foreign" multiculturalism and pacifism prohibiting aggressive wars. Second, as typical in Puritanism and its heir evangelicalism, like Islamic fundamentalism and perhaps all world religions, such demonization gives "Christian warriors" and "patriots" a sort of "license to kill" with Puritan self-righteousness ("good conscience") such international "evil" forces and their domestic "un-American" representatives in the "name of God and America", as epitomized by the self-righteous, unrepentant Oklahoma and Olympic bombers and virtually all "godly" and "patriotic" terrorists, including those murdering abortion personnel as a sort of God's commandment (as the 2010 Kansas case again showed). (The preceding factors of terrorism are summed up in Table 7.1.) Needless to say, US anti-abortion evangelical and other warriors vehemently deny or grossly overlook that individual liberty also includes what Tönnies calls freedom of "possession of one's *own* body and its organs" or the "physical qualities of the body" (Giddens 1984).

In regional terms, perhaps nowhere in the "Bible Belt" and "evangelical America" as a whole is the hostility and opposition toward the UN and its institutions and values more manifest and intense than in Texas, both among the "godly" repressive oligarchy and the general population, mostly due to a sort of "blissful ignorance" resulting from systematic conservative indoctrination persuading Texans with "pride and joy" that figuratively "Earth is still flat" or "revolves around the sun" (and some Texan and other US conservatives, likely the only ones in the Western world, literally believe this medieval religious dogma eventually abandoned even by the Vatican). For instance, the state of Texas, through its ultra-conservative governors and other officials, etc., has self-righteously rejected any decisions or opinions by some UN-affiliated agencies such as the World Court of Justice concerning its death penalty system, including executions of innocent persons or foreigners denied legal assistance (e.g., consular access) in violation of international rules that the US government demands other governments to apply to its citizens in identical situations. And this state does so not much on legalistic formalities but on the basis of these agencies being associated with the UN as an "evil" foreign power and being "international." Substantively, these international court decisions state or imply that the Texas death penalty and general penal system, especially documented executions and long imprisonment of innocent persons for fabricated sins-crimes, notably non-committed rapes and murders–as recently proven by DNA evidence in the Dallas county as the American and Western "leader" in this sense–amounts to a sort or proxy of state "selective terror".

For instance, the media reported in 2011 that a "DNA test on a single hair has cast doubt on the guilt of a Texas man who was put to death 10 years ago for a liquor-store murder—an execution that went forward after then-Gov. George W. Bush's staff failed to tell him the condemned man was asking for genetic analysis of the strand", commenting that "that would be an explosive finding, since it would corroborate what opponents of the death penalty have long argued: that the legal system is flawed and that capital punishment could result in a grave and irreversible error." In another case, a person from Fort Worth reportedly, "was convicted of rape and died in prison before DNA evidence cleared him". As sort of post-humous "consolation prize", the Texas Legislature passed in 2009 the Tim Cole Act, providing for monetary (lump-sum) compensation to wrongly imprisoned persons, though evidently doing virtually nothing to prevent such imprisonments from happening in the first place by revoking various outdated irrational moralistic-religious ("dumb") laws instead reproducing or encouraging such injustice with paranoid "tough on crime" measures and Draconian punishments. The Texas legislature has been over time so "productive and efficient" that through such religiously grounded laws has created no less than 2,000 felonies, subjected to typically Draconian punishments, in the "books" of the "lone star state," as have, in a sort of all-American contest in institutional reproduction of sins-crimes, other "Bible Belt" states, from Alabama and Tennessee to Oklahoma. So long as this condition persists, imprisoning and even executing innocent persons will likely continue in Texas and other "Bible Belt" theocratic or repressive states, because there is no institutional mechanism of preventing such outcomes, simply protecting the innocent. For example, prosecutors and judges in "Bible Belt" and other "red" states, driven by religious ("original sin" and like) fervor and electoral "tough on crime" Machiavellian

aims, act effectively as persecutors and crusaders, thus "Christian" variants of "jihadist politics" (Turner 2002), against the "infidel" and "sinful"
seeking to imprison or execute the accused at any cost and by any means
regardless of legal innocence for the "glory of God" and reelection, as do in
part juries.

In another instance, in the May of 2011 it was reported that "DNA testing has freed another wrongly convicted man in Dallas County [for] DNA
testing proves he is innocent." Reportedly, the person "pleaded not guilty
in 1984 but was convicted by a jury in the sexual assault" and "sentenced
99 years in prison", so "will be the 22nd man cleared by DNA testing in
Dallas County, which has more exonerations than any county in the
nation since 2001, largely because the county preserved more evidence
from past crimes. Like all but one of Dallas County's DNA exonerations,
[he] was convicted based on faulty eyewitness testimony." Lastly, Dallas
County District Attorney was reported to say that the above case "illustrates yet again the need for the Texas Legislature to pass bills reforming
eyewitness identification procedures and rules on the storage of evidence", in his own words, "I would ask that everyone who sees this travesty
do something about it", with "travesty" implying hypocritical moralistic
state terror, Texas-style of conservative-evangelical self-righteousness,
obstinacy, and un-repentance.

Notably, such and other criminal justice systems in the "Bible Belt"
commit, and dominant political and religious groups advocate, and
support, "holy" terror typically on "godly" fundamentalist grounds by
invoking the Bible ("eye for eye", "original sin", etc.), just as Islamic
theocracies like Iran, Saudi Arabia, and Taliban-ruled regions sanctify
their executions and other Draconian punishments for sins-crimes
through invocation of the Koran. Yet, it seems an impossible leap of faith
to expect that fundamentalist "godly" executioners or death-penalty
advocates in Texas and the "Bible Belt" overall, like their Islamic counterparts in Iran, Saudi Arabia, and Taliban-held regions, would realize,
let alone acknowledge, that their shared system of executions, as well
as life or long incarceration, for sins-crimes and of guilty and innocent
persons alike is a kind of state "holy" terror, as usually viewed in most
Western societies and the sociological literature (Jacobs et al. 2005;
King et al. 2009). Needless to say, within such state terror, like in any
type of terrorism, considerations of guilt or innocence are made irrelevant, notably subordinate to the "glory of God" and the "crusade for Christ"
(or the "jihad for Allah") by "godly" executions and other Draconian
punishments.

To take a relatively trivial yet indicative instance, reportedly a person in Texas "was sentenced to 30 years in prison" for the "possession" of 50 grams of methamphetamine ("with intent to deliver"). Cynics or comics may comment, "only 30 years?", given the Texas state and generally the "Bible Belt" tradition to sentence such and, especially sexual, sinners to, say, 99 and more years in prison, apparently "predicting" more than 100-year "life expectancy" for such offenders. Comparatively, nowhere in the West are such drug offenders and related sinners imprisoned, if at all, for that long, but only in Islamic theocracies like Taliban-ruled regions, Iran, and Saudi Arabia. Hence, such exceptional Draconian punishments for these and related sins operate or appear as the true or proxy syndrome of moralistic state terror from the stance of Western liberal democracies, not to mention the ruined or permanently disrupted individual lives; one wonders "what life?" for those after being imprisoned for 30 or so years, but this is absolutely immaterial for Puritan-rooted "Bible Belt" and Islamic penal systems with their shared depreciation and ultimately destruction of human life for the "glory of God". In strictly penal terms, the above is a punishment for the mix of a trivial crime-as-sin (possession of 50 grams of an illicit drug) and an Orwellian thought-crime ("intent to deliver"), with the effect of generating or sustaining the climate of terror or ambiance of fear among moral sinners, so conceivably most Americans.

Global-Cosmopolitan Society and Its Enemies and Global Terror

At this juncture, contemporary terrorism can be situated, explained, and possibly predicted within the context of modern globalized and universalistic, in particular open, liberal-democratic "cosmopolitan society and its enemies"[17] (Beck 2002). And, as indicated, of these enemies of open,

---

[17] Beck (2002:37) incorporates into cosmopolitan society's "enemies" nationalism, market-economic "globalism" and "democratic authoritarianism". In his view, first nationalism "has taken shape as the remaining real danger to the culture of political freedom at the beginning of the 21st century" in that it inevitably produces those "consequences which made the 20th century one of modernized barbarism" (Beck 2002:37). Second, market-economic globalism is a "powerful opponent of cosmopolitan societies" in that free market ideology/policy or global capitalism "undermines democratic politics and democratic identities" or the "culture of democratic freedom" through recreating social inequalities and dismissing the "principles of fundamental social justice and security" (Beck 2002:39). Third, democratic authoritarianism seeks to "compensate for the loss of democratic power by authoritarian means [with] the democratic façade" in the form of "capitalism without democracy". In particular, the "combination of ethnic nationalism and democratic authoritarianism adds up to a severe attack on liberty" (Beck 2002:40).

Table 7.1. Antagonism to Global-Cosmopolitan Modernity as the Factor of Contemporary Terrorism.

---

1. Anti-globalism
   Antagonism to economic, political, and cultural globalization
2. Anti-cosmopolitanism
   Antagonism to trans-national processes beyond nation-states
3. Anti-universalism
   Antagonism to universal liberty, equality, inclusion, and justice "for all"
4. Anti-multiculturalism
   Antagonism to cultural, including ethnic, religious, and linguistic, diversity
5. Anti-pacifism
   Antagonism to pacifism or peaceful resolution of inter-estate conflicts
6. Anti-humanism
   1–6 Shared by Islamic and American (and other) religious fundamentalism and cultural conservatism in general
7. Anti-internationalism
   antagonism to the UN and associated international institutions and conventions (the Geneva Convention for treatment of war prisoners, etc.).
   "exceptional" mostly for contemporary American fundamentalism, neo-fascism, and neo-conservatism

---

global-cosmopolitan–notably liberal-democratic, secular, rationalistic, and generally modernized–society, Islamic and US fundamentalist or ultra-conservative groups and regions are paradigmatic (though, of course, not sole) exemplars among contemporary societies. As also noted, the second forces represent even the most intransigent adversaries in this respect in virtue of their exceptional or unparalleled enmity toward the UN as the condemned agent and emblem of modern globalism and cosmopolitanism or secular internationalism, including pluralism, multiculturalism, and pacifism, and thus the perceived threat in the form of a "world government" or "new world order" to America's national "sovereignty, liberty, and democracy" as well as "faith", "godliness", and "morality". Generally, both Islamic and US fundamentalist forces and states, as paradigmatically exemplified by Taliban-ruled regions and the Southern "Bible Belt" respectively, exhibit a sort of instinctive hostility and revulsion for the reality or ideal of open, global-cosmopolitan society, because the latter tends to be liberal-democratic, secular, rationalistic, universalistic, and modernist overall, as their shared "worst nightmare".

For instance, a "Bible Belt" governor form Alabama reportedly proclaimed immediately prior to his inauguration in 2011 that "anybody here today who has not accepted Jesus Christ as their savior, I'm telling you, you're not my brother and you're not my sister", thus resurrecting or evoking the theocratic law of Puritanism that, as Tocqueville observes, "Whosoever shall worship any other God than the Lord shall surely be put to death."

As implied, the secondary difference between Islamic and US fundamentalism consists in their respective attitude and actions toward the UN. US "born again" fundamentalist, neo-fascist, and other ultra-conservative groups and regions, i.e., "red" states, especially in the hyper-nationalistic and xenophobic "Bible Belt" from Alabama and Tennessee to Texas and Oklahoma, show more intense and enduring enmity for the UN than do their Islamic counterparts and any extremist forces in contemporary societies, Western and non-Western. They demonize the UN as the perceived agency and symbol of cosmopolitan or transnational society construed as expressing "ungodly" internationalism that supposedly threatens to submit the "one nation indivisible under God" to the "new world liberal-secular order". To that extent, US revived fundamentalism, neo-fascism, and neo-conservatism overall presents itself as the foremost enemy of modern global-cosmopolitan society both as an ideal and emerging societal reality, the genuine "world leader" in anti-cosmopolitanism or anti-internationalism, including overt or implied anti-pluralism, anti-multiculturalism, and anti-pacifism. It is thus more extreme or radical in this respect than even Islamic and any other religious extremism, a seemingly unexpected ("shocking"?) yet manifest and salient moment in contemporary society and also implied, though not fully elaborated, in the sociological literature (Juergensmeyer 2003; Turk 2004).

Hence, contemporary terrorism, notably that perpetrated or advocated, incited, and supported by Islamic and American fundamentalism and ultra-conservatism in general, (also) arises and persists as the reflection and product of anti-globalism, anti-cosmopolitanism or anti-internationalism, and anti-universalism, including anti-multiculturalism. It does in the form of a radical adverse reaction by these fundamentalist and other conservative forces against global, open, cosmopolitan, and universalistic, including multicultural, Western modernity, as a long-standing liberal Enlightenment ideal, the relatively novel institutional arrangement, and a nascent historical period, including, as in the case of primarily American fundamentalism, the UN as the agency and symbol of detested liberal-secular internationalism.

Alternatively, in the form of a corresponding complex of anti-globalization, joined and mutually reinforced with anti-cosmopolitanism or anti-internationalism, and anti-universalism, including anti-multiculturalism, anti-globalism operates as the sociological determinant and predictor of contemporary terrorism, especially those terrorist acts perpetrated or advocated and incited by Islamic and American fundamentalism and conservatism overall. It does so in that anti-globalism engenders and predicts terrorist acts and agents as the nihilistic climax and face of the antagonism toward global, cosmopolitan, universalistic, and multicultural modernity, including, above all for American "reborn" religious fundamentalism and neo-conservatism overall, the UN as its international institutional epitome and symbol. In short, anti-globalism generates terrorism through producing violent, destructive revolt against globalism, cosmopolitanism, universalism, and multiculturalism, and, as with US fundamentalists and other neo-conservatives, their international institutionalization in the organization they "love to hate" with unparalleled intensity and passion, such as UN Universal Declaration of Human Rights.

At this juncture, it seems that US "born again" fundamentalists, neo-fascists, and other neo-conservatives do or would self-exonerate for their terrorist acts and thus attain, as they say, peace of mind or "good conscience". They do/would so on the ground of their strong negative "passions" against the UN and those cosmopolitan or international and universalistic and multicultural values and rules that this organization represents or entails, not to mention invoking "faith and God", as in the case of anti-abortion terrorists, as witnessed by the attempt of the murderer of an abortion-providing physician in America to justify and thus avoid punishment for the murder by "pro-life" beliefs at the time of writing these lines. For example, the murderer of an abortion physician in Kansas was convicted and sentenced to life in prison for first-degree murder in 2010, which would seem that the "pro-life faith" defense of this terrorist act did not work this time in the court, including the jury. However, this is correct only in part. Above all, premeditated, first-degree murders are usually in this and other ultra-conservative "red", and in Texas almost invariably, punished with the death penalty, but not in this particular case, which would give the opposite impression that such relative leniency was due precisely to the "pro-life faith" defense of the murder.

Second, this murder was never defined, either by the prosecutor and the judge or jury, as an act of terrorism, for arguably such a definition would result in a harsher punishment, including the death penalty. The omission thus continues the long-standing tradition of US authorities to avoid defining most acts of violence by "home-grown boys" as terrorism (Lutz and Lutz 2004) but rather as ordinary crimes, of course excluding those involving mass killings or destruction like the 1995 Oklahoma bombing, by contrast to those committed by foreigners or non-Americans. Counterfactually, one wonders had the murderer in question been a foreigner, whether the court would have defined the act as an ordinary crime or terrorism, more likely the second, given the observed past and present xenophobic or anti-foreign bias of most US, especially local and state, courts, including prosecutors/judges and juries. In sum, the above case reveals a double asymmetry, typical of the judicial system especially in US conservative "red" states. The first is the asymmetry between more harshly punishing ordinary first-degree murders than those like anti-abortion killings driven and justified by "holy" religious causes a la "pro-life beliefs". The second is the asymmetry between defining the same or comparable acts of violence as ordinary crime if committed by Americans and as terrorism if perpetrated by non-Americans, thus almost invariably more harshly punishing the second than the first offenses.

This open or overt tendency of fundamentalist self-righteousness or non-repentance in terror parallels and perhaps relates, for instance, to that of some courts in the "Bible Belt" like Texas to acquit or mildly punish murderers of their adulterous wives on the ground of "crimes of passion". Historically, both tendencies follow or evoke the venerable sanctimony of Puritanism, as the perennial model of American religious fundamentalism (Dunn and Woodard 1996; Munch 2001), transforming "evil into distorted good" (Habermas 2001) after the model of Salem's un-repented witch-trials and executions (Harley 1996) as the paradigmatic cases of the Puritan "reign" of state terror, self-righteousness, and non-repentance. They also perpetuate or reflect the tradition of Puritanism defining and punishing, just as does fundamentalist Islam, adultery and other sexual sins ("fornication", etc.) are graver offenses in the "mind of God" than both murders of other guilty or innocent humans *and* wars of extermination of entire societies or groups like Native Americans, as Puritans attempted (Gould 1996; Munch 2001) in one of the prototypical cases of genocide and thus inter-societal terror (Mann 2005). Recall that Tocqueville lists adultery, alongside blasphemy and witchcraft, but not murder, among the offenses punished with death by the "Puritan legislator" in New England (also, Dayton 1999). Legislators or courts in the "Bible Belt" like Texas seemingly retrieve this archetypical classification of Puritanism, just as Islam before and after, in their obsession with and Draconian punitive treatment of non-violent sexual sins as more serious offenses than murders of sinners as no "big deal", virtually exonerated as "crimes of passion" subject to probation at most, rarely brief imprisonment, never execution.

In this connection, terrorism, including civil and anti-liberal violent culture wars within society and offensive war against other societies, is Clausewitz's like logical continuation or ultimate escalation of the politics of opposition toward global, open, cosmopolitan, and universalistic, including multicultural, modernity, in particular, as with American fundamentalism and conservatism overall, the UN and its agencies and rules, by "other means" of violence, destruction, coercion, and repression. Terrorism continues or escalates anti-global, anti-open, anti-cosmopolitan or anti-international, and anti-universalistic, including, as with American fundamentalism and other conservatism, anti-UN, politics as well as by implication ideology and religion, by radical measures and violent actions. As the composite factor of terrorism, anti-globalism, anti-cosmopolitanism, and anti-universalism, particularly anti-multiculturalism–and, as for American fundamentalism and neo-conservatism, anti-UN antagonism–operates conjointly and mutually reinforcing with the previously considered factors, i.e., anti-liberalism and anti-democracy, anti-secularism, and anti-rationalism or anti-scientism. And, anti-globalism, anti-cosmopolitanism, anti-universalism, and these other factors indicate ("load on") anti-modernism as the overarching determinant and predictor of contemporary terrorism, while globalism, cosmopolitanism, universalism, and multiculturalism, as well as liberalism and democracy, secularism, and scientific rationalism indicating ("loading on") modernism.

The above suggests that contemporary terrorism and related acts and agents are often rooted in and thus explained and predicted by the antagonism to modern global, open, cosmopolitan, and universalistic, including multicultural, society, as sociological theory suggests and empirical research documents (Dahrendorf 1979; Friedland 2002; Habermas 2001; Juergensmeyer 2003; Popper 1973). Especially, such acts and agents of terrorism have their roots or rationales in the negative reaction to the processes of economic, political, and cultural globalization (Bendix 1984; Bergesen and Lizardo 2004; Fischer 2003; Smelser and Mitchell 2002; Turk 2004) and hence global liberalization and democratization, openness, pluralism, and multiculturalism, secularization and rationalization, and modernization as a whole (Inglehart 2004).

In particular, extreme conservative, "right-wing" ideologies and groups are observed to intensify and expand in adverse reaction reaching the point of radical, violent revolt against the process of modernization and globalization seen as threatening "existing institutions and patterns of governance" (Lutz and Lutz 2004) in contemporary society, especially Islamic and other non-Western countries, as well as in certain segments of Western societies, such as "red" Southern and other US states. Reportedly, religious nationalists such as Iranian and other Islamic fundamentalists *and* US evangelicals from the Southern "Bible Belt" and beyond, as well as neo-fascist groups in Europe and elsewhere, oppose and attack modern globalized capitalism not much as an "economic system in itself" but rather as a "carrier of an alien, profaning culture" (Friedland 2002). By assumption, this is the culture and prospect of openness, cosmopolitanism, and universalism, notably of multiculturalism, as well as of liberalism and democracy, secularism, and scientific rationalism, simply of Western liberal modernity. Particularly, in this account (neo) Nazism's anti-cosmopolitan and anti-universalistic, as well as anti-liberal, anti-rationalistic, and anti-modern, semiotic print" is a functionally equivalent match to that of US "religious nationalists" (Friedland 2002), notably "born again" fundamentalists as "American fascists" (Hedges 2006) epitomized by "Christian" neo-Nazi groups in the Southern and other "Bible Belt".

Therefore, one can infer and expect that those individuals, social groups, states, and societies or cultures that are antagonistic to global, open, cosmopolitan, and universalistic, including multicultural, modernity, including the expanding process of economic, political, and cultural globalization, as well as, primarily in the case of America, the UN, are more likely to commit, advocate, incite, and support in terrorism than are others. To be sure, the disclaimer is that not all individuals, social groups, states, and societies or cultures antagonistic to global, open, cosmopolitan, and multicultural modernity, including the process of globalization and the UN organization, conduct and endorse terrorism, and yet they exhibit a stronger and more persistent tendency for doing so than do others. The above argument and expectation applies to most types or instances of terrorism, in particular counter-state and state, religious and quasi- or non-religious, conservative and non-conservative, domestic and global, and within- and across-society, terrorisms.

As implied in the previous chapters, contemporary terrorism can particularly be attributed or linked to the antagonistic reaction against the "foreign", namely Western-style processes of political liberalization, democratization, and modernization, in particular pluralism in politics, and diversity in civil society and culture (Bendix 1984; Juergensmeyer 2003; Smelser and Mitchell 2002; Turk 2004). Such opposition is most manifest, intense, and persistent in the undemocratic and underdeveloped world, especially Islamic countries, with some rare exceptions like Turkey because of its Westernization, notably institutional secularism in the form of an atypically, within the Muslim world, secular state although recently undermined and threatened by resurgent Islamism both from within and outside. They are also observed among certain segments and regions in democratic, developed Western societies themselves. These include particularly America, such as the persistently "under-democratized" (Amenta and Halfmann 2001) South *cum* the "Bible Belt" threatening to place American democracy under the undemocratic "shadow of Dixie" (Cochran 2001) as the epicenter of religious nationalism (Friedland 2002), sectarianism, and theocratic fundamentalism (Hicks 2006; King 2008), and other ultra-conservative areas a la "red states" or middle America", not to mention Mormon-ruled Utah as a paradigmatic sectarian theocracy (Weisbrod 1999), thus the system of "holy" state terror and the "nightmarish world" (McCann 2000).

Closely related to the preceding, contemporary terrorism can be attributed or linked to the antagonistic reaction against the Western processes of cultural and economic liberalization and modernization–interrelated and mutually reinforcing with their political forms–including globalization in the economy and culture (Bendix 1984; Caplan and Cowen 2004; Juergensmeyer 2003; Lutz and Lutz[18] 2004; Smelser and Mitchell 2002; Turk 2004; also, Alexander 2004). As in the previous case, such opposition

---

[18] Lutz and Lutz (2004:17) remark that economic globalization and capitalism overall is perceived as causing "inequality among states as well as within countries [with] inequalities [fueling] frustrations within states and helped set the stage for appeals for violence by dissident groups. Modernization can also disrupt social structures by de-emphasizing old patterns of respect and social interaction as new economic and social elites develop." In their account, "modernization and globalization will also affect the structure of values and norms. Western culture and values are seen as threatening to local religions and cultures. The importance of modernization and globalization in contributing to terrorism (is) demonstrated by the fact that any symbol of modernization becomes a legitimate target for attack. [Also], modernization contribute(s) to terrorism by making economies and societies more vulnerable. The terrorism of the late 20th century [is] a manifestation of and a reaction to the process of globalization" (Lutz and Lutz 2004:18).

is most manifest, intense, and persistent in under-developed, especially Islamic countries, again with such exceptions as Turkey, with their grievances against developed Western societies within the world system[19] (Abadie 2006; Bergesen and Lizardo 2004) and generally a sort of "wishful thinking in development" mixing fascination with contempt and hostility[20] (Bendix 1984) for the West. In particular, such mixed feelings involve "ambivalence" toward America, mixing admiration for a "utopian America" of "immigrant communities" and opposition to its global dominance or world-system hegemony[21] (Smelser and Mitchell 2002).

However, the third-world style opposition toward cultural and economic liberalization and modernization is also found among certain groups and parts of the Western world itself. This includes especially conservative ("red") America, and within it most visibly and intensively the Southern and other "Bible Belt" with its long-standing cultural, religiously grounded, parochialism, closure, and hostility toward outsiders (Putnam 2000), including xenophobia, as well as its anti-cosmopolitanism, aggressive nationalism and bellicosity, economic traditionalism, isolationism, and protectionism, not to mention vehement anti-labor and anti-union and anti-minority sentiments, laws, and practices. Paradigmatic instances are "born again" fundamentalist "Christian", almost exclusively

---

[19] According to Turk (2004:283), however, the "world systems approach (seems) too abstractly conceptualized and too remote from specific political conflicts."

[20] Bendix (1984:117) elaborates that "to the person in the backward country the strength of the advanced country appears formidable; but that strength is also perceived as sapped by false values, corruption and spiritual decay, and "therefore" such country should not and cannot endure. Thus the dominance of the advanced country carries with it the seeds of its own destruction, whereas the backward people and the underdeveloped country possess capacities that are signs of a bright future. Such wishful thinking has been an important factor in nationalist efforts to achieve the social and economic development of backward countries by routes other than followed by the pioneering country."

[21] Smelser and Mitchell (2002:21) comment that "since the collapse of the [Soviet Union], the world system [is seen as] "the American hegemony." "However, they suggest that such a view is "misnamed, because the dominant powers are a complex combination of North American, West European, and East Asian powers. Nevertheless, the role of the US is paramount. Those who are dominated [or believe so] by stronger outside powers come to resent and oppose their oppressors" (Smelser and Mitchell 2002:24). Also, they observe (Smelser and Mitchell 2002:25) that "ambivalence toward the US is now found throughout the world [especially] Muslim societies" in that, first, "there is America the demon, the rich, godless, morally and sexually corrupt, imperialist country that has come to its wealth by exploitation, a power that dominates the world and forms alliances with the ruling elites in their own societies, a nation that is hypocritical in its assertions of equality when it is plagued with racism and poverty [etc.]", and second, a "utopian America" (of) immigrant communities".

Protestant,[22] militias" a la "Christian Identity movement" antagonistic
toward globalization, modernization, and international institutions,
notably the UN, and implicated or instrumental in the 1995 Oklahoma
and 1996 Atlanta Olympics bombing, anti-abortion attacks[23] (Lutz and
Lutz 2004), and other terrorist attacks in the US during recent times[24]
(Juergensmeyer 2003; Turk 2004). Reportedly, most of these terrorist
or fundamentalist groups in the US, just as their Islamic counterparts,
are driven by an anti-global and generally "anti-modernist" ideological-
political agenda, with "the extreme end of this religious rejection of modernism" including a wide assortment of groups, spanning from the
"American anti-abortion group Defensive Action" through "Christian
Identity movement" and other "Christian" militias to the Branch Davidian
sect in Waco (Juergensmeyer 2003). This includes antagonism toward the
Western welfare state construed, as "big government" and the element or
symbol of cosmopolitanism, globalism, and internationalism, as the cause
and rationale of contemporary terrorism, especially its counter-state form
committed or threatened and planed by US anti-government groups like
"Tea Parties", "Christian warriors", etc.

Consequently, terrorism is more likely to be advocated, committed,
and supported or justified by those individuals, social groups, states, and
societies in hostility and opposition toward modern Western liberal
democracy and society, including the process of political, cultural, and
economic liberalization and democratization than are by others. This
does not mean that all individuals, social groups, states, and societies hostile to and opposing liberal-democratic political, cultural, and economic
systems and processes necessarily perpetrate or justify terrorist actions,
yet they typically show a stronger tendency, persistence, and intensity
to do so than do others. Simply, anti-liberal, anti-democrat, and anti-
modernist, including anti-cosmopolitan or anti-global—i.e., conservative
in this sense–individual and collective agents tend to be more inclined
toward committing or justifying terrorism and other forms of violence,
destruction, and coercion than do others. The above helps account for

---

[22] Wimmer, Cederman, and Min (2009:318) also register the "emergence of Protestant militias and terrorist groups opposed to the nationalist project" in Northern Ireland.

[23] In the view of Lutz and Lutz (2004:247), "in the US anti-abortion violence has been at least partially successful because it has indeed become more difficult to get an abortion".

[24] Juergensmeyer (2003:34) notes that "Christian Identity militia" identifies the UN and the Democratic Party as "accomplices in the conspiracy to control the world and deprive individuals of their freedom".

and anticipate most types of contemporary terrorism, particularly anti-government and government, religious, conservative, domestic and transnational, within- and inter-society terrorisms. Specifically, this means within-society or domestic counter-state and state terrorism alike, and inter-society or global *state* terrorism against other societies through illegal wars of aggression (prohibited by the UN) and other unlawful violence and weapons of mass destruction (Juergensmeyer 2003; Habermas 2001; Schelling[25] 2006). Also, it applies to both individual and collective agents and acts of terrorism, and within the second category to terrorist groups or organizations on one hand, and governments and societies or "cultures of violence" on the other (Juergensmeyer 2003).

Societal Closure and Terrorism

Alternatively, what Weber calls social closure and related conditions such as exclusion, monopolization of material and ideal resources and life chances, and isolation in society, including nationalism, nativism, religious sectarianism, and ethnocentrism in relation to other societies, form another set of factors and predictors of contemporary terrorism. Contemporary terrorism often represents an extreme, violent expression and outcome of social closure, exclusion, monopolization, and isolation, particularly nationalism, nativism, religious sectarianism, and ethnocentrism. This complex of factors persists or resurges in adverse reaction and vehement opposition to modern open, global, and cosmopolitan, including multicultural, society, in particular the expanding and accelerating process of economic, political, and cultural globalization. As typical of the antagonistic-nihilistic trajectory, the intense and persistent antagonism

---

[25] Schelling (2006:929) observes that "there has never been any doubt about the military effectiveness of nuclear weapons, or their potential for terror". Notably, he registers the tendency for American conservatism, from paleo-conservatives in the 1950s (e.g., Dulles, Eisenhower) to neo-conservatives (Goldwater, Reagan et al.), to entertain the idea of "preemptive" nuclear war against "enemies", from Korea and the Soviet Union to Iran, China, and Russia. For instance, Schelling 2006:937) laments the fact that the conservative-dominated Senate rejected in 1999 the Comprehensive Test Ban Treaty in spite or rather because of the "potential of that Treaty to enhance the nearly universal revulsion against nuclear weapons", thus on apparent militarist and/or nationalistic grounds a la "American interests". He concludes that the "widespread taboo against nuclear weapons" is actually "in the American interest", and hence that "advertising a continued dependence on nuclear weapons, i.e., a U.S. readiness to use them, a U.S. need for new nuclear capabilities (and new nuclear tests)—let alone ever using them against an enemy—has to be weighed against the corrosive effect on a nearly universal attitude that has been cultivated through universal abstinence of 60 years" (Schelling 2006:937).

against openness, globalism, cosmopolitanism, and multiculturalism, tends to ultimately escalate or result in terrorism and violent nihilism overall in the form of violent revolt against and destruction or reversal of open, global, cosmopolitan, and multicultural modernity. In particular, such antagonism includes the opposition to the process of globalization, as well as, as mostly in the case of nationalistic and sectarian groups and regions in America, the UN as the perceived force of "anti-American" internationalism and multiculturalism.

In Clausewitz's words, terrorism, including violent repression or culture wars within society and aggressive war against other societies, represents the continuation or product of the politics of antagonistic, particularly nationalistic and sectarian, opposition toward open, global, cosmopolitan, and multicultural modernity, particularly the process of economic and cultural globalization and, as with US nationalistic forces, the UN and its underlying internationalism and multiculturalism by "other means". In general, terrorism continues and expresses through violent, destructive means and actions what Weber and Parsons call ethical and other societal particularism or anti-universalism in opposition to social universalism in the sense of Kant-Voltaire-Hume-Jefferson's Enlightenment principle of universal liberty, equality, inclusion, and justice ("for all") in society. In turn, Kantian and generally Enlightenment cosmopolitanism or internationalism develops as an inter-societal, global extension of social universalism (Beck 2001; Habermas 2001).

The latter is most intensely detested by particularistic or anti-universalistic forces, including nationalist and religiously sectarian groups and societies, of all times and places. They span from anti-Enlightenment "nation and God" medievalist conservatives a la Burke and Maistre in late 18th century Europe to "all-American" nativists and religious sectarians in contemporary America and Muslim nationalists in Islamic countries (Friedland 2001). Alternatively, societal particularism, including especially nationalism[26] (Brubaker 2009) and religious sectarianism, in virtue of being anti-universalistic antagonism tends to escalate or result in terrorism and nihilism overall in the form of violent revolt against and destruction or reversal of universalism, notably the Enlightenment ideal and social system of universal liberty, equality, inclusion, and justice.

---

[26] Brubaker (2009:29) includes terrorist attacks into ethnic, racial, and nationalist violence, alongside other forms such as violent protests, pogroms, feuds, lynchings, genocides, gang assaults, ethnic fights, and various hybrid forms".

Nationalism and Terrorism

The preceding especially holds true of religious sectarianism as discussed above and of nationalism[27] or nativism as the particular dimension of societal particularism in relation to other nations or national groups denied or deprived of the ideal and exercise of universal liberty, equality, inclusion, and justice on grounds of their imputed "evilness" or "inferiority" in favor of natives as paragons of "goodness" and "superiority". Thus, the typical trajectory of nationalism or nativism, especially its aggressive form, just as religious sectarianism, has been moving from anti-universalistic antagonism, including anti-cosmopolitanism or anti-internationalism and anti-multiculturalism, to terrorist nihilism through violence, coercion, offensive war, and destruction targeting other national groups or nations and cultures, and via militarism (Acemoglu and Yared 2010) and imperialism (Steinmetz 2005) or colonialism generally, as systems of inter-state terror in their own right.

As observed in history and presently, virtually always and everywhere aggressive nationalism or nativism, just as religious sectarianism, has ultimately metastasized or resulted in state and inter-state terrorism, i.e., violent repression of "evil" or "inferior" national groups within society and wars of extermination or genocide of other nations and cultures. This is simply a fusion of tyranny at home and war of aggression abroad in interconnection and mutual reinforcement. Tyranny or systematic government violent repression within society, as Simmel prophetically

---

[27] Apparently referring to WW I, Tawney (1920:32) registers the "terrors of nationalism", and Williams (1994) describes terrorism as one of the "main forms of collective ethnic conflict." Also, Heymann (1999:13) suggests that "when a society is already dangerously divided, terrorism can do great damage and is likely to be resistant to government efforts (more than) in democracies that enjoy strong support across the broad spectrum of their populations. [Terrorism] can affect the familiar dynamics of transition from a secure, multi-ethnic society into a dangerously divided society characterized by high levels of violence, hatred, and mistrust among ethnic groups (N. Ireland, Bosnia). A dangerously divided society is thus, for many separatist groups, a promising stage on the way to a separate national government, and terrorism can force the pace of this dangerous transition. Although ethnic tensions escalate into hatreds and then violence between members of opposing groups even without the encouragement of terrorists, the process can be speeded by terrorist attacks on an opposing group, inviting tit-for-tat responses and fanning the flames of hatred and fear." Similarly, Juergensmeyer (2003:6) observes that terrorist acts have also been "propelled by a desire for ethnic or regional separatism." Lutz and Lutz (2004:12) also note that "many active terrorist organizations have sought objectives related to a particular ethnic group, or linguistic group, or region of the country." They cite the case of "Albanian dissidents [who] eventually coalesced into the Kosovo Liberation Army (KLA), which began to fight back using both guerrilla and terrorist tactics" (Lutz and Lutz 2004:105).

observed and an Orwellian dystopia epitomizes, by striving what he calls "after a natural relief" tends to eventually result in offensive war against other societies, while such wars being subsequently used as the rationale for perpetuating and intensifying domestic tyrannical oppression that generated them in the first place on "we are at war" or "national security" grounds. In short, state terror causes or escalates into inter-state terrorism, and then the second as the effect or destination justifies the first as its cause or point of origin.

Such an outcome was epitomized by WW II involving, as in Germany and Italy, interlinked and mutually reinforced violent repression and wars of aggression, thus domestic and international terror, and essentially caused, as had been WW II, by the nationalistic aspirations and actions of European (German) conservatism, including Nazism as the "new conservatism" (Blinkhorn 2003). The above also applies to US wars of aggression like, for instance, those against Vietnam, Yugoslavia, Iraq II, and a myriad of others or military interventions typically by the neo-conservative government during recent times (Granada, Panama, etc.). First, these offensive or imperial wars (Abbott 2005) were invariably driven and justified by conservative, religiously grounded nationalism (Friedland 2002) or "superpatriotism" cum Americanism (Steinmetz 2005). Consequently, they were sanctified by Americanism's sacred basis and rationale, i.e., what Weber called "Protestant sectarianism" (Lipset 1996) traced back to Puritanism that he depicted as sectarian Calvinism or a Calvinist "pure sect" with its notion of America's "manifest destiny" necessitating, for instance, the genocide (Mann 2005) or "disappearance" of Native Americans (Gould 1996; Munch 2001). Second, these wars exemplify what Simmel sees as the typical pattern of any offensive war and militarism generally in relation to centralized tyranny and any form of violent repression, as inter- and intra-societal terror, respectively. Namely, these "patriotic" and proxy religious wars against "evil" and "ungodly" nations, including Vietnam, Yugoslavia and via an apparent projection "communist" Russia or China, etc., have proceeded in interconnection and mutual reinforcement with domestic violent, yet moralistic Puritan-style, repression and physical coercion and to that extent genuine or proxy state terror.

For instance, lie the Vietnam War, the 1999 US government's and generally NATO's admittedly illegal or UN-unauthorized (Bauman 2001; Giddens 2000) war against Yugoslavia often appeared as a proxy war against post-communist, perceived militarily weak Russia in the wake of the collapse of the Soviet Union–as did, incidentally, Russia's 2008 intervention in Georgia, as such a proxy versus the West–and to a lesser extent communist China (not just because of the "mistaken" bombing of the Chinese embassy). And recall to add insult to injury, the illegitimate attack on Yugoslavia was on behalf or in alliance with what US secretary of state initially admitted to be an "ethnic [Albanian" terrorist army" to become "freedom fighters" eventually stating something to the effect that what is the point of having such an "army" if do not use it. In this respect, the "mighty" American military and NATO overall operated as a kind of "overwhelming" air force for this ethnic-religious terrorist organization (Bauman 2001; Lutz and Lutz 2004), thus probably relegating this action into the infamy of history, at least for future historians.

Comparatively, such violent repression and coercion within society is conducted on a scale admittedly unknown or unparalleled among modern Western liberal democracies (Lipset 1996), including both European societies and America's neighbor Canada and other British former dominions like Australia and New Zealand. Recall such repressive practices have involved and continue to involve anti-liberal Puritan-style temperance wars (Munch 2001; Wagner 1997) in a long sequence from Prohibition to the "war on drugs" (Hill 2002), inflicting harsh Draconian punishments[28] (Cooney and Harbin 2008; Harris et al. 2011) on sinners-criminals as effectively prisoners of ethical conscience like nonviolent drug, alcohol, sexual, and other immoral offenders. As known, such punishments involve mass, long incarceration resulting the unprecedented explosion of the prison population (Uggen and Manza 2002) and widespread executions, often of innocent or sinful persons, on "godly" grounds by a religiously grounded conservative penal and death penalty system (Cunningham and Phillips 2007; Jacobs and Tope 2007; King 2008), paradigmatically exemplified by its fundamentalist type governed by "Biblical law" in the "Bible Belt" (and within it Texas), just as its functionally equivalent versions (Jacobs et al. 2005) in Iran and Taliban-regions are ruled by "Islamic law".

To that extent, contemporary terrorism, including violent intra-societal repression and offensive war in Simmel's reciprocal relation and reinforcement, often constitutes Clausewitz's like continuation or outcome of the politics of societal particularism or anti-universalism in the form of closure, exclusion, or monopolization of resources and opportunities

---

[28] Cooney and Harbin (2008) observe that in general "the severity of punishment increases with political absolutism—is almost certainly true. Penal law should be enhanced in areas where conservative political ideologies predominate [such as] sentence lengths and the death penalty."

within society and in relation to other societies, especially aggressive
nationalism or nativism and religious sectarianism, by "other means" and
actions of violence, destruction, and coercion (represented in Table 7.2).
This especially, though not solely, holds for Islamic and American religious fundamentalism and extreme conservatism overall. Namely, Islamic
and US religious fundamentalists and ultra-conservatives overall are
observed to be both the strongest nationalist (Friedland 2002) and sectarian, and thus by implication particularistic or anti-universalistic–i.e.,
closed, exclusionary, and monopolizing–groups *and* also the major forces
or supporters of terrorism, including violent repression at home and
"holy" wars against other nations (Juergensmeyer 2003; Turk 2004), in
contemporary societies.

Their shared intense religiously grounded nationalism (Friedland
2002), religious sectarianism (King 2008; Lipset 1996; Munch 2001), and in
extension particularism or anti-universalism through social closure,
exclusion, or monopolization reportedly tends to mutate or result in
religiously grounded and sanctified terrorism (Juergensmeyer 2003).
This comprises counter-state terrorist acts through anti-government

Table 7.2. Social closure, nationalism, and militarism as the composite
factor of contemporary terrorism.

Social exclusion, particularism, and anti-universalism
Aggressive nationalism and chauvinism
Jingoism
Nativism
"Americanism"
Xenophobia
Anti-immigration sentiments
Religious sectarianism
Sectarian Islam and Protestantism
Ethnocentrism
"American exceptionalism" from the Western (and entire) world cum superiority and supremacy
Militarism and imperialism
Military-industrial complex
"Holy" national wars (crusades and jihads)
Islamic world "empire"
American "empire of liberty"

violence a la the Oklahoma bombing and vigilantism in historical and contemporary America, as well as government systematic violent repression of certain "inferior" national out-groups and offensive wars of extermination, crusades and jihads in the broadest sense by evangelical and Islamic governments or non-governmental forces, against "evil" nations. Alternatively, their common religious terrorism cum total "holy" war ultimately continues or expresses the shared "politics" of religious sectarianism and consequently religiously based nationalism[29] and generally particularism or anti-universalism, including anti-cosmopolitanism and anti-multiculturalism, by "other means" of force, destruction, coercion, and violent repression.

Therefore, one can infer and expect that those individuals, social, particularly religious, groups, states, and societies that are closed, isolationist, exclusive, or monopolizing resources and life chances, including sectarian, parochial, nationalistic, ethnocentric, and particularistic, are likely to commit, advocate, incited, and support terrorism than are others. As before, this assertion is relaxed in stating that not all closed, isolationist, exclusive or monopolistic, parochial, nationalistic, ethnocentric, and particularistic social, including sectarian religious, groups, states, and societies conduct and endorse terrorism, but they tend to do more than others.

In short, social closure or particularism, especially aggressive nationalism and religious sectarianism, is a pertinent factor of terrorism, as

---

[29] According to Townshend (2002:74), "the framework for much modern terrorist action is ethnic or nationalist. Indeed, the emblematic terrorist act of the early 20th century (the assassination of Franz Ferdinand in 1914) was carried out by a Serbian nationalist. The vast bulk of subsequent terrorism (by governmental or other criteria) was similarly the work of nationalists". In this view, "nationalist movements have shown much greater resilience and destructive capacity than the small and fissiparous left-wing revolutionary groups. They tend to be significantly bigger (plus) to draw on a broader pool of recruitment; and though their "cause" – freeing or uniting the nation – is not necessarily more practicable than the revolutionary dream of total social transformation, nationalism has dominated modern politics precisely because it connects with a visceral, apparently natural force" (Townshend 2002:75). Arguably, "another dimension of terrorism (is) communal slaughter (or) "ethnic cleansing". Nationalists are intolerant of diversity or plurality. Once rooted, nationalist "causes" are astoundingly resilient – in modern times, despite predictions that the world is moving into a post-national age, they look virtually indestructible" (Townshend 2002:76). Townshend (2002:101–2) concludes that the "idea of fixing boundaries between religious and ethnic motivation is also problematic, since these boundaries are highly permeable. Indeed, the very notion of isolating the "religious" element in the motivation of a group, to establish whether or not it is 'predominant', is rooted in Western political culture, with its sharp division between church and state, sacred and secular. It may have limited value even in the West, where the syndrome of sacral or "holy nationalism" has been far more pervasive than most people have recognized."

historical and empirical research demonstrates as well as sociological theory posits (Bendix 1984; Munch 2001; Turk 2004; also, Parsons 1951; Popper 1973). This is in particular observed and posited for aggressive religiously grounded nativism (Merton 1939), nationalism (Friedland 2002; Juergensmeyer 2003), and sectarianism (Smelser and Mitchell 2002; also, Lipset 1996), as forms of social closure, exclusion, monopolization of resources and opportunities, and generally particularism or non-universalism rationalized on "sacred" grounds, and eventually the driving forces of terrorism through violent repression of selected national-religious out-groups within society and offensive war or militarism against entire nations. For instance, almost a century ago (Tawney 1920) warned about the "terrors of nationalism", religious and secular alike, in the aftermath and light of the nationalist-driven devastating WW I, and thus implicitly in anticipation of Nazism and its own even more destructive effect, WW II[30] (Lutz and Lutz 2004), as well as various post-WW II wars.

In turn, writing during the 1930s Merton (1939) identifies what he calls "American nativism" manifested initially as anti-Catholicism and subsequently in "anti-foreign sentiment" and a "religio- and ethno-centric pattern" in general originating in New England Puritanism as prototypical Protestant sectarianism (Lipset 1996; Munch 2001) or the Calvinist "pure sect", while continuing and expanding through 19th century, ("temporarily" culminating in the "Know-Nothing Party" of the 1850s). Notably, he observes that the "main outlines" of the pattern of Puritan-rooted American nativism and by implication religious (Protestant) sectarianism and fundamentalism, are analogous to fascist "nativist developments in Europe today", specifically Nazism in Germany. For instance, the "analogue" of the Puritan early "New England Primer" of nativism and religious sectarianism is found in the "various Nazi primers", namely the "displacement of aggression against a convenient out-group", especially during economic crises, "the impugning of out-group morality", and various other "myths and tactics" of "nativist movements before and since" (Merton 1939).

---

[30] Lutz and Lutz (2004:147) remark that the "Nazi party in Germany, both before it was in power and obviously afterwards, sought to incorporate the Germans in Czechoslovakia into a Greater Germany as well as seeking a union of Germany with Austria. Right-wing extremists also assassinated key figures in Germany. Foreign minister Rathenau was killed in 1922 for signing a treaty establishing diplomatic relations between Germany and the Soviet Union". In general, they suggest that "right-wing ideologies (aim) to force a government to attempt to acquire territory with related peoples or to intervene to protect the rights of an "oppressed" minority in a neighboring country" (Lutz and Lutz 2004:146–7).

Furthermore, Puritan- and generally Calvinist-inspired and fundamen-talism in America is observed or predicted to function as a sort of neo-fascism and thus pervaded by nativism, anti-cosmopolitanism, and anti-universalism, specifically religious extreme nationalism (Friedland 2002) or chauvinism (Hedges 2006), yet predictably adorned with the "Christian cross" and the American flag and elevated by the Pledge of Allegiance (Paxton[31] 2004). Consequently, its "born again" adherents, especially those adhering to the theology of Dominionism and generally Christian Reconstructionism inspired by theocratic Calvinism,[32] are described as "American fascists" calling for "moral and physical suprem-acy of a [fascist-like] master race" in America and the world as whole, of course in the face of US evangelicals cum sole "American Christians"[33] mastering and ultimately exterminating "nonbelievers" such as "secular humanists" or "liberals" (Hedges 2006). In sum, revived fundamentalism, notably, but not solely, Calvinist-rooted Dominionism, reportedly aims to reinstitute in America, following the New England Puritan and even Calvin's European theocratic model, "an American theocracy, a Christian fascism" (Hedges 2006; also, Phillips[34] 2006), thus the system of "holy"

---

[31] Paxton (2004) envisions "no swastika in an American fascism, buts Stars and Strips (or Stars and Bars) and Christian crosses. No fascist salute, but mass recitations of the Pledge of Allegiance." For example, such a remark is both diagnostic of KKK (Cunningham and Phillips 2007) and other old fascist groups and predictive of "Tea Party" and related neo-fascist or extreme-right movements.

[32] Hedges (2008:11) remarks that as a form of contemporary American fundamentalism Dominionism defined by the design of "Christian dominion" in society is a" theocratic set with its roots in a radical Calvinism. It looks to the theocracy John Calvin implanted in Geneva, Switzerland in the 1500s as its political model. It teaches that American Christian have been mandated by God to make America a Christian state".

[33] Hedges (2008:11) observes that American fundamentalism in the form of Dominionism "has, like all fascist movements, a belief in magic along with leadership ado-ration and a strident call for moral and physical supremacy of a master race, in this case, American Christians".

[34] Phillips (2006:2) observes that US "born again" evangelicals "actively seeking to dismantle the separation of church and state and indeed, such religious fundamentalists explicitly affirm that the United States is a Christian nation founded on Biblical prin-ciples – takes the Bible as the inerrant Word of God" and infers that "the seriousness and influence of this Religious Right cannot be discounted". In particular, he remarks the neo-conservative administration's "National Security Strategy" involving the war on terror and the "axis of evil", such as "regime change" in Iraq and the doctrine of preemptive war, "has garnered support among a high percentage of evangelical Christians because such policies appear congruent with their understanding of scripture." Also, he suggests that as the effect of "a surge of Christian fundamentalism and evangelical religiosity", neo-conservatism (the "Republican Right") captured political power and an "increasing num-ber" of neo-conservatives (Republicans) "are interpreting world events and shaping public policy around a Biblical (and even apocalyptic)" (Phillips 2006:2).

tyranny and terror, characterized with fascist-type nationalism a la "Christian patriotism" and totalitarianism overall.

Also, contemporary sociological analyses register the resurgence of the "apparently premodern specter of religious nationalism" (Friedland 2001). In this account, religious, including sectarian and theocratic, terrorists tend to be "almost all religious nationalists" in virtue of searching for an "alternative order" as the sacred basis of secular "state authority", thus "religious terrorism" being "only the most extreme form" of the tendency for redeeming "religion's inherent political powers" cum "final judgments" as a "general movement", particularly among Islamic fundamentalist groups and society and US evangelicals and "Christian" America. As regards these two, religious nationalism is reportedly "more likely" to resurge or persist in Islamic societies like Iran and even officially secular Turkey, as well as in the US, in virtue of all these societies being nations-states with a "civil religious", essentially theocratic tradition, to the effect that "religious nationalism" tends to attach "primacy to the family—not to democracy or the market" in opposition liberal-secular nationalism (Friedland 2002).

In particular, most "fundamentalist" Christians, typically evangelical Protestants claiming the "only true Christian" status, in America are observed to be "religious nationalists" (Friedland 2002), reflecting the essence of religious nationalism as the "public return of religion" in American politics and society, just as in Islamic settings. Generally, in another sociological account, modern extremely conservative or fascist ("right-wing") groups and ideologies in Western and other societies, including Europe and America, display and commit nationalistic and/or racist tendencies and activities by despising and targeting "minority groups" through attacks generating "terror"[35] (Lutz and Lutz 2004). Thus, the resurgence of extreme conservatism as equivalent or leading to fascism as the "radical right" in Europe and America is observed to be a negative "response" to economic and cultural globalization, with religion, notably religious fundamentalism, playing a "supportive role" in justifying and even reinforcing such antagonism to "outside influences", with the (second) Ku Klux Klan as the US or "Bible Belt" paradigmatic instance of

---

[35] Lutz and Lutz (2004:147) add that "the antipathy toward outsiders represents one facet of the need of the extreme right to create a stronger state. (They) are seen as weakening the state because they create divisions in society (including) opposition to foreign ideas and influences of all kinds."

a "right-wing movement"[36] (Lutz and Lutz 2004), basically of "godly" and racist proto-fascism (Cunningham and Phillips 2007).

Hence, terrorism often expresses and results from the nationalistic, sectarian, and ethnocentric opposition to global and cosmopolitan modernity, notably the process of economic, political, and cultural globalization and modernization (Bergesen and Lizardo 2004; Fischer 2003). This includes hostilities or grievances of nativist, isolationist groups in developing and authoritarian countries against wealthy, liberal-democratic Western societies (Abadie 2006; Bergesen and Lizardo 2004) resulting in violent revolt against the latter. As before, such tendencies are particularly observed in religious sectarianism (Smelser and Mitchell 2002), nativism or nationalism (Friedland 2002; Juergensmeyer 2003), and isolationism, paradigmatic instances being identified in Islamic and American "born again" fundamentalism and neo-conservatism overall, in opposition to the secular processes of economic and social globalization and modernization.

For instance, most Islamic as well as other non-Western societies are pervaded by the "widespread perception" of domestic religion and culture overall being "under threat of extinction", resulting in "revivalist or fundamentalist reactions" and consequently in the "religious character of much of recent terrorism" (Smelser and Mitchell 2002). Admittedly, while "this variant of terrorism" has particularly operated within the "context of a wider Islamic revival" during recent times, it is also linked with "revivalist and fundamentalist Christian movements" in contemporary America and "extreme Western political movements such as fascism" in interwar and postwar Europe (Smelser and Mitchell 2002). In this view, Islamic and Christian revivalism, sectarianism, and fundamentalism as the religious basis and sanctification of terrorism share certain common elements. These are, first, "a totalistic worldview" founded on a "sacred religious system", second, "a profound sense of threat, angst, and apprehension about the destruction of their society, culture, and way of life", third, "a specification of certain agents" as having "total responsibility for this deterioration", fourth, "an unqualified, and absolute, sense of rage" rationalized as

---

[36] Lutz and Lutz (2004:147–8) observe that the Ku Klux Klan opposed "increased immigration (particularly) Oriental, Jewish, or Catholic [as] carriers of foreign ideas (Lutz and Lutz 2004:147). Attacks on Jews, Catholics, and others with dangerous ideas were also frequent (or) immigrants in businesses that threatened the economic interests of white Protestants. The KKK [was involved] in the political process in terms of supporting candidates and seeking to influence policies (at the state level).

"morally legitimate", and fifth, a "utopian view of their own culture and society" cum an "imagined, glorious past" placed in total opposition to the "decaying and threatening" Western world (Smelser and Mitchell 2002; also, Alexander[37] 2004).

The last element includes, for instance, "religious indoctrination" through corresponding educational institutions such as madrassas[38] in some Islamic countries (Pakistan, etc.) (Krueger and Maleckova 2003; Turk 2004) and private religious schools or home schooling in America (Darnell and Sherkat 1997), especially the Southern "Bible Belt" and its extensions through, as a rule, ultra-conservative "red" states (Utah, Montana, Oklahoma, Nebraska, Idaho, Wyoming, the Dakotas, etc.) In particular, Muslim fundamentalist groups claim a sacred religious ground for terrorism in contending that Islamic God never engages in negotiation and discussions[39] (Smelser and Mitchell 2002), just as do their evangelical counterparts through equivalent claims about "Christian God", more precisely what Weber calls the "God of Calvinism", including English-American Puritanism, as a sort of "hard king" and merciless and capricious "Oriental despot" (Artz 1998) for whom even Puritan Milton had "no respect". Hence, Islamic and US fundamentalists seek and often succeed to "Islamize" and "Christianize" cum "Calvinize" (Clemens 2007) Muslim societies and American society, respectively. They do so by reconstructing them as "Islamic" and "Christian" sectarian republics, thus effectively as theocracies and systems of "holy" state terror, i.e., as governed by Koran and Biblical law[40] (Lutz and Lutz 2004), including executions and

---

[37] Characterizing terrorism in general as a "form of antipolitical action", Alexander (2004) suggests that "the terrorist attack (on NYC) and the counterattacks (were) an iteration of the performance/counterperformance dialectic that began decades, indeed centuries, ago in terms of the relation of Western expansion and Arab-Muslim reaction. The counterperformance of [Americans] develop[ed] an idealized, liminal alternative that inspired self-defense and outrage, leading to exactly the opposite performance results from those the al-Qaeda terrorists had intended."

[38] Turk (2004:279) comments that "Islamist fundamentalism depend(s) on radicalization through formal education consisting mostly of religious indoctrination (madrassas) (i.e.) the duty to engage in holy war (jihad) against all enemies of the true Islam. Inspired by the ideological messages, the charisma of leaders, the potential for material or status gains, or whatever else attracts them, others are likely to join."

[39] Smelser and Mitchell (2002:27) comment that "revivalist-like movements of a totalistic sort [to "Islamize" the religious community by imposing Islamic norms throughout all spheres of life] antedate deep Western influences ("Christian")". In their view, "the presence of extreme Islamic fundamentalism, like the demographic, economic, and political realities found in most Muslim societies, is part of the fertile seedbed in which a particular ideologically based brand of terrorism finds a supportive audience and some recruits" (Smelser and Mitchell 2002:28).

[40] According to Lutz and Lutz (2004:71), religious terrorism or extremism "can be a response to the stresses and change that come with modernization and greater

imprisonment for sins-crimes, so the shared and functionally equivalent death penalty and generally prison system populated mostly by sinners-criminals (Becky and Western 2004; Jacobs et al. 2005; Matsueda et al. 2006; Uggen and Manza 2002) such as non-violent drug, sexual and other sinful persons.

The above yields the inference and expectation that those individuals, social, in particular religious, groups, states, and societies that are opposed, on nationalistic or isolationist and sectarian grounds, to economic, political and cultural openness and globalization are more likely to commit, advocate, incite, and support terrorism than are others. This proposition is qualified in that not all individuals, social, including religious, groups, states, and societies opposing, on nationalistic and sectarian grounds, the process of economic, political and cultural globalization and openness conduct and endorse terrorism, but they reveal a more manifest and salient tendency for doing so than do others. The hypothesis can help explain contemporary terrorism in its various types or cases, in particular transnational or global, conservative, religious, and counter-state terrorisms, and in part their alternative forms.

---

globalization (i.e.,) as a "response to modernity." Most extreme religious groups see themselves to be battling with secularism [or] "secular humanism" in the West (e.g.,) efforts to make the Sharia the basis of law in Islamic countries" as well as Biblical law in "Christian America." In this view, "religious groups frequently seek to return to a purer past and to purge society of outside influences [and other] right-wing groups (fight) against changes [from] globalization [while] left-wing dissidents (battle) against global capitalism, sharing some of the same fears as religious groups and some ethnic groups" (Lutz and Lutz 2004:245–6).

CONCLUSIONS

Modernism, Anti-Modernism, and Modern Terrorism

Modern terrorism is probably best understood, explained, and predicted within the sociological framework and historical conjuncture of profound antagonism and vehement revolt against liberal Western modernity. Such antagonism and revolt against liberal modernity operates as the principal and overarching factor of most, though not all, terrorist agents and actions in contemporary societies. Hence, anti-modernity in its anti-liberal and anti-Western form and meaning crucially generates, explains, and predicts most contemporary terrorism, especially its dominant religious, more specifically fundamentalist forms observed in Islamic settings/groups, America, and to a lesser extent other societies. Alternatively, it is difficult, if not impossible, to fully understand, explain, predict, and conceivably solve the problem of terrorism, especially in its currently prevalent religiously conditioned form, without taking in due consideration anti-modernity as a composite of anti-liberalism and anti-democracy, as well as anti-secularism, anti-rationalism, and anti-globalism, anti-cosmopolitanism, and anti-universalism in conjunction and mutual reinforcement.

In this sense, most contemporary, particularly religiously grounded and sanctified, terrorism can be considered and predicted as in essence the radical act and/or product of anti-liberalism. Anti-liberalism may have become a sort of "badge of honor" or bumper-sticker, notably a political alchemy to attain and retain power (election, reelection, etc.), wealth, and status, for US conservatives since neo-conservatism, specifically Reaganism labeling and via the "great communicator" apparently convincing most Americans that liberalism was "un-American" and "foreign". In spite or perhaps because of its resurgence and dominance in American politics and society, as well as Islamic countries—virtually the only two major or most visible settings experiencing such anti-liberal revival and control–anti-liberalism has also firmly established itself as the prime mover of contemporary terrorism during the same period, namely since the 1980s through the 2010s.

Notably, anti-liberalism has operated as the major driving force and rationale of the dominant, religious form of terrorism in contemporary

America as well as Islamic countries or by Muslim fundamentalist groups in Western societies. Virtually all major terrorist agents and actions or threats in America during the 1990s-2010s as well as in Islamic settings or by Muslim fundamentalist groups have been essentially driven and/or rationalized by anti-liberalism in the sense of antagonism and revolt against liberal-democratic Western modernity as both an Enlightenment-based ideal and a social system, simply a prospective utopia and an institutional reality. Even if assuming multiple and complex intertwined factors and motivations (Smelser and Mitchell 2002; Smelser 2007), it is evident that nothing more intensively and persistently induces and/or self-justifies terrorist agents and acts in contemporary America and Islamic settings or by Muslim fundamentalist groups in Western societies than does anti-liberalism thus understood, conjoined and mutually reinforced with anti-secularism, anti-rationalism, and anti-globalism, anti-cosmopolitanism, and anti-universalism, as integral elements of anti-modernism.

The positive obverse (flip-side) of anti-liberalism and generally anti-modernism as a negativity through anti-liberal and anti-modern antagonism and revolt is primarily conservatism as the self-declared initial and perennial opponent of liberalism and modernism, which was born out of the ashes of medieval traditionalism turned "self-reflective" in encountering and opposing rising liberal modernity (Mannheim 1986). Consequently, if anti-liberalism is the prime negative sociological mover, justification, and motivation of terrorism, then conservatism represents the primary positive factor, rationalization, and inducement of the latter, especially its prevalent religious forms, in contemporary societies, including both Western societies like America and Islamic countries or Muslim fundamentalist groups acting in the West and beyond.

Analogously, virtually all, notably religiously based, terrorist agents and actions in America during the 1990s-2010s as well as in Islamic settings or by Muslim fundamentalist groups have been positively induced and rationalized by conservatism as the antagonistic force against liberalism and modernism generally. Conservatism has sought to destroy or revert, through anti-government violence and government violent repression alike, liberal-democratic Western modernity as both an ideal and a social system in favor of restoring or perpetuating medieval-based traditionalism as the conservative parent or point of origin and model of the "good society" (Dunn and Woodard 1996; Nisbet 1966). And even on the plausible assumption of multiple and complex entwined factors, justifications, and motivations, evidently no such factor, justification, and motivation more intensively and persistently induces and/or justifies terrorist agents and acts in contemporary America and in Islamic settings or by Muslim fundamentalist groups than does conservatism thus understood.

As indicated throughout, conservatism operating as the major positive factor and predictor of contemporary terrorism includes religious fundamentalism and sectarianism as reviving and expanding during recent times and especially shared, alongside the concomitant design and system of theocracy cum "godly" society, by Islamic fundamentalists and "Christian" evangelical groups in America and to a lesser extent other Western societies. Conservatism also includes neo-fascism (the far-right), including neo-Nazism, as resurging and even reasserting itself in Europe and America alike, typically, especially in the second, in alliance and eventual merger with religious fundamentalism and sectarianism, as exemplified by "Christian" theocratic neo-Nazi militias ("Christian Identity", "Christian warriors", etc.) and other "godly" and "all-American" fascists (Hedges 2006). Generally, conservatism incorporates neo-conservatism rising and becoming especially dominant or prominent in political-ideological terms within America (Jacobs and Tope 2007) since Reaganism through its sequels and in part Great Britain (Thatcherism) since the 1980s. Neo-conservatism has formed the underlying basis and generalized setting for "born again" fundamentalist and neo-fascist forces merged or allied (Hicks 2006; King 2008) within the neo-conservative "extended family" (or "big tent") to form a sort of neo-fascism with the composite of the Christian cross and the American flag (Paxton 2004). Recall the "I am one of you [evangelicals]'" declaration of Reagan, the father or icon–alongside with Goldwater (Baldassarri and Gelman 2008), while both being the "children" of McCarthyism (Plotke 2002)–of US neo-conservatism and a Presbyterian Puritan, to US anti-liberal or theocratic evangelicals during his political campaigns, as well as his publicly stated admiration for Winthrop, the master theocrat of American Puritanism and characterized with "austere Calvinism" (Kloppenberg 1998).

In sum, this yields the (re)discovery of anti-liberalism in the main form of conservatism, specifically neo-conservatism via fundamentalism and its "twin brother" neo-fascism, as the primary factor and predictor of contemporary, notably prevalent religious, terrorism, especially in America during recent times and Islamic settings or by Muslim groups against Western and other societies. And this rediscovery is purely a scientific or objective inference derived from observation and evidence, and not a political and arbitrary statement, viz., "pro-liberal" and "anti-conservative". "Liberalism", "anti-liberalism", "conservatism", and "neo-conservatism", including revived "fundamentalism" and "neo-fascism", are understood in Weber-Mannheim's manner as particular ideal types of ideology as well as of social system in a value-free, neutral sense–i.e., as not "good" or "bad" per se–and considered not in themselves but only with respect to their specific impact on contemporary terrorism. At this juncture "anti-liberalism" in the form of "conservatism" is simply what it objectively *does* in relation to contemporary terrorism, not what it claims or aims to be. In a way, one cannot emphasize enough, especially in the American context, the scientific, apolitical trust of the conclusion concerning what Weber would call referring to ascetic Protestantism and capitalism the "intimate relationship" of "anti-liberalism" cum "conservatism" with terrorism, yet a sort of "fatal attraction" given the grave consequences for human liberty and life (though some may find "political" connotations).

Namely, this is because in America since the 1980s and with the rise of neo-conservatism like Reaganism, "anti-liberalism" or "conservatism" has become a sort of "all-American" ideology, politics, and behavior. Notably, it has operated as the supreme formula for attaining and maintaining political power at all levels (Hill 2002; Jacobs and Tope 2007; King 2008; Matsueda et al. 2006), especially in the Southern "Bible Belt" (Baldassarri and Gelman 2008; Hicks 2006; Steensland 2006) and other evangelical or hyper-conservative ("red") regions, thus a sort of alchemy or winning formula in politics. Conversely, "liberalism" has been construed as a kind of "un-American", "foreign", or "European" polar opposite with a stigma or pejorative meaning ("L-word") almost in the sense and manner of McCarthyism that actually prototypically defined it in this way, to be followed by Goldwater (Baldassarri and Gelman 2008) and Reagan et al. (Plotke 2002). Simply, "anti-liberals" or "conservatives", including so-called "neo-cons"–partially discredited during the early 2000s but promising and even succeeding to stage another comeback via ultra-conservative movements a la "Tea Party" rising in adverse reaction to the 2008 Elections (as did in 1994)–declare themselves and are regarded by most Americans as "good", "true", even "only" Americans ("patriots", etc.). Conversely, they condemn "liberals" as anything but "American" and as equivalent to insane persons–as also were viewed their European versions by Nazism and communism–and stigmatized as "immoral", "ungodly", "blasphemous", and (so) "bad" people, including "unpatriotic", as witnessed since Reaganism through the 1994 conservative "revolution" to theocratic-fascist "Christian" militia and anti-liberal radical "Tea Party" groups since 2008.

In light of such prevalent social constructions of the alternative realities of "liberalism" and "anti-liberalism" in the form of "conservatism" in
America during recent times, the uncovering or inferring the "fatal attraction" or complicity of the latter with modern terrorism (Jacobs et al. 2005;
King 2008; King et al. 2009) is at first sight surprising. Conceivably, if by
any chance communicated to them, this finding would "shock" most
Americans "brain washed" (Beiner 1992) into believing the claim that
liberalism is "un-American" or "evil" and conservatism as "American as the
apple pie" or "unmitigated good", thus that they are a sort of "natural born"
and "forever" conservatives (if not, they are not "real Americans"), even if
in some accounts recent ideological-political trends in this respect are
more complex and ambivalent[1] (Besley and Case 2003). It is also likely to
"offend" or "upset" US neo-conservatives, including "born again" religious
fundamentalists and neo-fascists, though probably not their Islamic enemies in the contest for global religious-military dominance and yet "brothers in arms" in theocracy, who seem more open or less hypocritical than
these "all-American" Puritan descendants about their terrorist attractions,
links, and intentions or complicities. But if the saying that the truth is
often painful is correct, then it applies to the documented and thus
expected "fatal attraction" or close link and complicity, overt or covert,
between terrorism and conservatism as the main type of anti-liberalism.

While US conservatism attempts and succeeds to make its "attraction"
with counter-state and state terrorism the "best kept secret" in America by
keeping it, like its other workings and outcomes glorified as "American
exceptionalism", "out of sight and so out of mind" (Perrucci and Wysong
2008) for most Americans, it is uncovered or revealed, by analogy to the
proverbial emperor with no cloths, as the "worst kept secret" in the "exceptional nation" and modern Western societies. Simply, by now in Western
society likely "every schoolboy knows it", except perhaps for most
Americans made to believe in the "godliness" and so "goodness" of "all-
American" conservatives, just as the "fatal attraction" between Islamic
religious conservatism and terrorism has become universally known in
the world during recent times (Feldstein 2008). In short, it has become
painfully manifest that conservatism is to terrorism in America what
Islamic fundamentalism has been in this (September 11, 2001) and other
settings.

---

[1] Besley and Case (2003:22) find a "move toward a more conservative ideology" during
the 1980s, yet "followed by a return to a slightly more liberal stance in the 1990s", thus contradicting conservatism's construing of Americans as "natural born" conservatives.

At any rate, the above rediscovery or inference is devoid of and refuses to be attached any explicit political or partisan connotation and aims to be reasonably value-free or neutral in the Weberian methodological tradition. And if it "shocks", perhaps this is what Weber would call the inherent vocation and even unavoidable fate of science, as exemplified by the "seismic shocks" of non-scientific populations and the "offense" of religious conservatives generated by heliocentric astronomy (the "earth revolves around the sun") and Darwin's evolutionism, including sociology, economics, and other social sciences. Alternatively, it would scientifically irresponsible and dishonest, a betrayal of this intrinsic vocation of science *not* to make and present through a sort of "patriotic" or "godly" self-censorship the discovery or inference of the "fatal attraction" between anti-liberalism in the form of conservatism and terrorism when the compelling and overwhelming basis exists for doing so, just because "liberal" ideas, activities, and groups are attached the stigma of "un-American", and "anti-liberal" or "conservative" ones, are glorified as "all-American" in America during recent times (though not the 1960s). After all, such "patriotic" and "godly" avoidance or "head in sand" attitude" was not a sensible option even for many scientists and philosophers during the Dark Middle Ages of science and culture and their Inquisition, or the feudal *ancien regime*, as exemplified by Copernicus and Galileo, Hobbes and Spinoza, Kant, Voltaire, and Hume, and other "heretics" and "ungodly" figures. Hence, it is even less so in modern democratic society, though Islamic and US religious conservatisms seemingly strive and occasionally succeed, as in Iran, Taliban-ruled regions, and the "Bible Belt", to resurrect these societies and times as their shared perennial ideal from the "dead past" and recreate "New Dark Ages" (Bauman 2001; Berman 2000) through counter-state and state terror against liberal-democratic modernity.

In turn, anti-modernity or anti-modernism is conceived in the composite sense of an ideology, social system, and period antagonistic and destructive to modernity or modernism also understood in the triple meaning of an ideological, systemic, and historical phenomenon. Anti-modernism is understood by analogy to and as a negative form of what Weber calls traditionalism, including medievalism, as its extant historical basis or rationale, and modernism analogously to and as a setting of capitalism as its economic foundation or structure, both representing Weberian ideal types of ideology, social system, and historical conjuncture.

Therefore, for the purposes of this work anti-modernism incorporates, first, traditionalism, particularly feudalism, as its initial phase or anticipation, second, early or arch-conservatism born out of the former, especially medievalism, and third, fascism, including Nazism and other fascisms in interwar Europe, McCarthyism in postwar America, as the conservative extreme subtype. It also includes, as its fourth and recent element, contemporary or neo-conservatism, including the "new" fundamentalism and neo-fascism in American and European societies respectively, as revived and adapted types of the "good old" religious conservatism and fascism. In essence, anti-modernism is primarily (though not solely) conservative, both proto- and neo-conservative, including fascist and neo-fascist, anti-modernity, while taking account of secondary non-conservative anti-modernities (e.g., communist, neo-Marxist, post-modernist, feminist, etc.).

In turn, modernism involves, first, liberal democracy, second, secular politics and culture, third, rationalistic society, and fourth, a global-cosmopolitan and universalistic economic, political, and cultural system, i.e., liberalism, secularism, rationalism, and globalism, cosmopolitanism, and universalism, including globalized democratic (as distinguished from authoritarian) capitalism, respectively. Essentially, modernism is hence, first and foremost, liberal Western modernity both in the classical and contemporary sense of liberalism, while also keeping in mind non-liberal and non-Western "multiple modernities" as secondary phenomena for our purpose.

Against this background, the primary and most comprehensive source of most contemporary terrorism is conservative anti-modernism as an ideology, social system, and historical period initially arising out of medieval traditionalism in adverse reaction against and ultimately, through fascism and religious fundamentalism, seeking destruction or reversal of liberal modernism as an alternative ideological, systemic, and historical phenomenon. Contemporary terrorism is hence best explained and predicted as an extreme form or ultimate outcome of conservative anti-modernism's antagonism and revolt against and attempted reversal of liberal modernity, specifically modern liberal-democratic, secular, rationalistic, and global-cosmopolitan democracy, economy, and society. Terrorism as the radical, violent type of adverse anti-modernity reaction signifies extreme and destructive, including self-destructive or suicidal, counteraction or counterrevolution against liberal modernity expressing and carrying anti-modern antagonism or opposition to its ultimate nihilistic or deadly consequences.

The preceding is a relatively, though not completely, original or novel conception in relation to the current sociological and related literature.

It has a potential to significantly enhance our knowledge, understanding, and prediction of terrorism and for substantively contributing to the theory and research in the field by further theoretical elaboration and empirical tests and for providing a partly new approach to solving a growing problem in contemporary societies. The conception of anti-modernity through antagonism and revolt against modern Western liberal-democratic, secular, rationalistic, and global society, as the fundamental and the most general determinant and predictor of terrorism, is original or crucial in at least two related respects. First, it provides a more fundamental and general explanation, prediction, and consequently potential solution of the problem of terrorism in relation to the current literature. The conception significantly extends the present literature in which anti-modernity's critical role in terrorism is at best implicit (Juergensmeyer 2003; Smelser and Mitchell 2002; Turk 2004) but hardly ever explicitly stated, explicated, and investigated. Anti-modernity in the above sense is a more fundamental and comprehensive determinant and predictor of terrorism than any of the related and convergent or divergent determinants and predictors proffered in the literature, ranging from anti-democracy and anti-secularism and religious traditionalism to anti-rationalism and anti-capitalism and anti-globalization. In fact, "anti-modernity" comprises virtually all of these determinants and predictors of terrorism, namely anti-democracy, anti-secularism, anti-rationalism, and anti-globalization and anti-cosmopolitanism, including anti-capitalism.

Conversely, all these are the indicators or measures of (by "loading" on) anti-modernity as the underlying ("unobservable") general variable. Second, as a corollary, the above conception promises a greater explanatory potential and scope of application in relation to other conceptions in that it can help explain and predict most all forms or expressions of terrorism. Specifically, it may potentially explain and predict both counter-state and state, domestic and global oppositional, intra-and inter-society official terrorisms. In particular, it would apply to counter-state and state terrorisms alike, not only or mostly to counter-state terrorism as the focus of the current literature (Juergensmeyer 2003; Smelser and Mitchell 2002; Smelser 2007; Turk 2004).

Summary

To summarize, most contemporary terrorism is the violent, destructive expression of the hostility and revolt against modern liberal-democratic, secular, rationalistic, and global-cosmopolitan society. Terrorism is the product of the antagonism to Western liberal modernity turned anti-modern nihilism in the form of collective act of destruction[2] (Juergensmeyer 2003) typically by an organized group or organization, including ultimately self-destruction, and violence directed against modern society defined by these four interlinked and mutually reinforced sets of attributes and its basic values and institutions. While not every antagonism or opposition to liberal modernity necessarily becomes anti-modern nihilism or destruction, most contemporary terrorism results from and expresses an antagonistic, hostile view of modern liberal-democratic society and its basic values and institutions.

Alternatively, whenever and wherever antagonism to liberal modernity becomes anti-modern nihilism, this causes and predicts, just as defines and constitutes, contemporary terrorism. This renders contemporary terrorism (the form of) anti-modern nihilism or destruction derived from antagonism or opposition to liberal modernity. In Clausewitz's terms, like war, modern terrorism is the "continuation" of the antagonistic "politics" to liberal modernity by "other means", namely destructive instruments and violent actions. In this sense, modern terrorism is a sort of total war against liberal modernity "continuing" or expressing hostility toward the latter. And, in terrorism's prevalent religious-conservative variations, this war invariably assumes the form of the real-life, political manifestation of a "holy war" or "Divine warfare" a la jihad and crusade against modernity (Juergensmeyer 2003; Turk 2004). In short, anti-modernism acts as the main determinant and predictor of modern terrorism.

The preceding yields the following empirical generalization, inference, and prediction: The more a social group, state, and society is antagonistic to liberal Western modernity and modernization, the more likely it is to engage in terrorism and related destructive actions than are other groups, states and societies, and conversely. While not all groups (and individuals within them), states, and societies antagonistic to Western liberal modernism as an ideology, social system and time and modernization engage

---

[2] Juergensmeyer (2003:10) observes that "terrorism is seldom a lone act." For example, "when Hill stepped from a sidewalk in Pensacola, and shot Dr. Britton and his security escort as they prepared to enter their clinic, he was cheered by a certain circle of militant Christian anti-abortion activists around the country. Behind convicted bomber McVeigh [etc.] was a subculture of militant Christian groups that extends throughout the US" (Juergensmeyer 2003:11). Juergensmeyer (2003:13) adds that there were "Christians in America who supported abortion clinic bombings and militia actions such as the bombing of the Oklahoma City federal building."

in terrorism and related activities, those that are tend to do so more than others, and the other way round. Hence, this hypothesis applies to both counter-state and state, within-society (domestic) and inter-society or inter-state, terrorism, namely to terrorist groups and individuals, states or governments, and societies or "cultures of violence" (Juergensmeyer 2003).

Alternatively, terrorism is the extreme, violent expression of the rebellion or counterrevolution of traditionalism and its heir conservatism as the prime type of anti-modernism, notably anti-liberalism, against modernism. Traditionalism or conservatism in the sense the perpetuation or restoration of traditionalist or conservative social, including religious, values and institutions, functions as the factor of modern terrorism (Emerson and Hartman 2006; Juergensmeyer 2003; Smelser and Mitchell 2002; Turk 2004). The above yields the following alternative conclusion and prediction: The more a social group, state, and society seeks to perpetuate or restore and reinforce traditionalist or conservative social values and institutions, the more likely it is to engage in terrorism and related actions than are other groups, states, and societies, and conversely. While not all individuals, groups, states, and societies seeking to perpetuate or restore traditionalist or conservative values and institutions engage in terrorism and related activities, those doing so they tend to do more than others.

The above inference and prediction can be specified with respect to religious groups, states or political organizations, and societies. The more a religious group, state or political organization, and society seeks to perpetuate or restore traditionalistic values and institutions, the more likely it is to engage in terrorism and related violent actions than are other groups, states, and societies, and conversely. A further variation of this inference specifies the impact of religious revivalism, notably the revival of the social and political hegemony of traditional or conservative religion in modern society, on terrorism. Specifically, religious revivalism is a factor of terrorism, including the perpetuation or revival of the social and political dominance or influence of traditional religion (Juergensmeyer 2003). Religious revivalism includes "Islamic revival" and "revivalist and fundamentalist Christian movements" (Smelser and Mitchell 2002), specifically Protestant "revivals" (Juergensmeyer 2003), both seeking to revive traditional religion and its dominance in society and politics. In America, a paradigmatic exemplar was 18th century "Calvinist revivalism" via the Great Awakenings (Archer 2001; German 1995; Rossel 1970). This yields the inference and prediction that the more a religious group, state, and society is revivalist, notably seeking traditional, conservative religion's social and political revival, the more likely it is to commit terrorist acts than are others, and conversely. To be sure, not all religious groups, states, and societies that are revivalist, in particular seek traditional, conservative religion's sociopolitical revival, necessarily engage in terrorism and related violent activities, but those that are tend to do more than others.

As a specification of the previous, in particular terrorism as a violent rebellion or counterrevolution of medievalism, including feudalism, is a form or result of traditionalism's revolt against modernism. Notably, traditionalism involves medievalism after the model or image of the "Dark Middle Ages", particularly feudalism, in the sense of perpetuation or restoration of medieval, in particular feudal, values and institutions, as the factor of modern terrorism. The above yields the following inference and prediction specifying the previous. The more a social group, state, and society seeks to perpetuate or restore and reinforce medieval, including feudal, values and institutions, the more likely it is to engage in terrorism and related destructive violent actions than are other groups, states, and societies, and conversely. While not all social groups, states, and societies with medievalist or feudal properties and ideals conduct terrorism and related violent activities, they tend to do so more than others. A specification of the above with respect to religious groups, states or political organizations and societies yields the following inference and prediction. The more a religious group, state or political organization, and society seeks to perpetuate or revive medieval values and institutions, the more likely it is to commit or support terrorism and related violent actions than are other groups, states, and societies, and conversely.

Perhaps, as implied throughout, the ultimate, all-encompassing, and inherent reason why conservatism cum vehement anti-liberalism generates and eventually in the form of theocratic fundamentalism and fascism constitutes a design and system of terror is that it, to use Durkheim's word, awakens and encourages the worst in human beings, including contempt, disrespect, depreciation, intolerance, and notably hatred of the individual, group, and societal Other. Consequently, it commits or incites generalized "hate crimes" in the sense of hate-driven terror such as violent repression and severe coercion in society and offensive wars of extermination against other societies.

This especially applies to US neo-conservatism, including revived theocratic evangelicalism and neo-fascism, since obsessively anti-liberal Reaganism, although it has no monopoly on such attributes and actions, notably hatred and hate-driven action, in the "extended family" of conservatism encompassing religious fundamentalism and fascism overall. For instance, US neo-conservatism generated and encouraged, within modern Western societies, the most intense hatred of condemned "un-American" Presidents and Congress and beyond during 1992–2000 and even more 2008–2012, and consequently various hate-driven terror acts or plans against federal government, including the Oklahoma City 1995, 1996 Atlanta Olympic, and 2010 Texas bombings. And neo-conservative hatred and consequently hate-driven terror acts or plans targeted/target these US Presidents and related persons not only or mainly because of racism, manifest in the 2008–2012, but absent in the 1992–2000 case. They did and do so even more because of what these Presidents (plus Congressmen, etc.) were perceived to represent, liberal cum "big" government, as witnessed in these terrorist bombings, and generally liberalism condemned as an "un-American" ideology and social system after the pattern of McCarthyism and Reaganism.

On this account, in these and related cases of neo-conservatism's hate-complex what Weber calls "racial repulsion" or hatred is largely a secondary element and, analogously, ideological hatred or revulsion the primary in the form of (to paraphrase Comte) conservative abhorrence for liberalism (Van Dyke 1995) as the project of human liberation, dignified life, and happiness. Simply, it is not only race but, above all, liberal modernity that is the source and rationale for neo-conservative hatred and hate-induced terror acts or plans in America. Hence, this validates the argument that conservative anti-liberalism is the critical, ultimate source and predictor of terrorism in contemporary societies, including America, just as Islamic settings.

Historically, US neo-conservatism, notably revived evangelicalism, perpetuates or resurrects a major attribute and action of its acknowledged parent and perennial model (Dunn and Woodard 1996), Calvinist Puritanism's self-righteous hatred or what Weber calls "misanthropy" of humans and its hate-induced "reign of terror", as well as McCarthyism's similar traits and practices like allegorical "witch hunts". Comparatively, the intensity, persistence or recurrence, and ultimately insanity of such neo-conservative hatred of and hate-driven acts against "liberal" and "un-American" persons and ideas is unparalleled among modern Western democratic societies, and only rivaled by interwar fascism, notably Nazism's anti-liberal hostility and violence, in Europe and Islamic fundamentalism's anti-liberalism in Iran, Taliban-ruled regions, and other Muslim settings or groups. In other words, the underlying reason for its anti-modern and anti-liberal terror is that conservatism, in particular

US neo-conservatism, regenerates, stimulates, and epitomizes what Habermas (2001) denotes un-repented "evil as distorted good", prototypically exemplified by Puritanism and its self-righteous, godly "reign of terror" in early America. Alternatively, this is because conservatism, in particular theocratic fundamentalism and fascism, destroys and discourages the best or most humane attributes of humans, as the polar opposites of those that it awakens, reproduces, and encourages. In a sort of infinite regression, one may and often does wonder why conservatism awakens and encourages the worst in humans, notably "why so much hatred" in American neo-conservatism, including revived evangelicalism, leading to hate-induced actions, but this is the question that only US conservatives or "born again" evangelicals, and perhaps Freudian psychoanalysts, can answer.

At this juncture, conservatism, notably theocratic fundamentalism and fascism, appears as a sort of "naturalized", "rationalized", and "generalized" terror in the sense that its very nature, notably its hatred and sacrifice of humans to supra-and anti-human powers a la absolute God, totalitarian "leader", "nation", etc. generates, rationalizes, and generalizes terrorism in the entwined formula of intra-societal violent repression and inter-societal aggressive wars. In this sense, conservatism was (to paraphrase Dahrendorf 1959) "born decomposed" as the design and system of terror out of the "death" of the despotic, theocratic, irrational, and warlike Dark Middle Ages, viz., the feudal ancient regime during the French Revolution (Acemoglu et al. 2011; Markoff 1997), in hostile and violent reaction to the advent of liberal modernity as the societal and ideological Other. And it has continued to live as such ever since through interwar fascism and postwar neo-conservatism, revived religious fundamentalism, and neo-fascism, up to the present. Apparently, conservatism being engendered by–and then seeking to revive or perpetuate–the darkness of medievalism, including feudalism, did and conceivably could only generate terror in the twin conservative formula of societal violent repression and inter-societal offensive war. In Durkheim's words, the "genesis" of conservatism from despotic, theocratic, irrational, and warlike medievalism as its perpetual ideal to be resurrected from death caused by the advent of modernity–theocratic "paradise lost" to be found, as in the US "Bible Belt"–has determined and predicted its "evolution" and "functioning" as the design and system of terror in this double sense.

Alternatively, the reason why liberal modernity and thus liberalism is the best or the only viable long-term solution to terrorism, including violent repression within society and aggressive wars against other societies, is that, with secondary exceptions, it awakens and encourages what is the best in humans, including appreciation, respect, tolerance, love, and compassion of others and non-violent individual and collective action. By contrast to conservatism as its hostile reaction, liberal modernity/liberalism was "born composed" as the project and system of universal liberty, equality, and justice, as both the French and American (in its Jeffersonian dimension) Revolution proclaimed, from the Enlightenment overcoming the darkness of medievalism. Consequently, it originated as the most effective antidote and cure, at least in the long run, to the poison and death of terror in the dual conservative medieval-based formula of societal violent repression and inter-societal offensive war.

To that extent, what Weber would call the "adverse fate" of the Dark Middle Ages, including feudalism, and the triumph of the Enlightenment and its "child" liberal modernity likely augurs the equivalent "destiny" for conservatism as the medieval-rooted design, generator, and system of terror. Moreover, this outcome has materialized in early 21st century Western liberal modernity such as Europe (plus Canada, Australia, etc.) essentially overcoming conservative, notably "native" religiously based, counter-state and especially state terrorism. This holds with the striking–but probably not indefinitely sustainable–deviation of America during neo-conservatism, with both forms of terror, the first against "big" government and the second against the "ungodly" and "sinful" in the "Bible Belt" and other "red" states, persisting and intensifying at the time of writing these lines. This hence reveals the true face of *conservative*–as distinct from liberal–"American exceptionalism" as an extreme anti-liberal and so anti-Western, i.e., fascist- and Islamic-style aberration.

In general, hating subjects tend, as Simmel[3] suggests, to search for social objects of their inherent hatred or hostility, simply different Others–rather than the latter being the cause of it–just as loving agents look for the object of their need of love. This applies not only to inherently hateful, hostile, bigoted individuals. It also holds for conservative groups and societies pervaded and driven by what Simmel calls "social hatred", including racial hate and especially ideological hatred or hostility toward liberalism and modernity overall, thus liberal institutions and liberals

---

[3] Simmel proposes that the individual may have an 'inborn need for hating and fighting [which] injects into the objects it takes for itself their hate-provoking qualities', thus a 'formal hostility drive.' Similarly, he observes that 'it has been said that man does not have religion because he believes in God, but he believes in God because he has religion which is a mood of his soul' and also that 'love is not a mere reaction evoked by its object but we have a need of loving.'

hated, condemned, and to be exterminated as, both US evangelicals and Islamic fundamentalists say, "enemies of God and Nation", notably as "un-American" and "anti-Islamic". Simply, just as do hateful individuals, hatred-driven conservative, notably fundamentalist and fascist, groups and societies "naturally" have to invent their liberal-democratic collective "enemies" thereby to be subjected to violent repression and ultimately extermination.

To that extent, like hateful individuals, conservative groups and societies will always search for other collective objects of their anti-liberal and anti-modern social hatred—rather than these different collectivities being the cause of their hate–and consequently commit or advocate terrorist acts against liberalism and modernity, i.e., liberal institutions and liberals. Given the renewed ideological and political predominance of theocratic and generally oppressive religious-political conservatism in America since the 1980s through the 2010s, like the Muslim world, this is perhaps the true "American tragedy". It consists of conservatism's intrinsic and permanent "social hatred" of and hence persistent hatred-induced counter-state and state terror or generalized "hate crimes" against liberal modernity and liberals depending on whether conservatives are outside or in political power, functionally equivalent to the apparent Islamic "destiny" of religious anti-liberal and anti-modern hate-driven terrorism in both forms.

The Present/Future Vicious Circle of Anti-Liberalism and Terrorism and How to Break It

The preceding detects and predicts a sort of vicious circle of anti-liberalism in the major form of conservatism, including revived religious fundamentalism, neo-fascism, and neo-conservatism, with terrorism especially in America and to a lesser or diminishing degree other Western societies. The first stage of the circle consists in that (re) establishing and consolidating liberal-secular democracy, in particular the limited welfare state, including "liberal" Presidents and Congress, become or is construed, cum "big" government, as the agent provocateur of counter-state terrorism through anti-government violence and threats by anti-liberal conservative, including fundamentalist and fascists, forces a la "Christian warriors", "Tea Party" movements, and the like. Yet, in the second stage of the circle, eliminating or undermining and suspending liberal-secular democracy as "big" government, including electoral and other political victories and gains of anti-liberal conservatism, eventually generates "holy" state terror through systematic "godly" government coercion and violent repression of "liberals" and "ungodly" cum "un-American" ideas, persons, and activities, including executions and mass imprisonment for sins-crimes, as well as inter-state terrorism via wars of aggression against the "evil" world.

In a way, this is a sort of sociological "American tragedy" with a cycle of counter-state terrorism and state and inter-state terror depending on whether liberal-secular democracy is established or eliminated/subverted, and alternatively anti-liberal conservative, including fundamentalist and neo-fascist, forces are in violent opposition or authoritarian, notably theocratic, control of government. It is in a sense a "win-win" situation for conservative-generated and executed, especially religiously grounded and sanctified, terror moving back and forth between counter-state and state/inter-state terrorism, yet, conversely, a sort of "no-win" scenario or zero-sum game for stable democracy, peace, and human liberty, dignity, happiness, and life in America. This appears to be a peculiar "American exceptionalism". For no other Western society is characterized in the same degree and intensity with such a self-perpetuating cycle of anti-liberal conservative counter-state and state terror. Specifically, this is the cycle of violence against liberal-secular democracy *and* "godly" government violent oppression by conservative forces, for example "Christian warriors" seeking both to destroy, when in opposition, the first and, once capturing political power by "ballot or bullet", institute the second.

To be sure, conservative and other anti-liberal forces always and everywhere, including Western Europe, adversely react to modern liberal-secular democracy when in opposition and conduct systematic coercion and repression once seizing power, but nowhere with such vehemence, violence, extensiveness, persistence, and intensity, simply the degree of counter-state and state terror respectively, than in contemporary America. Simply, it is only or mostly in today's America that anti-liberal conservatives become agents or advocates and supporters of counter-state and state terror depending on their position within power constellations such as in opposition or government control, at least more so than in other Western societies. This is a striking and perhaps shocking rediscovery and inference which reveals a sort of new anti-liberal conservative-reproduced American exceptionalism within the Western world and alternatively convergence or commonality with Islamic fundamentalism also sharing such a pattern of counter-state terrorism versus liberal-secular democracy (Turkey during recent times, etc.) and "holy" state terror once established in theocratic power (as in Iran, Taliban-ruled regions, etc.).

Hence, the question arises as how, if ever, to break the anti-liberal conservative cycle of counter-state and state terror especially, if not solely, typifying America among modern Western societies and seemingly predestining the new nation to an enfolding "American tragedy," unlike the despised "old world" and like Islamic countries. One scenario is to drastically dilute, if not relinquish, liberal-secular democracy as "un-American" or "anti-Islamic" (e.g., Turkey, Egypt) through adapting it to religious revivals and demands, including "Christian" and Islamic fundamentalism, by recognizing and permitting the greater "public role" of religion rather than relegating it to the private sphere as done by liberalism (Juergensmeyer 2003), thus essentially reconciling democracy with theocracy, state with church, by placating would-be-theocrats.

However, this scenario would not only end liberal democracy "as we know it" or change it beyond recognition, but likely would not eliminate terrorism, by placating would-be theocrats or fundamentalists. For terrorism would only likely change its form and domain from counter-state to "holy" state and inter-state terror committed by fundamentalist, theocratic forces once capturing government or, as US evangelicals like to say, "influencing" and reconstructing the latter according to their beliefs to make it conform with "Biblical law" (Lindsey 2008), as demonstrated by Protestant fundamentalism in the "Bible Belt" and in extension "Christian America" and by its Islamic counterpart in Iran, Saudi Arabia, Taliban-ruled regions, and other Muslim theocracies. Also, this is what exactly happened, minus the open theocratic or fundamentalist dimension, in interwar Germany, namely by "adapting" democracy to Nazism's demands and placating the Nazis by making Hitler the chancellor, Nazi anti-government violent putsches changed, expanded, and intensified into Nazi totalitarian state and inter-state terror.

On this account, the scenario of "adapting" liberal democracy to religious fundamentalism, just as fascism, by satisfying fundamentalists' theocratic demands for the greater "public role" of religion through ending or diluting the church-state separation, as well as those similar of neo-fascists, amounts to the "kind of cure that cures the disease by killing the patient". Of course, the latter means liberal, democracy and human liberty and eventually life eliminated by "holy", religiously sanctified state and inters-state terror via government violent repression in society and aggressive wars against other societies. For evidently US and Islamic fundamentalism's "appetite" for theocracy, like fascism's for totalitarianism, further increases with consuming theocratic and totalitarian "food", just as does that of liberal-democratic forces for democracy with "eating" or tasting its democratic alternative (Beck 2000).

In economic terms, US and Islamic fundamentalists', like interwar and postwar European fascists', the "marginal utility" of additional "units" of theocracy, just as of totalitarianism, increases rather than, as with material goods, decreases. To that extent, this ever-increasing "marginal utility" of theocratic "goods" makes any concessions to their shared demand for the "greater public role of religion" self-destructive or suicidal and naïve, resulting ultimately in the destruction of democracy, liberty, and eventually life via "holy" state terror and war, once fundamentalism or sectarianism captures government, just as it happened when fascism did in interwar Europe, notably Nazism in Germany. Simply, if one does not know this adverse outcome until one sees it, then looking at Taliban-ruled Islamic regions and the evangelical-sectarian Southern "Bible Belt" (plus Mormon-ruled Utah), both resulting from and fulfilling demands for the "greater public role of religion", can help to understand the past and present and predict the future.

In a way, for US, Islamic, and any religious fundamentalism or sectarianism there is *no* such thing as a "stopping point" in its seemingly legitimate demands for the "greater public role" of religion or "faith-based" government, just as for fascism in its similar requests for recognition in interwar Europe and neo-fascism in postwar European and American societies. In essence, Protestant and Islamic religious fundamentalism or sectarianism does *not* stop in its demands and desist in its counter-state terrorism until and unless seizing power and establishing "holy" state and inter-state terror. As Weber, like Comte, J.S. Mill, and Troeltsch, observes for Puritanism, the Puritan "pure sect", while self-righteously demanding "liberty of conscience" and "tolerance" for itself when not in government, invariably wants, seeks, and succeeds to capture via anti-government violence the state and once in power institutes "holy" terror through "unexampled tyranny" or "violent repression" eliminating religious and all liberties and toleration, as in England and the "theocracy of New England", just as do Islamic fundamentalist sects. Like Puritanism, Puritan-rooted US evangelical, as well as Islamic fundamentalist, sects are extremely power-hungry-and-thirsty strictly organized groups for that purpose which never have been, are, and will be satisfied in their demands and cease their counter-state terrorism unless and until capturing and exercising total societal power and thus instituting "holy" state and inter-state terror and tyranny overall, just as are Nazi and other fascist factions. In short, like Puritans and Calvinists overall, US evangelicals and Islamic fundamentalists never stop short of making their sectarian "laws" and beliefs the "law of the land", as did and do Nazis and other fascists.

On this account, the pacification or accommodation of American Puritan-inspired sectarianism and evangelicalism and Islamic fundamentalism within modern liberal-secular democracy has the same degree of probability of success as pacifying or accommodating Nazism and other fascism in interwar Germany and Europe and neo-Nazism and neo-fascism in the postwar period—approximately zero. Hence, accommodating inherently theocratic and in that sense terror-prone, i.e., violent, repressive, coercive, and warlike, religious fundamentalism and sectarianism, like intrinsically totalitarian and thus terrorist Nazism and fascism, represents what master novelist-sociologist Balzac called "lost illusions", although might have been part of the "age of great expectations" until say, the 1995 Oklahoma bombing or September 11, 2001.

Another scenario in breaking the anti-liberal conservative cycle of counter-state and state terror is the demise or decline of anti-liberalism, specifically conservatism, including religious fundamentalism and fascism, in relation to liberalism and its system of liberal-secular democracy. The likely result will be the concomitant demise or decline of both counter-state and state and inter-state terrorism, as witnessed by and large in contemporary Western Europe, especially Scandinavia, by comparison with America and Islamic countries or groups. Hence, this is the most realistic scenario and effective way to solve the problem of contemporary terrorism. Namely, whenever and wherever conservatism and anti-liberalism overall has declined and will decline in relation to liberal-secular modernity, so has and will both counter-state and state and inter-state terrorisms, as paradigmatically witnessed in most of Western Europe, excluding exogenous Islamic terrorist agents and actions.

A third possible scenario of breaking the anti-liberal cycle of counter-state and state terror is "liberalizing" or tempering conservatism, including fundamentalism and fascism, to become less antagonistic and thus less violent toward liberal-democratic modernity. But this scenario does not seem very realistic given that conservatism originally defined and still defines liberalism as its "immediate" and perpetual antagonist and that the conservative original and perpetual desideratum or dream has been that, as Michels remarks, liberal-secular democracy "must be eliminated" by virtually any available means, strategies, and methods, from democratic procedures like free elections to anti-government violence and subversions, thus counter-state terror. So long as conservatism, particularly religious fundamentalism and fascism, remains what has always been—i.e., vehement anti-liberalism, anti-secularism, and anti-modernism—it will generate and even become itself counter-state and state terrorism depending on whether it is in opposition to or has eliminated and subverted liberal-secular democracy. Simply, there is *no* such thing as conservatism, at the minimum religious fundamentalism and fascism, that is non-violent or non-radical in opposition to liberal-secular modernity, and non-coercive and non-repressive once in power, and to that extent not committing, inciting, advocating, or supporting the complex of counter-state and state/inter-state terror, respectively.

Generally, there is no such thing as conservatism, at least religious fundamentalism and fascism, that does not awaken the worst in humans, including contempt, intolerance, and hatred of different persons, groups, and societies, and consequently hate-driven terror, so generalized "hate crimes", in the form of violent repression and coercion within society and war of extermination or genocide against other societies. Conversely, there is no such thing, with minor qualifications, as conservatism, notably religious fundamentalism and fascism, that does not destroy the best in humans, including tolerance, love, and compassion for other human beings, groups, and cultures, as well as non-violent conflict resolution within and across societies. The latter is a sort of "task" that especially US conservatives avoid as beneath their "honor and pride" and left instead to Western "un-American" liberalism resulting in a sort of conservative-liberal division of labor in the reproduction of opposite outcomes for modern society.

Hence, to expect that either counter-state or state terrorism will somehow miraculously disappear and even diminish in contemporary liberal societies while anti-liberalism in the form of conservatism, notably revived religious fundamentalism and/or neo-fascism, being "still well and alive", as in America and Islamic countries ("Christian" and "Muslim" warriors), is merely a human hope or wishful thinking rather than a "rational expectation". The opposite outcome of "more of the same" is more likely in the future, viz., counter-state and state and inter-state terrorism. This holds so long anti-liberalism via religious-political conservatism remains, and even revives and rejuvenates itself, as via "Tea Party" and related anti-liberal and fundamentalist movements in America from 2008 to the 2010s, in fanatical opposition to "ungodly" liberal-secular democracy deceptively defined and condemned as "big" government, or it dominates and recreates "godly" politics and society, respectively.

The above vicious circle or dualism is exactly witnessed in America in which the first scenario of counter-state remains and even reinforces in a sort of counter-revolution or adverse reaction to the 2008 Elections of a "liberal" and so ":anti-American" President and Congress, and the resulting "big" government with its economic stimulus package, health care reform, etc., as it did in opposition to the 1992 Elections of the identical forces of "liberalism" and "anti-Americanism". The second is virtually institutionalized in the theocratic form of "faith-based" politics and society in the South and other vehemently anti-liberal, ultra-conservative "red" regions a la the "Bible Belt", just as is in Islamic societies. It may be disconcerting or shocking for most Americans to realize that they have shared in the past, share in the present, and are likely to share in the future with Islamic peoples this vicious circle of perpetual counter-state and state terror primarily depending on whether anti-liberalism cum religious-political conservatism is in opposition to established liberal-secular democracy or captures political power, and ultimately eliminates or perverts democratic government via "godly" politics.

Yet, the sociological distance is shorter than usually assumed or wished by most Americans between "Christian soldiers" and "Islamic warriors" in counter-state terrorism via anti-government violence, and between the "Bible Belt" (plus Mormon-ruled Utah) and the "Islamic Republic of Iran" or Taliban-ruled regions in "holy" state terror through government violent repression, coercion, and war for the "glory and love of God", including in both cases, as Pareto predicted, killing humans "in the name of the Divine master". No wonder that the evangelical design of "Christian America" governed by "Biblical law", especially the Southern "Bible Belt", has sometimes been experienced or described as a sort of "Christian Taliban" or "Christian Iran" (Bauman 1997; Mansbach 2006) in terms of 'holy" terror in the form of mass imprisonment for sins, executions of also innocent persons, and global war on "evil", thus destruction of human liberty and life, ultimately total annihilation as the path to "salvation" (Adorno 2001) after the scenario or image of nuclear MAD (mutually assured destruction).

Finally, the authors do not propose, however, what "should" or "should not" be done in this respect—i.e., whether or not to pacify Islamic and US fundamentalists by satisfying their demands for the "greater public role" of religion in politics and society. This is a type of value judgment and decision to be made by appropriate political institutions and agents, thus beyond reasonably value-free sociological and other scientific analysis in Weber's sense. Instead, the authors only register and predict on the basis of past experience and present trends, making statements of fact, what has happened, does, and will happen *if* such demands for the "greater public role" of religion are met and thereby Islamic and US fundamentalists are placated by modern democratic, secular governments. One cannot emphasize enough that this has been, is, and likely will be the system of "holy" state and inter-state terror combining total and systematic violent repression, including mass executions and imprisonment for sins-crimes, within society and "cosmic" war a la jihad and crusade against "evil" societies, and operating as the most effective means of establishing and perpetuating, as US fundamentalism claims (Hedges 2006), "God's Dominion" in society (Hedges 2006). Ultimately, this is simply a sort of "Islamic Taliban" and "Protestant Taliban" (the "Bible Belt") respectively, sharing the complex of "holy" intra-societal terror and inter-societal war. Conversely, so long as American evangelicalism is driven by the Calvinist design of "God's Dominion" in society ruled by "Biblical law"— and US evangelicals would not be what they if not literally driven by such a vision into a state of permanent effervescence a la Durkheim or insanity in Pareto's terms and revolution–the evangelical long-dreamed and attempted seizure of government (Lindsey 2008) will immediately or ultimately result in the system of "holy" terror, tyranny, and warfare, as has at least in part in the Southern "Bible Belt." The same holds true of Islamic fundamentalisms and its equivalent or comparable idea of "godly" society governed by Koran law.

To that extent, the above tempers or dispels any "rational expectations" or optimistic hopes that the political triumph, "influence", or societal expansion of American evangelicalism–recall at least one third of Americans are evangelicals in virtue of biblical literalism–and Islamic fundamentalism witnessed in recent times and literally while writing these lines does not or will not necessarily represent or generate 'holy" state and inter-state terror but "just" the "greater public role" of "faith" in society. Such expectations and hopes are as rational or realistic as those that the political victory or societal expansion of fascism, including Nazism, in interwar Europe would not necessarily, as many hoped underestimating or dismissing Hitlerism and other fascist forces, represent the system of state terror and inter-state war, or will not so in today's European and American societies—near-zero degrees of rationality and realism. As has been said of Nazism and all fascism since, American and Islamic fundamentalism never has been, can, and likely will be underestimated in its theocratic design and action, "word and sword" with impunity, and conversely, always and everywhere eventually with cruel punishment, i.e., "holy" terror, war, destruction, and mass death, as paradigmatically exemplified by the "Bible Belt" and Taliban-ruled regions. As a disclaimer, the "Bible Belt" and Taliban rule are *not* equated, the second being more extreme or radical than the first. Still, both are extremes within a definite societal context, the "Bible Belt" within Western society and Taliban the non-Western, Islamic world. To that extent, the differences between the two are the matter of different quasi-statistical "degrees of un-freedom", and not of substance of illiberty, shared theocratic coercion and violent repression defining "holy" state terror.

The following observation illustrates the above with respect to America: "When I came to this country as a bride 50 years ago, I was aware that there was a "conservative" element in the U.S. that seemed suspect to me, but at that time it also seemed well-contained and not connected to the mainstream. Now it seems to have tentacles everywhere. I believe totalitarianism is a real possibility here. I think those that dismiss the Republican Right as a minority are underestimating the threat. Older people like myself who remember the fear and catastrophe of totalitarianism in Europe during the Second World War will understand. History will repeat itself if we do not wake up" (TIME June, 2010 blogger). Needless but still instructive to say, conservative totalitarianism or simply fascism established once religious-political conservatism captures political power to realize its demands for the "greater public role of religion", is nothing more or less than a system of total state and inter-state terror religiously driven and sanctified.

And the prospect for such total, notably theocratic "holy", terror by a "godly" government is low or rapidly diminishing in modern liberal-secular Western Europe (with minor exceptions like post-communist theocentric Poland), but substantial and even ever-increasing, literally while writing these lines, in conservative-evangelical America to the point of being more or less realized in some regions (the "Bible Belt", Utah, and most other "red" states). For instance, one can predict or expect with a high statistical probability, if not almost mathematical precision, that if conservative-evangelical forces, as they constantly dream (Lindsey 2008), capture federal government at all levels (Presidency, Congress, Supreme Court) in the near or foreseeable future, as well as the remaining states beyond the Southern and other "Bible Belt", the outcome will be total "holy" terror in the usual double form of governmental Puritan-style or Islamic-like moralistic "godly" repression and coercion, including ever-increasing imprisonment for sins and executions of innocent people, within society and offensive global wars of extermination against "evil' societies resulting in mass death and perhaps total MAD (mutually assured destruction).

In comparative terms, this is conservatism's deliberate and proud (though never so called) Islamic-type theocratic, anti-liberal, and anti-individualistic—rather than, as in ethnocentric triumphalism, "libertarian", democratic", and "individualistic"—"American exceptionalism" or deviation from demonized "ungodly" liberal-secular Western society, just as Iran, Saudi Arabia, Taliban regions, and other Muslim theocracies deliberately and proudly demonize and deviate from the "infidel" West. In historical terms, it returns to or evokes the "Dark Middle Ages", specifically Calvin's medieval theocracy as the perennial inspiration of American evangelicalism (Hedges 2006), including proxy Inquisition-style practices like widespread executions, often of innocent persons, and mass long imprisonment of non-violent moral sinners as innocent prisoners of ethical conscience, just as medieval heretics were ones of religious and political conscience. To that extent, it is difficult to observe or imagine a more sinister "American tragedy" or "American exceptionalism", because such a prospective and in part instituted, as in the "Bible Belt" and Mormon-ruled Utah, Islamic-style and medieval-like theocratic "holy" terror destroys or perverts America's liberal-Jeffersonian ideals of "liberty and justice for all", the "pursuit of happiness", ultimately human wellbeing, dignity, and life, thus the "land of freedom" itself. At this juncture, anti-liberalism cum conservatism presents itself and operates as a kind of "curse" in the "promised" land through "holy" state and inter-state terror once in political power, as well as counter-state terrorism when not in control of government, a theme for further theoretical elaboration and empirical investigation.

Still, this "bad news" from and for modern and future America—i.e., so long as anti-liberalism via conservatism persists or expands, so does and will terror—logically and empirically points to a "good news" coming from and for virtually all other Western societies. This is that so long as liberal democracy and modernity prevails over anti-liberalism like conservatism, including fundamentalism and fascism, endogenous, domestic counter-state and state and inter-state terror does and will substantively decline and perhaps eventually disappear. No wonder that religiously driven and sanctified endogenous, as distinguished from exogenous, mainly Islamic, counter-state or state and inter-state terror is virtually non-existent or rapidly diminishing in all modern Western liberal-democratic societies, and only or mostly observed in America during revived fundamentalism and neo-conservatism overall, revealing

"American exceptionalism" in this respect. Yet, so long as the project and reality of liberal democracy and modernity ultimately prevails over anti-liberalism such as conservatism even in America itself (Munch 2001), "holy" terror, both religiously based anti-government violence and "godly" government violent repression, will likely decline or perhaps vanish in the latter and so will such "American exceptionalism". If this outcome materializes, the news is not entirely "bad" from and for America in the long run so long as it remains part of or becomes reincorporated into—conditional on conservative non-Western Islamic-style theocratic or religious "American exceptionalism" being "gone with the wind"—Western liberal modernity and civilization. Therefore, liberal Western modernity, while initially the agent provocateur of modern, especially religiously motivated and sanctified, terror as its poison, ultimately operates as the most effective antidote to the latter.

REFERENCES

Abadie Alberto. 2006. Poverty, Political Freedom, and the Roots of Terrorism. *American Economic Review* 96, 50–56.

Abbink, Klaus, Jordi Brandts, Benedikt Herrmann, and Henrik Orzen. 2010. Intergroup Conflict and Intra-group Punishment in an Experimental Contest Game. *American Economic Review* 100, 420–47.

Abbott, Andrew. 2005. Linked Ecologies: States and Universities as Environments for Professions. *Sociological Theory* 23, 245–274.

Acemoglu Daron. 2005. Constitutions, Politics, and Economics: A Review Essay on Persson and Tabellini's The Economic Effects of Constitutions. *Journal of Economic Literature* 43, 1025–1048.

———. 2010. Institutions, Factor Prices, and Taxation: Virtues of Strong States? *American Economic Review* 100, 115–19.

Acemoglu Daron and James Robinson. 2008. Persistence of Power, Elites, and Institutions. *American Economic Review* 98, 267–293.

Acemoglu, Daron, and Pierre Yared. 2010. Political Limits to Globalization. *American Economic Review* 100, 83–88.

Acemoglu, Daron, Davide Cantoni, Simon Johnson, and James Robinson. 2011. The Consequences of Radical Reform: The French Revolution. *American Economic Review* 101, 3286–3307.

Adorno, Theodor. 2001. *The Stars Down to Earth and Other Essays in the Irrational in Culture.* New York: Routledge.

Akerlof, George. 2002. Behavioral Macroeconomics and Macroeconomic Behavior. *American Economic Review* 92, 411–433.

Alesina Alberto and Eliana La Ferrara. 2005. Ethnic Diversity and Economic Performance. *Journal of Economic Literature* 43, 762–800.

Alexander, Jeffrey. 1983 *Theoretical Logic in Sociology.* Berkeley: University of California Press.

———. 2004. From the Depths of Despair: Performance, Counterperformance, and September 11. *Sociological Theory* 22, 88–105.

Amenta, Edwin and Halfmann, Drew. 2000. Wage Wars: Institutional Politics, WPA Wages, And The Struggle For U.S. Social Policy, *American Sociological Review* 65, 506–528.

Amenta, Edwin, Chris Bonastia and Neal Caren. 2001. US Social Policy In Comparative And Historical Perspective: Concepts, Images, Arguments, And Research Strategies. *Annual Review of Sociology* 27, 213–234.

Angel, Leonard. 1994. *Enlightenment East and West.* Albany: State University of New York Press.

Archer, Robin. 2001. Secularism And Sectarianism In India And The West: What Are The Real Lessons Of American History? *Economy and Society* 30, 273–287.

Arendt, Hannah. 1951. *The Origins of Totalitarianism.* New York: Meridian Books.

Artz, Frederick. 1998 [1968]. *The Enlightenment in France.* Kent: Kent State University Press.

Bahr, Peter. 2002, Identifying The Unprecedented: Hannah Arendt, Totalitarianism, And The Critique Of Sociology. *American Sociological Review,* 67, 804–31.

Bailey, Amy and Karen Snedker. 2011. Practicing What They Preach? Lynching and Religion in the American South, 1890–1929. *American Journal of Sociology* 117, 844–887.

Baldassarri Delia and Andrew Gelman. 2008. Partisans without Constraint: Political Polarization and Trends in American Public Opinion. *American Journal of Sociology* 114, 408–46.

Baldwin, Eric. 2006. The Devil Begins to Roar': Opposition to Early Methodists in New England. Church History 75, 94–119.

Barnes, Barry. 2000. *Understanding Agency*. London: Sage Publications.

Barnett, William and Michael Woywode. 2004. From Red Vienna to the Anschluss: Ideological Competition among Viennese Newspapers during the Rise of National Socialism. *American Journal of Sociology* 109, 1452–99.

Bartley, Tim. 2007. Institutional Emergence in an Era of Globalization: The Rise of Transnational Private Regulation of Labor and Environmental Conditions. *American Journal of Sociology* 113, 297–351.

Baudrillard, Jean. 1994. *The Illusion of the End*. Stanford University Press.

——. 1999. *America*. London: Verso.

Bauman, Zygmunt. 1997. *Postmodernity And Its Discontents*. New York: New York University Press.

——. 2001. *The Individualized Society*. Cambridge: Polity Press.

Baumer Eric, Steven Messner and Richard Rosenfeld. 2003. Explaining Spatial Variation in Support for Capital Punishment: A Multilevel Analysis. *American Journal of Sociology* 108, 844–875.

Beck, Ulrich. 2000. *The Brave New World Of Work*. Cambridge: Polity Press.

——. 2002. The Cosmopolitan Society and its Enemies. *Theory, Culture and Society* 19, 17–44.

Becky, Pettit and Bruce Western. 2004. Mass Imprisonment and the Life Course: Race and Class Inequality in U.S. Incarceration. *American Sociological Review* 69, 151–169.

Beiner, Ronald. 1992. *What's The Matter With Liberalism?* Berkeley: University of California Press.

Béland, Daniel. 2005. Insecurity, Citizenship, and Globalization: The Multiple Faces of State Protection. *Sociological Theory* 23, 25–41.

Bell, Daniel. 1977. The Return of the Sacred? The Argument on the Future of Religion. *British Journal of Sociology* 28, 419–449.

—— (ed.) 2002. The *Radical Right*. New Brunswick: Transaction Publishers.

Bendix, Reinhard. 1970. *Embattled Reason*. New York: Oxford University Press.

——. 1977. *Max Weber*. Berkeley: University of California Press.

——. 1984. *Force, Fate and Freedom*. Berkeley: University of California Press.

Benson, Rodney and Abigail Saguy. 2005. Constructing Social Problems in an Age of Globalization: A French–American Comparison. *American Sociological Review* 70, 233–259.

Bergesen, Albert and Lizardo, Omar. 2004. International Terrorism and the World-System. *Sociological Theory* 22, 38–52.

Berman, Morris. 2000. *The Twilight of American Culture*. New York W.W. Norton.

Besley, Timothy and Anne Case. 2003. Political Institutions and Policy Choices: Evidence from the United States. *Journal of Economic Literature* 41, 7–73.

Besley, Timothy, and Torsten Persson. 2009. Repression or Civil War? *American Economic Review* 99, 292–97.

Bittner, Rüdiger. 1996. What Is Enlightenment? In Schmidt James (ed.). *What Is Enlightenment?* (pp. 345–358.). Berkeley: University of California Press.

Black, Antony. 1997. Christianity and Republicanism: From St. Cyprian to Rousseau. *The American Political Science Review* 91, 647–656.

Black, Donald. 2004. The Geometry of Terrorism. *Sociological Theory* 22, 14–25.

Blattman, Christopher, and Edward Miguel. 2010. Civil War. *Journal of Economic Literature* 48, 3–57.

Blee Kathleen and Kimberly Creasap. 2010. Conservative and Right-Wing Movements. *Annual Review of Sociology* 36, 269–286.

Blinkhorn, Martin. 2003. *Fascists and Conservatives*. London: Taylor & Francis.

Blomberg, Brock and Joseph Harrington. 2000. A Theory of Rigid Extremists and Flexible Moderates with an Application to the U.S. Congress. *American Economic Review* 90, 605–620.

Bloom, Allan. 1988. *The Closing of the American Mind*. New York: Simon and Schuster.

Bluestein, Gene. 1977. The Brotherhood of Sinners: Literary Calvinism. *The New England Quarterly* 50, 195–213.

Boles, John. 1999. The Southern Way of Religion. *Virginia Quarterly Review* 75, 226–247.

Borgeson, Kevin and Robin Valeri [eds]. 2009. Terrorism in America. Sudbury, Mass.: Jones and Bartlett.

Boudon, Raymond. 1982. *The Unintended Consequences of Social Action.* New York: St. Martin's Press.

Bourdieu, Pierre. 1998. *Acts of Resistance.* New York: Free Press.

——. 2000. *Pascalian Meditations.* Stanford: Stanford University Press.

Bourdieu, Pierre and Hans Haacke. 1995. *Free Exchange.* Stanford: Stanford University Press.

Bowles Samuel, Herbert Gintis and Meliss Osborne. 2001. The Determinants of Earnings: A Behavioral Approach. *Journal of Economic Literature* 39, 1137–1176.

Brady David, Jason Beckfield, Martin Seeleib-Kaiser. 2005. Economic Globalization and the Welfare State in Affluent Democracies, 1975–2001, *American Sociological Review* 70, 921–948.

Brady, David, Jason Beckfield, and Wei Zhao. 2007. The Consequences of Economic Globalization for Affluent Democracies. *Annual Review of Sociology* 33, 313–34.

Braudel, Fernand. 1979. *Civilisation, économie et capitalism.* Paris: Armand Colin.

Bremer, Francis. 1995. *The Puritan Experiment.* Hanover: University Press of New England.

Breitenbach, William. 1984. The Consistent Calvinism of the New Divinity Movement. *The William and Mary Quarterly*, Third Series, 41, 241–264.

Buchanan, James. 1991. *Constitutional Economics.* London: Basil Blackwell.

Buchanan James and Gordon Tullock. 1962. *The Calculus of Consent.* Ann Arbor: University of Michigan Press.

Burns, Gene. 1990. The Politics of Ideology: The Papal Struggle With Liberalism. *American Journal of Sociology* 95, 1123–1252.

Byrne, James. 1997. *Religion and the Enlightenment.* Louisville: Westminster John Knox Press.

Cable, Sherry, Thomas Shriver, and Tamara Mix. 2008. Risk Society and Contested Illness: The Case of Nuclear Weapons Workers. *American Sociological Review* 73, 380–401.

Calhoun, Arthur. 1925. Social Development. *Social Forces* 4, 43–56.

Calhoun, Craig. 1993. Nationalism and Ethnicity. *Annual Review of Sociology* 19, 211–39.

Campbell, Bradley. 2009. Genocide as Social Control. *Sociological Theory* 27, 150–172.

Caplan, Bryan and Tyler Cowen. 2004. Do We Underestimate the Benefits of Cultural Competition? *American Economic Review* 94, 402–07.

Ceobanu Alin and Xavier Escandell. 2010. Comparative Analyses of Public Attitudes Toward Immigrants and Immigration Using Multinational Survey Data: A Review of Theories and Research. *Annual Review of Sociology* 36, 309–328.

Cetina Knorr Karin and Urs Bruegger. 2002. Global Microstructures: The Virtual Societies of Financial Markets. *American Journal of Sociology* 107, 905–50.

Chase-Dunn, Christopher, Yukio Kawano and Benjamin Brewer. 2000. Trade Globalization Since 1795: Waves Of Integration In The World-System. *American Sociological Review* 65, 77–95.

Clairmont Frederic. 1993. US State Terrorism: Another Criminal Act. Economic and Political Weekly 28, 1423–1424.

Clemens, Elisabeth. 2007. Toward a Historicized Sociology: Theorizing Events, Processes, and Emergence. *Annual Review of Sociology* 33, 527–49.

Coats, A.W. 1967. Sociological Aspects of British Economic Thought. *Journal of Political Economy* 75, 706–729.

Cochran, Augustus. 2001. *Democracy Heading South.* Lawrence: University Press of Kansas.

Coffey, John. 1998. Puritanism and Liberty Revisited: The Case for Toleration in the English Revolution. *The Historical Journal* 41: 961–985.

Cole, Wade. 2005. Sovereignty Relinquished? Explaining Commitment to the International Human Rights Covenants, 1966–1999. *American Sociological Review* 70, 472–495.

Coleman, James. 1990. Foundations of Social Theory. Cambridge, Mass. The Belkhap Press of Harvard University Press.

Collins Patricia. 2010. The New Politics of Community. *American Sociological Review* 75, 7–30.

Collins, Randall. 2004. Rituals of Solidarity and Security in the Wake of Terrorist Attack. *Sociological Theory* 22, 153–87.

Cooney, Mark. 1997. From Warre to Tyranny: Lethal Conflict and the State. *American Sociological Review* 62, 2, 316–338.

Cooney, Mark and Callie Burt. 2008. Less Crime, More Punishment. *American Journal of Sociology* 114, 491–527.

Crabtree, Steve and Brett Pelham. 2009. What Alabamians And Iranians Have In Common. GALLUP http://www.gallup.com/poll/114211/Alabamians-Iranians-Common.aspx.

Cragin, Kim and Peter Chalk. 2003. *Terrorism & development*. Santa Monica, CA: Rand.

Cunningham David and Benjamin Phillips. 2007. Contexts for Mobilization: Spatial Settings and Klan Presence in North Carolina, 1964–1966. *American Journal of Sociology* 113, 781–814.

Dahrendorf, Ralph. 1959. *Class and Class Conflict in Industrial Society*. Stanford: Stanford University Press.

——. 1975. *The New Liberty*. London: Routledge and Kegan Paul.

——. 1979. *Life Chances*. Chicago: Chicago University Press.

Danigelis, Nicholas, Melissa Hardy, Stephen Cutler. 2007. Population Aging, Intracohort Aging, and Sociopolitical Attitudes. *American Sociological Review* 72, 812–830.

Darnell, Alfred and Darren Sherkat. 1997. The Impact of Protestant Fundamentalism on Educational Attainment. *American Sociological Review* 62, 306–15.

Davis, Nancy and Robert Robinson. 2006. The Egalitarian Face of Islamic Orthodoxy: Support for Islamic Law and Economic Justice in Seven Muslim-Majority Nations. *American Sociological Review* 71, 167–190.

——. 2009. Overcoming Movement Obstacles by the Religiously Orthodox: The Muslim Brotherhood in Egypt, Shas in Israel, Comunione e Liberazione in Italy, and the Salvation Army in the United States. *American Journal of Sociology* 114, 1302–49.

Dayton, Cornelia. 1999. Excommunicating the Governor's Wife: Religious Dissent in the Puritan Colonies before the Era of Rights Consciousness, in McLaren John and Coward, Harold (eds.), *Religious Conscience, the State, and the Law* (pp. 29–45). Albany: State University of New York.

Delanty, Gerard. 2000. The Foundations of Social Theory: Origins and Trajectories, in Bryan Turner, ed., *The Blackwell Companion to Social Theory* (pp. 21–46). Malden: Blackwell.

Desai, Mihir. 2005. The Degradation of Reported Corporate Profits. *Journal of Economic Perspectives* 19, 171–192.

Dessí, Roberta. 2008. Collective Memory, Cultural Transmission, and Investments. *American Economic Review* 98, 534–560.

Deutsch, Kenneth and Walter Soffer (eds.). 1987. *The Crisis of Liberal Democracy*. Albany: State University of New York Press.

Diamond, Douglas and Raghuram Rajan. 2009. The Credit Crisis: Conjectures about Causes and Remedies. *American Economic Review* 99, 606–10.

Dobbin Frank, Beth Simmons, and Geoffrey Garrett. 2007. The Global Diffusion of Public Policies: Social Construction, Coercion, Competition, or Learning? *Annual Review of Sociology* 33, 449–72.

Dombrowski, Daniel. 2001. *Rawls And Religion*. New York: State University of New York Press.

Dugger, William. 1998. Against Inequality. *Journal of Economic Issues* 32, 286–305.

Dunn, Charles and David Woodard. 1996. *The Conservative Tradition in America*. Lanham: Rowan & Littlefield.

Edelman, Benjamin 2009. Markets: Red Light States: Who Buys Online Adult Entertainment? *Journal of Economic Perspectives* 23, 209–20.

Edgell, Penny, Joseph Gerteis and Douglas Hartmann 2006. Atheists as Other: Moral Boundaries and Cultural Membership in American Society. *American Sociological Review* 71, 211–234.

Eggertsson, Gauti. 2008. Great Expectations and the End of the Depression. *American Economic Review* 98, 1476–1516.

Einolf, Christopher. 2007. The Fall and Rise of Torture: A Comparative and Historical Analysis. *Sociological Theory* 25, 101–121.

Eisenstadt, Shmuel. (ed.) 1986. The Origins and Diversity Of Axial Age Civilizations. Albany: State University of New York Press.

——. 1998. The Paradox of Democratic Regimes: Fragility and Transformability. *Sociological Theory* 16, 211–38.

——. 1999. *Fundamentalism, Sectarianism, And Revolution*. New York: Cambridge University Press.

——. 2003. *Comparative Civilizations and Multiple Modernities*. Leiden: Brill Academic Publishers.

Eisenstadt, Shmuel and Sachsenmaier Dominic (eds). 2002. *Reflections on Multiple Modernities*. Leiden: Brill.

Eliasoph, Nina and Paul Lichterman. 2003. Culture in Interaction. *American Journal of Sociology* 108, 735–794.

Elwood, Christopher. 1999. *The Body Broken*. New York: Oxford University Press.

Emerson, Michael and David Hartman. 2006. The Rise Of Religious Fundamentalism. *Annual Review of Sociology* 32, 123–141.

Esping-Andersen, Gosta. 1994. Welfare States and the Economy, In Neil Smelser and Richard Swedberg, eds., *The Handbook of Economic Sociology*. Princeton: Princeton University, pp. 711–732.

Evans John and Michael Evans. 2008. Religion and Science: Beyond the Epistemological Conflict Narrative. *Annual Review of Sociology* 34, 87–105.

Feldstein, Martin. 2005. Rethinking Social Insurance. *American Economic Review* 95, 1–24.

——. 2008. Designing Institutions to Deal with Terrorism in the United States. *American Economic Review* 98, 122–26.

Fishback, Price. 1998. Operations of Unfettered Labor Markets: Exit and Voice in American Labor Markets at the Turn of the Century. *Journal of Economic Literature* 36: 722–765.

Fischer, Stanley. 2003. Globalization and Its Challenges. *American Economic Review* 93, 1–30.

Fiss Peer and Paul Hirsch. 2005. The Discourse of Globalization: Framing and Sensemaking of an Emerging Concept. *American Sociological Review* 70, 29–52.

Fligstein, Neil. 2001. *The Architecture of Markets*. Princeton: Princeton University Press.

Fourcade, Marion and Kieran Healy. 2007. Moral Views of Market Society. *Annual Review of Sociology* 33, 285–311.

Frey, Bruno. 1997. Rational Choice in Religion and Beyond. *Journal of Institutional and Theoretical Economics* 153, 279–284.

Friedland, Roger. 2001. Religious Nationalism And The Problem Of Collective Representation. *Annual Review of Sociology* 27, 25–52.

——. 2002. Money, Sex, and God: The Erotic Logic of Religious Nationalism. *Sociological Theory* 20, 381–425.

Friedman, Benjamin. 2011. Economics: A Moral Inquiry with Religious Origins. *American Economic Review*, 101, 166–70.

Friedman, Milton. 1982. *Capitalism and Freedom*. Chicago: University of Chicago Press.

——. 1997. Economics of Crime. *Journal of Economic Perspectives* 11, 194.

Fromm, Erich. 1941. *Escape from Freedom*. New York: Holt, Rinehart and Winston.

Garrard, Graeme. 2003. *Rousseau's Counter-Enlightenment*. Albany: State University of New York Press.

German, James. 1995. The Social Utility of Wicked Self-Love: Calvinism, Capitalism, and Public Policy in Revolutionary New England. Journal of American History 82, 965–998.

Gibbs Jack. 1989. Conceptualization of Terrorism. *American Sociological Review* 54, 329–40.

Giddens, Anthony. 1979. *Central Problems in Social Theory.* Berkeley: University of California Press.

——. 1984. *The Constitution of Society.* Berkeley: University of California Press.

——. 2000. *The Third Way And Its Critics.* London: Polity Press.

Glaeser, Edward. 2004. Psychology and the Market. *American Economic Review* 94, 408–13.

Goldstone, John. 1986. State Breakdown in the English Revolution: A New Synthesis. *American Journal of Sociology* 92, 257–322.

——. 2000. The Rise of the West—or Not? A Revision to Socio-economic History. *Sociological Theory* 18, 175–94.

Goode, William. 1972. The Place of Force in Human Society. *American Sociological Review* 37, 507–19.

Goodwin, Jeff. 2006. A Theory of Categorical Terrorism. *Social Forces*, 84, 4, 2027–2046.

Gorski, Philip. 2000. The Mosaic Moment: An Early Modernist Critique of Modernist Theories of Nationalism. *American Journal of Sociology* 105, 1428–1468.

——. 2003. *The Disciplinary Revolution.* Chicago: University of Chicago Press.

Gorski, Philip and Ates Altinordu. 2008. After Secularization? *Annual Review of Sociology* 34, 55–85.

Gould, Philip. 1996. *Covenant and Republic.* New York: Cambridge University Press.

Grim Brian, Roger Finke. 2007. Religious Persecution in Cross-National Context: Clashing Civilizations or Regulated Religious Economies? *American Sociological Review* 72, 633–658.

Grossman, Henryk. 2006. The Beginnings of Capitalism and the New Mass Morality. *Journal of Classical Sociology* 6, 201–213.

Gouldner, Alvin. 1970. *The Coming Crisis of Western Sociology.* New York: Avon.

Guillen, Mauro. 2001. Is Globalization Civilizing, Destructive Or Feeble? A Critique Of Five Key Debates In The Social Science Literature, *Annual Review of Sociology* 27, 235–60.

Habermas, Jürgen. 1971. *Knowledge and Human Interests.* Boston: Beacon Press.

——. 1989. *The New Conservatism.* Cambridge: MIT Press.

——. 2001. *The Postnational Constellation.* Cambridge: MIT Press.

Habermas, Jürgen, Cronin Ciaran and De Greiff, Pablo. 1998. *The Inclusion of the Other.* Cambridge: MIT Press.

Hamilton, Gary. 1994. Civilizations and The Organization Of Economics. In Neil Smelser and Richard Swedberg (eds). *The Handbook of Economic Sociology* (pp. 166–180). Princeton: Princeton University Press.

Harley, David. 1996. Explaining Salem: Calvinist psychology and the diagnosis of.... American Historical Review 101, 306–330.

Harris Alexes, Heather Evans, and Katherine Beckett. 2011. Courtesy Stigma and Monetary Sanctions: Toward a Socio-Cultural Theory of Punishment. *American Sociological Review* 76, 234–264.

Harrold, Frederick. 1936. The Nature of Carlyle's Calvinism. *Studies in Philology* 33, 475–486.

Hayek, Friedrich. 1941. Review of *Nationalokonomie* by L. Von Mises. *The Economic Journal* 51, 124–127.

——. 1948. *Individualism and Economic Order.* Chicago: University of Chicago Press.

——. 1955. *The Counter-Revolution of Science.* New York: Free Press of Glencoe.

Hayagreeva Rao, Lori Qingyuan Yue, and Paul Ingram. 2011. Laws of Attraction: Regulatory Arbitrage in the Face of Activism in Right-to-Work States. *American Sociological Review* 76: 365–385.

Hedges, Chris. 2006. *American Fascists.* New York Free Press.

Heller, Henry. 1986. *The Conquest of Poverty.* Leiden: Brill.

Heymann, Philip. 1999. *Terrorism and America.* Boulder, Colo.: NetLibrary, Inc.

———. 2003. *Terrorism, freedom, and security*. Cambridge, Mass.: MIT Press.

Hicks, Alexander. 2006. Free-Market and Religious Fundamentalists versus Poor Relief. *American Sociological Review* 71, 503–510.

Hicks, Alexander and Joya Misra. 1993. Two Perspectives on the Welfare State: Political Resources and the Growth of Welfare in Affluent Capitalist Democracies, 1960–82. *American Journal of Sociology* 99, 668–710.

Hill, Steven. 2002. *Fixing Elections*. New York: Routledge.

Hillmann, Henning. 2008. Mediation in Multiple Networks: Elite Mobilization before the English Civil War. *American Sociological Review* 73, 426–454.

Hirschman, Albert. 1982. Rival Interpretations of Market Society: Civilizing, Destructive, or Feeble? *Journal of Economic Literature* 20, 1463–1484.

Hummels, David. 2007. Transportation Costs and International Trade in the Second Era of Globalization. *Journal of Economic Perspectives* 21, 131–154.

Horkheimer, Max and Theodor Adorno. 1993. *Dialectic of Enlightenment*. New York: Continuum.

Houen, Alex. 2002. *Terrorism and modern literature*. Oxford: Oxford University Press.

Hout, Michael and Claude Fischer. 2002. Why More Americans Have No Religious Preference: Politics and Generations. *American Sociological Review* 67, 165–190.

Howitt, Peter. 2000. Endogenous Growth and Cross-Country Income Differences, *American Economic Review* 90, 829–846.

Hudson, Kenneth and Coukos, Andrea. 2005. The Dark Side of the Protestant Ethic: A Comparative Analysis of Welfare Reform. Sociological Theory 23, 1–24.

Hull, Mary. 1999. *Censorship in America*. Boulder: NetLibrary.

Infantino, Lorenzo. 2003. *Ignorance and liberty*. New York: Routledge.

Inglehart, Ronald and Wayne Baker. 2000. Modernization, Cultural Change and the Persistence of Traditional Values. *American Sociological Review* 65, 19–51.

Inglehart, Ronald (ed.). 2004. *Human Beliefs and Values*. México: Siglo XXI.

Jackman Mary R. 2002. Violence In Social Life. *Annual Review of Sociology* 28, 387–415.

Jacobs, David, Jason Carmichael, Stephanie Kent. 2005. Vigilantism, Current Racial Threat, and Death Sentences. *American Sociological Review* 70, 656–677.

Jacobs, David and Daniel Tope. 2007. The Politics of Resentment in the Post–Civil Rights Era: Minority Threat, Homicide, and Ideological Voting in Congress. *American Journal of Sociology* 112, 1458–94.

Jacobs David, Zhenchao Qian, Jason Carmichael, and Stephanie Kent. 2007. Who Survives on Death Row? An Individual and Contextual Analysis. *American Sociological Review* 72, 610–632.

Janssen, Susanne, Giselinde Kuipers, Marc Verboord. 2008. Cultural Globalization and Arts Journalism: The International Orientation of Arts and Culture Coverage in Dutch, French, German, and U.S. Newspapers, 1955 to 2005. *American Sociological Review* 73, 719–740.

Jenness, Valerie. 2004. Explaining Criminalization: From Demography and Status Politics to Globalization and Modernization. *Annual Review of Sociology* 29, 147–71.

Jepperson, Ronald. 2002. Political Modernities: Disentangling Two Underlying Dimensions of Institutional Differentiation. *Sociological Theory* 20, 61–85.

Jonsson, Jan, Grusky, David, Di Carlo, Matthew, Pollak, Reinhard, and Brinton, Mary. 2009. Microclass Mobility: Social Reproduction in Four Countries. *American Journal of Sociology* 114, 977–1036.

Juergensmeyer, Mark. 1994. *The New Cold War?* Berkeley: University of California Press.

———. 2003. *Terror In The Mind Of God*. Berkeley: University of California Press.

Kaplan, Benjamin. 2002. 'Dutch' Religious Tolerance: Celebration And Revision, In Hsia Po-chia and Henk van Nierop, eds., *Calvinism and Religious Toleration in the Dutch Golden Age*. New York: Cambridge University Press, pp. 8–27.

Kaufman, Jason. 2008. Corporate Law and the Sovereignty of States. *American Sociological Review* 73, 402–425.

Keister, Lisa and Stephanie Moller. 2000. Wealth Inequality In The United States. *Annual Review of Sociology* 26, 63–82.

Keister, Lisa. 2008. Conservative Protestants and Wealth: How Religion Perpetuates Asset Poverty. *American Journal of Sociology* 113, 1237–71.

Kestnbaum, Meyer. 2009. The Sociology of War and the Military. *Annual Review of Sociology* 35, 235–54.

Keynes, John M. 1960 [1936]. *The General Theory of Employment, Interest and Money*, London, Macmillan.

King, Mervyn. 2004. The Institutions of Monetary Policy. *American Economic Review* 94, 1–13.

King, Ryan. 2008. Conservatism, Institutionalism, and the Social Control of Intergroup Conflict. *American Journal of Sociology* 113, 1351–93.

King, Ryan, Steven Messner, Robert Baller. 2009. Contemporary Hate Crimes, Law Enforcement, and the Legacy of Racial Violence. *American Sociological Review* 74, 291–315.

Kloppenberg, James. 1998. The *Virtues of Liberalism*. New York: Oxford University Press.

Korpi, Walter. 1978. *The Working Class in Welfare Capitalism*. London, Routledge and Kegan Paul.

Krueger, Alan and Jitka Maleckova 2003. Education, Poverty and Terrorism: Is There a Causal Connection? *Journal of Economic Perspectives* 17, 119–144.

Krugman, Paul. 2009. The Increasing Returns Revolution in Trade and Geography. *American Economic Review* 99, 561–71.

Kuran, Timur. 2004. Why the Middle East is Economically Underdeveloped: Historical Mechanisms of Institutional Stagnation. *Journal of Economic Perspectives* 18, 71–90.

Leijonhufvud, Axel. 2004. Celebrating Ned. *Journal Of Economic Literature* 42, 811–821.

Lemert, Charles. 1999. The Might Have Been and Could Be of Religion in Social Theory. *Sociological Theory* 17, 240–263.

Lenski, Gerhard. 1994. Societal Taxonomies: Mapping the Social Universe. *Annual Review of Sociology* 20, 1–26.

Levy, Marion. 1998. Thorstein Veblen's absentee ownership, *Society*, 35, 64-/68.

Lichterman, Paul. 2008. Religion and the Construction of Civic Identity. *American Sociological Review* 73, 83–104.

Lindsay, Michael. 2008. Evangelicals in the Power Elite: Elite Cohesion Advancing a Movement. *American Sociological Review* 73, 60–82.

Lipset, Seymour. 1955. The Radical Right: A Problem for American Democracy. *The British Journal of Sociology* 6, 176–209.

——. 1996. *American Exceptionalism*. New York: Norton.

Lipset, Seymour and Gary Marks. 2000. *It Didn't Happen Here*. Norton.

Loveman, Mara. 2005. The Modern State and the Primitive Accumulation of Symbolic Power. *American Journal of Sociology* 110, 1651–1683.

Lucas, Jr. Robert. 2000. Some Macroeconomics for the 21st Century. *Journal of Economic Perspectives* 14, 159–168.

Lutz James and Brenda Lutz. 2004. *Global Terrorism*. London: Routledge.

Madsen, Richard. 2009. The Archipelago of Faith: Religious Individualism and Faith Community in America Today. *American Journal of Sociology* 114, 1263–1301.

Mannheim, Karl. 1936. *Ideology and Utopia*. New York: Harcourt, Brace & World.

——. 1967. *Essays on the Sociology of Culture*. London: Routledge & Kegan Paul.

——. 1986. *Conservatism*. London: Routledge and Kegan Paul.

Manent Pierre. 1998. *Modern Liberty and Its Discontents*. Lanham: Rowman & Littlefield Publishers.

Mann, Michael. 1993. *The Sources of Social Power*. New York: Cambridge University Press.

——. 2005. *The Dark Side of Democracy*. New York: Cambridge University Press.

Mansbach, Richard. 2006. Calvinism as a Precedent for Islamic Radicalism. Brown Journal of World Affairs 12, 103–115.

Markoff, John. 1997. Peasants Help Destroy an Old Regime and Defy a New One: Some Lessons from (and for) the Study of Social Movements. *American Journal of Sociology* 102, 1113–1142.

Martin, John. 2002. Power, Authority, and the Constraint of Belief Systems. *American Journal of Sociology* 107, 861–904.

Matsueda, Ross, Derek Kreager, and David Huizinga. 2006. Deterring Delinquents: A Rational Choice Model of Theft and Violence. *American Sociological Review* 71, 95–122.

Maurer, Heinrich. 1924. The Sociology of Protestantism. *American Journal of Sociology* 30, 257–286.

Mayway, Leon. 1984. In Defense of Modernity: Talcott Parsons and the Utilitarian Tradition. *American Journal of Sociology* 89, 1273–1305.

McBride, Michael. 2008. Religious Pluralism and Religious Participation: A Game Theoretic Analysis. *American Journal of Sociology* 114, 77–108.

McCann, Sean. 2000. *Gumshoe America*. Durham: Duke University Press.

McGiffert, Michael. 1988. From Moses to Adam: The Making of the Covenant of Works. *The Sixteenth Century Journal* 19, 131–155.

McLaughlin, Neil. 1996. Nazism, Nationalism, and the Sociology of Emotions: Escape from Freedom Revisited. *Sociological Theory* 14, 241–261.

Means, Richard. 1966. Protestantism and Economic Institutions: Auxiliary Theories to Weber's Protestant Ethic. *Social Forces* 44, 372–381.

Mencken H.L. 1982. *A Mencken Chrestomathy*. New York: Vintage Books.

Merrill, Louis. 1945. The Puritan Policeman. *American Sociological Review* 10, 766–776.

Merton, Robert. 1939. Review of Ray Billington. *The Protestant Crusade, 1800–1860*. *American Sociological Review* 4, 436–438.

———. 1968. *Social Theory and Social Structure*. New York: Free Press.

Messner, Steven, Robert Baller, Matthew Zevenbergen. 2005. The Legacy of Lynching and Southern Homicide. *American Sociological Review* 70, 633–655.

Michels, Robert. 1968. *Political Parties*. New York: The Free Press.

Miliband, Ralph. 1969. *The State in Capitalist Society*. New York: Basic Books.

Mises, Ludwig von. 1950. *Socialism*. New Haven: Yale University Press.

———. 1957. *Theory and History*. New Haven: Yale University Press.

———. 1966. *Human Action*. Chicago: Henry Regnery.

Mokyr, Joel 2009. Intellectual Property Rights, the Industrial Revolution, and the Beginnings of Modern Economic Growth. *American Economic Review* 99, 349–55.

Moller, Stephanie Alderson, Arthur and Nielsen, François. 2009. Changing Patterns of Income Inequality in U.S. Counties, 1970—2000. *American Journal of Sociology*, 114, 4, 1037–1101.

Morrill Calvin, Mayer Zald, and Hayagreeva Rao. 2003. Covert Political Conflict In Organizations: Challenges from Below. *Annual Review of Sociology* 29, 391–415.

Moore, Barrington. 1993. *Social Origins of Dictatorship and Democracy*. Boston: Beacon Press.

Moore, Tyler, Richard Clayton, and Ross Anderson. 2009. The Economics of Online Crime. *Journal of Economic Perspectives* 23, 3–20.

Munch, Richard. 1994. *Sociological Theory*. Chicago: Nelson-Hall Publishers.

———. 2001. *The Ethics Of Modernity*. Lanham: Rowman & Littlefield.

McMurtry, John. 1999. The Cancer Stage Of Capitalism. London: Pluto Press.

Myles, John. 1994. Comparative Studies in Class Structure. *Annual Review of Sociology* 20, 103–124.

Nisbet, Robert. 1966. *The Sociological Tradition*. New York: Basic Books.

Nischan, Bodo. 1994. *Prince, People, And Confession*. Philadelphia: University of Pennsylvania Press.

Norris, Pippa and Ronald Inglehart. 2004. *Sacred and Secular*. New York: Cambridge University Press.

Oberschall, Anthony. 2004. Explaining Terrorism: The Contribution of Collective Action Theory. *Sociological Theory* 22, 26–37.

Olick Jeffrey K. 1999. Collective Memory: The Two Cultures. *Sociological Theory* 17, 333–48.

Owens Timothy, Dawn Robinson, and Lynn Smith-Lovin. 2010. Three Faces of Identity. *Annual Review of Sociology* 36, 477–499.

Pager, Devah. 2003. The Mark of a Criminal Record. *American Journal of Sociology* 108, 937–975.

Parsons, Talcott. 1951. *The Social System*. New York: The Free Press.

———. 1967. *The Structure of Social Action*. New York: McGraw-Hill.

Patell, Cyrus. 2001. *Negative Liberties*. Durham: Duke University Press.

Paxton, Robert. 2004. Anatomy of Fascism. New York: Knopf.

Perrucci, Robert and Earl Wysong. 2008. The New Class Society. Lanham: Rowman & Littlefield.

Phelps, Edmund. 2007. Macroeconomics for a Modern Economy. *American Economic Review* 97, 543–561.

Phillips, Kevin. 2006. *American Theocracy*. New York: Viking.

Phillips, Scott and Mark Cooney. 2005. Aiding Peace, Abetting Violence: Third Parties and the Management of Conflict. *American Sociological Review* 70, 334–354.

Pillar, Paul. 2001. *Terrorism and U.S. foreign policy*. Washington, D.C.: Brookings Institution Press.

Piven, Frances. 2008. Can Power from Below Change the World? *American Sociological Review* 73, 1–14.

Plotke, David. 2002. Introduction, In Daniel Bell, ed., The *Radical Right*. New Brunswick: Transaction Publishers, pp. vi-lxxvi.

Popper, Karl. 1966. *The Open Society And Its Enemies*. Vol. 1. London: Routledge and Kegan Paul.

———. 1973. *The Open Society And Its Enemies*. Vol. 2. London: Routledge and Kegan Paul.

Prechel Harland and Theresa Morris. 2010. The Effects of Organizational and Political Embeddedness on Financial Malfeasance in the Largest U.S. Corporations: Dependence, Incentives, and Opportunities. *American Sociological Review* 75, 331–354.

Pryor, Frederic. 2002. *The Future of U.S. Capitalism*. New York: Cambridge University Press.

Putnam, Robert. 2000. *Bowling Alone*. New York: Simon & Schuster.

Quadagno, Jill. 1984. Welfare Capitalism and the Social Security Act of 1935. *American Sociological Review* 49, 632–47.

———. 1999. Creating a Capital Investment Welfare State: The New American Exceptionalism. *American Sociological Review* 64, 1–11.

Reuter, Peter. 2005. Review of Jeffrey Miron. Drug War Crimes. Oakland: Independent Institute. *Journal of Economic Literature* 43, 1075–1077.

Roche de la, Roberta Senechal. 2001. Why is Collective Violence Collective? *Sociological Theory* 19, 126–44.

———. 2004. Toward a Scientific Theory of Terrorism. *Sociological Theory* 22, 1–4.

Romer, Paul. 2010. What Parts of Globalization Matter for Catch-Up Growth? *American Economic Review* 100, 94–98.

Rossel, Robert. 1970. The Great Awakening: An Historical Analysis. *American Journal of Sociology* 75, 907–925.

Ruiter, Stijn and Frank van Tubergen. 2009. Religious Attendance in Cross-National Perspective: A Multilevel Analysis of 60 Countries. *American Journal of Sociology* 115, 863–95.

Rydgren, Jens. 2007a. The Sociology of the Radical Right. *Annual Review of Sociology* 33, 241–62.

———. 2007b. The Power of the Past: A Contribution to a Cognitive Sociology of Ethnic Conflict. *Sociological Theory* 25, 225–244.

Rutherford, Andrew. 1994. Crime Control as Industry: Towards Gulags, Western Style? *British Journal of Criminology* 34, 391–2.

Sachsenmaier Dominic with Shmuel Eisenstadt (eds). 2002. Reflections on multiple modernities: European, Chinese, and other interpretations. Leiden: Brill.

Samuelson, Paul. 2004. Where Ricardo and Mill Rebut and Confirm Arguments of Mainstream Economists Supporting Globalization. *Journal of Economic Perspectives* 18, 135–146.

Savelsberg Joachim and Ryan King. 2005. Institutionalizing Collective Memories of Hate: Law and Law Enforcement in Germany and the United States. *American Journal of Sociology* 111, 579–616.

Schelling, Thomas. 2006. An Astonishing Sixty Years: The Legacy of Hiroshima. *American Economic Review* 96, 929–937.

Schmidt James (ed.). 1996. *What Is Enlightenment?.* Berkeley: University of California Press.

Scitovsky, Tibor. 1972. What's Wrong with the Arts Is What's Wrong with Society. *American Economic Review* 62, 62–69.

Schofer, Evan and John Meyer. 2005. The Worldwide Expansion of Higher Education in the Twentieth Century. *American Sociological Review* 70, 898–920.

Schumpeter, Joseph. 1991. *The Economics and Sociology of Capitalism*. Princeton: Princeton University Press.

Schutz, Eric. 2001. *Markets And Power*. Armonk: Sharpe.

Scott, Richard. 2004. Reflections On A Half-Century Of Organizational Sociology. *Annual Review of Sociology* 30, 1–21.

Seed, John. 2005. The Spectre Of Puritanism: Forgetting The Seventeenth Century in David Hume's History of England. *Social History* 30, 444–462.

Shamir, Ronen. 2005. Without Borders? Notes on Globalization as a Mobility Regime. *Sociological Theory* 23, 2, 197–217.

Smart, Barry. 2000. Introduction – Postmodern Traces. In Turner, Bryan (ed.). *The Blackwell Companion to Social Theory* (pp. 447–480). Malden: Blackwell Publishers.

Smelser. Neil. 2007. The *Faces of Terrorism*. Princeton: Princeton University Press.

Smelser, Neil and Mitchell, Faith. 2002. *Terrorism*. Washington: National Academies Press.

Smith, Brent. 1994. *Terrorism in America*. Albany: State University of New York Press.

Smith, Christian. 2000. *Christian America*? Berkeley: University of California Press.

Sorokin, Pitirim. 1970. *Social & Cultural Dynamics*. Boston: Porter Sargent Publisher.

Sorrel, George. 1919. Reflections sur la violence. Paris, M. Riviere.

Spilerman Seymour and Guy Stecklov. 2009. Societal Responses to Terrorist Attacks. *Annual Review of Sociology* 35, 167–89.

Sprunger, Keith. 1982. *Dutch Puritanism*. Leiden: Brill Academic Publishers.

Steensland, *Brian*. 2006. Cultural Categories and the American Welfare State: The Case of Guaranteed Income Policy, *American Journal of Sociology* 111, 1273–1326.

Steinberg Marc. 2003. Capitalist Development, the Labor Process, and the Law. *American Journal of Sociology* 109, 2, 445–95.

Steinmetz, George. 2005. Return to Empire: The New US Imperialism in Comparative Historical Perspective. *Sociological Theory* 23: 339–367.

Stiglitz, Joseph. 2002. Information and the Change in the Paradigm in Economics. *American Economic Review* 92, 460–501.

——. 2010. *Freefall: America, Free Markets, And The Sinking Of The World Economy*. New York: W.W. Norton & Co.

Stivers, Richard. 1994. *The Culture of Cynicism*. Cambridge: Blackwell.

Straughn Jeremy. 2005. Taking the State at Its Word: The Arts of Consentful Contention in the German Democratic Republic. *American Journal of Sociology* 110, 1598–1650.

Sutton, John. 2004. The Political Economy of Imprisonment in Affluent Western Democracies, 1960–1990. *American Sociological Review* 69, 170–89.

Swidler Ann. 1986. Culture in Action: Symbols And Strategies. *American Sociological Review* 51, 273–86.

Symonds, Michael and Jason Pudsey. 2006. The Forms of Brotherly Love in Max Weber's Sociology of Religion. *Sociological Theory* 24: 133–149.

Tawney, Richard. 1920. The Acquisitive Society. New York: Harcourt, Brace and Company.
——. 1923. Religious Thought on Social and Economic Questions in the Sixteenth and Seventeenth Centuries. The Journal of Political Economy 31, 804–825.
——. 1962. Religion And The Rise Of Capitalism. New York: Harcourt.
Teall John. 1962. Witchcraft and Calvinism in Elizabethan England: Divine Power and Human Agency. Journal of the History of Ideas 23, 21–36.
Throsby, David. 1994. The Production and Consumption of the Arts: A View of Cultural Economics. Journal of Economic Literature 32, 1–29.
Tilly, Charles. 2004. Terror, Terrorism, Terrorists. Sociological Theory 22, 5–13.
Torpey, John. 1998. Coming and Going: On the State Monopolization of the Legitimate Means of Movement. Sociological Theory 16, 239–59.
Townshend, Charles. 2002. Terrorism. Oxford: Oxford University Press.
Tilman, Rick. 2001. Ideology and Utopia In The Social Philosophy Of The Libertarian Economists. Westport: Greenwood Press.
Tiryakian, Edward. 2000. Tiryakian, Edward. Parsons's Emergent Durkheims. Sociological Theory 18, 60–83.
——. 2002. Review of Richard Munch. The Ethics of Modernity. American Journal of Sociology 107, 1629–1631.
Trigilia Carlo. 2002. Economic Sociology. Malden: Blackwell Publishers.
Turk, Austin. 2004. Sociology of Terrorism. Annual Review of Sociology 29, 271–86.
Turner Bryan. 2002. Sovereignty and Emergency: Political Theology, Islam and American Conservatism. Theory, Culture & Society 19, 103–119.
Uggen, Christopher and Jeff Manza. 2002. Democratic Contraction? Political Consequences of Felon Disenfranchisement in the United States. American Sociological Review 67, 777–803.
Vaisey Stephen. 2009. Motivation and Justification: A Dual-Process Model of Culture in Action. American Journal of Sociology 114, 1615–75.
Van Dyke, Vernon. 1995. Ideology and Political Choice. Chatham: Chatham House.
Vasi Bogdan and David Strang. 2009. Civil Liberty in America: The Diffusion of Municipal Bill of Rights Resolutions after the Passage of the USA PATRIOT Act. American Journal of Sociology 114, 1716–64.
Wacquant, Loýc. 2002. Scrutinizing the Street: Poverty, Morality, and the Pitfalls of Urban Ethnography. American Journal of Sociology 107, 1468–1532.
Wagner, David. 1997. The New Temperance. Boulder: Westview Press.
Wakefield Sara and Christopher Uggen. 2010. Incarceration and Stratification. Annual Review of Sociology 36, 387–406.
Walder, Andrew. 2009, Political Sociology and Social Movements. Annual Review of Sociology 35, 393–412.
Wall, Steven. 1998. Liberalism, Perfectionism And Restraint. New York: Cambridge University Press.
Wallerstein, Immanuel and Sharon Zukin. 1989. 1968, Revolution in the World-System: Theses and Queries. Theory and Society 18, 431–449.
Walzer, Michael. 1963. Puritanism as a Revolutionary Ideology. History and Theory 3, 59–90.
——. 1965. The Revolution of the Saints. Cambridge: Cambridge University Press.
Weisbrod, Carol. 1999. The Law and Reconstituted Christianity: The Case of the Mormons, In McLaren John and Coward, Harold, eds., Religious Conscience, The State, And The Law (pp. 136–153). Albany: State University of New York,
Western Bruce and Jake Rosenfeld. 2011. Unions, Norms, and the Rise in U.S. Wage Inequality. American Sociological Review 76, 513–537.
Williams, Robin. 1994. The Sociology Of Ethnic Conflicts: Comparative International Perspectives. Annual Review of Sociology 20, 49–79.
Wimmer, Andreas, Lars-Erik Cederman, and Brian Min. 2009. Ethnic Politics and Armed Conflict: A Configurational Analysis of a New Global Data Set. American Sociological Review 74, 316–337.

Woodard, James. 1938. The Relation of Personality Structure to the Structure of Culture. *American Sociological Review* 3, 637–651.

Wolff, Edward. 2002. *Top Heavy*. New York: New Press.

Wuthnow, Robert. 1998. *After Heaven*. Berkeley: University of California Press.

Zaret, David. 1989. Religion and the Rise of Liberal-Democratic Ideology in 17th century England. *American Sociological Review* 54, 163–79.

INDEX